Men's College Athletics and the Politics of Racial Equality

Five Pioneer Stories of Black Manliness, White Citizenship, and American Democracy

Gregory J. Kaliss

TEMPLE UNIVERSITY PRESS   PHILADELPHIA

TEMPLE UNIVERSITY PRESS
Philadelphia, Pennsylvania 19122
www.temple.edu/tempress

Copyright © 2012 by Temple University
All rights reserved
Published 2012
Paperback published 2014

Library of Congress Cataloging-in-Publication Data

Kaliss, Gregory J.
  Men's college athletics and the politics of racial equality : five
pioneer stories of Black manliness, White citizenship, and American
democracy / Gregory J. Kaliss.
      p. cm.
  Includes bibliographical references and index.
    ISBN 978-1-4399-0856-3 (hardback) —
ISBN 978-1-4399-0858-7 (e-book)   1. College sports—United
States.   2. Racism in sports—United States.   3. Discrimination in
sports—United States.   4. African American athletes.   5. United
States—Race relations.   I. Title.
    GV351.K35 2012
    796.04'30973—dc23

                                                    2011047603

ISBN 978-1-4399-0857-0 (paperback : alk. paper)

Printed in the United States of America

021814P

Men's College Athletics
and the Politics of Racial Equality

For Leigh and Holly

Contents

Acknowledgments

W riting this book required the support of countless individuals and institutions. The following funding made the completion of this project possible: the Mowry Dissertation Fellowship for Research from the University of North Carolina (UNC) History Department; the Off-Campus Dissertation Research Fellowship from UNC's Graduate School; generous funding from the Historical Society of Southern California, which supported a research trip to the University of California at Los Angeles (UCLA); valuable summer research funding and the McColl Dissertation Year Fellowship from the Center for the Study of the American South; and timely research funding from Franklin and Marshall College. Many librarians and archivists also provided support. I am very grateful for the help of individuals at the North Carolina Collection and the Southern Historical Collection at UNC, the UCLA University Archives in the Charles E. Young Research Library, the William Stanley Hoole Special Collections Library and the Paul S. Bryant Museum at the University of Alabama at Tuscaloosa, and the University Archives in the Archibald S. Alexander Library at Rutgers University. I found the librarians at each of these institutions to be friendly, knowledgeable, and helpful, and I thank them for their efforts. I offer special thanks to Rebecca Schulte and Deborah Dandridge of the University of Kansas Archives in Spencer Research Library. Both were immeasurably helpful in sifting through the range of materials regarding Wilt Chamberlain and in pointing me toward the papers of Dowdal Davis.

Many scholars shared their knowledge and offered aid, including William Chafe, Lewis Erenberg, Peter Filene, Aram Goudsouzian, Bethany Keenan, Pam Lach, Tim Marr, David C. Ogden, Joel Nathan Rosen, David Sehat, Blake Slonecker, and Maren Wood. I thank them, as well as the anonymous readers of the *Journal of Sport History* and the *Journal of American History*, who offered perceptive and helpful comments on articles related to Charlie Scott and the 1939 UCLA football team, respectively. I am also grateful to my peers at Franklin and Marshall College, including Dennis Deslippe, Matt Hoffman, Alison Kibler, and David Schuyler, who helped me navigate the book publishing process and offered comments on my project and proposal. A few individuals deserve special thanks. Fitz Brundage helped conceive the project and offered invaluable professional advice along the way. My graduate school advisor, John Kasson, who supported this project from the start, has also been my sharpest critic, helping me draw broader inferences from the material at hand and providing countless helpful suggestions along the way. He has also been a warm friend, commiserating in times of distress and offering encouragement and support throughout the process. Patrick W. O'Neil probably read more drafts of this work than any other person; without his careful editing and insightful commentary, I would have been at a great loss. More important still, he has been a good and faithful friend to me.

Finally, and above all, I thank my family. My parents, Edward and Millie Kaliss, were loyal cheerleaders as I wrote and edited this book. They kept my spirits up in the tough times and offered hearty congratulations in the good times. My mother-in-law, Patti Butler, and her husband, Paul, provided moral support of their own. But most of all, I am indebted to my wife, Leigh, and my daughter, Holly, to whom I dedicate this book. The long hours and trying phases of writing and research can make writing a book a lonely endeavor, but at the end of each day, it is always a joy to have my family to come home to. They make all the effort worthwhile, and I thank them, with love, for everything.

Introduction

College Sports, "Fair Play,"
and Black Masculinity

I n November 1939, the editors of the *Crisis*, the monthly publication of the National Association for the Advancement of Colored
People (NAACP), nominated a rather unusual "honor roll." Instead
of successful black students, or even black businesses or schools, the
list consisted of predominantly white southern universities: Southern
Methodist University, Texas Christian University, Duke University, the
University of Oklahoma, and the University of Maryland. What had
these schools, many of which would not admit African American students until decades later, done to deserve such an honor? All had played
football games in the previous year against racially integrated teams
from schools in the North and West. Considering the tenacious hold
of Jim Crow segregation over the South, and the exclusion of African
American athletes from every major professional sport, including Major
League Baseball (by far the most popular and lucrative professional cir-
cuit), these contests were indeed significant developments in the realm
of sports. But the editors of the *Crisis* saw implications beyond the playing field, writing, "Fair play in sports leads the way to fair play in life.
May the honor roll increase!"[1]

The NAACP's emphasis on encouraging racial integration in American society helps explain the editors' eagerness to assign larger meanings to
these football games. But they were hardly alone in believing in the potential of sports to model fairness in American life. In countless publications
and forums, observers throughout the twentieth century identified the "level
playing field" of sports as a realization of the "American dream" of equal

opportunity. The notion of a meritocracy, deeply embedded in American culture, seemed best realized in athletic competition, an arena many hoped could be free from the racial prejudice that abrogated millions of Americans' opportunities in business, politics, and social life. When barriers to participation fell—when, for example, blacks competed against, or later for, white southern schools—the path seemed clear for players to succeed on the playing field or court by merit alone. Their effort and ability, not the color of their skin, would determine their standing as athletes. Observers on both sides of the color line clung to this ideal as proof that the American democratic system could work, that an equal-opportunity society was, in fact, possible.

That faith constitutes the central theme of this study, which explores how Americans responded to changes in the nation's racial politics. By analyzing the public discourse surrounding men's college athletics from 1915 to 1973—in black and white newspapers, national magazines, school publications, memoirs, legal documents, and correspondence—I trace how Americans of all stripes used sports to discuss and contest issues of race, equality, citizenship, and masculinity. The range of these diverse reactions can be seen in my five case studies: Paul Robeson at Rutgers College, 1915–1919; the 1939 University of California at Los Angeles (UCLA) football team; Wilt Chamberlain at the University of Kansas (KU), 1955–1958; Charlie Scott at the University of North Carolina (UNC), 1966–1970; and the integration of football at the University of Alabama, 1969–1973. As the varied responses to these pioneering athletes illustrate, sports, and college sports in particular, were central to how many people conceived of American society.[2]

Although residing in the leisure-time realm of "fun" and "play," and supposedly remote from the everyday world and its consequences, spectator sports grew tremendously popular in the late nineteenth century and into the twentieth century, often mirroring the altered rhythms of everyday life as American society shifted and changed. In watching sports, in reading about the games, and in discussing the performances afterward, people drew entertainment value from the competition, but they also used sports as a shared cultural language to help them understand their world.[3] Inevitably, race was a central topic of these discussions. More than any other marker of identity, including gender, class, and sexual preference, race has been intertwined with sports history from its earliest origins in American life. From the first American boxing championship contender, Tom Molineaux, to the early dominance of the Kentucky Derby by black jockeys, to the struggles of pioneers such as Jackie Robinson, to contemporary athletes such as professional golfer Tiger Woods, sports figures have embodied racial politics in myriad ways.[4] Scholars and casual observers alike have looked to these athletes for their ability—or inability—to change racial beliefs. This topic has dominated sports history, particularly in recent years, as historians, sociologists, and journalists have sought a middle ground between two competing, and often overly simplistic, arguments. On the one hand, some analysts and commentators have found sports to be an advanced model for social change, in which the "even field of fair play . . . serves to break down social divisions and boundaries."[5] On the other hand, other scholars have emphasized the limitations of sports as agents of change and have even suggested that sports act more effectively as barriers to progress. According to this mind-set, sports contribute to beliefs in black intellectual inferiority, maintain traditional power relationships in which whites control most of the ownership and management positions, and provide false hopes for impoverished African American youths hoping to escape poverty.[6]

College sports provide a unique opportunity to explore these contrasting beliefs. In an era when professional basketball and football had yet to reach a broad national audience and achieve the heightened levels of income and stardom we know today, college sports were tremendously popular and important to many communities, as fans connected team success to a sense of civic pride. Football games, for example, were often surrounded by weekend-long social events that brought fans from across an entire state together. Since fans often saw local college stars as emblematizing how their team, school, and even region were better than those of their competitors, college athletes were particularly intense receptacles for hopes and anxieties. That these athletes were also students further heightened the significance of the games. College represented a path to upward mobility through education, and many viewed these young men as representing the best and brightest in their respective communities and their communities' ambitions for recognition and respect. Thus, college star athletes were icons to their fans, who followed their exploits closely, and all the black athletes discussed in this book were superior talents widely recognized for their skills. Men's basketball and football, both in the past and into the present day, constituted the most popular and financially lucrative sports in the collegiate realm and generated the most discourse. A few features of these sports made them especially relevant for discussions of racial equality. Both basketball and football were team sports that required individuals to work together at nearly all times on the field and court. They were also contact sports, in which bodies collided frequently, and organized violence was part and parcel of the games. The sports therefore provided rich symbolic examples of blacks and whites working together and overcoming differences.

The location and timing of these five stories also provides unique insights into the intersection of sports and race. There were certainly other noteworthy star black athletes in the college ranks, including Jesse Owens at the Ohio State University in the 1930s, Bill Russell at San Francisco University and Jim Brown at Syracuse University in the 1950s, and Lew Alcindor at UCLA in the 1960s. However, the five case studies in this book follow the overall pattern of sports desegregation across the nation. Since the Northeast tended to integrate its athletics teams first, Robeson, one of the first black stars as newspaper sports coverage matured, and a figure who earned significant media coverage because of his proximity to New York, makes a compelling starting point for the project. Similarly, the other case studies generally followed the broader trend of integration in the collegiate athletics realm, moving from the North to the West (with the 1930s UCLA football team) to Middle America (with Chamberlain in Kansas in the 1950s) and then finally to the upper and lower South (with Scott at UNC and the Alabama football team in the late 1960s and early 1970s). Because these athletes were pioneering figures at their institutions *and* in their regions of the country, they faced additional pressure and engendered heightened dialogue about their roles.

Racial integration in sports, including college athletics and even some of the stories told here, has become a hot topic in recent years for scholars, journalists, and Hollywood film producers alike, but much work remains to be done.[7] A number of biographies have been written about Robeson, including Martin Duberman's thorough account and Lloyd Brown's exploration of his younger years.[8] However, no works consider in any depth the public reception to Robeson's athletic accomplishments, especially the disparities in reporting between the mainstream and black presses. Similarly, although Michael Oriard and others have mentioned the remarkable 1939 UCLA football team in passing, and Lane Demas summarizes the team in his work, a substantial analysis of some of the most pivotal events of their story—including a remarkably racist homecoming display and the employment of derogatory nicknames—has gone unwritten.[9] For all his celebrity, Wilt Chamberlain's experiences at KU have been surprisingly underreported, with only Aram Goudsouzian's narrative history of his time at the school.[10] Charlie Scott has received good coverage in Barry Jacobs's journalistic account of the first black basketball players in the two major athletic conferences in the South, but Jacobs's work lacks the scholarly analysis to situate Scott's story in regard to racial politics and competing definitions of masculinity.[11] Finally, of the many books about Alabama football, only Andrew Doyle has taken a scholarly approach, and his work fails to consider the story of Alabama's integration in connection with some of the key larger developments of the time, including the controversies over affirmative action and contested notions of black manliness.[12]

More generally, this book departs from these other accounts in two major ways. First, my emphasis here is less on what individual athletes and coaches *did* and more on what people *said* about their actions and performances. To that end, in addition to sifting through correspondence and university documents, I have systematically explored the local mainstream and black press response to each of these figures. This analytical focus provides a much more thorough engagement with people's conceptions of fairness and equality in American life. The black press's coverage of these athletes provides a startling contrast to the mainstream press in its assessment of athletic achievement, black male leadership, and the process of integration, a viewpoint often neglected (or only marginally explored) in these other works. The national scope of this book also sets it apart from most of its peers. Although many fine regional studies have been commissioned in recent years, this book provides a broader picture of college sports integration, and thus Americans' changing sense of equality, by comparing and contrasting the responses of New York–area residents to those of southerners, midwesterners, and people on the West Coast. By following the process of big-time college athletics integration, from the early pioneers in the Northeast in the late nineteenth and early twentieth century until the last holdouts in the Deep South in the 1970s, we get a sense of how sports integration fit into *national* debates regarding race, manliness, equality, and citizenship. Indeed, these case studies need to be put into dialogue with one another in order to best understand their significance. Pulling these five case studies together, over such a wide range of time and space, provides a more thorough understanding of the interrelated nature of sports integration, the quest for civil rights, national and international politics, gender ideals, and debates regarding higher education.

As people discussed these athletes, several key themes emerged, shedding light on some of the major issues that divided, and continue to divide, Americans regarding civil rights and the nation's egalitarian ideals. These themes included (1) regional and temporal variations in ordinary Americans' sense of racial politics, (2) contested notions of black masculinity, (3) differing perspectives on citizenship and race, such as access to the roles of breadwinner and citizen-soldier, and (4) competing models of sports as a blueprint for how equality might be achieved, including issues related to leadership in broader society.

The nationwide reach of college sports made them especially apt sounding boards for issues of racial equality. The most prominent professional team sports, including Major League Baseball (MLB), were largely confined to the northern half of the country until the late 1950s. But college games took place at schools in all regions of the nation. Thus, their contests illuminated responses to desegregation in locations and time periods often absent from traditional civil rights histories. In fact, surprising continuities and contrasts emerge when looking at these five case studies. One thread that tied all of these case studies together across time and space was the surprisingly strong gravitational pull of the South's strict Jim Crow segregation—which, in addition to college athletics in North Carolina and Alabama, also affected athletic contests in the New York area in the 1910s, Southern California in the

1930s, and even the National Collegiate Athletic Association (NCAA) men's basketball tournament in the 1950s. But there were peculiarities for each location and time period as well. North Carolina's reputation as a "progressive" state with regard to race affected the discourse surrounding integrated athletic competition in ways that differed profoundly from, say, the coverage of Wilt Chamberlain in Kansas. From these different reactions, we can see more clearly how Americans adjusted to the changes in racial politics that took place throughout the twentieth century.

The athletes being discussed in these varied locations were almost exclusively male—a sign of traditional gender assumptions and the dearth of opportunities available to female athletes. The gendered nature of these sports naturally affected people's perceptions of athletic achievement, especially because of the circumscribed position of black men in American society.[13] Systematically denied access to many of the conventional attributes of manliness—including the right to vote and the capacity to be the breadwinner for their families—black men looked for hopeful signs of progress wherever they could be found, including in the realm of athletics. White men, on the other hand, expressed their anxieties about a loss of stature, as black male athletic success portended competition in other arenas of life—most notably the workforce. Thus, sports coverage could refute stereotypes that paradoxically labeled black men as shiftless and inconsequential yet also sexually charged and menacing—or it could uphold those stereotypes for the sake of buttressing white men's privileged position in society.[14] This tension would be played out numerous times and in numerous ways as individuals discussed these college athletes' accomplishments and shortfalls.

Black athletic success was also seen to have important ramifications for citizenship itself. Although athletics were seemingly far removed from the realms of politics and the law, they had the potential to alter people's conceptions of African Americans' place in society, what the political theorist Judith Shklar has referred to as the idea of citizenship as "standing."[15] Having a black man earn praise and recognition as a star athlete indicated a certain level of respect to which most African Americans, and other suppressed minority groups, aspired. This understanding of citizenship helps explain why so many black leaders continued to believe in the transformative possibilities of athletics, despite numerous setbacks over the years: public respect and admiration for African American achievements and contributions to society revealed blacks and whites on an even plane, overcoming symbolic and legal barriers that relegated African Americans to an inferior position.[16] Claims for African Americans' right to serve in the military—as was the case in Paul Robeson's time—stemmed directly from an attempt to affirm black men as full citizens, with all the rights and responsibilities of their white peers. Understanding citizenship as standing in this way also underscores why whites beholden to Jim Crow attempted to minimize or denigrate the achievements of black athletes—threats to the privileged position of the white male citizen were not taken lightly.

The role of the media in situating sports and race deserves special mention. Given the many contradictory readings that observers made of integrated sports competition—including proof of black male potential, a justification for the continued degradation of African Americans, and, as we will see, a host of responses in between—it is no small wonder that commentators on both sides of the color line continued to turn to sports as a powerful symbol of equal opportunity in action. Generally speaking, I have divided analysis of press coverage between that of the mainstream (or white) press and that of the black press. Clearly, these two institutions had different biases and goals that affected their perceptions and their editorial decisions. The mainstream presses, owned almost exclusively by white men with ties to the local business communities in which their papers operated, faced market pressures as they sought to keep up with their competition. As this book shows, those market pressures helped shape the discourse regarding racial conflict—especially in the Jim Crow South. Generally speaking, mainstream white newspapers did not promote athletics as a way to advance black civil rights. However, they nonetheless consistently praised sports as an arena free from prejudice and bigotry, where sportsmanship dictated fair play between all participants. Often ignoring racial slights and the verbal and physical abuse levied on black athletes (and employing racially coded language of their own), these publications held fast to the idea of sports as a color-blind institution in American life.

The black presses, on the other hand, were smaller in number and size but occupied a particularly important place in the black community. As one of the few options available for black voices to be heard in public, black newspapers did more than report and entertain. Many black editors and publishers saw themselves as the voice of the black community and used their papers as sounding boards for issues neglected in white political, intellectual, and cultural circles.[17] Not surprisingly, then, these men and women often invested sports coverage with greater meanings than that of harmless entertainment, hoping to use sports to push for pressing issues to African Americans. Pursuing a strategy of "muscular assimilation," many black leaders hoped black success in sports would lead white Americans to recognize the potential of African Americans to contribute meaningfully in all aspects of society.[18] As my research reveals, black publications across the country, including the *Crisis* in New York, the *Baltimore Afro-American*, the *Pittsburgh Courier*, the *Chicago Defender*, the *Kansas City Call*, and the *California Eagle*, celebrated black athletic achievement, lamented incidents of discrimination, and expressed their hopes that sports would open up ever more areas of American life to equal black participation. Those hopes would become more cautious in the 1960s and 1970s, and articles in the *Carolina Times* and the *Birmingham World* reflected the growing unease with integration's unintended effects on black-run institutions. But even these publications still found hope in black athletic success and expressed some degree of faith in its transformative capabilities.

That both black and white sportswriters, given these different sets of circumstances, would turn to sports as a model for American society speaks to the allure of the level playing field. However, these shared hopes for the inherent fairness of sports, expressed by writers across the nation and over the course of many decades, often masked very different readings of some key ideals. In particular, the malleability of the term *equality* made it possible for observers to assign different meanings, and draw different lessons, from the achievements of black sports figures. Even when a variety of people all lauded sports as being a proving ground for equality, or equal opportunity, they often had conflicting ideas of what those terms meant. Indeed, as political theorists such as Bernard Williams have noted, even bigots generally believe that all human beings share certain fundamental characteristics that make them deserving of fair and equal treatment. Prejudiced people simply operate from the assumption that something such as a person's race correlates with other factors that make those people "deserving" of an inferior place in life.[19] This way of thinking helps explain how white southern writers could praise the "democracy" and "equality" of the United States while still supporting the legal system of Jim Crow segregation that relegated African Americans to an inferior position in society. Their visions of "democracy" and "equality" rested on rarely stated assumptions of white superiority in a variety of human characteristics. However, as commentators discussed black stars in their respective contexts, they often outlined a more precise vision of those ideas, circumscribing athletics' importance or "explaining" success by falling back on damaging stereotypes.

Even among those opposed to segregation or the idea of racial bigotry, the notion of "equal opportunity" was slippery enough to accommodate a wide range of meanings. As Williams argues, although most express support for "the . . . equal opportunity for *everyone in society* to secure certain goods," a variety of interrelated factors often make achieving that goal impossible and open the door to a wide range of interpretations.[20] For example, a state university could consider black students for admission on equal terms with whites and insist that it was fulfilling the goal of equality of opportunity. However, if most black high school students in the state went to underfunded, segregated schools, leading to lower test scores and admission rates, one might wonder if black students in the state truly had "equal" access to state schools.[21] Complexities such as these were rarely discussed in the press, but sports provided an opening for this dialogue. In their competing interpretations of these athletes' careers, black and white writers (often unwittingly) wrestled with competing definitions of equality and equal opportunity precisely because of the widespread belief in sportsmanship and the level playing field. As a result, they naturally identified different ways in which sports served as a model for an equal opportunity society.

College sports, then, provided a particularly compelling arena (pun intended) in which to discuss racial identities, manliness, citizenship, and equality. A popular activity among diverse spectators—young and old, men and women, black and white—college sports served as a lingua franca for many Americans, a more accessible mode of communication than the relatively abstract languages of law and politics. When people discussed the experiences of these black athletes, they articulated their sense of how American society worked and how it ought to work. At other times, however, these discussions masked contentious debates, inhibiting a thorough analysis of the thorny issues still inhibiting the attainment of a color-blind and racially equitable society.

Chapter 1, "'Our Own "Roby"' and 'the Dark Cloud,'" explores reactions to Paul Robeson's career as an All-American football player at Rutgers College from 1915 to 1919. Although Robeson would earn considerable fame later in life as an actor, singer, and activist, his first entry in national public discourse came from his considerable talents on the football field, where he helped pull perennial also-ran Rutgers briefly into the ranks of the elite. In the waning years of "Muscular Christianity," just after black boxer Jack Johnson's loss of the heavyweight championship, and as the United States prepared for war in Europe, Robeson's extraordinary career inspired black and white observers, although the terms by which they discussed his career suggested very different conceptions of black men's proper place in the nation.

Chapter 2, "'Harbingers of Progress' and 'the Gold Dust Trio,'" studies responses to the very successful football squad fielded at the University of California at Los Angeles in the fall of 1939. With three black starters—Kenny Washington, Woody Strode, and Jackie Robinson—this team offered hope to many blacks and whites who saw the New Deal era as an ideal time to craft a new civic nationalism that could welcome the contributions of ethnic and racial minorities. The increasing threats of Hitler's fascist regime and its hate-filled rhetoric fueled discussions of how this team might (for good or ill) represent an expanded sense of American egalitarian democracy.

Chapter 3, "'A First-Class Gentleman' and 'That Big N——r,'" explores the extraordinary response to Wilt Chamberlain, the legendary seven-foot basketball player, during his time at the University of Kansas. As the modern civil rights movement began in earnest, with the 1954 U.S. Supreme Court ruling in *Brown v. Board of Education* acting as a catalyst, Chamberlain's reception by blacks and whites prodded observers to consider the barriers to full black male citizenship. Recruited explicitly by area black leaders to help improve "race relations" in the area, Chamberlain attempted to perform a number of tasks in the glaring media spotlight that accompanied him: lead his team to a national championship, set a good example for African American youths, and persuade whites to abandon racial segregation (which existed in the supposedly "free state" of Kansas).

Chapter 4, "'Our Colored Boy' and 'Fine Black Athletes,'" analyzes the experiences of black basketball star Charlie Scott at the University of North Carolina at Chapel Hill. Although North Carolina, and the town of Chapel Hill, especially, had reputations for "progressive" attitudes regarding race and equality, Scott's experiences revealed the resistance of southern whites to black claims for civil rights. Attempting to balance his desires to help his team, convince southern whites that racial integration was feasible, and advocate on behalf of African Americans, Scott found little support in the state's mainstream media, which avoided generating conflict and refused to discuss racial issues frankly. Scott's frustrations spoke to the challenges faced by African Americans attempting to break through the numerous, and often invisible, barriers of the Jim Crow South.

Chapter 5, "'Those Nigras' and 'Men Again,'" analyzes the long process of desegregating the University of Alabama's football team, one of the South's most popular teams. Celebrated head coach Paul "Bear" Bryant's hesitance to integrate his highly successful squad angered many, particularly because his stature, esteem, and racially moderate views appeared to make him an ideal candidate for such a task. Hemmed in by the words and actions of avowed segregationist governor George Wallace, however, Bryant cautiously waited to welcome black athletes to his squad. In the summer of 1969, the Afro-American Association student group took matters into their own hands, filing a lawsuit in federal court to force the school to seek out black athletes for its prestigious program. In the years that followed, the team showed both the possibilities and limitations of sports in modeling an integrated society in the Deep South, as debates over affirmative action and black activism presented considerable obstacles for southern whites and blacks to overcome in the waning years of the civil rights movement.

Despite the very different cultural, political, and economic contexts these pioneer athletes lived through, observers on both sides of the color line consistently turned to them as symbols of change, some seeing them as models of hope for an equitable society and others as harbingers of doom for an established way of life. These diverse reactions help us understand the issues that were at stake as these athletes moved onto previously privileged courts and fields—nothing more or less than the definitions of U.S. citizenship, the place of athletics in American life, the proper roles of universities and colleges, changing definitions of gender and racial identities, and the fundamental contours of American democratic society. As these players achieved great success—all of them earning the rank of "All-American" on at least one occasion—while facing racial abuse and idealized praise, they channeled ordinary Americans' aspirations of what their nation might be.

The changing tenor of responses to these celebrated black athletes reveals the gradual evolution of Americans' sense of egalitarian democracy. When Paul Robeson took the field for Rutgers in the 1910s, prominent northern and southern white leaders had no qualms marking out full citizenship as the exclusive preserve of white, educated men. Many key black leaders, including Robeson himself, limited their own calls for black equality to basic legal, political, and economic rights, willing to forgo, for the moment, social integration. By the late 1930s, many black and white Americans hoped for a more expansive civic nationalism that welcomed the contributions of previously disparaged minorities, including African Americans. The negative response to Jackie Robinson and his teammates at UCLA indicated that that vision of American democracy had not yet taken hold as the dominant ideal.

But by the mid-1950s, after the pivotal events of World War II and the start of the modern-day civil rights movement, increasing numbers of black and white Americans called for a society in which blacks and whites shared not only equal legal protection but also access to the same social spaces. Although some attempted to cling to segregated society, support was slipping. However, certain issues remained contentious—who would lead this newly integrated society? Whose social spaces and economic institutions would remain intact when the walls of segregation came down? What steps were necessary to ensure African Americans' economic equality with whites? These debates increased in urgency from Wilt Chamberlain's time in Kansas, to Charlie Scott's career at UNC, to the torturous process of integration at the University of Alabama. In many ways, those questions have been left unanswered. The color-blind society aspired to by supporters of an expansive civic nationalism has been attained in some respects—in laws prohibiting discrimination in public accommodations, education, and housing—but has proved elusive in others. Although many white Americans continue to affirm the reality of the American dream of equal opportunity, most African American leaders and other social critics are more skeptical. The dialogue surrounding the experiences of these black athletes helps explain why those significantly different interpretations exist, revealing the contentious issues surrounding civic leadership, social activism, and affirmative action that divide Americans even to this day. And they point to the possibilities—and failures—of college sports, and sports in general—to facilitate the dialogue that will best solve these vexing issues.

1

"Our Own 'Roby'" and "the Dark Cloud"

Paul Robeson at Rutgers, 1915–1919

Spectators at Ebbets Field in Brooklyn, New York, on the afternoon of November 24, 1917, witnessed a remarkable sight: deliriously excited white Rutgers College football fans storming the field and carrying a black player by the name of Paul Robeson on their shoulders in celebration. The occasion was Rutgers's stunning 14–0 victory over the Newport Naval Reserves, a veteran All-Star squad that had dominated some of the best teams in the Northeast. That the upstart Rutgers College team won was quite an achievement; that its best player was a black man, the only black player on either squad, made the event even more significant. In an era when African American men were often depicted as mindless brutes or shiftless criminals, and as the nation's armed services joined the fight to "save democracy" in World War I, Robeson's achievements engendered debates about the meanings of equality and had the potential to upend conventions of manliness and race. Indeed, his success in this contest, and the white fans' postgame enthusiasm, inspired one black writer to suggest sending an article about the game to Assistant Secretary of the Navy Josephus Daniels, who had recently snubbed black men for prime positions within the U.S. Navy.[1] Leading an integrated team to victory, and earning the praise and adulation of white fans and media members alike, Robeson, in this moment and throughout his career, provided an entry point into ongoing debates about the nation's sense of its egalitarian ideals, debates that nearly always intersected with gender and racial beliefs.

Robeson's career, and the many responses to it, reveals the increasing importance of sports to discussions of fairness and equality in American life in the early twentieth century. Although Robeson was not the first African American to participate in major college sports, he was among the first national black stars in college football, rising to prominence in the sport as it reached an ever wider audience and earning significant media coverage because of his proximity to the numerous publications centered in New York City. As black and white observers, especially newspaper writers, covered Robeson's career, they drew lessons that extended well beyond the playing field. At the tail end of the era of "muscular Christianity," during the build-up and commitment to World War I, and directly immersed in a time of white male anxiety about cultural supremacy (particularly in the wake of the controversial African American heavyweight boxing champion Jack Johnson), Robeson's achievements generated discussions that were freighted with meaning beyond just points scored and tackles made. Through the numerous voices, on campus and off, that discussed this athlete over the years 1915–1919, we hear black voices clamoring for racial equality, full citizenship as soldiers, and new visions of African American masculinity. Yet, as we shall see, even in the urban North, far removed from the Jim Crow South, those claims were met by whites with a mixture of frosty silence, verbal hostility, and even outright violence.

Muscles, Race, and War: U.S. Culture in the 1910s

The years surrounding U.S. entry into World War I provide a particularly rich historical moment to consider the deeper meanings of interracial college sports. These years marked the denouement of the religious cultural movement dubbed "muscular Christianity."[2] Stemming from religious leaders' worries regarding the deleterious effects of city life, adherents to muscular Christianity promoted a vision of godliness that entailed vigorous physical activity and a reaffirmation of manly behavior. Their efforts increased the popularity of groups such as the Young Men's Christian Association (YMCA), spawned new organizations such as the Boy Scouts, and led to the popularity of such noted preachers as former baseball player Billy Sunday.[3] By the late 1910s, this movement had attained widespread popularity across the country, particularly with white Protestant Christians.

Many supporters of muscular Christianity linked this idea with broader concerns about white manliness in general, fearing that the Anglo-Saxon stock was losing its physical vigor. As more women moved into the workforce and clamored for the right to vote, and as African Americans sought equality in American democratic institutions, many Anglo-Saxon white men felt threatened, fearing that they were losing the status and power associated with their privileged place in the nation's citizenry. As a result, these white men made repeated efforts to promote the virtues of white masculinity in a variety of cultural outlets, such as sports, the World's Fair, and fictional figures such as the popular Tarzan of the Apes.[4] Cultural definitions of manhood were changing as well, for both blacks and whites, as Victorian ideas of manliness based on character and production shifted to a modern masculinity based on consumption and the body.[5]

In this climate, sports had potentially far-reaching implications. Many African American leaders hoped to pursue a strategy of "muscular assimilation," in which black success in sports would lead white Americans to recognize the potential of African Americans to contribute meaningfully in all aspects of society.[6] Anxious white Americans, alternatively, often saw white success in sports as affirmation of white males' supposed intrinsic superiority. Two events in the 1910s drew particular attention to these issues and made the careers of athletes such as Robeson strike an even more resonant chord: Jack Johnson's retention of the heavyweight championship in 1910 and U.S. involvement in World War I. Johnson was not only the first black heavyweight boxing champion but also a man who delighted in thumbing his nose at racial mores.[7] Marrying white women, driving expensive cars, and wearing fine clothes, Johnson refused to accept any limitation imposed on him because of his race—an attitude that greatly upset many white observers.[8] When on July 4, 1910, Johnson defeated former white boxing champion James Jeffries (who had been coaxed out of retirement solely to "restore" the championship to the white race), his victory inspired blacks across the country even as it thoroughly shook many whites. In the wake of the fight, numerous race riots broke out across the nation as white men indiscriminately attacked black people, threatened by Johnson's symbolic victory.[9] Coming in the immediate aftermath of Johnson's defeat for the heavyweight championship by white boxer Jess Willard in 1915, Paul Robeson's athletic career garnered extra attention because of the racial controversies associated with Johnson's rise to prominence. Now that Johnson was no longer champion, would another black athlete challenge white male prerogatives?

World War I also raised the stakes for Robeson's athletic career. Even before the United States officially entered the conflict in the spring of 1917, buildup for the war effort had begun, and numerous commentators saw the war as an opportunity to prove American virtue and hardiness on the battlefield. In the climate of muscular Christianity, even ministers joined in the fray, overwhelmingly supporting the war.[10] Military leaders saw sports as helpful training exercises for prospective soldiers, believing that rope climbing, gymnastics, boxing, swimming, and other athletic contests would create healthier men and would improve their "smartness, activity, and precision."[11]

Sports could also help undo the feminizing effects of civilized society, creating a "harder, stronger masculinity" among the troops.[12]

As discussions of manliness pervaded wartime discourse, many black leaders saw the war as an opportunity for black men to challenge stereotypes that labeled them shiftless and unruly and to forcefully call for full citizenship rights. Although black leaders had been burned in the past by this strategy—black service in the Spanish-American War had led to a backlash against returning servicemen—many black leaders nonetheless hoped that wartime service would, in the words of African American author and activist James Weldon Johnson, "strengthen" the race's "claim to equal citizenship."[13] These beliefs regarding military service carried over to support for sports participation as well. Although some athletic programs, such as those at Harvard and Yale, canceled their football seasons to focus on war preparation, the military generally supported the continuation of both professional and college sports during the war, affirming their value as a training ground for future soldiers.[14] In this light, the achievements of black athletes could either support or refute black claims for equality in a broad spectrum of manly activity, including war making. As the metaphors of war circulated through sports discourse, including the use of terms such as *bomb*, *clash*, and *battle*, athletic contests such as football games seemed to indicate the capacity of the races to participate in the protection of the nation—in other words, to determine who qualified to serve as a citizen-soldier.

As black and white commentators described the athletic achievements of stars such as Robeson, they linked these men's performance on the gridiron to the broader concerns of their time, a reflection of the utility of sports to channel a wide range of issues. The location of Robeson's accomplishments ensured considerable media attention—the local mainstream New York papers picked up on the story of his successes, as did local and national black newspapers. But differences in the coverage of these two groups marked significantly differing perspectives on racial equality. Black writers consistently saw athletics as an arena in which African American male equality could be tested.[15] Therefore, they attempted to use integrated athletic competition as a model for other aspects of society, in which allowing blacks to compete equally would enable African Americans to prove their equality with whites. They also used the careers of African American scholar-athletes to contest long-held pejorative stereotypes of black men by emphasizing these athletes' well-rounded characters. White observers, on the other hand, appeared to support egalitarian ideals, suggesting that sports were free from racial prejudice, but were often uncomfortable with using sports to instill lessons for other aspects of life. As a result, they tried to minimize black athletic achievement by assigning credit to other white teammates or coaches, or by emphasizing "primitive" qualities that supposedly enabled black success.[16] Although there were exceptions, both groups tended to see athletics as an arena in which male vigor and virtue could be tested; their desired outcomes, however, were quite different. While one group hoped to indicate African American equality in all walks of life through athletic excellence, the other desired to minimize the implications of that excellence as much as possible by confining its relevance to a fairly limited area. Meanwhile, Robeson added another powerful voice to these debates, outlining his own vision of blacks' capabilities. In the end, these debates, tethered as they were to the world of sports, spotlighted the limits of egalitarianism in the North, the rather stiff definitions of manliness and citizenship that excluded African Americans, and the considerable cultural weight of the Jim Crow South—even in the New York metropolitan area.

A Black Athlete at a White School: Unwelcome Guest, Beloved Star

Paul Robeson was the youngest of six brothers and sisters, the son of a minister. Born in Princeton in 1898, he and his father (his mother died when he was very young) moved to Somerville, New Jersey, in 1910, where he attended an integrated high school. Excelling as a student at sports, academics, and the arts, Robeson also learned, according to biographer Martin Duberman, "that accomplishment [could] win respect and applause but not full acceptance," and he carefully controlled his demeanor so as not to seem too boastful or proud.[17] Robeson was also unable to participate in social activities with white students, a division he seemed to accept without complaint but which certainly caused him inner tension and turmoil.

When Robeson arrived at Rutgers on an academic scholarship, the all-male private college had an enrollment of 484 students, and Robeson was the only African American student.[18] Although not recruited by the team's coaching staff, Robeson decided to try out for the football team in his freshman year and persevered through brutal (and apparently racially motivated) hazing from his future teammates. When Robeson decided to try out for the Rutgers squad, he must have been aware of the challenges he would face as the lone black player on the squad, but the physical abuse he suffered at the hands of his future teammates shook him deeply. Although all rookies hoping to make the varsity squad faced tough hazing from veteran players, Robeson took a vicious beating from the others on the field, who piled on him after plays had ended and targeted him for extra-rough physical treatment. Suffering from a number of injuries, Robeson was bedridden for a week and considered quitting. When he returned, one player deliberately stepped on his outstretched hand at the conclusion of a play, stripping the fingernails off his hand and nearly breaking multiple bones. Infuriated, Robeson responded by targeting that player in subsequent drills, attacking him so aggressively that head coach George Foster Sanford halted play to let Robeson know that he had made the team in an effort to calm him down.[19]

Eslanda Goode Robeson's account of these events, published in 1930, suggests some of the reasons why her husband's white teammates responded as violently as they did. She related how the white players "were surprised" when a black man showed up for practice and were still "even more surprised and disconcerted" when Robeson excelled in practice competition with the scrubs, fearful that they might "lose" their position on the team "to a Negro."[20] For men raised in a culture that lauded white male superiority and viewed physical prowess as a defining attribute of that superiority, Robeson's accomplishments on the field emasculated his white teammates by pulling them down from their privileged position. As sociologist Michael Kimmel has argued, white men were often beset by anxiety over their own manliness, and the college environment, with young men newly from home seeking to prove their masculine worth in an all-male enclave, would have heightened these feelings of inadequacy. In this context, Robeson's dominance on the field would have had unsettling implications.[21] Robeson's experiences also pointed to some of the unacknowledged limits of sports as a level playing field. Far from being given the same opportunities as his white teammates, Robeson was made to undergo trials above and beyond the norm, a complaint that numerous black athletes would repeat throughout the twentieth century.

Gradually earning his teammates' acceptance, Robeson earned increased playing time during his freshman and sophomore seasons and became one of the team's top players as a junior and senior. As he did so, the university administration monitored his progress, apparently concerned how the school's lone black student was faring in the company of all-white teammates and how he was representing the university in off-campus contests. M. A. Blake, the school's horticulturist and the treasurer of the Rutgers Athletic Association, occasionally reported on Robeson to President William Demarest, noting Robeson's growing cadre of friends and his healthy lifestyle.[22] Apparently concerned that Robeson would not fit in, or perhaps worried that a black man would be poor company for white elites, the administration seemed pleased (and perhaps surprised) that Robeson enmeshed himself so well in the football team. After Rutgers's game against Fordham in October 1917, Blake reported the praise of one Fordham fan and alum, who applauded Robeson's "great game" and "clean" style of play. Reports of this sort must have mitigated anxieties about Robeson's representation of the school; they also showed the impact Robeson had on white fans outside Rutgers. One can hear a certain pleasant surprise in the talk of Robeson's sportsmanship and "clean" playing. Within the locker room, meanwhile, Robeson had clearly endeared himself to his teammates; in that same letter, Blake wrote that after the team had supper together following the game, the players "asked Robeson to sing."[23]

The extra attention given to Robeson by school administrators and opposing fans speaks to the added pressure he faced as a lone black athlete in an all-white school. Robeson was under constant scrutiny as a curiosity to white fans and a symbol of hope and achievement to many black leaders (including his own father). While the Fordham fan expressed admiration that Robeson played as "clean" as he did, there was, in a sense, no other option for him. With all eyes on him, Robeson had to play cleaner, and live cleaner, than his white counterparts in order to maintain his (relatively) privileged position and continue to earn the support and esteem of the black community. The extra burdens must have been difficult for the eighteen-year-old to shoulder.

Although the administration seemed pleased with Robeson's performances on the field and off, an incident in Robeson's sophomore year starkly revealed the limits of the school's egalitarianism and highlighted the power of Jim Crow segregation even in the urban Northeast. As the school approached its weekend-long sesquicentennial celebration, Washington and Lee University, Rutgers's scheduled football opponent, demanded that Robeson not play in the upcoming contest. Although the southerners were visitors to New Brunswick, they insisted that their customs and norms be followed. Since their entire social structure of legally sanctioned segregation depended on an affirmation of white racial superiority, they were unwilling to accept a black player as a worthy opponent or to put their manhood to the test against Robeson. Grudgingly, Coach George Foster Sanford agreed to sit Robeson out, despite the player's disgust and protests. Financial implications help explain the decision: the school was hoping to raise "a million dollars in endowment and property" for its 150th anniversary, and losing the revenue from the football game, if Washington and Lee backed out, would have significantly impinged that fund-raising drive.[24] As a result, Sanford indicated that Robeson had been injured in practice and would not play in the game, an excuse that many in the local press accepted without question.[25]

Robeson was deeply disappointed by the experience and pondered quitting the team in protest.[26] He was not alone in feeling betrayed by the team and school; two and a half years later, as Robeson graduated from Rutgers, fellow black alumnus James D. Carr wrote Demarest to complain about Robeson's treatment, inspired to do so by a similar event that had recently occurred at the University of Pennsylvania. Complaining that the school "prostituted her sacred principles" by agreeing to hold Robeson out of the game, Carr thought it was bitterly ironic that the school would accede to the demands of southern men, "whose progenitors tried to destroy this Union" and in the process took away "equality of opportunity and privilege" from a black student "whose progenitors helped to save the Union."[27] Robeson's absence hindered the team's fortunes in the contest, which ended in a 13–13 tie, and his bitter disappointment about being denied the chance to participate was almost certainly heightened by the game's symbolic significance. As the centerpiece of the university's three-day celebration, preceded by a number of parades and followed by a gala reception, the football game meant more than an ordinary contest.[28] With the stadium filled with past and present students and luminaries, Robeson's forced absence highlighted the persistence of racial intolerance and bigotry despite his presence on the team. And, as Carr noted, the benching also prevented Robeson from using the contest as a showcase of black "athletic ability, and, perhaps . . . athletic superiority." Understanding the circumstances—the large crowd in attendance and the game's special importance because of the celebration—Carr was particularly distressed that Robeson could not prove publicly African Americans' worth on the football field. "Equality of opportunity" was denied Robeson strictly because of his race.[29]

Although the university administration did not live up to the ideals of the level playing field, at least Robeson's fellow students seemed to embrace him (and the fame he brought the school) with earnest enthusiasm.[30] In covering Robeson's football career, the writers for the school newspaper, the *Targum*, consistently lauded Robeson's accomplishments. Stories often referred to Robeson by his widely used, and affectionate, campus nickname, "Roby," and credited him as a highly skilled performer.[31] A wrap-up of the 1917 football season, Robeson's junior year, spotlighted Robeson's importance and accomplishments in a number of ways, with a large photograph of him catching a pass, a reference to him as "the first of all ends" in the country, and a spotlight of his individual accomplishments (one of only five players to receive such an honor).[32] The paragraph-long assessment of Robeson reveals the esteem and friendly familiarity felt by the students toward him:

Our own "Roby." As a football man he stands out as the best in the country to-day. As a receiver of forward passes he stood out head and shoulders above all others. As defensive quarterback he is in a class by himself. His greatest compliment comes from Coach Sanford, who says he is the greatest player of all times. . . . He has been picked as the leading player in the country and as All-American end by practically every foot-ball authority throughout the east. As everybody knows, "Roby," you're there.[33]

Despite the abuse Robeson suffered when he attempted to join the team, this passage suggests that many Rutgers students felt a kinship with him as he rose to fame. In referring to Robeson as "Our own 'Roby,'" the newspaper's staff embraced him as one of their own, even if the parental tone betrayed a hint of condescension. Of course, part of Robeson's appeal was that he "knew his place," as he did not attempt to attend mixed-race social events and he refrained from joining the glee club because of racial dynamics.[34] As the only black man on campus for much of his time at Rutgers, Robeson hardly threatened the dominant social order that placed whites in a superior position—one exceptional black man did not necessarily portend an upheaval of white men's privileged place. Still, even this limited acceptance and praise of Robeson was remarkable in some ways for its apparently color-blind perspective.[35]

Those warm feelings extended beyond the football field. Over the course of Robeson's career, particularly as he approached graduation, the *Targum* and the school yearbook, *The Scarlet Letter*, effusively praised the wide range of his accomplishments. Entries in the yearbook celebrated Robeson for bringing "fame" to Rutgers on the football field and baseball diamond and also highlighted his academic achievements—his acceptance into Phi Beta Kappa and his numerous victories as an orator.[36] The *Targum* was even more enthusiastic about Robeson's wide-ranging achievements, praising him at length as he graduated in June 1919. Lauding Robeson for being an excellent athlete, a tremendous student, and a morally upright person, the newspaper's editors were especially impressed that Robeson "starred in both" academics and athletics. At the same time, the editors' precise wording reveals both the high esteem and the race-specific expectations that students at the school had for him. The writers appeared to go against the grain of beliefs in white male supremacy by writing that Robeson was "a man through and through." But their conclusion contained some implicit reservations:

> Now Paul, as you pass from our midst, take with you the respect and appreciation of us who remain behind. May your success in life be comparable to that of college days. In you other members of your race may well find a noble example, and this leadership is your new duty.[37]

Certainly impressed by Robeson, and willing to acknowledge Robeson's manliness, the newspaper editors nonetheless saw a relatively limited leadership role for Robeson, one specific to African Americans. That perspective was embodied in his class prophecy as well. Looking approximately twenty years into the future, prophecy writer Francis Lyons predicted, "Paul Robeson is the governor of New Jersey. He has dimmed the fame of Booker T. Washington and is the leader of the colored race in America."[38] For these white students, who were undoubtedly bowled over by Robeson's many athletic and academic accomplishments, there was still a limited realm in which Robeson could express his influence. On the one hand, they foresaw a great future for Robeson as the leader of the state; on the other, they could not get past seeing him primarily as a leader of black men.

The issue of leadership similarly impacted students' coverage of Robeson's athletic feats. On multiple occasions, *Targum* writers and editors hesitated to identify Robeson as the best player on the football team, the one most responsible for its success, despite the fact that he was the most decorated player in the school's history. After the victory over the Newport squad, which brought the spotlight to both Robeson and Rutgers football in general, the *Targum* did not single out Robeson for praise, even though nearly every other major newspaper highlighted his starring role: "It would be difficult to choose from the varsity any individual star. There was one huge star—the team."[39] Following the 1918 season, the paper fretted that "individual mention is a dangerous thing. It seems to give much of the credit to a few," but then pinpointed Coach Sanford as "the man who has done more for the athletics and spirit of this college than any other."[40] Perhaps individual mention of a black man was a "dangerous thing," whereas acknowledging a white male leader was acceptable. Other evidence supports this interpretation: despite being the best player by far on the football team, Robeson was not elected team captain during his senior year. According to his son's account, "His name was never even mentioned from the floor during the nominations."[41] As much as his fellow Rutgers students welcomed Robeson's contributions to their school, they appeared uncomfortable with positioning him as a school leader, unwilling to put him in a position of authority over white students.

African American Newspapers: Robeson and "Fritz" Pollard as "Race Men"

Although Robeson was very much alone as a black man on the Rutgers football team, he was not the only black college football star at the time. His career intersected with that of Frederick "Fritz" Pollard of Brown University, a remarkably agile halfback who earned widespread coverage and acclaim during the 1915 and 1916 seasons. Because the two were often discussed in connection with one another by both the black and white press, Pollard's relatively brief career at Brown provides a useful comparison and helps to illustrate broader patterns regarding black athletes.[42]

Frederick Douglass "Fritz" Pollard, named for the former slave and most famous African American leader of the nineteenth century, was born in 1894 in Chicago and raised in the Rogers Park section of the city, a northern, nearly all-white area. The Pollards were a relatively well-to-do and accomplished African American family, with many of Pollard's seven siblings achieving noteworthy successes in both athletic and nonathletic fields. Fritz Pollard, playing for the integrated Lane Tech High School in Chicago, starred in a number of sports and earned a modicum of fame throughout the city.[43] For two years after graduating high school, however, he was a vagabond student-athlete, traveling from college to college in the hopes of getting accepted so that he could play football. In the end, after stops at Northwestern, Brown,

Dartmouth, Harvard, and Bates College, Pollard was finally admitted to Brown as a full-time student and enrolled in the spring of 1915. At the time, Brown was a fairly small school with only about a thousand undergraduate students, and Pollard was one of only two African American students on campus.[44] After a rocky start, straightening out his eligibility issues and dealing with his own teammates' racism, Pollard quickly became a star on campus, where students gleefully celebrated his remarkable runs on the football field. In particular, Pollard's role in Brown's victories over Yale and Harvard during the 1916 season vaulted him to national fame and earned him a spot on football innovator and leading national football commentator Walter Camp's All-American team—only the second African American ever to make the team, and the first from the more celebrated backfield positions.[45]

Pollard's and Robeson's achievements on the football field proved especially inspiring to many in the black community because of the nature of integrated team competition and the amount of press devoted to the popular sport. Black leaders and black newsmen certainly celebrated black athletic achievement in segregated sports—indeed, sports pages in African American newspapers devoted considerable attention to football games involving schools such as Howard University, Morehouse College, and the other all-black schools that had emerged as a result of racial segregation. But members of the black press took particular delight in trumpeting the achievements of black athletes in integrated team sports in order to impart broader lessons about the potential for African American advancement, seeing these contests as models of broader integrated cooperation.[46] Thus, many black newspaper editors and writers depicted star athletes on integrated teams, such as Pollard and Robeson, as "race men," the natural leaders of African Americans at large. In this context, black newspapers represented Pollard and Robeson not merely as superior athletes but as well-rounded individuals who affirmed the capabilities of black men.

Pollard and Robeson were ideal models for this tactic, as both provided ample material for black newspaper editors and writers. After Pollard's scintillating performance in Brown's surprising 21–0 upset victory over Harvard in 1916, for example, the *New York Age* devoted one of its main editorials to him, praising Pollard for his ability to overcome "obstacles and handicaps" to become "the center of all eyes in the athletic world." Clearly finding value in Pollard's performance beyond his role in his team's victory, the editorial concluded, "Mr. Pollard is doing a very great deal to help solve the race problem."[47] Similarly, in 1915, the *Chicago Defender* championed Pollard and other black athletes, placing them in the "galaxy of race men" on account of their roles in pushing forward African American progress.[48] Just how was Pollard advancing the black race and solving the race problem? Part of the answer lay in his ability to overcome the many barriers erected to prevent black athletic advancement—which many saw as representative of the legal and social restrictions placed on blacks in economic, political, and everyday life. Thus, many of the stories printed and reprinted in black newspapers emphasized Pollard's determination, his hard work on and off the field— including the tailoring business he ran to help pay his way through school.[49]

The *Chicago Defender*, particularly attuned to Pollard's achievements because he had been a high school star in Chicago, devoted numerous stories and photographs to the star, emphasizing qualities that contradicted stereotypes of black men as lazy, violent, and unintelligent. Thus, Pollard was not only "a player of wonderful ability" but also "a clean sportsman" and "a scholar."[50] Similarly, another story emphasized that Pollard was "a quiet, unassuming lad" who "talks little, works hard with his books and his pressing shop."[51] Implicitly contrasting his character with that of the brash former heavyweight champion Johnson, the paper set Pollard up as a role model for both blacks and whites—a modest, hardworking athlete who succeeded by persevering. This characterization fit well with the ideals espoused by black leader Booker T. Washington, who emphasized black self-uplift through hard work and moderation. By stressing other aspects of Pollard's life off the playing field, using athletics as a conduit to illustrate larger points about him, these black papers attempted to open even more realms of civic life to black participation. Black men could be hard workers, could be responsible citizens, and could accomplish great things.

Black papers pursued a similar strategy in documenting Robeson's accomplishments, emphasizing his intelligence on the football field and depicting him as a football player who succeeded more because of his brain than his brawn. Although white newspapers also noted this aspect of Robeson's play, their coverage tended to emphasize his (for the time) "giant" stature—six feet, two inches in height, and weighing approximately 190 pounds.[52] Black papers instead emphasized his mental acuity, no doubt to counter stereotypes of black men as mindless brutes. In this light, the *New York Age* made sure to credit Robeson's accomplishments to "his superb strength augmented by a knowledge of both the theory and practice of the finer points of football,"[53] and the *Baltimore Afro-American* argued that the success of Rutgers owed much to "the brilliancy of [Robeson's] execution and the alertness of his brain."[54]

The *Crisis*, at the time edited by black scholar W.E.B. Du Bois, paid special attention to Robeson's wide-ranging scholastic achievements, finding him to be an excellent candidate for the role of race man. When the paper named Robeson as one of its "Men of the Month" in March 1918, the editors praised his "high scholastic record" and noted that he had "won the class oratorical prize for two years, a feat never before accomplished in the school." The paragraph also mentioned his other sports achievements and singing skills.[55] By depicting Robeson as a well-rounded individual, the *Crisis* used his celebrity as an athlete to draw attention to the intellectual and artistic capabilities of African American men in general. The editors would repeat that emphasis when he graduated in 1919, giving the black star special billing in the publication's annual issue about black graduates. Although most students simply had their name listed and, occasionally, their yearbook photograph, Robeson received a fairly lengthy write-up listing his numerous accomplishments on and off the athletic field alongside his yearbook photograph.[56] The attention paid to Robeson in the *Crisis* and elsewhere clearly registered with many readers; some black New Jersey residents recalled being specifically told to emulate his academic and athletic success.[57]

Those claims extended to specific issues of African American male citizenship that became contentious during World War I. When the war started in 1914, most black newspaper editors and writers, like most Americans in general, were hesitant for the United States to get involved in the conflict. However, by the time the United States officially entered the war in April 1917, most black papers (with some notable exceptions) had lent their support to the war effort. Although their motives varied, most black leaders had two goals in mind: to prove their race's loyalty to the nation (in the hopes of reaping postwar rewards) and to prove blacks' competence as soldiers, especially because many white southerners attempted to restrict black men from the manly role of citizen-soldier.[58]

In this context, sports could play a key role in validating black men's capabilities to serve. Black and white writers, such as Edwin B. Henderson in the *Crisis*, had long linked participation in sports with the development of a "strong, virile manhood."[59] War training, of course, offered a similar potential. In the fall of 1917, Rutgers Athletic Association treasurer M. A. Blake argued that the team's football players (including, apparently, Robeson) were "certainly receiving training that will be of great value to them if they later serve at the front," and Coach Sanford chided his team for not earnestly devoting themselves to their military drills.[60] The Rutgers students also supported the importance of athletics to military matters: in the wrap-up of the 1917 football season, the *Targum*'s editors argued in defense of continuing football the following fall, believing that if any of the players were drafted into the armed services, "their physical training will have fitted them better to serve their country."[61] Black leaders linked these two streams of thought, arguing that African Americans' success in integrated team sports revealed blacks' capacity to serve in the military—and, by extension, their manly capabilities more generally. In March 1917, for example, the *Crisis* featured a photograph of Pollard in between a photograph of a statue of Abraham Lincoln and a photograph of Lieutenant Colonel Charles Young, a hero of the Spanish-American War and one of the few black military officers in the nation's history.[62] In this representation, Pollard was part of a continuum of heroic figures who were fighting, or who had fought, for black equality. Although black leaders became increasingly frustrated by white military leaders' hesitance to employ black soldiers in combat duty, they still hoped that World War I would open new doors to African Americans. Black leaders thus supported the placement of celebrities such as Pollard with military units, a role he took up after his college career ended, even if these notable athletes and entertainers were there primarily as peacekeepers sent to soothe racial tensions among troops.[63] The symbolic value of having a star athlete such as Pollard in a leadership role as a YMCA physical director was too noteworthy to pass up.

By the fall of 1918, the connections between military service and on-campus activities were made stronger by the military's presence at the school. Robeson signed up, along with 450 other Rutgers men, for the Student Army Training Corps (SATC), which essentially took over the campus in the fall of 1918, converting buildings into training facilities and storage sites. Members of the SATC received $30 a week from the government and went through a rigorous schedule that involved morning reveille at 6:00 A.M., followed by room inspection and then a series of drills and duties.[64] It is little wonder, then, that a *Targum* staff writer employed military metaphors in covering Rutgers's loss to the Great Lakes Naval Reserve squad that fall. The writer saw a valuable lesson in the fact that the team had continued to fight even as the outcome of the game was no longer in doubt, writing that the "spirit" the players showed was a sign of "an unquenchable interest and a determination to stand with our team through thick and thin." He equated it to the refusal of a soldier to "[give] up when his armies face defeat."[65]

Given the enthusiasm of these white administrators and students to connect athletic excellence to military prowess, it makes sense that black newsmen would eagerly employ black athletic success in support of black male military capabilities. The best example of that enthusiasm came in the November 29, 1917, issue of the *Age*. When Josephus Daniels, the assistant secretary of the navy, issued a letter calling for "several thousand . . . only white men of good physique" to join the navy to work in the engine room and "about fifteen hundred Negro mess attendants to serve as officers' servants," the newspaper's editors howled with rage. Recognizing that Daniels's demeaning letter attempted to relegate African American men to a second-class role in the war, the paper's main editorial for that day vigorously protested the unequal recruiting strategies, arguing that black men had the capacity to do anything that whites did, that they were not fit for only servile positions.[66] For black leaders who hoped that the war would prove black male capabilities and challenge stereotypes, slights such as Daniels's letter could not be ignored, and they proudly recounted past military exploits by black soldiers.[67]

The paper found the perfect way to prove its argument about African American men's equality in that week's sports section. Describing the biggest victory of Robeson's career, Rutgers's triumph over the Newport squad in November 1917, Lester A. Walton argued that Robeson's performance had earned him a spot "in the athletic hall of fame alongside" other black athletes such as former Harvard football player William Henry Lewis and Pollard. After quoting, at length, two white newspapers, the *Brooklyn Eagle* and the *New York Tribune*, in their praise of Robeson, Walton concluded the article, "At the close of the contest Robeson and Whitehill, left end and full back for the New Jersey team, who scored the only touchdowns of the game, were carried off the field by a wildly serpentining [*sic*] mob of rooters." Clearly pleased by this image, Walton added, "P.S.—The above paragraph, in fact, the entire article, is respectfully referred to Secretary of the Navy Josephus Daniels for perusal."[68] In Robeson's achievement, and in his ability to work with and be embraced by white people, Walton saw a lesson for how black people could play a prominent and successful role in the war. Robeson had led his team to victory and had earned the acclaim of his white peers; his athletic success proved the inaccuracy of stereotypes that labeled black men as shiftless or capable of performing only menial tasks. Robeson had joined with his white teammates to achieve a brilliant victory. He had followed the "orders" of his head coach. He had used his physical prowess and his savvy to lead his team to victory over the "enemy" team—a team composed, no less, of naval reserves. In short, Robeson's athletic achievements proved that African American men could be effective leaders and soldiers.

Because black leaders invested so much in praising successful African American athletes, they took special delight in noting examples when white audiences, and particularly white leaders, appeared to recognize black men as equals. In a 1915 article about black football player Gideon Smith at Michigan Agricultural College (later Michigan State University), for example, writer Phil Waters reprinted a letter from Michigan governor Woodbridge N. Ferris to Smith:

> I like you because you are a success in football. . . . I am sure that you are now realizing in a measure of your ambition, and I am also sure that the future is rich with promise for you. I congratulate [Michigan Agricultural College] upon having a man of your ability on their team.[69]

Even though the note from the governor was a rather qualified letter of praise (Ferris congratulates Smith on his "success in football" and his "ability" rather than his character or intellect), Waters chose to reprint it in its entirety. Doubtless, he and his editors found special significance in the state's governor recognizing the achievements of a black athlete. By praising Smith, Ferris acknowledged, to some degree, the athlete's humanity and manliness. Had any members of the black press been present at the pep rally following Brown's 21–0 thrashing of Harvard in November 1916, they almost certainly would have been interested to hear Brown University president William Herbert Perry Faunce praise the "manhood" of the football team and remark that "there is no bigger white man on the team than Fred Pollard."[70] Affirming Pollard's equality with his white teammates by referring to him as a "white man," Faunce of course fell back on cultural conventions that affirmed white male superiority and whiteness as the highest standard of civilization. But he also did what many black press leaders hoped that whites in positions of power would do after viewing athletic success: he affirmed Pollard's equality, as a man, with his white teammates.

Delighting in such affirmations, the black press took a particular interest in emphasizing the applause of white fans during Pollard's and Robeson's careers. The account of white fans carrying Robeson on their shoulders after Rutgers's win over Newport Naval resonated for this reason, and thus was a particularly appropriate passage to send to Assistant Secretary of the Navy Daniels. Countless other stories in the *Age* and the *Afro-American* paid special attention to the enthusiastic applause that Pollard and Robeson received, especially from white fans of rival schools such as Yale and Harvard.[71] There was a symbolic value in white fans gleefully cheering on the exploits of black athletes; therefore, the *Defender*'s article about Pollard's placement on Camp's All-American team also highlighted the fact that he had earned rousing ovations from both the Harvard and Yale crowds.[72] African American newsmen eagerly highlighted these examples of white fan admiration because they showed that athletes could transcend, at least temporarily, the barriers of racial prejudice, earning respect for black manliness.

The designation of a player as an "All-American" carried particularly heavy weight with black newsmen. The title itself elevated athletes to the highest esteem, suggesting their membership in an exclusive club of the nation's elite. Earning a spot on Camp's team was especially prestigious. Considered by many as the leading spokesman for football, an advocate of football's virtuous effects on American manhood, and a former confidant of President Theodore Roosevelt, Camp was revered by most sportswriters and fans. His team, in short, represented for many a cross section of the manliest young Americans. These factors help explain why the *Defender* printed a front-page photograph with accompanying caption announcing Pollard's selection to Camp's All-American team, what they called "the highest award in the football world."[73] Pollard, earning his position on Camp's team one year before Robeson, was treated like royalty by the black leaders of the day, having a banquet in his honor at the Libya club in New York (an event attended by famous bandleader

James Reese Europe and *Age* editor James Weldon Johnson, among others)[74] and being "'lionized' by the society debutantes" in Chicago.[75]

Although the black press earnestly sought to use athletic success to over-turn conventional images of black men and to affirm the rights of black males as full citizens, writers in the white press made no such efforts. Clearly writing from a different perspective—and with different goals in mind—white writers instead subtly undercut black male athletic achievement in a number of ways. After all, these writers operated in a culture dominated by the belief in white racial supremacy. And their anxieties about the deeper meanings of sports were especially heightened because of Jack Johnson's recent success and his refusal to accommodate to white racial norms. For all the laudatory coverage of black athletic achievement, then, there were also numerous reminders of prejudice in the language used to describe black athletes and in the papers' hesitance to feature African Americans positively in photographs.

Nevertheless, white reporters could—and did—praise African American athletes for their talents and even intellect on the playing fields. Writers for mainstream papers such as the *New York Tribune* and the *New York Sun* lauded Pollard and Robeson as being "brilliant" and "the best" at their respective positions.[76] *Tribune* writer Louis Lee Arms indicated that Rutgers head coach George Sanford called Robeson "the smartest man he has ever seen on a grid-iron," and Arms himself praised Robeson for "diagnosing plays and holding aloof from tricks and threats."[77] Furthermore, following Rutgers's stunning upset victory over the Newport Naval Reserves, the *Tribune* even referred to Robeson as "a veritable Othello of battle, who led the dashing little Rutgers eleven to a 14 to 0 victory."[78] Closer to home, the praise continued in ear-nest. The New Brunswick *Daily Home News* particularly lauded Robeson for his many achievements while in school. After Robeson graduated, the news-paper printed a brief farewell to the big star, sad to see him depart Rutgers, and lamented, "There passed from the undergraduate ranks one of the big-gest all-around college men and athletes that this country has ever known." Especially impressed that Robeson was one of the few who were "great ath-letes" and "great scholars" at the same time, the unnamed writer concluded by writing, "A man who has accomplished so much as an undergraduate in so many different lines ought certainly to make good when he gets out into the world."[79] Such praise seems genuine in retrospect—white writers were deeply impressed by both the physical skills and mental attributes that Pollard and Robeson possessed. In praising these athletes so effusively, these white writ-ers lent credence to the idea that sports could be free from racial prejudice. Using militaristic terms ("Othello of battle") and acknowledging intellectual capabilities indicated, on some level, an acceptance of the idea that black men could measure up to white men as well-rounded individuals.

However, white newspapers revealed their own anxieties (and, presumably, those of many in the white community) about black men's potential as social and political equals in their deployment of language and photographs. The employment of natural imagery and animal metaphors upheld pervasive beliefs in African, and African American, primitivism and reinforced damaging stereotypes about African American men. Although sportswriting in general from this time period employed (in contemporary terms) over-the-top metaphors and overly descriptive language for nearly every athlete and sport, white papers tended to use naturalistic and animalistic language more frequently in covering black athletes—and certainly used that language more frequently than black newspapers did. For example, the *Yale Alumni Review* referred to Pollard as "a human eel" after he helped lead Brown to victory over Yale in 1916.[80] Similarly, the *Philadelphia Inquirer* used a host of (rather mixed) animal metaphors to describe Pollard's performance against Yale: Pollard was "the lion of the day," according to the paper. The Yale would-be tacklers, according to the *Inquirer*, were like "cats . . . and pounced on [Pollard] whenever they had a chance, but he was as elusive a greased eel."[81] Although the paper used cats to describe the white Yale players as well, Pollard's skills seem to come from his association with the primitive, the animalistic; his elusiveness as a "greased eel" was not intellectual, but natural.

White writers used similar language in describing Robeson's exploits, although instead of comparing Robeson to a beast, they often linked him to storms and shadows. Charles A. Taylor, writing for the *Tribune*, extensively employed the metaphor of a "dark cloud" in writing about Robeson's performance against Fordham University in October 1917. In describing Robeson's impact on the game, for example, Taylor wrote, "The dark cloud was omnipresent," and "The dark cloud used up three opponents in the course of the battle." His conclusion returned to Robeson and the "dark cloud" metaphor: "It would be wrong to say that Robeson is the entire Rutgers team. The aggregation is too well balanced for that, but it was this dark cloud that cut off all the sunshine for the Fordham rooters yesterday."[82] Depicting Robeson as a menacing shadow, even in admiration, had the potential to reduce him to a natural phenomenon, instead of a thinking, hardworking human being. Other writers employed similar language; Louis Lee Arms wrote that Robeson "rode on the wings of the frigid breezes; a grim, silent and compelling figure" in describing his performance against the Newport Naval Reserves.[83] An unnamed *Tribune* writer referred to Robeson as "a dark streak" in covering another Rutgers game.[84] Even Harold E. O'Neill, describing the Newport game in the *Daily Home News*, called Robeson "the incarnation of fury."[85] Similarly, nearly every mention of Robeson in the *New York Times* referred to him as "giant"—not necessarily an offensive term but one that, when used repeatedly, seemed to indicate that Robeson was something other than human.

By depicting Robeson as a force of nature, the *Tribune* and other papers undercut their own praise of Robeson's intellectual abilities. The consistent use
of natural imagery fit in well with contemporary racial beliefs among many
whites who saw African Americans as more primitive and thus able to connect
to a sort of primordial but uncivilized strength.[86] It also diminished these athletes' claim on the qualities and prerogatives associated with white manliness.

Beyond overtly metaphoric language, even mundane descriptions in these
newspapers carried with them the freight of racial prejudice. The consistent
use of terms such as *dusky* to refer to Pollard and Robeson were an attempt to
mark out for readers that these athletes were African Americans—as though
white writers were drawing arrows to the race of these players, making an
extra effort to note their racial exoticism, their otherness. The *Daily Home
News* coverage of Robeson's final game for Rutgers, a 5–1 baseball victory
over Princeton, for example, praised Robeson effusively as he concluded his
career, despite the fact that he had had little impact on that particular victory. However, the unnamed writer still felt the need to point out Robeson's
race *twice* in two paragraphs, referring to him as "the big colored fellow from
Somerville," and "the dusky giant."[87] Coach Sanford, when reaching for a
player to compare Robeson to in November 1917, selected Bemus Peirce,
a famous tackle, even though Robeson played the different position of end.
Why would he select Peirce? Because Robeson's "all around work always"
reminded him "of that great Indian player."[88] In connecting Robeson to past
stars, Sanford could not help but select another member of a racial minority.
These examples, in and of themselves, did not necessarily indicate prejudice
or the employment of stereotypes, but they did reveal the importance of race
to these players' identities in white minds, and the ways in which all members
of racial minorities were marked, no matter what uniform they wore.

The notation of race could also subtly, or explicitly, undercut black players'
achievements, particularly as race related to issues of leadership. A *Brooklyn
Daily Eagle* story that genuinely celebrated Robeson's accomplishments in the
1917 season and his academic prowess off the field also referred to him as "the
colored boy, who George Foster Sanford has developed into an end with All-
American possibilities."[89] In this instance, the white coach received the credit
for the success of the "colored boy," fitting in well with contemporary beliefs in
the need for whites to control and manage darker peoples. Mainstream papers
also, from time to time, employed overtly demeaning terms; one example was
a *Tribune* story that referred to Robeson as "the towering darky end" for the
Rutgers team.[90] By the 1910s, *darky* was an offensive term to many black
leaders, who vigorously protested its use.[91] Although a comparatively rare phenomenon, referring to Robeson and Pollard with terms such as *darky* enabled
white papers to reach out to white readers who wanted to dismiss the accomplishments of star athletes such as Robeson and Pollard.

White newspapers also subtly diminished African American athletes' achievements by minimizing the inclusion of their photographs, even for acknowledged stars, in their coverage of collegiate sports. Too pervasive a pattern to be merely coincidence, the absence of photographs of black athletes was particularly noticeable in the coverage of Robeson in the *Tribune* (among other newspapers that showed a similar bias). One clear example came at the close of the 1917 football season, when the *Tribune* featured an article by Louis Lee Arms in which he chose the season's best eleven players. One of them was Robeson, whom Arms praised as "the best football player I have seen this season." Although Arms also applauded a Rutgers player named Rendell, he clearly pegged Robeson as the superior player.[92] As if to counterbalance this apparent openness to Robeson and his race, however, the paper also featured five football "stars" in a photo montage that accompanied Arms's story. Not only was Robeson's picture conspicuously absent, but one of the players who was pictured was the white Rendell.[93] One might dismiss a single example as an oversight, but such omission occurred repeatedly throughout Robeson's career. Although the *Daily Home News* identified Robeson as the "star" of the 1916 game against Washington and Jefferson, he was not pictured. Two white players were instead.[94] Even more egregiously, early in Robeson's senior year the *Tribune* finally featured a photo montage of the Rutgers team (the first time it had done so, as previously, the paper had had printed photographs of only Coach Sanford)—with one picture in the middle of their starting eleven and five individual photographs of "star" players from the team. Robeson, stunningly, was not one of the five stars pictured. Although Robeson was present in the team photograph, at the end of the line and looking up at the camera, the newspaper excluded him in an individual portrait, despite the fact that he was universally considered the best player on the team.[95] There were limits to how far white newspapers would go in praising black manliness—and providing a flattering photograph of a black athlete in a starring role apparently crossed a line at the *Tribune*.

Coverage of Pollard's career showed similar trends. Even when Pollard was a star athlete in high school, he was not immune from unflattering depictions in the white-run media; a cartoon from the school newspaper depicted him in his track outfit with exaggerated lips and wild, kinky hair.[96] For all the hopes that black leaders had for athletic accomplishments to undermine stereotypes, this and other examples reflected the reality, the ways in which whites clung to long-held beliefs and prejudices. In later years, Pollard would be conspicuously absent from mainstream newspapers' photographs, just as Robeson.[97] The image of a black man triumphing over white athletes was too threatening, a visible reminder of the fallacies of white supremacy.

In contrast, African American newspaper editors went out of their way to include photographs of black athletic success. The *Crisis* featured very few photographs, particularly in its early years, but offered pictures of both Pollard and Robeson on multiple occasions. The *Defender* featured photographs of Pollard on its *front page* numerous times.[98] In fact, the *Defender* even reprinted photographs of relatively obscure football games such as the Tufts-Harvard game from 1916, simply because Tufts had two African American players on its team—and the paper drew in arrows to point out the black players in action.[99] An image of black men physically dominating whites instantly challenged stereotypes of black men as shiftless, lazy, and weak.[100]

In violent collisions, scampering runs, and joyful celebrations, then, college football offered a variety of tableaus in which to see black men and white men competing with one another and working together. These rich moments offered exciting potential for black leaders and distressing possibilities for many whites. The contestation over the description and depiction of these athletes, then, struck at the heart of larger debates—the place of black men in the American body politic.

The Many Meanings of Fair Play in Life: Competing Models of Sports

The attempts to mark out roles and capacities for black men were not the only larger issues discussed through the careers of individuals like Pollard and Robeson. More generally, black and white sportswriters also differed in their interpretations of the model that sports offered for American democracy. Although both black and white sportswriters often praised the egalitarian qualities of the sporting world, of the level playing field, their different approaches revealed contested visions of the contours of American society and politics.

Although generally celebratory of the egalitarian opportunities in sports, hoping that the level playing field could be extended to other realms of life, black newspapers were also attuned to the fact that the games themselves did not always illustrate the proper behavior of good sportsmanship and fairness. Indeed, one of the major differences in coverage between black and white papers was the willingness of black writers to point out examples of unsportsmanlike behavior. While white writers tended to shy away from anything that depicted sports in an unsavory light, black writers made sure to note when black athletes were being treated unfairly. After all, sports worked as an integrationist metaphor only if whites actually provided blacks equal opportunities and afforded them equal treatment on the playing field.[101]

The ongoing inequality of college sports, however, was often revealed in the hesitance of some universities to schedule games against teams that had black athletes, a trend revealed in the Robeson benching against Washington and Lee. Black newspapers were much more likely to call attention to these incidents, distressed that sports were not as color-blind as many wished to believe. The lead editorial of the *Age* on November 23, 1916, denounced

Princeton University for purportedly refusing to schedule a game against Brown because of Pollard's presence on the team. Editors saw this event as reflective of the "influence" of Woodrow Wilson—a southerner, former Princeton president, and of course, U.S. president—who was described as "an enemy of the Negro."[102] This story did not appear in mainstream white papers. Similarly, when Washington and Lee University refused to play against Rutgers in 1916, the white press largely ignored the racist demands of the southern school, but black newspapers such as the *Age* made certain to mention the snub. In a recap of the 1916 season, the paper revealed that Robeson "played every minute of every game Rutgers played . . . except the game with Washington and Lee of Virginia, which team refused to play against him because of his color."[103] The paper, unlike the local white press, would not let this slight go unmentioned. Because sports could serve as a metaphor for black equality only if whites agreed to participate against African Americans, black papers emphasized what they saw as violations of the tenets of fair competition.

Harsh treatment of African Americans on the playing field manifested white racism and ongoing inequality in another way, and the black press paid careful attention to examples of white abuse. The *Defender* selected excerpts from white papers, for example, that described the unnecessary roughness committed by Harvard players against Pollard during the Brown-Harvard game of 1916. After Pollard dazzled the crowd with several long runs, three Harvard players tackled him out of bounds in the second half, driving him up against the stadium wall and earning a fifteen-yard roughing penalty (Pollard, fortunately, was unharmed).[104] Although some of the major white newspapers (such as the *Tribune*) made no mention of the violence, the *Defender* selected papers that noted the rough play, allowing its readers to see the difficult conditions that black athletes faced as they tried to integrate popular sports. Indeed, earlier in that season, the *Defender* had printed a distressing account of a Princeton-Tufts game in which the all-white Princeton team had violently targeted two black players on the Tufts squad. Although the Princeton team grudgingly agreed to play Tufts, its players "went after both" African Americans "with vengeance, determining to put them out of the game." According to the account, one of the black players "went into convulsions" because of the violence against him. Meanwhile, the other black player complained several times to the referee about "the filthy and vile language the Princeton players were using against him."[105] Unwilling to sugarcoat the experiences of black athletes, papers such as the *Defender* made sure to highlight these examples of ongoing inequalities in order to make whites abide by principles of good sportsmanship and fairness. In this way, a cleaned-up sports world could be an effective model for an egalitarian American society.

By contrast, white newspapers hesitated to reveal the limits of fair play and decorum in sports. Although white writers often lauded the level playing field of sports as a representation of American meritocracy, they were less interested in identifying the wide-ranging impacts of race. When Robeson was roughed up and verbally taunted by the Great Lakes Naval Training School in 1918, the *Tribune* made no mention of the violence against him even though the *Defender* claimed it was "one of the most outrageous occurrences that has happened on the gridiron in many a moon." Indeed, Robeson's teammates were so upset by the "injustice and unsportsmanlike tactics" that "they began slugging" and were penalized as a result.[106] White newspapers could have pursued this story as a sign of teammates coming together, crossing racial lines, but they did not. It was left to the black press to show the ongoing difficulties faced by black athletes trying to get fair play on the football field. African Americans knew all too well the many double standards employed against them in everyday life, and while sports could be a helpful sign of progress, they also provided a cautionary tale about the slow pace of change.

The unwillingness of white papers to address the halting steps needed for a meritocracy to be realized in the sporting world, let alone general society, spoke to the different visions many blacks and whites had regarding the nature of American democracy in the early decades of the twentieth century. As the coverage of Robeson and Pollard reveals, most white sportswriters tended to emphasize sports as a fair testing ground for people of all races and praised sports as being free from prejudice. In this way, they appeared to agree with their black peers, who saw sports as a model for U.S. society. On the other hand, these white writers deliberately skewed their coverage, as the preceding examples indicate, to "prove" the idea of the inherent fairness of sports. As a result, they often failed to acknowledge the limits sports offered for social transformation and implicitly supported the current status of American society, in which racial distinctions actually meant a good deal to one's chances for success in life. By minimizing the persistent limits to black advancement, these newspapers (perhaps unwittingly) contributed to an ongoing belief that African Americans could lift themselves out of poverty if only they worked hard enough—after all, writers seemed to imply, black sports stars had achieved success; why couldn't everyday African Americans?

White newspapers, of course, betrayed their own ambivalence about the broader lessons of sports in failing to report white abuse of black athletes on playing fields and by not commenting on incidents when racial politics prevented contests from taking place or players from suiting up. Even poor fan behavior—the use of racial slurs, for example—went unreported by the white newspapers. For example, white writers turned a deaf ear to Yale fans screaming, "Catch that nigger" or "Kill that nigger" every time Pollard returned a punt in the 1915 matchup between the two schools.[107] Although the legal notion of "hate speech" had not yet entered legal discourse in the United

States, white sportswriters clearly knew that such language was offensive, demeaning, and indeed threatening.[108]

Political theorist Judith Shklar's concept of a liberalism of fear helps explain this behavior by white fans and the hesitance of white newsmen to report it. In Shklar's formulation, a truly liberal society—by which she means a fair and just democracy—would enable all people to make decisions based on their personal interests and beliefs, without the threat of fear from others or from a government agency. Recognizing two "basic units of political life," "the weak and the powerful," a truly liberal state would "secure . . . freedom from the abuse of power and intimidation of the defenseless this difference invites."[109] From this perspective, the white fans, players, and coaches who employed racially motivated verbal threats and created an atmosphere of hostility toward these athletes affirmed their strength as a group over the weaker racial minority. They publicly exercised their greater power in society. Because most white sportswriters consistently praised the fairness and openness of American society and of the sporting world in particular, they did not report this unsportsmanlike language. Doing so would have indicated the limitations of sports to effect lasting change and would have pointed out that the "level playing field" was fraught with inequalities, as black athletes had to endure taunts and abuse that their white counterparts did not.[110] When viewed from that perspective, sports as a metaphor for society at large would have revealed that systemic changes needed to occur before African Americans could achieve social and economic equality with whites. That was a lesson even liberal whites were not, on the whole, interested in exploring, and so they kept these issues out of their coverage.

In fact, these newspapers at times went overboard in emphasizing the inherent fairness of sports. In one breathless paragraph about Rutgers's 1916 game against West Virginia, Harold E. O'Neill in the *Daily Home News* described the game, and the players, as being "clean" five different times. In addition, he called the action "perfect football," with teams playing "fair" and with players acting "like gentlemen."[111] This account contradicts the recollection of Robeson, who remembered the game as being particularly rough because some West Virginia players were upset about competing against him.[112] Was O'Neill covering for the behavior of the West Virginia players? O'Neill's assertion that he "hoped that relations [would] be continued" in the future between the two teams suggests that he was inspired that a game featuring Robeson against a southern school had proceeded without any major incidents and may explain his eagerness to paint a positive picture of the game's action.[113]

Then, too, O'Neill and other white writers likely wrote from the perspective that the American dream of equal opportunity had been attained, or very nearly so; therefore, they did not look to sports as a model for how society *should* be but, rather, as a representation of how society *was* at its best. White writers ignored racial troubles because they would have reflected that the American dream was no more than a dream and that whites were given substantial privileges in nearly every aspect of life. These two ideas of the value of the level playing field—as a road map for the rest of society or as a reflection of society—help explain how both blacks and whites could write about the egalitarian possibilities of sports but then subscribe to quite distinct racial politics. In the translation of racial politics to sporting coverage, however, those distinctions were often missed by writers and readers alike.

Robeson's Perspectives on "Loyalty" and the Quest for Equality

The voices of newspaper writers, university administrators, and fellow students were not the only ones to comment on Robeson's significance in the context of black aspirations for equality, World War I, and changing conventions of manliness. Robeson himself, as a scholar and speaker, also publicly outlined his beliefs in a number of forums. Through public speaking contests, his honors thesis, and his commencement address, Robeson charted a moderate path for black advancement, outlining a civil society in which whites would recognize the contributions and untapped potential of African Americans in broader American society, even if they were unwilling to embrace blacks as social equals.

Robeson was a skilled orator, sweeping to victory every year in class oratory contests, and he often engaged many of the key issues circulating in public discussion of athletics.[114] Although those speeches were not recorded, the *Targum* printed a rather lengthy account of his junior year entry, when he selected "Loyalty and the American Negro" as his topic, and we can get a sense of how Robeson positioned African Americans in relation to World War I. After outlining the valorous deeds (and devotion to country) of black soldiers in both the Revolutionary War and the Civil War, Robeson turned his attention to the current conflict. According to the *Targum* account, he indicated:

> In the present war, more than ever before, negroes are showing the loyalty and the results of their American training. They are being given commissions and are formed into large and effective units of our armed forces.
>
> After the war the negro will still show his loyalty and . . . a new growth of democracy will gain a place never before attained in this country.[115]

As many of the era's black leaders had hoped, Robeson articulated a vision whereby black accomplishment and devotion during World War I would persuade white Americans to expand democracy to include African Americans as full citizens. By calling attention to the past and current service of loyal black soldiers, Robeson attempted to mitigate fears of black radicals even as he pushed for "a new growth of democracy" that was clearly meant to be a radical reconfiguring of American society. The audience was deeply moved, and Robeson "was applauded to the echo."[116] Robeson's rather moderate political tone likely earned him support from both blacks and whites—he emphasized a united body politic, one in which democracy could connect people across the color line and in which patriotism motivated all Americans.[117]

Robeson's last words on these issues as a Rutgers student came in his commencement address, titled "A New Idealism," at his graduation in June 1919. Speaking to his fellow students, their families, and university administrators, Robeson articulated his vision of a civil society in which blacks and whites could coexist peacefully and equally.[118] Showing his savvy as an orator, Robeson eased his way into the issue of race relations, first explaining that the postwar era was "an unparalleled opportunity for reconstructing our entire national life and moulding it in accordance with the purpose and the ideals of a new age." Only after praising U.S. soldiers for preserving "freedom" through their heroic sacrifices in World War I and lamenting the loss of courageous young men in service to their country did he make his way toward race and segregation. To preserve the freedom soldiers had fought and died for, Robeson argued, the nation needed to unite all its individuals by providing "full opportunities for the development of everyone, both as a living personality and as a member of a community upon which social responsibilities devolve." Referring to Lincoln's Gettysburg Address, Robeson challenged his listeners to make the soldiers' sacrifices count by striving to "carry to successful fruition the ideals for which these honored ones have sacrificed."

Robeson then addressed race explicitly, saying that he would do his "little part in helping [his] untutored brother." But, given the predominantly white audience, Robeson carefully used the language of Booker T. Washington, affirming, "We of this less favored race realize that our future lies chiefly in our own hands." Plugging into the American ethos of self-help and hard work, Robeson seemed to eschew aid from white America. Or did he? Even as he argued for the importance of individual effort, he listed a host of factors that made African American advancement particularly difficult:

We are struggling on attempting to show that knowledge can be obtained under difficulties; that poverty may give place to affluence; that obscurity is not an absolute bar to distinction, and that a way is open to welfare and happiness to all who will follow the way with resolution and wisdom; that neither the old-time slavery, nor continued

prejudice need extinguish self-respect, crush manly ambition or para-
lyze effort; that no power outside of himself can prevent a man from
sustaining an honorable character and a useful relation to his day and
generation.

While emphasizing "that races like individuals must stand or fall by their
own merit," Robeson simultaneously highlighted the ongoing impact of racial prejudice, slavery, and poverty to black advancement. In order for African
Americans to achieve equality, Robeson argued, whites needed to exercise
"compassion," to help African Americans and to help build a stronger "community spirit." Simply providing equal access to opportunities would not be
enough, no matter what sportswriters had argued throughout his career.

In encouraging whites to help blacks achieve political and economic
equality, Robeson was careful not to argue for an entirely integrated society. Instead, he wanted a civil society, one in which blacks could rise out of
poverty and enjoy material comfort and basic legal rights. Blacks and whites
could share a "fraternal spirit which does not necessarily mean intimacy, or
personal friendship, but implies courtesy and fair-mindedness." Here Robeson stipulated that merit, that equal opportunity, did not currently dictate
a person's fate in American society. Only after whites acknowledged African
Americans' "fellow-citizenship and fellow-humanity" could there be a nation
"in which success and achievement are recognized, and those deserving
receive the respect, honor and dignity due them." Robeson reached out to his
audience by couching his remarks in the language of American egalitarianism
but was clear on the point that that ideal was far from a reality. He had reason
to be cautious in his tenor. Events such as the July 1917 race riots in St. Louis,
when white male workers, upset at the growing number of black employees
in local factories, went on a rampage in the city's black section, attacking
and killing black men and women and destroying countless homes and businesses, showed that the black quest for economic equality could spark vicious
reprisals from whites.[119]

As if to ward off any rustling in the seats from those who might have
resented his subtle jab at the nation's currently unegalitarian society, Robeson
then returned to patriotism, lauding the dead soldiers and echoing the Gettysburg Address in promising to "consecrate ourselves . . . to the furtherance of
the great motives for which they gave their lives." But his conclusion stressed
the importance of equality again, arguing that the soldiers' goals would not be
fulfilled "until in all sections of this fair land there will be equal opportunity
for all, and character shall be the standard of excellence." Although he did not
name race as a key factor in how people were judged, his more astute listeners
must have surely recognized his point. If they did not, his list of the qualities
of his "ideal government" made his intentions clear. In Robeson's America,

"an injury to the meanest citizen is an insult to the whole constitution." In an ideal society, "black and white shall clasp friendly hands in the consciousness of the fact that we are brethren and that God is the father of us all."[120]

Robeson's moderate political stance in this speech is striking, in part, because of his later radical beliefs.[121] But they also point to the context—a time when most blacks were still trying to determine the best way to advancement, still hopeful that compassionate whites and compliant courts could open doors wide enough that blacks would be able to achieve status and wealth commensurate with that of their white peers. Robeson built on the self-help ethos of Booker T. Washington even as his own wide-ranging academic interests better represented the ideals of W.E.B. Du Bois. At this moment, fresh from a full career at Rutgers and preparing to attend law school in the fall, Robeson was not yet ready to turn his back on the country of his birth, still hopeful that America could fulfill its democratic and egalitarian promise.

Conclusion: Black Masculinity's Contested Meanings

Paul Robeson was many things during his time at Rutgers: an unwelcome freshman tryout for the football team, a beloved senior All-American, a well-liked singer who entertained his peers at various events, and a social outcast who could not attend any of the dances held after his singing engagements. In these roles, and others, he attracted the attention of countless observers, black and white, on campus and off. As the star football player on an integrated team, in a sport becoming increasingly popular across the nation, he carried particularly weighty cultural baggage. When the nation entered the fray of World War I, he became an even more potent symbol—for good or ill, according to the observer—of what black men could accomplish in an integrated, competitive setting.

Inevitably, different observers drew different meanings from Robeson's accomplishments and those of his contemporary Fritz Pollard. But as black and white people discussed his significance, they continually circled back to sports as a model of egalitarianism. No one, it seems, could escape the allure of sports as a realm where equal opportunity could be seen in action, where the notions of fair play and sportsmanship seemed to epitomize the nation's larger political ideals and social promise. As a college athlete, supposedly free from the taint of commercialism, Robeson could represent the possibilities of a system that rewarded merit regardless of race, creed, or color. If some black observers saw the model as still incomplete, they nonetheless subscribed to its potential, hopeful that even an imperfect realization of equal opportunity could lead to greater access to the political, economic, and social privileges still reserved almost exclusively for white men. That Robeson himself made no allusions to sports in his own speeches and writings about equality, even in his commencement address, suggests that he was well aware of the limitations of sports. But as he left Rutgers after four years replete with praise and honor, nearly anything must have seemed possible to those who watched him say his final words as a collegian and exit the spotlight (for the moment): an All-American athlete, a scholar, a black man, a Rutgers alum, a walking representation that maybe, just maybe, the nation could deliver on its promises.

Neither Robeson nor the black and white observers attending graduation that day in June 1919 could have known that the nation would erupt in violence in the ensuing months as whites viciously assaulted returning black servicemen and black factory workers who hoped to capitalize politically and economically on their wartime service.[122] The brutal race riots of 1919 showed emphatically that the nation was not yet amenable to equal black citizenship, no matter the accomplishments of Robeson and other black athletes. That these riots took place in all regions of the country—from the South to the Midwest to the Northeast—further amplified the mixed reactions to Robeson in the metropolitan New York area. Even in the North and even in mixed-race urban spaces, the time for fair play in American civic life would have to come later.

2

"Harbingers of Progress" and "the Gold Dust Trio"

Kenny Washington, Woody Strode, Jackie Robinson, and the 1939 UCLA Football Team

n the November 18, 1939, issue of the *Washington* (D.C.) *Afro-American*, sports editor Sam Lacy could not contain his excitement. As the college football season wound down, it was not the local black colleges and universities, such as Howard University, that inspired Lacy's enthusiasm; nor was it any of the East Coast schools that featured black players, such as Cornell University. Instead, Lacy turned his attention to the University of California at Los Angeles (UCLA), then a relatively young school with few athletic accomplishments to its credit. The UCLA squad was undefeated, and it seemed likely that a season-ending game against crosstown rival the University of Southern California (USC) would determine which school would be invited to play in the annual Rose Bowl game, at the time the most prestigious and financially rewarding postseason college bowl game. Lacy wrote that he would "give anything . . . to see the Los Angeles lads trim the wicks of the lamps of their Trojan rivals." There were three reasons why Lacy felt so passionately about the UCLA squad: Kenny Washington, Woody Strode, and Jackie Robinson, the remarkably talented trio of African American men who starred for the team. In an era when integrated team athletic competition was still relatively rare, to have three black starters on one squad at a predominantly white school was unprecedented. As Lacy wrote, if UCLA earned a trip to the Rose Bowl, the game would be "overrun with sepia flesh" as never before. Thrilled by the possibility, he urged his readers to support him in saying, "C'mon UCLA!"[1]

Lacy's cross-country reaction gives some sense of the close attention paid by many to the 1939 UCLA football squad. With three black starters and a key black reserve among its active roster, the UCLA team epitomized (optimistically to some, and despairingly to others) the possibilities of a multiracial and multiethnic America.[2] A number of factors made this team an especially rich one to continue—and amend—the conversations regarding race and sports that had taken place during Robeson's time at Rutgers. The time period altered the dialogues regarding race and sports considerably. As New Deal policy makers and left-wing activists attempted to craft a new civic nationalism that welcomed the contributions of previously disparaged minorities, sports such as college football provided an ideal testing ground for a racially integrated America. College football's increasing popularity and media coverage in the 1930s, even in the midst of the Great Depression, also made the sport a particularly compelling outlet for discussions of racial politics. That this UCLA team played its games just as the Nazis began their campaign of terror halfway across the globe, one predicated on racist beliefs, only heightened this rhetoric. Finally, UCLA's location in Southern California also affected the discussions of racial politics. Though removed from the worst violence and abuses of the Jim Crow South, the mixed-race city of Los Angeles nonetheless had its own struggles, trying to define a civic culture that could accept peoples of European, African, Mexican, and Chinese descent.

In a racially mixed city during turbulent times, then, Washington, Strode, Robinson, and their teammates engendered a number of different reactions from fans, newspaper writers, and students—black and white, men and women. While some saw this integrated team's success as a true representation of American democracy, others attempted to circumscribe or undermine their achievements. Issues of leadership, representations of black men, competing visions of American civic life, and the ability of sports success to last beyond the limited time frame of college and the enclosed space of the football field—all of these issues spoke to the tenuous position of racial minorities in the supposedly improved temporal climate of the New Deal and the geographic environs of Southern California. The numerous obstacles encountered by UCLA's black stars, on the field and off, starkly outlined the limits of the nation's new civic nationalism. Old fractures—between the haves and have-nots, the privileged and the oppressed—proved too significant for sports achievements to heal entirely.

Southern California, UCLA, and 1930s American Democracy

Late 1930s Southern California was a rich setting for the discussions of race, equality, and democracy surrounding the 1939 UCLA squad. Although the Los Angeles area would not experience its most substantial population boom until the start of World War II, the area had been growing consistently since railroads first brought a significant number of immigrants to the area in the 1880s. Located on the periphery of the U.S. mainland, the area attracted a multiracial population that included Mexicans, Chinese, African Americans, Jewish Americans, and midwestern Protestant European Americans. Although whites constituted the majority group, this diverse ethnic population made the area a particularly appropriate location to test the limits of American democratic society's inclusiveness.

The Los Angeles area had a long-standing reputation for harboring progressive racial attitudes and offering an abundance of opportunities for African Americans, and the relatively high level of home ownership for African Americans was one key positive trend. However, the city's black residents still faced discrimination in a number of facets of life, including restrictive racial covenants in housing and segregated businesses and public facilities. In the realm of employment, black men in particular found jobs scarce, with employers preferring to hire whites first, and then ethnic groups other than blacks second. Although black women could find work as domestic servants, black men were often passed over for jobs in factory work, which was the major employment opportunity in the prewar years. Black men instead had to find work as domestic servants, porters and waiters on trains, and janitors, and perhaps in entertainment as musicians. Even Hollywood offered few opportunities. So, although the city was largely free from the excessive racial violence of the South, African Americans still faced a number of social and economic limitations. By the 1930s, these factors combined to form a climate in which many blacks tenaciously clung to the few advantages Los Angeles had to offer, while increasing numbers of whites resented black achievement and success.[3]

The unsettled character of the city led to wide variances in racial politics, where blacks could be welcomed participants in society by some whites and brutally disparaged by others. Rachel Isum Robinson, a UCLA student in the 1940s and widow of Jackie Robinson, recalled the racial climate in the city as being "Northern-style bigotry . . . unlike the South, incidents of discrimination were often unexpected and inexplicable—you never knew when they would happen."[4] Businesses posted signs in their windows that announced, "We reserve the right to refuse service to anyone," code for their distaste for black and other minority customers. Certain sections of the city— Inglewood, and Pasadena, where Jackie Robinson and his family lived—were more prejudiced than others.[5] But other sections of the city, where blacks and other ethnic groups such as Italian Americans lived, proved to be at least tolerant of racial diversity, with fewer signs of discrimination and animosity. This mixed character to the city's racial attitudes profoundly influenced coverage of the 1939 UCLA team, as responses, even among whites, vacillated between unabashed celebration of black athletic achievement and violent antipathy.

These differences in the city's racial attitudes were also reflected in the distinct biographical circumstances of the team's three black stars. Strode, the oldest of the three at age twenty-five in 1939, had grown up in the south-central section of Los Angeles, a predominantly African American area. Although he had encountered some racism as a youth, he remembered sports being one aspect of his life largely free from racial "grudges, especially between the players." Washington, Strode's best friend on the team, hailed from the mostly white Lincoln Heights section of Los Angeles. Washington's high school friends were nearly all of Irish or Italian descent, and Strode said that as far as he knew "the Washington family was the only black family in the neighborhood." Although Washington's father was largely absent from his life, his uncle Rocky, a well-liked lieutenant on the L.A. police force, served an important role as a mentor. Kenny Washington was a star football player coming out of high school and had a number of scholarship offers, including one from crosstown rival USC, but chose UCLA because of its better record with black athletes.[6]

Jackie Robinson selected UCLA for similar reasons to those of Washington, although his background and life experiences were quite different from those of his two black star teammates. Growing up in Pasadena, Robinson faced bitter racism at an early age. One of his first recollections was of a rock fight with his white neighbor across the street when he was eight years old, after the young girl called him a "nigger." In later years, Robinson would see firsthand the adulation black athletes could receive from white fans but also the ongoing discrimination and limited avenues of advancement opened to blacks. Older brother Mack Robinson was feted nationally and locally after winning a silver medal in track at the 1936 Olympics. A few years later, he was working as a janitor, one of the few jobs open to black men. Another older brother, Edgar, was arrested on trumped-up charges and viciously beaten by Los Angeles police during the annual Tournament of Roses Parade on January 1, 1939. Robinson also had bitter personal experiences with the police. On two separate occasions, Pasadena law enforcement officials arrested Robinson under dubious circumstances. The first involved a fight after a high school football game, when Robinson threw a punch at an opposing player who had used a racial slur against him. The second incident occurred just before he left for UCLA. While he was driving home with friends after a summer baseball game, some white youths insulted Robinson and his companions. When teammate Ray Bartlett slapped one of the offending whites with his baseball mitt, a crowd of African Americans gathered around the two cars. A local police cruiser stopped to investigate the situation, and Robinson alone was jailed, most likely because of his local celebrity as an athlete, despite his having thrown no punches in the incident. These experiences, and others like them, made him suspicious of local whites. As Strode later recalled, Robinson "had a little more hate going than the rest of us" because of his upbringing in Pasadena.[7]

Despite these varied backgrounds, UCLA was, on the whole, a good fit for the three black stars. A relatively young school, UCLA was nonetheless big and growing by the late 1930s. In the fall of 1939, the school's 9,762 total students made it smaller than its sister school, the University of California at Berkeley (Cal), which had just over fifteen thousand students, but still a fairly large institution. Nonetheless, the school had ground to make up to compete with rivals such as Cal and USC, larger and older schools with traditions of athletic success. Those factors perhaps explain UCLA's willingness to accept black athletes, even in the 1920s. Just before the school joined the Pacific Coast Conference (PCC), the dominant athletic conference in the region, African American Ralph Bunche, who would go on to fame as a UN ambassador, was a star basketball player and track athlete for the school from 1925 to 1927. By the mid-1930s, USC owned the dominant athletic program in the area but had a reputation for being prejudiced against black players. UCLA thus offered a local institution for African American athletes such as Strode, Washington, and Robinson to participate in big-time college sports; in turn, these stars played key roles in making the UCLA Bruins competitive in the PCC.[8]

As UCLA tried to build up its athletic programs, black sports stars across the country continued to make their mark on amateur and professional athletics. Track star Jesse Owens and boxer Joe Louis earned special acclaim, providing hope for black newspaper editors and writers. Owens became a national star after his performance in the 1936 Berlin Olympic Games, when he symbolically disproved Adolf Hitler's assertions of Aryan superiority by winning four gold medals. Louis became a hero by claiming the heavyweight championship in 1937, making him the first black champion in the division since the controversial Jack Johnson, and by defeating German boxer Max Schmeling in their rematch in 1938. Unlike Johnson, Louis and Owens were generally well regarded in both the white and black communities because they avoided public bravado, incendiary political talk, and, of course, white women.[9] Such esteem was always tenuous, however. One editorial from the Raleigh, North Carolina, *News and Observer*, for example, praised the two black stars for their "brawn" but cautioned that their "conduct" and not their "fame" would "serve to help or hurt the race." Outspoken black athletes would clearly not be acceptable to these white men's standards.[10] Jesse Owens knew this tightrope all too well. Although he had been a national hero following the Olympics, he quickly alienated many of his supporters by leaving the national team before a series of meets in Europe, attempting to cash in on his success and earn money for his family. As a result of this supposed betrayal of the national team, Owens's commercial endorsement opportunities dried up and he found himself desperate for work. Like Louis and Owens, UCLA's black stars would have to negotiate the pitfalls of public perception as they embarked on their athletic careers. Although not performing in the Jim Crow South, they nonetheless encountered numerous examples of that mind-set, and of racial bigotry in general, in their experiences on the West Coast, as Jim Crow's reach extended far beyond the boundaries of the old Confederacy.[11]

The effects of southern racial mores were mitigated to some extent by the national political climate surrounding these pioneering stars. As the historian Gary Gerstle has argued, many white policy makers in the 1930s were motivated by a sense of civic nationalism that embraced ethnic pluralism. Amid the ravages of the Great Depression, "the 1930s called for a kinder and gentler" approach to immigrants and other minority groups, one that emphasized the need "to bring diverse groups of Americans together rather than split them apart." A number of cultural forms seemed to pick up on this shift in government attitude: swing music featured black and white performers (at times in integrated concerts) and absorbed a variety of influences, including Jewish klezmer music and even hillbilly instrumentation. Sports were another arena where this inclusive mind-set could be made manifest. Historian Lewis Erenberg argues that Louis's victory over Schmeling was so compelling, in part, because Louis "became a hero to a growing number of white Americans" as well as blacks, particularly those who "were wrestling with a new civic nationalism . . . that was far more inclusive than previous American self-definitions rooted in Anglo-Saxon white supremacy." The participation of the UCLA stars in integrated team competition, as opposed to the individual sports played by Louis and Owens, took on added significance in this context. The UCLA team captured so much attention because it had the potential to model how a new civic culture—with blacks and whites working together—might operate.[12]

Preludes: Race, Democracy, and Athletic Achievements before 1939

Strode, Washington, and Robinson all earned plaudits in the years leading to their breakthrough season, and certain key moments anticipated some of the positive and negative reactions they would encounter. Washington and Strode earned attention for their performance with the UCLA team in their sophomore and junior years (the 1937 and 1938 seasons, respectively). Although UCLA had a positive reputation regarding racial egalitarianism in the black community, Strode and Washington faced their share of racial bigotry in their early years with the squad. When the two joined the freshman team in the fall of 1936, they were the first black football players on the squad in a number of years. The two received a lukewarm and at times hostile response from some of their teammates—experiences that mirrored those of Robeson at Rutgers some twenty years earlier. Although there were apparently no racial incidents among the freshman players, rumors reached Washington and Strode that there were "some players on the varsity saying they don't want to play with any niggers." When the two moved up to the varsity squad in 1937, two players, Walt Schell and Celestine Moses "Slats" Wyrick, recoiled at the two black players' presence on the team. Wyrick, a lineman from Oklahoma, was the primary culprit. When Strode and Wyrick were slated to line up next to one another in practice, Wyrick refused to take the field, explaining to Coach Bill Spaulding, "I can't play next to a nigger because my folks would disown me." Spaulding then placed the two across from one another. When the whistle blew, Strode knocked Wyrick down, and the irate Oklahoman called Strode "a black son of a bitch." Strode began to pummel the white lineman until the coaches called him off.[13]

Although Strode later wrote that he and Wyrick became good friends after the incident and that racial troubles vanished on the team, his memory may have been tinged by nostalgia. A university report on the football team, commissioned after the 1937 season, highlighted "prejudice among some against the colored boys" as one of the key problems on the team throughout the season. Local newspapers picked up on these tensions. A column by J. Cullen Fentress in the *California Eagle* from 1939 revealed that the UCLA squads in 1937 and 1938 had been "characterized" by "dissension," a likely reference to racial tensions within the team. Similarly, Rube Samuelsen, writing in the *Pasadena Post* in 1938, wrote that that year's team's "morale is not of the best," causing the team to be "unpredictable."[14] That both black and white writers would hesitate to identify racial hostility spoke to the longstanding faith in sports as a model of an integrated society. For black writers such as Fentress, the UCLA team *had* to work in order to show that the civic nationalist rhetoric of the Roosevelt administration could be fulfilled. For white writers such as Samuelsen, ignoring racial hostility spoke to either a resigned acceptance of bigotry or an effort to insulate sports from the realm of the political, a vision of sports as a realization of American meritocracy. These competing interpretations existed just below the surface of sports coverage, reflecting similar, and yet distinct, approaches to the idea of a racially integrated America.

Strode and Washington were well aware of the limitations of sports. Area journalists and opposing fans, players, coaches, and even cheerleaders consistently called attention to the black athletes' racial otherness, mocking and even threatening them. Opposing players sometimes tried to rub Washington's eyes in the lime they used to mark the fields. Strode fought players who called him a "nigger." On one occasion, even the Washington State University football *coach* shouted that term at Washington as he ran down the sideline, which caused Washington to charge the offender. Games against Southern

Methodist University (SMU) and the University of Missouri were especially contentious. SMU players seemed intent on injuring Washington and Strode, and the Missouri cheerleaders heightened their vitriol when the black players were on the field.[15] As with the hostile fans faced by Pollard and Robeson, these white players, cheerleaders, and fans attempted to affirm their stronger position in American society through physical and emotional abuse.

Apart from the physical pounding and verbal taunting that Strode and Washington endured in their early years with UCLA, numerous incidents and accounts showed how stereotypes of blacks as clowns and buffoons infiltrated the supposedly egalitarian realm of athletics. One example of this tendency was in the well-worn nickname "the Gold Dust Twins," used widely in the mainstream media for Strode and Washington and later for Robinson and Washington. Although seemingly harmless on the surface, the nickname came from a brand of soap called Fairbank's Gold Dust Soap Powder, whose label featured two children in the style of blackface minstrelsy. Similarly, one of the major nicknames employed for Washington was "Kingfish," a reference to one of the main black characters on the (in)famous *Amos 'n' Andy* radio show.[16] These nicknames identified the players as black, marking out their race for white readers, and they also fit into a long tradition of white humor aimed at mocking blackness and black pretensions. In the case of the soap powder, blackness was linked to being dirty (and perhaps infantile). That connection may explain why the *Eagle* never used the nickname in its coverage of the UCLA team, and why black UCLA student Tom Bradley fretted in a letter to the editor to the *Eagle* that "the entire country knows us as 'Gold Dust Twins' and other names which designate only Negroes." He did not like this emphasis because, he argued, "We can only have a true democracy when all races are forgotten and each human is accepted as a man offering real contributions . . . to the progress of our country."[17] The humor in *Amos 'n' Andy*, meanwhile, derived from black characters' inability to function successfully in their modern world and from the comedy of their pretensions to white middle-class status.[18] No wonder, then, that the *Eagle* refrained from using this nickname as well. Even as black athletes such as Washington earned acclaim for their performances on the field, these tongue-in-cheek nicknames subtly mocked their achievements.[19]

Other uses of stereotypes were less subtle. The United Press (UP) story about Kenny Washington's first varsity game with UCLA described how the team was "sparked by Kenneth Washington, a 200-pound Negro left half, who defied the superstitions of his race and wore a huge golden '13' on his blue jersey."[20] Later that season, Stanford's football coaches applied burned cork to the face of their scout team halfback so that he could better simulate Washington in their preparations for their game against UCLA. The local *Pasadena Post* reprinted the UP account in a humorous light.[21] Braven Dyer employed similar humor in one of his columns the following month. Writing from the perspective of an alter ego named Pigskin Peter, a supposed professor of football, Dyer at first praised Washington, UCLA's "dark destroyer." But the praise was laden with demeaning stereotypes:

> The lad's a wow in boldface caps, but it's mostly what he doesn't do on a football field that impresses me. He doesn't overwork, he doesn't get excited, he doesn't get those black steel muscles busy until it counts. In short, Kenny has the complete relaxation of his race. You never saw a member of his race eat a po'k chop and then go into a heavy campaign of worrying about where his next one is coming from. No, sah; he may bear down on that po'k chop, but when it's gone he just unlaxes until the next po'k chop comes along. Well, K. Washington plays football like that, if you see what I mean.[22]

The malapropisms (e.g., "unlaxes" instead of "relaxes") were pulled from blackface minstrelsy and its many descendents, such as *Amos 'n' Andy*. And the characterization of Washington as relaxed and unconcerned about the future made him a passive figure, one incapable of leadership. He did not direct the team's fortunes but was rather pulled along by his white teammates. Black male physical superiority had to be qualified through humor and diminished by linking it to stereotypes of racial inferiority.

Despite these rather appalling trends, sportswriters on both sides of the color line still found validation for the New Deal in these athletes' experiences—a sign of the value of sports to many as a model of fairness and equality, facts be damned. From this perspective, some fans and journalists praised Washington and Strode's athletic accomplishments from the moment they first took the field for UCLA. Fans of the team quickly fell in love with Washington; by September 1937, his first season on varsity, he was already pictured on the front page of the school newspaper, the *Daily Bruin*, next to the story about his team's triumph over Oregon. The photograph's caption even referred to him as "GENERAL KENNY WASHINGTON"—certainly a more positive nickname and one that would especially circulate in the black papers and the *Bruin*.[23] Linking Washington to the nation's first president emphasized his capacity as a leader and citizen-soldier.[24] Similarly, the cheering crowds for Washington's on-field heroics spoke to a certain level of acceptance—just as they had for Pollard and Robeson.[25] Washington's seventy-two-yard pass to receiver Hal Hirschon, completed in an early December 1937 game against USC, was considered the longest pass play in college history up to that time. As a result, it generated national attention and earned Washington significant praise in the mainstream and black press.[26] One unidentified *Eagle* reader was so pleased with Washington's record-setting pass that the reader submitted a letter to the editor that linked Washington's "herculean" pass to "the wonderful legs of Jesse Owens . . . the wonderful arms of [black boxer] Henry Armstrong, and also that fast ball of [black pitcher] Satchel Paige. They can never dig up anyone who can outclass these Black boys."[27]

Underlining much of this praise was the familiar hope, among black and white writers, that sports represented a model for democracy. Thus, Braven Dyer, who made the allusion between Washington's running and a black man eating a pork chop, drew considerable meaning about the democratic potential of sports from one play in UCLA's victory over the University of Washington in October 1938. When white player Jack Montgomery intercepted a pass, he passed the ball to Washington and continued downfield to block, a set of events Dyer saw as being representative of "the true spirit of American football. Montgomery is white and Washington black, but true sportsmanship and team play draws no color line."[28] Similarly, *Eagle* sports editor Almena Davis spotlighted fan reaction at one 1938 contest between UCLA and the University of Wisconsin as being particularly meaningful. He found "the most inspiring bit" to be the reactions of a white "blonde" Wisconsin fan in the stands when Washington struggled to stay in the game after being pummeled by the opposing team's defenders:

> As our hero limped to the sidelines, the crowd and the blonde paid him tribute.
>
> "He wanted to stay in and give his all," she, the blonde wailed.
>
> And to their feet the Badgers were leaping on the field, forming a gauntlet of congratulatory expressions, pumping our hero's hand, slapping his back, shoving him on to the next. . . . Good old American sportsmanship.[29]

These moments showed that whites and blacks could come together on the athletic field and could recognize one another's shared spirit and humanity. But note, too, that Davis spotlighted a moment when sportsmanship extended beyond the playing field to the fans watching. For black writers, emphasizing the transcendent possibilities of sports was the key. Sportsmanship limited to the playing field was nice but not an end to itself.

Reactions to Jackie Robinson's athletic exploits at Pasadena Junior College (PJC) show similar themes, although Robinson's unique circumstances complicate the story considerably. A phenomenal athlete even in high school, Robinson was sought after by many major colleges but chose to attend PJC to be closer to his mother. While there, Robinson dazzled fans in his one and a half years at the school. An exceptional all-around athlete, excelling at football, basketball, track, baseball, and tennis, Robinson earned the most plaudits for his performance with the PJC football squad. Although an injury derailed the first half of his freshman year, he performed well in the second half of the season. In the fall of 1938, his second and final year with the team, he was simply extraordinary, scoring more points than any football player in the country, leading his team to an undefeated season and a mythical junior college championship and earning praise from local black and white newspaper writers alike. One writer for the *Pasadena Post* called Robinson "probably the greatest junior college player to ever don the moleskins." With Robinson leading the way, the PJC squad scored 369 points in eleven games that year, with only 70 scored against them.[30]

Some of this coverage must have proved especially hopeful to those who saw sports as a model of fair play. As had been the case with Robeson and Pollard, the black press took special delight in noting white esteem for black accomplishments on the athletic field, as they reflected an appreciation and recognition of black masculinity. Thus, the *Eagle* delighted in the record-setting crowd of fifty thousand on hand to watch Robinson star in a 20–7 victory over Compton Junior College. When Robinson scored on a spectacular forty-five-yard run in the game, the newspaper delighted to note that "wave after wave of cheering swept the crowded stands."[31] The praise for Robinson was not exclusive to the black press. Rube Samuelsen in the *Post* even campaigned for Robinson to be named as an All-American player, an honor traditionally denied to junior college players.[32] That a white journalist would make such a bold claim for a black athlete spoke to the possibilities of sports transcending race, a sign of sports leading to recognition for black male accomplishments.

So, too, did Robinson's postseason awards. At the PJC team banquet, sponsored by the local Elks Club, Robinson was named the team's Most Valuable Player, receiving a trophy and a gold football.[33] The *Post* celebrated his award by publishing a line drawing of a smiling Robinson, with no exaggerated features, and a laudatory caption that called him one of the "greatest all-around athletes in history of Pasadena school athletics."[34] A clay model made by two white football team members to celebrate the season, meanwhile, emphasized Robinson's importance by depicting him running with the ball at the top of the trophy while ten other players constituted the statue's base.[35] Thrilled by Robinson's astonishing performance, blacks and whites celebrated his remarkable season euphorically. Voters chose him "by unanimous selection" to play on a junior college all-star team that would compete against an all-star team from the East Coast.[36] And the Scott M. E. Church of Pasadena even held a "Jack Robinson Day," where the athlete received a "handsome gold loving cup."[37]

However, there were signs that Robinson's accomplishments were still bracketed by the limitations of racial prejudice. Despite his considerable ability and intellect, Robinson was not named team captain for his second and final year at PJC, a slight all too familiar to black athletes (such as Robeson at Rutgers) throughout most of the twentieth century.[38] The local press also ignored the fact that Robinson did not have his choice of four-year schools to which to transfer after his brilliant junior college career. USC, the most prestigious football powerhouse in the region, was off-limits because of its unofficial policy against black athletes, but the press ignored that barrier.[39] By not mentioning that issue, the local papers—black and white—ignored the problem. As with the silence regarding Robeson's snub at the Washington and Lee football game, the lack of commentary in the press supported, by default, an "equal" society in which blacks were systematically discriminated against in often unspoken ways. These newspapers accepted as a given the presence of Jim Crow racism in their midst on the West Coast, a sign of segregation's reach and a reminder of the limitations facing black Americans in their day-to-day lives.

Any euphoria Robinson felt as a result of his award-winning season and his future career at UCLA must have been short-lived, as two events in the ensuing months troubled him deeply and cast in stark relief the racial prejudice that still marked much of Southern California life. The first was the aforementioned arrest of his brother Edgar at the Tournament of Roses parade. Edgar Robinson, like many black and white residents, rented chairs to set up along the parade route for a day of lighthearted revelry. However, when two police officers asked him to produce his permit for the chairs, he was beaten and arrested before he even had the opportunity to produce the paperwork. Hauled down to the local station, a battered and bruised Robinson was booked on charges of resisting arrest and violating a city ordinance, robbed of more than $10, and forced to pay an additional $10 fine. Only the *Eagle* reported the miscarriage of justice, devoting a front-page story to the "latest instance of flagrant discrimination and brutal treatment of colored citizens in Pasadena by the police." That the brother of Olympian Mack and up-and-coming star Jackie would be treated so poorly spoke to the racial animosity in Pasadena and beyond.[40] The second event was Robinson's own arrest in September 1939, just before the start of UCLA's fall semester. Although Robinson had been little more than a bystander to the angry confrontation between blacks and whites, his celebrity made him an easy target for the police to single out, and he was hauled off to jail. These experiences and others led him to affirm that if his mother did not live in Pasadena, he would "never come back."[41]

By the time Robinson started the school year at UCLA, he was in a sour mood, troubled by the limits of democracy and saddened by the accidental death of his closest brother, Frank. Frustrated by unequal treatment in the law and suspicious of white people, Robinson cut something of a solitary figure.[42] In contrast to the gregarious and affable Washington, Robinson seemed aloof to some. Combined with his recent arrest, this demeanor led some whites to see him as representative of, according to biographer Arnold Rampersad, "the stereotype of the lawless, shiftless black buck."[43] What would people make of a black man who would not back down, who regarded whites suspiciously? How would teammates and fans respond to a dark-skinned black man who, as graduate manager Bill Ackerman remembered, "always seemed to have a chip on his shoulder"?[44]

The Season Begins: Black Stars, National Coverage, and Disgruntled Fans and Teammates

As the 1939 season arrived, the black stars on the UCLA squad found themselves at the center of local and even national attention. When it became clear that the squad would start three black players, African American newspapers across the country followed the team's fortunes closely. Even before they had played a game, the integrated team had attracted the attention of national black publications: the *Chicago Defender* devoted multiple stories to the team and included a massive photograph of Strode (labeled "A Bronze Hercules" as he threw a discus in track) and one of Robinson showing up for the first day of football practice.[45] Locally, the *Eagle* bubbled over with enthusiasm, delighting that five of the sixty-one players trying out for the varsity football squad were black—according to the *Eagle*, "the largest number ever to play on a major university team."[46] One sign of the *Eagle*'s enthusiasm was its decision to publish a photograph of Bartlett, Robinson, Strode, and Washington posed around Coach Babe Horrell. The four-column-wide photograph, at the top center of the sports page, must have stood out to readers.[47] The "colorful" quality of the team led to a deluge of coverage in the newspaper, far more than any other college football (even all-black) teams.[48] Just before UCLA's first game of the season against Texas Christian University (TCU), Fentress explained, "We devote a lot of space to the UCLA entry because it is the only major institution on the coast on whose football squad there are four Negro athletes. We hope that in the future other institutions follow the Westwood lead."[49]

If white newspapers did not explicitly call for the UCLA team to serve as a trailblazer for other institutions' football squads, they nonetheless buzzed with excitement over the team's potential. Before the team's first game, the *Daily Bruin* printed a photograph of Strode, Washington, and Robinson wearing their uniforms and smiling under the heading "Gold Dust Trio." Given the relative rarity of sports photographs in the newspaper, the attention paid to the black players spoke to fans' excitement.[50] One story noted that Robinson and Washington would likely start together, which meant "that the greatest possible power will be tossed into the Bruin scoring engine at the same time."[51] It also meant that the two most prestigious skill positions on the field—the left and right halfback roles—would be filled by black players, a fact the newspaper did not mention but one that would have been apparent to sports fans.[52]

Although the mainstream newspapers did not emphasize the preponderance of black players on UCLA's team (there were no stories in the *Los Angeles Examiner*, *Los Angeles Times*, or *Pasadena Post* that discussed the unprecedented number of African American stars on the team, nor did they print the photograph of the black players with Coach Horrell), they did hint that there was racial harmony on the squad. One story in the *Examiner* noted that the team's attitude had improved from previous years. An unnamed veteran player was quoted as saying that "he has never known such a harmonious spirit on the club." Similarly, Samuelsen, writing in the *Post*, indicated that the UCLA team "showed a 100 per cent improvement in morale over last year."[53] Even in not naming race, the emphasis on depicting a united squad spoke to the possibilities of integrated teamwork, a point that fit in well with the widespread hopes for a pluralistic civic nationalism.

And yet for all of the stories emphasizing the possibilities embodied in this squad, a cloud seemed to follow Robinson because of his recent arrest. Although many of the area newspapers did not cover the incident, the *Los Angeles Times* did, printing a brief story in the back pages of its main news section. Beneath a headline reading "Pasadena Grid Player Arrested," a subheading called attention to the locally famous football player: "Jackie Robinson Held on Charge of Resisting Motorcycle Officer." The story evinced little sympathy, indicating that Robinson "assertedly [*sic*] resisted the officer's attempts to disperse a group of Negroes who were threatening a white man."[54] The events were well known and cast Robinson in a negative light. The arrest "followed me all over and it was pretty hard to shake off," Robinson recalled wistfully in later years.[55] By the time Robinson's case finally went to trial, he was in the midst of football season, and UCLA boosters arranged to have the case dismissed in exchange for Robinson changing his plea to guilty and forfeiting his bond. Unaware that the arrangements were taking place, Robinson was relieved to find that the case was over with and recognized that his stature as an athlete had given him favorable treatment. Others in the community were not so pleased. One white female UCLA fan, Billie C. Schindhelm, wrote University of California president Robert Sproul to complain that "the scrapes some of [the football players] have gotten into" reflected badly "upon a university such as ours."[56] James R. Bowen was less circumspect, sending a clipping of the *Pasadena Star-News* coverage of the case dismissal along with a letter calling Robinson "a very undesirable citizen in Pasadena. There have been other disorders which have not appeared in the papers." He added that Robinson was in need of "a good citizen class" in order to become "a worth while boy" and warned that "further praise will ruin him."[57] Distaste for Robinson also led some to believe, according to Davis J. Walsh of the *Examiner*, that he "was a prima donna who fretted and became fractious" while playing a secondary role to Washington.[58]

Robinson's demeanor and personality explain why he elicited such responses. He refused to play the role of the compliant black who accepted insults and slights without responding, which made him threatening to some whites.[59] Instead, Robinson embodied a more threatening black male persona, an outspoken and resolute figure who would not bow down to white authority. The local newspapers did not help. The stories about Robinson's case being dismissed made no mention of the fact that police arrested Robinson for little more than being present at an argument between other young men. Only the *Eagle* reported that Robinson "reportedly essayed the role of peacekeeper" in the incident.[60] Robinson's supposed bad attitude and "bad nigger" persona would have significant consequences as the season unfolded, a counterbalance to the supposed racial harmony on the team.

As that drama played itself out behind the scenes, the season started impressively for the squad, with a 6–2 upset victory over TCU, the de facto defending national champion.[61] As the team continued to succeed on the field, the local and national black media ramped up their coverage, barraging readers with stories and photographs and delighting in the team's racial makeup. No team had ever been so racially mixed in big-time college sports. Thus, the *Defender's* game story of the TCU win emphasized that the three black stars had all been in the game "at one time" against "the Texas team."[62] Here, then, was a chance to see blacks and whites working together and succeeding (and defeating an all-white team). To that end, even papers such as the Washington *Afro-American*, which generally focused its sports coverage on southern black schools, boxing, and Negro league baseball, followed the 1939 UCLA outfit from the start and continued to provide more prominent and more expansive updates on the UCLA team than on any other national college sports team.[63]

As the team continued to win games, the effusive praise in the black and white press suggested that sports might in fact reveal the possibilities of an integrated, pluralistic society. White and black writers, opposing white coaches and players, and fans of both races lauded the black athletes on the team for their performances. In the *Examiner*, Bob Hunter gave Robinson and Washington credit for "almost single handedly" leading the team to victory over TCU and later praised Washington for being an "All-American" performer.[64] Fentress, writing in the *Eagle*, delighted that "Kenny and Jackie had the stands in an uproar" over their remarkable offensive performance in that same game. The black writer speculated that "every [African American] football fan, loyal as he may be to his favorite club," would be "pulling for the lads from the hills of Westwood."[65] He was probably correct; when the team traveled to Washington for a game in early October, the Brown Bombers, a local black band, held a "football jam session" to honor Washington, Strode, and Robinson.[66] Opposing players were inspired by the black players' skills as well: according to Al Santoro, players for Oregon State University "were convinced Kenny Washington was all the All-American everybody on the Coast believes him to be."[67] Paul Zimmerman, writing in the *Times*, argued that "you have to throw racial prejudice out the window when a couple of gentlemen like Jackie Robinson and Kenny Washington do the things they do."[68] These moments, and other examples of the enthusiasm these black athletes generated, the "ravings and rantings" they inspired, suggested that sports could be a place free from racial prejudice and bigotry.[69]

It was left to the *Eagle*, however, to forcefully draw the connection between the integrated team's success and the contours of American democratic society. Inspired by the performances of "Messrs Washington, Strode, and Robinson of the UCLA Bruins," the newspaper devoted an editorial to them, praising the athletes as "glorious symbols of rising Negro Youth, harbingers of a new era of economic, political and social recognition." The editors hoped that "the three gentlemen" would be "stalwart torch bearers in the forward march of Racial Progress (!)." Recognizing that those "high sounding analogies" might be a tad overdrawn, the editors affirmed that, on a more simple level, they were "very proud of these boys."[70]

One week later, Fentress made his own case for the black players' significance off the field. Looking ahead to the possibility that the team might play in the Rose Bowl, Fentress argued that UCLA's appearance in the prestigious game would be a wonderful event not only for West Coast college football but also for "the nation" because, in Fentress's view, sports were the "most logical media through which to effect world peace." Linking the struggles against fascism abroad to the team's performance, Fentress hoped for UCLA's continued success that season in order to "prove to this nation that its peoples can play together in the most approved manner as sportsmen, upholding as they do so the democratic principles as outlined by the signers of the Declaration of Independence."[71] To Fentress and the other editors of the *Eagle*, the black stars of the UCLA team were significant because of their athletic ability and team success, but only insofar as that success proved the feasibility of a pluralistic society that welcomed contributions from all of its peoples, regardless of race, and that accepted black men in leading roles. As the season went on, that message came to dominate the newspaper's coverage of the team. It helped to mitigate the bad news coming from UCLA's campus—such as the report that black students were being denied promotions in the Reserve Officer Training Corps (ROTC) program.[72] When Washington, Strode, Robinson, and other black athletes were feted at a mixed-race banquet held in their honor in mid-November, it proved that "sportsmanship and fair play" might yet help bring about a society that provided opportunities for all and recognized achievements equally.[73]

Those messages not only failed to make it into the white mainstream press; they also were undercut by familiar slips in language and photographs that echoed the earlier coverage of Robeson and Pollard. In addition to the tendency to employ variations on the "Gold Dust Twins" nickname, many of the newspapers frequently inserted phrases and terms to highlight the players' race in derogatory ways. A UP story in the *Post* from October 1939, for example, referred to Robinson and Washington as "the midnight express twins."[74] An *Examiner* story from the same day called Washington "Shufflin Kenny Washington," an allusion to the comic black characters of minstrel shows and Hollywood films.[75] Examples such as these were sprinkled throughout the mainstream newspapers, marking race and often making references to black stereotypes. For many whites, these comic stereotypes from minstrelsy were their only "encounter" with African Americans, so it was no wonder that they surfaced in sports coverage. And although some newspapers, such as the *Examiner*, did not shy away from including photographs of the black UCLA players in action, the *Post* almost never depicted the black stars in its pages. When photographs accompanied stories about the UCLA team, they almost invariably featured white players or the team's all-white coaches—just as had been the case with Robeson.[76] No matter the coast, it seems, white writers and editors were loath to credit black men for their achievements, especially in photographs.

A second, and to some degree more distressing, sign of the limitations of sports to model equality and a pluralistic society came when Robinson was injured in practice on November 1. As Robinson neared the sideline, two members of the team's "goof" squad—the scout team that mimicked the opposing team's offense and defense—tackled him forcefully, severely spraining his knee in the process. Although injuries were and are a regular part of football because of the game's physical nature, evidence suggests that the white players in fact targeted Robinson and attempted to hurt him. Hank Shatford, then a writer for the *Daily Bruin*, insisted in later years that the players deliberately set out to hurt Robinson, explaining that many felt Robinson was an uppity player getting too much press. According to Shatford, UCLA coaches were "furious" after the incident, recognizing that the injury had been intentional.[77] Bob Hunter's reports in the *Examiner* support Shatford's claim. He wrote, "Robinson was tackled viciously near the sidelines by two members of the goof squad and arose limping. Ray Richards, line coach, was actually white about the mouth and Babe Horrell and Jim Blewett were shaky for the rest of the day." His use of the adverb *viciously*, which was not a word he used regularly in his writing, suggests that he saw deliberate intent.[78]

None of the other papers reported the specific circumstances of Robinson's injury, likely because they did not have reporters covering a midweek practice. Regardless, the story would have been a troubling one to publish in the mainstream press; for all of the talk of sportsmanship modeling fair play in American life, even Robinson's own white teammates appeared to resent his success and his uncompromising attitude. What lesson did that offer for the rest of society?

These many contrasting examples of the egalitarian possibilities and ongoing limitations of sports were also manifested in two letters fans sent to University of California president Robert Sproul in December 1939. Billie C. Schindhelm was not pleased by the presence of "so many colored boys on the U.C.L.A. football team," and apparently she was not alone. According to her, this facet of the team was "the chief topic of conversation for the entire season." In fact, Schindhelm was so distressed by the number of black players on the 1939 team that when she went to her first game that year, against Stanford in Palo Alto, "so many colored boys turned up that we were forced to throw our support to Stanford." Token integration did not appear to bother Schindhelm—in one of the two versions of her letter she sent Sproul she praised Washington as "outstanding . . . a very fine gentleman and a clever football player." But apparently seeing three starters on the UCLA squad was too much for her—and others—to take: letters from fans in the East, according to Schindhelm, cautioned that "unless you curb the Negro rush to the U.C.L.A. team you will eventually find it difficult to schedule games." If Schindhelm was willing to accept some degree of integration, she clearly was not in favor of a pluralistic society in which blacks played significant roles; only token participation by African Americans would place institutions "above reproach."[79]

Michael Joseph Hart's letter to Sproul featured an entirely different reading of the UCLA squad. A resident of Phoenix, Arizona, Hart found the success and example of the black athletes on the UCLA team to be inspirational. Explaining that he was writing "because of the remarkable colored players on the U.C.L.A. team," Hart believed that their presence on the squad proved "U.C.L.A.'s consistency with Old Glory's principles and our beloved Democracy." In contrast to Schindhelm's anxiety about the mixed-race quality of the team, Hart's enthusiasm for the team rested on their fulfillment of American democratic ideals. He celebrated the "white folks" on the team who were "with those fine colored comrades 100%."[80] Although hopeful that the black players would be "humble, modest and proud," he also insisted that they "avoid any *inferiority complexes*" (his emphasis). The team was a model of interracial cooperation, in which whites and blacks participated equally. In short, UCLA's mixed-race team showcased "sincere patriots" and "decent citizens" working together to achieve a common goal.[81]

The Season Ends: The Homecoming Display, the All-American Controversy, and the Big Game

Although Robinson's injury weakened UCLA's explosiveness on offense, the team continued to perform admirably throughout the season. On offense and defense, Robinson, Washington, and Strode provided most of the spark. Washington was a fast, burly, and strong runner who could both power over would-be tacklers and outrace them. Robinson provided a good compliment as a lightning-quick, elusive open-field runner who specialized in evading would-be tacklers with last-second changes in direction. Strode, meanwhile, provided physical play on the line on both offense and defense and continued to be one of the best receivers on the team (along with Robinson), using his considerable height of six feet, five inches, to snare passes over the heads of defenders. In addition to beating favored TCU, UCLA also defeated a good University of Oregon team (16–6), convincingly beat perennially strong Cal (20–7), and earned hard-fought ties against Oregon State and independent power Santa Clara. Robinson returned to play in the team's final two games leading up to the USC matchup, the 13–13 draw against Oregon State and a 24–7 win over Washington State University. Students reveled in the team's success and even "jammed auditoriums to watch film footage from road games."[82]

As the team headed into the final game of the season, their record stood at six wins, no losses, and three ties. USC, meanwhile, entered the final game with a record of seven wins, no losses, and one tie, making the two squads the only undefeated teams in the PCC and thus the favorites to earn their conference's bid to play in the prestigious Rose Bowl. It was understood that whoever won the game would then play against one of the East's best teams (and receive the Rose Bowl's large financial payout). As the game approached, local newspapers, black and white, gushed with enthusiasm. In the dailies, stories appeared every day in the week leading up to the game, previewing various angles of the contest. Students at both schools exulted in their respective team's success, celebrating with rallies and with acts of vandalism against the other school.[83] As the enthusiasm began to build, a number of subplots emerged, each calling into question the ideal of sports as a model of fairness and equality.[84]

The first event that explicitly addressed the pluralistic nature of UCLA's football team occurred two weeks before the game, during USC's homecoming week. As part of the weeklong festivities, the school's Phi Kappa Psi fraternity created a memorable display saturated with racial and ethnic bigotry and meant to mock UCLA's team. The *California Eagle*, alone among the local newspapers, reported the display's existence and the furor it generated. The scene featured three "grass huts," one titled "Alpha African" (a reference to the Alpha Phi Alpha fraternity to which UCLA's black players belonged) with "gaudily painted figures of black savages wearing football helmets" looking out from inside the huts. Meanwhile, one of the huts bore a sign indicating that it was "Cantor and Cohen Food Shoppe, Inc.," which referred to two Jewish players on the UCLA squad, Leo Cantor and Jack Cohen. A replica of a ship, captained by a Trojan, was in front of the huts; the ship bore the name "S.C. Slave Ship." The fraternity brothers also "nailed grotesque figures to a giant palm tree in the center of the lawn." These figures, with "features . . . distorted to produce a minstrel effect," were apparently intended to represent Strode, Washington, and Robinson, since their football numbers were included. Effigies of the Jewish players also hung from the tree by their necks.[85]

Predictably, some local residents responded with outrage, but their specific responses—and those of the fraternity—reveal how sports could fit into broader discourse about the nature of American society. Tellingly, the *Eagle* explicitly linked the outrageous imagery to Nazism, equating American racial prejudice to Hitler's brutal fascist regime. The story's headline referred to the display as a "Nazism Attempt," and writer Fay Jackson called the exhibit "one of the most flagrant displays of Hitlerism ever offered under the aegis of an American university group."[86] Building on Joe Louis's popularity as an American symbol in contrast to German boxer Max Schmeling, these efforts attempted to make use of unease with the Nazi regime to call attention to racial prejudice at home.[87] Others made that connection. A number of groups, including the NAACP, Alpha Phi Alpha, Delta Sigma Theta (an African American sorority), and the Hollywood Anti-Nazi League, all protested the display, eventually causing the university administration to force the fraternity to take it down.

Curiously, the local daily newspapers made no mention of the controversy in their reporting. Although both the *Post* and the *Examiner* commented on various USC homecoming activities during the week, the fraternity display and reaction against it earned no coverage—perhaps because the incident pointed to the failure of sports to bridge racial and ethnic divides. Only when reader Warren Morton wrote a letter to the editor in the *Post* did the news make the white newspapers. Morton, disgusted by the behavior of the USC students, wondered how it was that "the sons of our 'bettah' people" had joined a fraternity that "seemed to have a brain of its own and it happened to have been hatched, originally, somewhere in the deep South or in Nazi Germany." He saw the display as "just a glimmer of the danger to civil liberties for minorities that can be found resting gently under the surface of even this institution of higher learning."[88] Another reader, Charles Amin, responded to Morton's letter, questioning the value of sports in higher education. He disputed those who argued that sports promoted good sportsmanship, noting that he "heard [his] fellow S.C. alumni acrimoniously referring to U.C.L.A.

as 'Harlem University.'" He lauded Morton for calling attention to the incident and for criticizing it, believing "that sort of spirit that will help save real Americanism, if it is saved."[89] For these men, and for the members of the *Eagle* and the various groups that protested, the struggles of UCLA's multiracial and multiethnic team represented a wider struggle—that of minority groups in a pluralistic society. The homecoming display was one more sign of the resistance to a democracy that welcomed the contributions of all of its constituents.

The response of the Phi Kappa Psi brothers to the episode reveals an alternate perspective. On the one hand, the denigration of Strode, Washington, Robinson, Cantor, and Cohen was meant to mark the UCLA team as inferior because of its racially and ethnically diverse team. Black players were connected to the primitive and savage, and the Jewish players linked to miserly store owners. As with the hate speech directed at Pollard and Robeson more than twenty years earlier, the figures hung in effigy were meant to intimidate—to remind minorities like the black UCLA stars of their weaker position in society. One might read this as a distinctly anxious response to the pluralism of American society—the preserves of white Christian male citizenship seemed under attack.[90] But the Phi Kappa Psi brothers went one step further, implicitly outlining a hierarchy of supposed inferiors in their response. When reprimanded by the school in the wake of the protest, the fraternity initially attempted to resolve the situation by removing the caricatures of the Jewish players and leaving the black figures untouched. Perhaps sensing that the Hollywood Anti-Nazi League would curtail its efforts once disparaging references to Jews were removed, the fraternity brothers must have been disappointed when protests continued. Michael Elkins, working for the Hollywood Anti-Nazi League, did not take the bait, saying, "The Lampooning of Negroes is just as horrible to us and we shall continue our protests in their behalf." When their attempt to fracture the coalition of ethnic and racial groups failed, the fraternity removed the scene altogether and put up a "censored" sign in its place.[91] For the moment, a more inclusive vision of American society had won out, but the display itself, and the mainstream media's silence regarding it, suggested that many sympathized with, or at least condoned, the fraternity brothers' perspective on racial equality. And it should be noted that no one publicly called out the failure of sports to bridge the racial divide in this instance, either. Indeed, one reading of the event would have been that sports competition potentially *fosters* racial animosity, as rabid fans gleefully employed racial terms to mock their opponents. The drawbacks to competition—tied as they were to the market ideology of the nation—remained removed from criticism.

Another controversy began to brew just as the furor over the homecoming display was quieting down: the role of race in the selection of the most prestigious All-American teams. Kenny Washington was at the heart of the story. As the season drew to a close, nearly all of the local media outlets, including the mainstream papers the *Examiner* and the *Times* and the black *Eagle*, campaigned for Washington to earn first-team All-American status, an honor he had narrowly missed out on in previous years.[92] Recognizing Washington's value to the undefeated UCLA team and rewarding his status as a senior player in his final year of football, these media outlets all considered him as deserving of first-team status.

When the major teams were announced, however, Washington's name was not on them; instead, he was named to the second team by most major organizations. Even more surprising to many was that Grenville Lansdell, a white starting back for USC, had been named a first-team player on the Hearst All-American team, one of the most prestigious squads in the country. Supporters of Washington were outraged. In the *Bruin*, Milt Cohen lamented Washington's exclusion from the first team, noting that Washington was far superior to Lansdell. In his opinion, "nine out of ten" western newsmen "would tell you that Lansdell couldn't walk on the same field with Washington."[93] Others were less strident, but still disappointed. In the *Eagle*, Fentress complained that the All-American teams announced by NEA, UP, and Hearst (among others) failed "to give Kenny Washington his just due," and he was particularly baffled by Lansdell's selection.[94] In the *Times*, Dick Hyland wrote that he was sorry "that Washington was not given the credit he deserved and earned on the football field before our eyes."[95] Walsh in the *Examiner* tried to be diplomatic, writing that both Washington and Lansdell deserved to make the Hearst first team (which he had helped to choose).[96]

However, for all of the support Washington received from these local writers, they hesitated to blame racism—one obvious explanation—for Washington's failure to earn first-team honors. In yet another example of the limitations of sports as a model for a meritocracy, sportswriters continued to turn a blind eye to the impacts of racial politics. In the *Bruin*, Cohen chalked up the poor voting to "eastern pickers" unfamiliar with West Coast football, and an editorial in the paper similarly blamed East Coast bias for the vote.[97] Other writers, including Fentress in the *Eagle*, offered no explanation as to why Washington had not been selected. Walsh was the only writer to mention the specter of bigotry explicitly, and he dismissed it outright, writing that there could "be no question of discrimination." He believed that Pollard's selection as an All-American in 1916, even when he had a poor game late in the year, proved the color blindness of the selection process, as did the choice in later years of Iowa University's Duke Slater.[98] Of course, one or two awards over the course of more than twenty years hardly marked the end of discrimination, but Walsh seemed to think it proved the egalitarian nature of sports. Beholden to the myth of the level playing field, to a vision of sports as an arena free from prejudice, most of these writers ignored the elephant in the room. For every writer like Hyland, who criticized "political" All-American teams (an apparent reference to racial politics), there were two or three who simply let the insult slide.[99]

It is unclear what Washington himself felt about the snub. Both the *Times* and the *Examiner* devoted lengthy stories to him as he approached the end of his career, but he made no comment on the All-American selections, even though the early results had started to trickle in. Instead, he reflected on his time at UCLA and his plans for the future. Ever the moderate, Washington told *Times* writer Chester Hanson that he hoped he could help his "people" after he finished school: "I think I can do something there. I think I have the confidence of the white people and also of the Negroes. I think that both sides to the problem are sometimes 'off side' and I might be able to help out there." He also demurred when asked if black players received more abuse on the field because of their race (a fact he surely knew to be true), noting that the opposing players "go after" white players "pretty hard" as well.[100] If Washington had been frustrated by the lack of recognition he received, he did not indicate it in these interviews, nor did he confide in his close friend Strode. In later years, Strode wrote, "If it ever bothered Kenny I don't know, he never showed it."[101] But Washington surely must have been disappointed.

However, there were some moments of redemption for Washington. After he was snubbed by the sportswriters for All-American honors, his peers voted him in unanimously in *Liberty Magazine*'s All-American team, which was voted on by 1,659 players.[102] Bill Stern, a radio broadcaster whose team appeared in *Life* magazine, also selected Washington as a first-team player, an event that generated national acclaim in the black press.[103] Finally, the venerable *Crisis* would not let the slight go by unmentioned. Although the publication had not followed Washington and Robinson as closely as it had Robeson and Pollard, its editors were clearly aware of the 1939 team's story. In its January 1940 issue, an editorial lamented the numerous affronts Washington had received. Although Washington "led the nation in ground gaining" and "sparked his team through a hard schedule," he did not receive his just due. The editorial argued that Washington fulfilled all the criteria for an All-American selection, except for "one thing wrong with him: he was several shades too dark."[104] The attention of this national publication to the event marked the importance of equal recognition to leaders in the black community: fair play and equal opportunity meant that all shared in their deserved rewards, regardless of race.

As the USC game drew nearer, then, Washington's slight and Lansdell's selection added intrigue to a contest already laden with meaning. Showing how even minor details could color people's perceptions of athletic performance, two thumbnail images of Lansdell and Washington in an *Examiner* story about the upcoming game conveyed markedly different messages. Lansdell looked off to the side at a three-quarter angle, a look of determination on his face, with no helmet on. Washington, on the other hand, was wearing a helmet, and the profile shot featured him with mouth open, as though yelling. It was a study in contrast between the cool, collected, and determined Lansdell and the emotionally charged and wild Washington. Even though the story praised both players for "the All-American recognition" they received, the images told a different story.[105] Black men, no matter how accomplished and beloved, were still hemmed in by a culture suffused with the stereotypes of blackface minstrelsy.

One final issue associated with the game drew attention to the significance of UCLA's racially integrated team: the possibility of a Rose Bowl bid. On the whole, African Americans delighted in the possibility that the integrated team might play in the Rose Bowl, hopeful that the team's success would open other doors to black advancement. Thus, Lacy in the *Afro-American* gushed about the potential game, wondering rhetorically "who . . . wouldn't like to see those three colored boys . . . given a chance in the feature event of the annual Tournament of Roses."[106] Hart's letter to Stroud showed a similar enthusiasm. The Phoenix native hoped that the team would defeat USC and earn a berth in the game so that they could "produce the greatest color and sensation ever produced in the Rose Bowl." The popularity and pageantry of this event marked an important public moment to recognize black achievement and to, in Hart's words, reaffirm "Old Glory's principles and our beloved Democracy."[107] Closer to home, Fentress saw larger ramifications from the team's success: "UCLA's democratic football team should be a hint to local promoters of professional football and baseball teams. Fans turn out to watch talent, not red talent, or blue talent, but TALENT."[108] Cleverly substituting the U.S. flag colors of red and blue for race markers of black and white, Fentress explicitly saw the team as the embodiment of the nation's citizenry and as proof that people of different races could work together as equals and succeed. He urged the power brokers in American sports to grant equal opportunity regardless of race.

Not everyone was so enthusiastic about that potential outcome. Across the nation, many worried that racial politics might complicate the selection of teams for the Rose Bowl, another sign of the weight of Jim Crow segregation. The University of Tennessee was considered by most to be the best team in the eastern half of the country, and thus most deserving of an invitation to the game, but many worried that southern Jim Crow politics would prevent them from playing against the Bruins. White writers addressed the issue in the days leading up to the game, as rumors swirled first that Tennessee was unlikely to play against UCLA, and then that they would play whoever won, since there was precedent for southern teams to play integrated squads outside the South.[109] That argument was perhaps overly optimistic—although certain southern teams had played integrated squads outside the South, such as the University of North Carolina taking on New York University and their star black football player Ed Williams in 1936, those events were still the exceptions to the rule. Many southern teams continued to refuse to play against black players, no matter the location, and no school in the Southeastern Conference (SEC), Tennessee's conference, had *ever* squared off against a black player, no matter the circumstances.[110]

To black writers, the possibility that Tennessee might not accept an invitation would certainly have been galling. Although they did not address the issue in their papers before the game (apparently hopeful that the matter would be resolved amiably), black sportswriters and fans expressed outrage when schools did enforce Jim Crow segregation in sports. When Boston University held its black player Charlie Thomas out of a game against Western Maryland University in November, Art Carter in the *Washington Afro-American* criticized the school for permitting "jim crowism . . . to creep into the collegiate athletic picture."[111] In a letter to the editor in response to that same incident, reader Dawsey Johnson, of Newark, New Jersey, wondered whether "southerners" would have the same attitude toward blacks during the (seemingly inevitable) war: "Will they say put the colored boys on the bench and let us win the war?"[112] When Boston College similarly held its star black player out of the prestigious Cotton Bowl game against Clemson University, *Defender* writer J. Don Davis labeled the school's decision an "un-American" one.[113] In short, the black press saw these moments of Jim Crow segregation in sports as representative of broader inequalities in American society.

Rarely did white writers critique Tennessee for even considering backing out of the game, despite its obvious violation of the tenets of fair play and sportsmanship. Most reported the dilemma without comment, passing up an opportunity to consider the limitations of sports. In the *Pasadena Star-News*, Charles Paddock merely wrote that Robinson, Bartlett, Strode, and Washington "could not qualify under the strict eligibility rules made necessary by Tennessee's geographic location," accepting segregation's potential influence on the game.[114] Only Hyland in the *Times* criticized the white southern mind-set—and even he refrained from directly addressing racism or bigotry. What angered Hyland was a column in the Birmingham, Alabama, *Post* that lamented that Tennessee and Tulane University (another strong team that year) would probably be unable to play in the bowl game should UCLA win. The column also suggested that if forced to play against the black players, the southern whites would likely set out to injure UCLA's black stars, a point that agitated Hyland significantly. Arguing that the *Post* story "never should have been written," he called on his readers to respond "as they are motivated by each respective conscience."[115] Far from an explicit attack on southern bigotry, Hyland's column at least publicly expressed disappointment with the situation. The larger point here is not that white newsmen were bigots or even cowards for refusing to take a stand on the matter. Rather, one could see that Jim Crow politics were so ingrained in American society—even on the West Coast—that even in obvious instances when they prevented fair play, when they undermined sports as a model for equality of opportunity and a pluralistic society, white newsmen accepted the situation without comment.

The mainstream newspapers also did not print any letters from white fans anxious that a racially integrated squad would earn the prestigious Rose Bowl bid, although there were surely many who had that mind-set. Schindhelm's letter to Sproul included one anecdote that revealed this perspective. According to her, a UCLA graduate "connected with the Navy in high command" and living in Washington, D.C., had written her expressing his belief that a UCLA appearance in the Rose Bowl "would be a disgrace" because the school would be "represented by so many Negroes."[116]

Finally, as these various controversies swirled around the two teams, the day of the game arrived: December 9, 1939. That day, the *Examiner* devoted *eight* stories to the contest, an indication of its cultural relevance to the Los Angeles community.[117] On a typical Southern California day, sunny and warm, the only two undefeated squads in the PCC squared off before more than 103,000 fans in the Los Angeles Coliseum, with 14,000 African Americans in attendance.[118] Strode recalled the overflowing crowd: "All the Hollywood royalty showed up. . . . And the noise was deafening, like the static from a blank TV station times a hundred thousand."[119] The first half belonged to USC, but they were unable to capitalize by putting points on the scoreboard. Using their superior line, the Trojans ran the ball well against UCLA's defense, and a Washington fumble gave USC excellent field position. A few plays later, however, as Lansdell ran for the end zone, Robinson flew in from the secondary, hitting him so hard that the USC back fumbled for the first time all year, and Strode recovered the ball. As the game entered the fourth quarter, it remained a scoreless deadlock. With only minutes left in the game, Washington's passing and Robinson's running drove UCLA inside the USC five-yard line. A touchdown and surefire berth in the Rose Bowl seemed imminent. But the USC defense tightened, and on fourth down from the two-yard line, the UCLA players (in a six-to-five vote in the huddle) decided to try for the touchdown instead of kicking a field goal. Washington's pass was batted away, and USC took over. It was the last best scoring chance for either team, and the game ended in a 0–0 tie that left the spectators breathless and the UCLA team crushed. With a final record of 6–0–4, compared to USC's 7–0–2, there would be no Rose Bowl for the remarkable UCLA squad.

In the days that followed, sportswriters across the nation debated the decision to try for the touchdown. However, UCLA had struggled with extra points in the preceding games, so the decision was not as puzzling as it might seem in contemporary times.[120] But no one—white or black—faulted Washington, Strode, or Robinson for failing to win. Indeed, the tie with a USC team considered deeper and stronger than UCLA impressed many observers. The black press, disappointed in the outcome, nonetheless praised the team effusively. The *Washington Afro-American* called the tie "a moral victory" for the school.[121] In the *Eagle*, Fentress admitted that UCLA's failure to win and earn a Rose Bowl bid left "an empty sort of feeling way down deep in us," but he also lauded Washington's play in the game and Robinson's role in forcing the crucial fumble.[122] *Defender* sports editor Fay Young was happy that the black players "had come through—and gloriously."[123] Having performed well on a national stage, the black players had made the black press proud. After all, the team finished with an undefeated record, ranked number seven in the nation by the Associated Press.[124]

One final event made its way into both the black and white coverage of the game and must have been heartening to those who saw the UCLA team as validation of a new kind of pluralistic civic nationalism. With fifteen seconds to play, and no opportunity for UCLA to score, Coach Horrell substituted for Washington so that the crowd could pay its respects to the player as his career ended. As he left the field, tens of thousands of fans stood and applauded, a deafening ovation that dazzled black and white sportswriters. Lansdell and USC teammate Harry Smith (a fellow All-American lineman) stopped Washington to shake his hand. It was, Strode later wrote, "the most soul-stirring event I have ever seen in sports."[125] For the moment at least, the biracial crowd joined in celebrating one of the most remarkable black athletes ever to play football on the West Coast.

That Washington's professional opportunities were far more limited than those of either Smith or Lansdell probably occurred to few that day, although they were a reality he would have to live with as his career ended. For the moment, the game provided people such as *Examiner* reader Robert C. Hume an opportunity to put aside the ongoing racial inequalities in American civil society and to have hope for a future when racial difference would not determine the limits of opportunity. In a letter to the editor headlined "Still Hope Here," Hume wrote:

> There is still hope for America when 103,303 rabid football fans forget home, business, friends and worry to enjoy to the fullest one of our national sports. . . . And those two teams, magnificent to a man, fighting heroically to the last second for victory and their alma mater. The display of real sportsmanship and fairness during those

60 minutes of tense excitement and strain deserves the plaudits of every football fan in the country. Forgetting color, race or creed, they carried on splendidly.[126]

In the wake of the momentous game and Washington's stirring ovation, such an appraisal seemed plausible, a heartening sign of what the nation might be.

Across the country, the reaction of the black newspaper the *New York Amsterdam News* to Washington's stunning ovation took on a different tone. In an editorial reprinted in the *Eagle* two weeks after the game, the editors of the *News* celebrated Washington's career and the fans' embrace, ecstatic that "103,000 bankers, politicians, movie stars, clerks, laborers, reliefers—the cross section of America—rose as one and applauded him for 10 minutes." But the *News* editorial lamented that most of the fans did not consider "the paradox" of the moment: the ongoing presence of discrimination in the nation, an affliction, the editors wrote, that "gnaws at the vitals of our democracy." After all, "despite Kenny's ability, courage, honesty" and other positive personality traits, he was "denied many privileges and rights which . . . make U.S. citizens the most blessed in the world." Because of his race, "thousands of jobs," including professional football, would be "closed to him." The writer wistfully considered "how much better off America would be" if the people in the stands considered these ongoing inequalities and then, even better, acted to correct them. If they did so, the writer mused, "it would fill a void in the lives of many, many Kenny Washingtons whose sole desire is to become illustrious and worthwhile Americans. It would make America a still greater nation and our democracy nearer perfect."[127] Building on the American ethos of hard work and self-sufficiency by emphasizing the desire of many black American men to be "illustrious and worthwhile," the editorial nonetheless called on white Americans to make equality a reality, to see the lack of opportunities in professional sports as a cautionary sign of American democracy's limitations.

After the Season: Awards, Limited Opportunities, and the Struggles of 1940

The season's end, disappointing as it was, did not conclude the story of the 1939 UCLA football team and certainly did not mark the end of the spotlight for its three black stars. In the days, weeks, and months that followed the "moral victory" over USC, people continued to comment on the team, a sign of the squad's symbolic resonance. Postseason award voting marked the first major event that thrust the three black stars back into the spotlight. When the East-West Shrine Game announced the rosters for the annual contest on New Year's Day in San Francisco, Kenny Washington's name did not appear among the invitees. As the game drew nearer, committee members for the game explicitly acknowledged race's role in the decision to exclude Washington, believing that "an invitation" to him "might cause friction with the Southern players on the Eastern team."[128] Many in the media, black and white, lambasted the Shrine Game organizers for acceding to Jim Crow customs, but the black press was particularly vocal and ascribed a great deal of significance to the story. In the *Eagle*, Washington's snub was the second most prominent story in the December 28, 1939, issue. According to the story, a host of organizations and individuals complained bitterly about Washington's absence from the game, including the UCLA Student Committee on Civil Liberties and Academic Freedom, the American Student Union at UCLA, the Maritime Federation of the Pacific (a labor organization), and two white sportswriters—Dick Hyland of the *Los Angeles Times* and Ned Cronin of the (Oakland) *Evening News*.[129] Fentress also denounced the reasoning of the game's officials, arguing that if the players who were selected for the teams had "not learned . . . the spirit of tolerance and fair play" during their four years in college, "then education . . . is a failure."[130] For these activists and writers, this case represented a breakdown in the nation's ideal of equal opportunity for all in a multiracial America. Even in northern California and in the supposedly color-blind realm of sports, the South's Jim Crow politics continued to influence everyday life for African Americans.

Curiously, some white reporters refused to pick up the story, hesitant to critique southern racial politics even when those biases were readily apparent. Walsh's silence in the *Examiner* was particularly significant. After all, he had quickly assured readers that prejudice had not been the cause of Washington's All-American snub; now, when it was clear that racial animosity was the sole reason Washington was not invited to the Shrine game, he declined comment. His coworker at the *Examiner*, Bob Hunter, wrote that Washington "was rudely spurned by officials of the East-West game in San Francisco," but he neglected to identify race's role.[131] As in countless newspapers across the country over the course of the twentieth century, these men did not discuss the racial inequities in assessing athletic performance, unwilling to undermine the potential of sports as a model for fairness and equality. At this historical moment, such a revelation would have indicated that the quest for a new kind of civic nationalism would require more than simply opening doors for opportunity; it would require citizens to change their beliefs, to shed traditional conceptions of race and male citizenship. In short, it would require hard work on the part of white Americans to remove the many unstated barriers to black advancement in American society and culture.

The limited professional opportunities for Strode and Washington (and black athletes more generally) also spoke to the numerous obstacles blacks faced in American life and provided another opportunity for observers to consider the limits of American democracy in the late 1930s. Although feted after the season by various local groups, senior starters Washington and Strode faced difficult decisions as their college careers ended.[132] How could they best capitalize on their fame and athletic ability? Unlike their white USC counterparts, who were observed by scouts from the National Football League during the big game between the two schools, Washington and Strode could not aspire to play for the most prominent professional league in the country, as an unwritten agreement barred blacks from competition.[133] The lack of professional sports opportunities must have been galling. Widely regarded as two of the finest football players on the West Coast, the pair had to settle for being paid on a game-by-game basis in exhibition contests against hastily assembled squads.[134]

Some in the press noted these inequalities. A lengthy story by Walsh cast a sympathetic light on Strode's decision to turn professional. Strode poignantly described the economic woes facing his family, as neither his brother nor his father could "find work," presumably on account of their race. Strode even sold his tickets to the UCLA-USC game in order to provide a good Christmas for his family.[135] That a college student should feel pressured to support his family was a poignant sign of the lack of employment opportunities for black men in the Los Angeles area. In late December, Fentress reprinted a radio address by Sam Balder, a national sports commentator, who lambasted NFL teams for failing to draft Washington. Balder called the decision "a source of bitter disillusionment" to him and to "the millions of American sports fans who believe in fair play and equal opportunity." Fentress agreed with that assessment, arguing that Major League Baseball's ongoing ban against black players also violated "American principles" such as "equality for all."[136] Across the country, writers in the black press highlighted these cases of obvious racial discrimination as proof that African Americans were not given a fair chance in American life. Although many political and social leaders called for a new, pluralistic America in the New Deal era, some black and white observers saw, through sports, a system in which avenues for advancement were either partially or fully closed to racial minorities.

Although the stars of the 1939 team went their separate ways—Strode and Washington to professional football exhibitions, Robinson to athletic stardom in basketball, track, and baseball for UCLA—issues of equality and fairness continued to follow them. The following fall, when Washington played with a group of former college all-stars against the Chicago Bears of the NFL, the *Defender* used the moment to call for an end to "Jim-crow in baseball and football. . . . It is un-American, it is un-democratic. There is no element of American fair play about it."[137] When Robinson failed to make the first-team all–Pacific Coast Conference basketball team in February 1941, despite being the leading scorer in the conference, UCLA student writer Hank Shatford dubbed the voting as "a flagrant bit of prejudice" and called Cal coach Nibs Price's failure to include Robinson on his ballots for first, second, and third teams "a miscarriage of justice."[138]

There were hopeful signs, too, in the months following the game against USC. Washington cashed in on his athletic stardom by signing a film contract in January 1940 and would star in one all-black film and appear in others in the years that followed, providing supplemental income for his burgeoning professional football career. UCLA also hired Washington as an assistant football coach for the 1940 season, a move that earned the school a spot on the "Honor Roll in Race Relations" put out by the Schomburg Collection at the New York Public Library. L. D. Reddick, the curator of the collection, wrote President Sproul that "efforts such as yours are doing a great deal toward making real the American Dream of a true democracy."[139] Published in the *New York Times*, broadcast over radio by the BBC in England, and mentioned by Eleanor Roosevelt in her regular column "My Day," the honor served notice that black athletic achievement could lead to other opportunities, that it might open doors previously closed to talented African Americans. Strode played professional football locally and also worked for the city's district attorney's office, using the connections he made at UCLA to great effect. He would later go on to have a lucrative career as an actor in a variety of action films. Although the 1940 UCLA team struggled, winning only one game, Robinson continued to dazzle writers and fans with his remarkable speed and agility. His performance against Washington State, when he accounted for 339 yards of total offense, ran for two touchdowns, passed for one other score, intercepted three of the opposing team's passes, and kicked all four of UCLA's extra points, was a particularly inspiring performance.[140]

Throughout the 1939 season, and in the months following it, numerous observers on both sides of the color line hoped that sports offered an arena in which players of multiple races and ethnicities could work together to achieve a common goal, a powerful symbol for a nation struggling to put into place a new, inclusive civic nationalism. How vexing, then, that time and again racial bigotry kept appearing—in prejudice's impact on award voting, in the stereotypical nicknames used by whites for beloved black stars, in the memorable homecoming display on USC's campus, and in the lack of professional opportunities for these young men as their college careers ended. Was the story of the 1939 UCLA team one of hope or despair? How could one decide? After all, only four months after tens of thousands stood to cheer Kenny Washington in the Los Angeles Coliseum, the Ku Klux Klan led a parade in downtown Los Angeles.[141] These contradictions revealed the conflicting responses to a multicultural America at a time when the nation was attempting to redefine the contours of American democracy. They reflected the fragmented nature of the American body politic and the challenges to crafting a civic nationalism that could welcome all the nation's citizens.

Milt Cohen could not have known he was being prophetic in May 1940 as he penned one of the final columns of his career at the *Daily Bruin*. Inspired by the performance of UCLA's black athletes that year, he wrote an "Open Letter to President Lincoln" about the problem of ongoing "prejudice," particularly as it related to black athletes. Wide-ranging in its description of the obstacles faced by African American athletes, Cohen's column somberly noted that sports were not free from bigotry: "The same barriers and prejudices that haunt [black athletes] elsewhere also follow them into the sports world." Not all schools were as enlightened as UCLA, Cohen noted; some refused to accept black students at all, and others used "a subtle 'discouraging process'" to prevent African Americans from participating in school sports programs. He reserved his strongest words for the bigotry of professional sports leagues. Although "fans would welcome a chance to see men like Jackie Robinson and Kenny Washington play big league baseball," Major League Baseball's "unwritten law" denied them the opportunity. Looking into the future, he wrote, "Some day a man will come along who will sign a Negro to play for his team—and then this so-called tradition will be shattered." Of course, UCLA's own Jackie Robinson would end up being the first black player signed, and his trail-blazing role would gradually open up the rosters of other baseball teams and other sports leagues. The same year Robinson played his first game with the Brooklyn Dodgers, the Los Angeles Rams signed the first two black players in modern NFL history: two Los Angeles–area residents named Kenny Washington and Woody Strode. Looking back, it seems clear that the 1939 UCLA team played a key role in building momentum toward the integration of professional sports. The national attention these black athletes and their white teammates received showed that blacks and white athletes could succeed together at the highest levels. But Cohen hoped that the "new era" he envisioned would "not apply to sports alone," that sports would "lead the way" for change in other aspects of American life, "for it is in the world of sports that our people are the most broadminded."[142]

Were sports ahead of society, as Cohen and many others hoped? Could equality on the field, however imperfectly reached, lead to more egalitarian American politics, economics, and society? As policy makers and pundits tried to craft a new, more inclusive version of American civic culture, as Los Angeles residents tried to create a civil space for their multiracial city, and as the Nazis began their campaign of terror halfway across the globe, Kenny Washington, Woody Strode, Jackie Robinson, and their teammates on the 1939 UCLA football team provided numerous opportunities for ordinary Americans to articulate more explicitly their beliefs regarding inclusiveness and fairness in American democracy. There were no easy answers. Certainly this team showed the capacity of whites to hold black athletes in esteem—and perhaps black men more generally—but the persistence of stereotypes and the troubling award voting suggested that black male leaders would not be welcome. Even on the West Coast, far from the cotton fields of the Deep South, Jim Crow segregation and its attendant racial attitudes continued to affect athletic contests—and everyday life—in significant ways. While the national climate created by FDR and his advisors may have been more welcoming for sports achievement to model an equitable society than it had been in Robeson's day, resistance remained strong. Events in ensuing years would continue to raise questions about the capacity of sports to model fairness and equality in American life, even as black and white sportswriters continued to cling to sports as a model (albeit in often different ways). For the moment, though, the 1939 UCLA team showed that a pluralistic team could, at least, achieve great things, no small feat for a tumultuous time.

3

"A First-Class Gentleman" and "That Big N——r"

Wilt Chamberlain at the University of Kansas, 1955–1958

tanding more than seven feet tall and moving with an agility and grace uncommon to big men, Wilt Chamberlain nearly always attracted the attention of those around him; he quite literally stood out in a crowd. Even on the basketball court, surrounded by other tall players, he dominated action as fans, coaches, and his fellow competitors all marveled at his on-court exploits. But Chamberlain did more than excel at basketball—as one of the first black basketball stars in the Midwest when he played for the University of Kansas (KU), he also profoundly influenced contemporary discussions of race in a pivotal era of civil rights activism. Indeed, shortly after his death in 1999, one white Kansas resident recalled, "Growing up in small-town Kansas, Wilt Chamberlain was the first black man in public life whose name I knew. He was a hero to us small-town sports fans."[1] He seemed larger than life to others as well. When the university town of Lawrence, Kansas, faced pressure to integrate all of its restaurants in the winter and spring of 1957, white resident Kathryn Harris wondered how townspeople could celebrate Chamberlain and black teammate Maurice King as "athletic heroes" and then prevent them from "ordering a meal in a downtown restaurant."[2] Chamberlain's race and celebrity—and the abundant media coverage of integrated basketball he inspired—forced observers and commentators to address publicly issues of race, masculinity, athletics, and equality.

Reactions to Chamberlain's career reveal more than just basketball's centrality to many Kansans or evolution in the game's style and popularity.

Instead, the many responses to his brilliant talents and unfulfilled college career indicate Americans in the heartland struggling to articulate their own definitions of *equality* and *equal opportunity* in the postwar era and as the modern civil rights movement gained momentum. Numerous people—black and white, old and young, men and women—employed Chamberlain as a form of cultural currency, using his status as a star athlete and black man to consider the implications of a truly equitable and perhaps color-blind society. People often did not agree in their assessment of those goals, or even the definitions of them, and discussions of Chamberlain's career as a college basketball star reveal contentious debates about the nation's sense of its democratic and egalitarian ideals. While most southern (and some midwestern) whites fought to maintain Jim Crow segregation, many whites had begun to view racial segregation with distaste, feeling that it violated the tenets of American egalitarian democracy at the heart of U.S. identity in World War II and the Cold War.

However, the discussion of Chamberlain's career reveals the conflicting notions of equality that existed even between black leaders and sympathetic whites. On the one hand, local black leaders expressly hoped that the spindly-legged young man would "improve area race relations" by disproving stereotypes of black male inferiority through his leadership of the basketball team, thus inspiring whites to abandon segregation. On the other hand, area white leaders and commentators supported Chamberlain's mission to solve "the race problem" on the assumption that he would provide a model of hard work and discipline for area blacks to follow—a vision of racial uplift that asked little of whites. Talking past one another, both groups saw sports as a model for society, but their very different interpretations revealed the tensions underlying changes in the nation's racial politics. At this key moment in history, and in a location largely unknown for its civil rights struggles, these divisions anticipated some of the fractures that would develop in the coalition that drove the civil rights movement. They also reflected the undue burdens that observers could heap on sports—and on athletic stars in particular—as they looked for resolution to the thorny issues of equality in American life.

Chamberlain in Context: The (Not Actually) Free State and Cold War America

Wilt Chamberlain was quite possibly the most publicized high school basketball player in the history of the game. Born in 1936 into a large family in Philadelphia, one of nine surviving children, Chamberlain grew to seven feet tall. His great height, combined with his remarkable coordination and competitive spirit, made him an excellent basketball player. By the time he was a senior at Overbrook High, he had become a national sensation, as national magazines such as *Life* published feature stories about him. Playing in one of the most competitive high school basketball conferences in the nation, Chamberlain led his team to three all–public school championships and two all-city championships, setting numerous records in the process. In one game as a senior, for example, he scored ninety points to lead his team to victory. Professional success, however, would have to wait; since the National Basketball Association (NBA) prohibited players from joining its professional league until after a player's class had graduated college, Chamberlain had to continue his career at the collegiate level or with a traveling team such as the Harlem Globetrotters. Given Chamberlain's on-court prowess, the competition for his services was intense; more than 120 schools offered him a scholarship (and other inducements that were technically against the rules set forth by the National Collegiate Athletic Association [NCAA]).[3] A media frenzy surrounded Chamberlain's college decision, as many believed that the school Chamberlain attended would win multiple national championships. Surprising many, in May 1955, Chamberlain selected KU.[4]

KU offered an alternative option for Chamberlain because it was located away from the prying East Coast media and because its head coach, Forrest "Phog" Allen, was generally considered one of the best in the nation. However, the university's own history of black athletes in sports—and with black students in general—might have given Chamberlain pause had he known of it. Although the school never had an official policy against admitting black students, their enrollment was sporadic and uneven from the time the university opened in 1867.[5] By the time Chamberlain arrived in the fall of 1955, the school averaged only 149 black students out of a total enrollment of 9,597.[6] This small population of black students often faced discrimination in a number of forms at the school and locally. Although the town of Lawrence had always prided itself on its progressive stance toward African Americans, conditions in the 1920s had been so bad that black student Loren Raymond Miller published a prize-winning essay in the *Crisis* outlining the discrimination that black students faced at KU.[7] Even by the mid-1950s, most public accommodations, including hotels, restaurants, and hospitals, remained segregated, as did local neighborhoods.[8] Segregation extended to the campus as well, where white fraternities and sororities refused to admit black students.[9]

Segregation and racial discrimination extended to athletics. While there had been black athletes in KU's past, including brothers Grant Harvey, Fred Harvey, and Ed Harvey, who had participated and starred in a number of sports around the turn of the century, the school agreed to exclude black students from its athletic teams at an early meeting of the Big Six Conference in 1912.[10] In 1924, athletic director Phog Allen, Chamberlain's future coach, removed the requirement for black students to pass a swimming test in order to graduate, just so that black and white students would not have to swim together.[11] The school also segregated black fans at sporting events. Although Ed Harvey and others protested bitterly, the university administration ignored their pleas.[12]

Gradually, school leaders became more sympathetic to black students. Following World War II, the Congress on Racial Equality (CORE) and other activist groups began to assault Lawrence's and KU's segregated facilities, businesses, and practices, although they faced vigorous opposition from business owners and town residents.[13] Soon after these early attempts at desegregation, Franklin D. Murphy, a firm supporter of racial equality, took over as chancellor in 1951 and used his influence to end segregation on campus and push for integration in the town of Lawrence. Change was brewing in KU's athletic department as well. Although Phog Allen had been a leading proponent of segregation as athletic director in the 1920s, he recruited the school's first black scholarship athlete, LeVannes Squires from Wichita, Kansas, in 1950. Squires made his varsity debut in 1952 and was a little-used reserve on Kansas's 1952 team that won the national championship.[14] Allen's second black recruit, Maurice King from nearby Kansas City, turned out to be a gifted player who was a senior starter when Chamberlain made his varsity debut for the 1957 season.[15]

Even with the progress being made in Lawrence and on campus, conditions were less than ideal when Chamberlain arrived at the school in the fall of 1955. Black students in the 1950s later remembered being told by professors on the first day of class that they could expect no better than a final grade of C because of their race. The Negro Student Association (NSA) formed in 1950, largely for the purpose of arranging social events for black students on campus since they were denied access to many events their white peers could attend, including the still-segregated fraternities and sororities.[16] Restaurants and hotels remained segregated in Lawrence. Even nearby Kansas City, a city with a sizable black population, continued to have segregated eating places, although efforts by black leaders had integrated hotels, theaters, and municipal parks.[17]

Nationally, the historical moment of Chamberlain's career at KU was a particularly rich one for testing and debating issues of equality and the terms of black male citizenship. A number of circumstances framed Chamberlain's arrival and thrust racial politics into the national consciousness, including the landmark U.S. Supreme Court rulings in the two *Brown v. Board of Education* rulings of 1954 and 1955 that ordered the integration of public schools. The case resonated locally: its title case was *Oliver Brown et al. v. The Board of Education of Topeka, Kansas*, a NAACP suit targeting the segregation policies in Topeka, less than thirty miles west of Lawrence. The murder of fourteen-year-old Emmett Till, a black teen in Mississippi, who was killed for allegedly whistling at a white woman, and the subsequent acquittal of his murderers by an all-white jury, occurred just before Chamberlain's arrival in Lawrence and deeply shook the nation. Meanwhile, as the United States fought the Cold War with the USSR, issues of civil rights and equality became increasingly important at the national and international levels. Policy makers fretted over negative publicity regarding race relations as incidents of bigotry undermined the claim of the United States as the land of the free, particularly as the nation worked to establish ties with African and Asian nations.[18] A lot was at stake then, then, as Chamberlain arrived. The modern civil rights movement had begun in earnest and would continue to gain momentum; national and international attention to incidents of bigotry would grow. And through it all, Chamberlain would galvanize attention as the biggest star in college sports.

Waiting Is the Hardest Part: Recruiting Chamberlain and His Arrival in Lawrence

Getting Chamberlain to Lawrence required a well-coordinated recruiting campaign to land the prized athletic star. Kansas coach Phog Allen's interest in recruiting Chamberlain was unexceptional (after all, nearly every major program hoped to land the big man), but his efforts to have black alumni participate in the process—and their willingness to help—illustrate the importance of race to Chamberlain's decision and the symbolic value some black leaders attached to him. In his autobiography, Chamberlain noted that Allen was "smart enough to play the black angle for all it was worth" in his recruitment of the Philadelphia big man.[19] To that end, he enlisted black KU alum Dowdal Davis, managing editor of the *Kansas City Call* and a prominent speaker and community leader. Davis played a vital role in the process, coordinating the efforts of a number of black leaders and KU alumni.[20] In February 1955, Davis also accompanied Allen to visit the Chamberlain home in Philadelphia and helped arrange the big man's two visits to Lawrence in February and April.[21] During the process, Davis also enlisted two other influential black alums—Etta Moten, a well-known concert singer, and Lloyd Kerford, a Lawrence-area businessman—to write Chamberlain, extolling the virtues of the university and also his potential importance to improving race relations.[22]

Although no record exists of the communication between Davis, Moten, Kerford, and Chamberlain, a number of recollections shed light on the appeals these black alumni made. When Chamberlain decided to leave KU in 1958, he described his recruitment in some depth, and explained that Davis, Moten, and Kerford all "told me I could help my race by attending K.U., and their arguments were convincing."[23] Other sources help illuminate how these black leaders hoped Chamberlain might "help" African Americans. Roy Edwards, a prominent white KU booster, recalled that Davis "pointed out

that much could be done to break the color line in this area, and he personally felt that Chamberlain could make a most outstanding contribution to his
race." Similarly, according to Edwards, Lloyd Kerford, on one of his "several"
trips to visit the Chamberlains, spent "four hours at one time visiting with
them and trying to explain how important it was that Wilt should come to
the midwest." These black leaders were not alone, as Edwards noted that "at
least five to six hundred letters were received from interested people" including many "from the colored race . . . with the underlying request that Chamberlain come to Lawrence."[24] Davis also told Ernest Mehl, the sports editor
for the *Kansas City Star*, that he "talked to Chamberlain of the prestige and
effectiveness of the University of Kansas, the boy's own potential importance
and how he might fit into a role which could not be duplicated by any other
person."[25] The *Call* (along with the *Lawrence Daily Journal-World*) covered
Chamberlain's recruitment in much greater detail than any other publication
in the area, even the school newspaper, printing numerous photographs and
columns in the wake of Chamberlain's two visits to the area. Clearly, black
leaders such as Davis had high hopes that Chamberlain could play a vital role
in ending local segregation.

An Associated Negro Press (ANP) article about Jackie Robinson's speaking engagement at a St. Louis high school in September 1955, just after
Chamberlain arrived, sheds light on the symbolic role that black leaders
hoped Chamberlain would fulfill. According to the story, Robinson argued
that integrated baseball "proved to lawmakers . . . that people can get along
together regardless of race, creed, or religion." The other positive impact of
sports, in Robinson's opinion, was one of uplift: he saw baseball as providing
"a new incentive" to African Americans "by making them feel that if they
have ability they can strive for professions and opportunities which were previously denied them because of race."[26] For area black leaders, Chamberlain
could perform similar cultural labor by proving the efficacy of integrated
society (thus undermining segregation) and providing a positive role model
for blacks and whites.

Those were lofty goals for sports figures, and certainly for an eighteen-
year-old basketball player far from home. However, when Chamberlain
announced his decision to attend KU on May 14, 1955, nearly anything
seemed possible to the local media, who celebrated gleefully with lead stories
on the sports page or even the front page.[27] And although area newspapers
primarily emphasized Chamberlain's impacts on the basketball court, they
also discussed the importance of race in his decision. The *Call*, no doubt
inspired by Davis's active role, celebrated local African Americans' involvement in bringing the star out west. Chamberlain acknowledged that "the
Negro people interested in Kansas had an awful lot to do with" his decision
and specifically mentioned Davis, Moten, and the Kerfords as being particularly

important.[28] The widely circulated Associated Press story regarding Chamberlain's decision featured Allen's praise of the "outstanding alumni of the Negro Race" for helping bring Chamberlain to KU.[29] The importance of race to Chamberlain's decision was unavoidable in newspaper coverage, an apparent recognition of the ongoing struggles with Jim Crow segregation in the region.

A closer look at the discourse surrounding Chamberlain's announcement, however, suggests that black and white observers were often talking past one another as they discussed the importance of race in these stories. Black leaders hoped that Chamberlain, as a nationally known athletic superstar, would inspire area whites to integrate their communities (including, of course, the still-segregated town of Lawrence). By dominating interracial, on-court competition, Chamberlain could show whites the fallacy of a color system that rested on assumptions of black inferiority. However, while black leaders wanted Chamberlain to serve as a role model to whites, convincing them that segregation was morally and ethically wrong through his feats of athletic excellence on an integrated team, many white Kansans hoped Chamberlain would be a "good" role model for African Americans and would show the university's and region's liberal racial attitudes. Bill Mayer in the *Journal-World*, for example, emphasized Chamberlain as a sign of progress and a role model for the black community at large. Mayer discussed the significance that race played in the recruiting process: "In past interviews, Chamberlain has said one of his primary goals in going to college is the furtherance of the Negro race. He has deep convictions here and states emphatically he hopes his future actions will reflect great credit on his people." Mayer believed that "the Negroes couldn't have a finer emissary in this area" because Chamberlain was "a first-class gentleman in every respect, possessed with great social poise, a sharp sense of humor and high intelligence in addition to his athletic ability." From Mayer's viewpoint, Chamberlain would be a model of humbleness and virtue and would prove that blacks could be responsible citizens. Indeed, he praised the Kerfords for their role in the process and said they were "outstanding citizens of their community for many years." He guessed that Chamberlain "saw how much this family had done for its race and was inspired by the fact he might be able to do likewise out West."[30]

From Mayer's perspective, Chamberlain could improve race relations not by revealing the injustices of the color line, but rather by living responsibly, working hard, and setting a good example for other African Americans to follow. Mayer either missed or purposefully reinterpreted African American leaders' hopes for Chamberlain. From the perspective of black leaders, after all, *whites* needed changing and inspiration, not African Americans. Like Coach Allen, who thought that Chamberlain was persuaded to attend the school because of its "fine points" for African Americans, Mayer focused on what the university and town could provide Chamberlain, and Chamberlain's potential as a role model for blacks, and not what Chamberlain could do to influence area whites.[31] These differing expectations reflected altering perspectives on who was responsible for bringing about racial integration in the region—whites or African Americans—and on whose terms.

That such conflicting interpretations existed reflected the nation's changing racial politics. By the mid-1950s, many white Americans had begun to support black claims for equality with more enthusiasm (or, at the least, with less overt hostility). But thorny issues remained: How would a racially integrated society work? Who would set the rules and provide the models for others to follow? For Mayer and others, white middle-class society was the ideal, a standard to which blacks and others—presumably foreign communists and third world countries—should aspire to reach.

With this cultural backdrop, Chamberlain arrived in Lawrence for the start of his freshman year in September 1955. Although a barrage of publicity surrounded his arrival, narratives of race had largely disappeared. Instead, the local press celebrated Chamberlain's celebrity and marveled at his size.[32] One photograph circulated widely in the newspapers: that of Chamberlain standing next to five-foot, five-inch KU football player Don Pfutzenreuter. The (Lawrence) *University Daily Kansan*, the *Kansas City Star*, the *Topeka Daily Capital*, and the *Lawrence Daily Journal-World* all published a version of this photograph, usually with a headline similar to the *Lawrence Daily Journal-World*'s: "Long and Short of K.U. Sport."[33]

The photograph documented Chamberlain's first full day in Lawrence, September 5, 1955, when he stopped by the football team's media day. These newspapers delighted in the comedic, almost clownish, possibilities of Chamberlain's height even as they tried to convey to readers his extreme size. Perhaps sensing the comic, and in some ways demeaning, implications of Chamberlain towering over the diminutive football player, the *Call*, alone among the area newspapers, did not print the photograph. There was certainly no apparent ill will in the mainstream papers' coverage of Chamberlain's arrival; indeed, several writers such as Dick Snider praised Chamberlain for being good-humored despite the fact that "it was only about the 9,768th time in his life he has been asked to pose for a picture with some little guy."[34] But the subtle difference in the *Call*'s coverage—the first photograph their editors printed of Chamberlain after he arrived was of him with white high school teammate Doug Leamon, who had also come to Kansas—suggested that Chamberlain's arrival meant more than fun and games to them.[35]

Leamon actually figured in the most remarkable aspect of Chamberlain's long-awaited entrance to the university town—a story that would be heard years later, only after Chamberlain left the school and went on to a stellar NBA career. Chamberlain and Leamon had driven together from Philadelphia to Lawrence, a long and exhausting trip. As they neared their destination, they stopped one last time at a diner in Kansas City for dinner. But, because of Chamberlain's race, they were refused service. Chamberlain was furious. Driving straight to Allen's house, Chamberlain pounded on the door, waking up Allen and his wife. A surprised Allen told Chamberlain to "forget about those people" and offered to put him up for the night. He also had some KU students bring over take-out food for them—it turned out later that he had done this so that Chamberlain did not realize that Lawrence was segregated as well. None of the newspapers printed this story; nor did Chamberlain publicly express his disgust and surprise. However, behind the scenes, Chamberlain angrily told Allen and others that he "had no intention of playing basketball for K.U." if he was forced to stay and/or eat apart from the team. After that warning, the team canceled games for the freshman team against Rice, SMU, and Louisiana State, and a game against TCU for the following season was taken off the schedule. After talking with his "advisors" in the area (presumably Davis), Chamberlain conducted his own one-man campaign to integrate area restaurants by demanding to be served in previously segregated establishments. According to his autobiography, he was never refused.[36] Local newspapers entirely neglected to cover these strenuous efforts.

And so it was a privately disgruntled Chamberlain who adapted to a town that was, in his own words, "infested with segregation."[37] On campus, Chamberlain fit in well with his peers despite his celebrity status, playing table tennis, engaging in competitions with other athletes, and clowning around. Student John Novotny recalled, "Wilt was never aloof, or a prima donna. . . . He was one of the gang."[38] As the news media focused on his positive public persona, missing the story of his discontent and his tumultuous arrival, they continued to bombard readers with various stories and images of the larger-than-life Chamberlain, reveling in his celebrity and massive physique.[39] The *Call* also devoted considerable attention to Chamberlain but resisted the impulse to emphasize Chamberlain's clownish traits. Instead, the black paper often depicted Chamberlain as part of a continuum of black success. In October 1955, for example, the *Call* printed a photograph of Chamberlain standing with three other black athletes at the school, including King and Charles Tidwell, "a freshman track star."[40] The newspaper took special delight in the increasing presence of black athletes on KU's varsity teams and used coverage of Chamberlain to illuminate this trend.

When it came time for Chamberlain's debut before a public audience in the annual varsity-freshman scrimmage, area newspapers covered the event in great detail, all reveling in Chamberlain's astonishing display of skill and athleticism. For the first time in the event's thirty-year history, the freshman squad defeated the varsity, with Chamberlain scoring forty-two points in the 81–71 victory in front of a record crowd of fourteen thousand fans. The area's white newspapers deluged readers with a flood of stories and photographs from the scrimmage, clearly dazzled by Chamberlain's dominance.[41] Photo montages showed Chamberlain in action, and columnists gushed about KU's national championship aspirations.[42] KU students responded similarly. A six-photograph spread of Chamberlain in the *Kansan* was the central feature of the newspaper's annual Thanksgiving photo supplement, which came out just after the scrimmage. Images depicted him in a variety of activities, including dunking a basketball, studying, and sitting on the court in his practice attire, his legs stretching across the two pages of the spread. The accompanying text joyfully predicted that KU would "become a major basketball power once again," thanks to Chamberlain.[43] Chamberlain's dunking earned special attention, as a number of papers printed photos and montages of Chamberlain stuffing the ball through the hoop.[44] As historian Aram Goudsouzian has noted, Chamberlain's style of play made significant progress in changing the nature of the game, emphasizing the more free-form style developed in African American communities. Although other players had been tall, and others had dunked, no one had dunked with the regularity and the flair that Chamberlain did.[45] His ability to dunk with ease and in the flow of the game amazed spectators; thus the many photographs.

Although Chamberlain's athletic exploits clearly registered with the editorial board of the *Call* as well—who featured multiple stories and photographs just as the predominantly white papers did—the black editors of the *Call* saw more than KU's basketball prowess at stake in Chamberlain's accomplishments.[46] Sports editor John I. Johnson took the moment of Chamberlain's scrimmage debut to ponder the state of affairs for black students at KU:

> It has been only recently that Negro athletes have chosen to attend the University of Kansas. There has existed a feeling in the past that a colored athlete had little chance to enter fully the athletic program.
>
> But it all seems to have changed in recent years. The change began a few years ago when LeVance [*sic*] Squires advanced from the freshman to the varsity basketball team. It moved forward this year under Coach Chuck Mather when three Negro boys became members this season of the varsity football team. This spring will see another step forward when Charles Tidwell, and probably others, get an opportunity to compete in track under the Jayhawk colors.
>
> This year for the first time a Negro girl became a candidate for the homecoming queen. Progress in human and athletic relations is being made at the University of Kansas. A new day has come to Mt. Oread.
>
> Wilt (The Stilt) will advance these good relations and other Negro students will follow. . . . Just the chance to make good is all a worthy athlete desires.[47]

Johnson saw Chamberlain as part of a continuum of black athletes who were opening doors for others, who were making "progress in human and athletic relations." Given that there was no "official" policy that prevented blacks from competing at KU, it was important to have concrete examples of black success—such as Chamberlain's smashing debut—to open the door. Chamberlain's success could give other African Americans "the chance to make good."

These alternate readings of Chamberlain's importance—as a basketball savior on the one hand and a sign of racial progress on the other—were not necessarily mutually exclusive. Clearly, black sportswriters recognized Chamberlain's importance to KU's basketball team as much as white writers did, and they would over time discuss his centrality to the team's fortunes. And there would be times when the white press pondered racism and ideas of equal opportunity through Chamberlain's career as well. However, the different emphases in press coverage at this particular moment, Chamberlain's first public performance in a KU uniform, reveal the heightened expectations many in the black press had for Chamberlain's starring role.

At the Center of the Athletic World: Chamberlain and KU's 1957 Season

Chamberlain's debut with the varsity squad for the 1956–1957 season, his sophomore year, contained a number of triumphant moments and gut-wrenching disappointments for KU fans and members of the team alike. Although hopes were high for the Chamberlain-led KU squad, some worried that the forced retirement of longtime head coach Allen would hinder the team's chances. Allen, a major reason Chamberlain selected the school, had reached the mandatory retirement age of seventy, and his appeal for one more year of coaching had been denied, much to his shock and dismay.[48] Still, Chamberlain's on-court prowess generated an enormous amount of media attention from both the black and white press. That attention started early, as the anticipation for Chamberlain's varsity debut on December 3, 1956, built up in the local newspapers. Some local papers printed photographs of Chamberlain dunking in practice, and some featured front-page preview stories and banner headlines in the days leading up to his first game.[49] Clearly people were excited to see the big man in action, and he did not disappoint. In an 87–69 victory over Northwestern University, Chamberlain put to rest any doubts skeptics had about his ability as he poured in a record-setting fifty-two points and dazzled fans and opponents alike with his agility and strength.[50]

In game coverage the next day, the local newspapers delighted in celebrating Chamberlain's accomplishments. The *Call*'s banner headline in the sports section announced, "Bill Russell Is Gone, but the Stilt Has Arrived," and its story proclaimed Chamberlain the new "king" of college basketball, celebrating his ascendance to the throne in the wake of the black Bill Russell's graduation from the University of San Francisco.[51] If the other newspapers did not call Chamberlain a "king," they nonetheless marveled at his feats. The editors of the *Star* believed Chamberlain had lived up to the hype: "Wilt 52, It's All True," a headline declared.[52] The fans apparently agreed with that assessment; according to the game story, "the crowd of 15,000 was more preoccupied by what Chamberlain was doing than with the progress of the game."[53] As they analyzed Chamberlain's first performance, writers celebrated more than Chamberlain's physical skills. Bill Mayer, for example, writing in the *Journal-World*, thought Chamberlain's ability "to adapt and adjust quickly to a given situation," such as when he changed his strategy in defending Northwestern center Joe Rucklick, revealed his "sharp mind and tremendous native talent." Mayer was also impressed by Chamberlain's strength and "tremendous stamina."[54] For a fan base eager for another national championship, after two consecutive years of mediocrity,[55] and newsmen excited to have a sensation who would sell more newspapers, Chamberlain appeared to deliver the athletic goods in his stunning debut.

Undoubtedly, Chamberlain's dazzling display of strength and athleticism proved disquieting to some observers even as it excited others. Anxious rule makers and fans, clearly distressed that a tall black man would dominate the sport (as his peer Bill Russell had done), modified the game's rules before his first varsity season: a widening of the lane to prevent big men from hanging out too close to the basket, a rule outlawing jumping from the foul line to shoot free throws, offensive goaltending (so Chamberlain could not tip in missed shots by teammates), and a rule against throwing inbound passes over the backboard.[56] The numerous dunk photographs in the local papers similarly would have been distressing to many whites, as they often depicted Chamberlain physically dominating white opponents. One photo in the *Journal-World*, for example, displayed Chamberlain dunking the ball forcefully through the hoop, his mouth open as though letting out a primal scream, while three players watched, one Marquette athlete unmistakably cowering at his power and size.[57]

This photograph, and others like it, had the potential to be quite destabilizing. Although theories of white male supremacy were not nearly as widespread in 1950s America as they had been at the turn of the century, Jim Crow segregation rested on fundamental assumptions of black inferiority that were often tied to stereotypes of black male shiftlessness and inadequacy. Images of Chamberlain dominating white competition clearly undermined these stereotypes.

Or did they? Another stereotype of black men revolved around the image of the "brutal black buck," which the film historian Donald Bogle describes as "big, baaddd niggers, over-sexed and savage, violent and frenzied as they lust for white flesh."[58] For these viewers, Chamberlain's on-court dominance might well have "proven" bestial physical prowess and little more. There were certainly Kansas sports followers who were eager to discount Chamberlain's greatness. Mayer later felt the need to defend the big man against some "capricious fans" who believed Chamberlain to be "washed up and probably never . . . really great at all" after he scored only twelve points in a narrow one-point win over Iowa State in the Big Seven tournament. After praising Chamberlain's defense, rebounding, and teamwork in KU's win, Mayer also had a few choice words for those who criticized Chamberlain "for missing several key free throws—five in the second half." He wondered whether those fans noticed that Gary Thompson, the "celebrated" star guard (and a white player) for Iowa State, also missed four free throws "in a crucial game," despite the fact that he was "noted for his coolness under fire."[59] Chamberlain's excellence went only so far in convincing skeptical observers of the inaccuracy of certain stereotypes, even when he clearly dominated the competition night in and night out. Chamberlain might be the star player on the court, but "scrappy" white players might be more "clutch" or "cool" under pressure.

These subtle differences aside, most fans and media members marveled at Chamberlain's athletic accomplishments but, in doing so, forgot or neglected Chamberlain's pioneering role as a race leader. Max Falkenstein, the long-time radio broadcaster for the KU men's basketball team, recalled that Chamberlain's "size and agility made him an entertaining oddity . . . for many of the wide-eyed Kansas faithful, fans who were still getting accustomed to the concept of a black man on the floor." Although some fans had misgivings about his race, according to Falkenstein, Chamberlain's talent—and the fact that he was playing for KU—made "Jayhawks fans more than willing to expand their capacity for acceptance."[60] A *Journal-World* front-page story about fans' reactions to Chamberlain's debut supports Falkenstein's perceptions. Men and women, such as the local sheriff and a female foreign exchange student, all marveled at Chamberlain's grace on the court, calling him "the best ever!" While some fans worried Chamberlain would get injured or become ill, no one expressed any concerns about his race.[61]

In the context of these celebratory reactions, from the media and fans alike, it is especially noteworthy that only one local publication printed Maurice King's assessment of Chamberlain's debut. As the other black player on the KU team, King was clearly excited by Chamberlain's potential impact on the team's fortunes, but he also considered some larger issues. According to student writer Bob Lyle of the *Kansan*, King hoped Chamberlain would "do a lot to improve racial relationships through his athletic career."[62] In theory one of the main reasons for Chamberlain's decision to play for KU, that aspect of his story largely vanished as writers employed hyperbole and editors scrambled for photos of thunderous dunks. Had those other publications merely been paying lip service to those lofty goals? Did they hope that angle of Chamberlain's story would be forgotten? Or did they hope that not mentioning Chamberlain's race would actually improve racial relations by treating his star presence as an unexceptional development? Certainly readers and writers would have been familiar with the burgeoning civil rights movement taking place across the South. The Montgomery bus boycott, which received significant attention from the national media, concluded in December 1956, just as Chamberlain played his first varsity game. Perhaps white Kansas and Missouri civic leaders avoided commenting on racial issues to depict their region of the country more positively, as unfettered by the unrest that marred the turbulent South. The hesitance to discuss the racial aspect of Chamberlain's debut at the least suggests an anxiety among whites in squarely addressing the racial meanings of Chamberlain's presence and performance, one that would resurface throughout his career. This was part of a larger, and troubling, pattern in the mainstream press. In not naming the problem of racism, in ignoring the larger issues at stake, these writers lent tacit support to the status quo, just as they had done in insisting that Kenny Washington had been denied All-American honors for reasons other than his race.

As the season progressed, Chamberlain continued to garner a great deal of media attention, nearly all of it complimentary of him on and off the court. However, some subtle differences in the coverage of the local newspapers reflect some alternate approaches to Chamberlain's role on the team. While the *Call* praised Chamberlain unequivocally as KU's team leader and considered his accomplishments in the context of the successes of other black athletes and black coaches, other newspapers focused on Chamberlain's leadership in various statistical categories: scoring, rebounds, and blocked shots. Even as these papers acknowledged the centrality of Chamberlain to KU's success, they shied away from praising him as the inspirational leader of his integrated team. To do so would have meant significantly altering long-held stereotypes about black men—something white press members seemed especially hesitant to do.

The writers and editors of the *Call* placed Chamberlain at the center of their coverage of KU, writing from the perspective that whatever successes the team enjoyed were due primarily to Chamberlain's presence. In sports editor John I. Johnson's wrap-up for 1956, for example, the final athlete mentioned was Chamberlain, "who has done a big part in pacing the team to a string of early victories and who may, barring misfortune, lead the squad to high national honors."[63] From Johnson's perspective, Chamberlain set the pace for his teammates, leading them almost single-handedly to their successes. That emphasis was echoed in the *Call*'s game story about the Jayhawks' second meeting with Colorado, which indicated that Chamberlain "turned in another leadership job" in his team's 68–57 victory.[64] The emphasis on Chamberlain as a black leader fit into a broader pattern of coverage in this newspaper. When Tennessee State became the first black school to win the National Association of Intercollegiate Athletics (NAIA) basketball tournament (a tournament featuring the best teams from some of the nation's smaller schools) on March 16, 1957, Johnson enthusiastically praised Tennessee State's black head coach, Johnny B. McLendon. He was heartened by the success of a black male head coach because it continued to prove that "given an equal opportunity," African Americans could succeed in "almost any field of activity."[65] To Johnson, Chamberlain and McLendon both embodied successful black male leaders who had proved their worth competing against whites, a powerful message for the newspaper's editors and writers. Just as black writers had turned to Robeson as a symbol of black male potential, this commentary framed Chamberlain as a figure of not only remarkable physical prowess and ability but also broader talents and character.

Other publications tended not to emphasize that message. Although the major publications in the Lawrence area all lauded Chamberlain's accomplishments on the court, praising his scoring, rebounding, and defense—and saw him as a leader of sorts off the court—his role as a leader of an integrated team was rarely mentioned. Instead, Chamberlain earned praised for setting "a good example for all young adults and teen-agers" by getting his second polio vaccine shot—which both the *Journal-World* and the *Capital* depicted in photographs.[66] Although the *Kansan* referred to Chamberlain as the "hero" of certain games, and Mayer mentioned Chamberlain's "loose" nature in the locker room before big games, even these newspapers did not suggest that Chamberlain was the leader of the team.[67] Nor did they assign this label to Maurice King, the other black player on the team and a senior starting guard. In fact, the team's co-captains were white senior starters John Parker and Gene Elstun. There may have been reasons beyond race as to why these two players were selected instead of King, but the decision fit into a broader pattern—going back to Robeson at Rutgers—where team leadership positions were occupied by whites. As the civil rights movement evolved, these types of issues became more and more contentious. Who would lead the newly integrated American society? One final example visually depicted many observers' notions of a proper leader: before the Big Seven preseason tournament, which KU would eventually win behind Chamberlain's record-setting ninety-three points over its three wins, the *Capital* printed a cartoon of white Iowa State player Gary Thompson. The caption read, "A Real Leader."[68] No similar cartoon appeared for Chamberlain throughout his two-year career.

Although Chamberlain's role as a racial leader had been largely forgotten in the coverage of Chamberlain's debut, Bill Mayer did return to that aspect of his career three weeks after the season's start. Praising the big man effusively, Mayer continued to see Chamberlain as a leader for black people and not for whites:

> Wilt, by the way, deserves some orchids for something he's been do-
> ing in addition to playing great basketball. When the towering Negro
> came west from Philadelphia, he did so with the idea that by being a
> great performer on the court and a good citizen—a gentleman—off
> the maples, he might be able to contribute toward the advancement
> of his people. So far everything he has done has reflected tremen-
> dous credit to his race, and Negroes everywhere have every right to
> be proud of him.
>   Despite the constant pestering by newsmen and photographers,
> he's remained calm and polite and usually smiling and jovial, always
> ready with a quip. Though battered and booed on the court, he's
> never lost his poise and composure. . . . Those who have been skepti-
> cal have ended up admiring him for his ability AND his gentlemanly
> ways.[69]

Mayer certainly seemed genuine in lauding Chamberlain's character, and he undoubtedly saw Chamberlain as an important figure in area race relations. However, Mayer declined to identify who needed to be led by Chamberlain, whose behavior needed to be changed, as he remained vague about how Chamberlain could "contribute toward the advancement of his people." Im- plying that the onus for racial change lay with blacks, that they needed to follow Chamberlain's model of persevering, remaining composed, and avoid- ing public pronouncements on controversial issues, Mayer outlined a narrow view of Negro uplift that asked little of whites.

Chamberlain's popularity and starring role made the absence of com- mentary about his leadership especially significant. After all, Chamberlain's arrival at KU had led to a marked increase in attendance at home and on the road and to more televised games than ever before in the school's history.[70] On one occasion, fans called Ivan Travis, the business manager for the Uni- versity of Washington, and asked for tickets to the upcoming "Washington- Chamberlain game," suggesting fans' desire to see the big man in action.[71] People, particularly children, were fascinated by Chamberlain and longed to see him in person. A *Journal-World* front-page photograph of Chamberlain walking hand-in-hand with a young white fan after one of the Big Seven tournament games was headlined "The Luckiest Kid in the World?" And the image's caption noted that Chamberlain "was mobbed most of the time dur- ing the Kansas City tournament by autograph seekers," a sentiment echoed in the *Star* as well, which reprinted the image of Chamberlain and the child.[72] These newspapers readily acknowledged (and celebrated) Chamberlain's popularity, and these interracial photographs seem to evidence a heartfelt interest in promoting racial goodwill.

That hope for interracial harmony, however, often belied the actual experiences of KU's two black players, Chamberlain and King, on the court. In later years, Chamberlain's white teammate John Parker recalled the racism black players had to deal with: "Wilt and his brash talent came along, and racial tensions, particularly in the traditionally Southern states like Missouri and Oklahoma, escalated. It seemed everywhere we went we heard 'nigger,' 'nigger lover,' and worse. Officials would often ignore blatant fouls committed against black players, and opposing schools waved Confederate flags and played 'Dixie.'"[73] There was almost no coverage of this behavior in any of the local newspapers. Occasionally, stories would refer to "partisan" crowds in Missouri or other locations, but there was never a hint of racial bigotry underlying fan behavior. The one exception to the rule was Mayer's commentary following Kansas's game against the University of Wisconsin in December, when a number of the Wisconsin players (and even the trainer, apparently) "started yelling nasty remarks" about King and Chamberlain. According to Mayer, "there were definite racial overtones."[74] Chamberlain and King both dismissed the incident as unimportant, but it is notable that none of the other white or black presses picked up the story. The persistent faith in sports as a model for interracial equality dictated that these publications not dwell on racial incidents at any length.

Bigotry in the Spotlight: The 1957 NCAA Tournament

Kansas concluded the 1957 regular season in impressive fashion, with a 21–2 record and an 11–1 mark in the Big Seven. Chamberlain finished the year averaging 29.52 points per game, easily the best in team history, and set a variety of other team records. Chamberlain dwarfed his opponents in multiple ways. He was not only larger than just about anyone else in the game; he was stronger, quicker, and more graceful. Films show him running the floor with ease, shooting fade-away jump shots with touch, and intimidating opponents by blocking their shots from nearly every spot on the court.[75] He was named to first-team All-American squads by every major news and sporting publication, including the prestigious Associated Press team.[76] KU's team was ranked number two in the nation, behind only the undefeated squad from the University of North Carolina, and many picked Kansas to win the national championship tournament.[77] In order to play for the title, however, the team would have to survive two western regional games in Dallas, Texas, including an opening-round game against hometown Southern Methodist University.

Although in 1957 the NCAA men's basketball tournament had not yet become a multimillion-dollar sporting event, it had nonetheless begun to garner major media attention both locally and nationally, particularly because of Chamberlain's presence. In Lawrence, advertisements in the *Kansan*—one paid for by local businesses and one sponsored by KU fraternities and sororities—praised the team's regular-season success and offered good luck for the NCAA tournament.[78] Meanwhile, thanks to the efforts of an enterprising group of students and local businessmen called the Jay Watchers, who worked to arrange television broadcasts of the team's games, students were able to crowd around television sets in the student union and in fraternity houses to watch the regional games in Dallas.[79] At least in Lawrence, Chamberlain and his teammates were the center of attention as they headed for the NCAA tournament.

The players and the fans were unaware of the challenges the team would face once it arrived in Texas. The team's living accommodations were the first sign of trouble. Instead of staying in downtown Dallas with the other three teams, the Jayhawks booked rooms in Grand Prairie, a suburb nearly thirty miles away. No hotel in Dallas would book the integrated team. The local media did not report the reason for the choice of housing.[80] Even the players were apparently unaware: Chamberlain wrote in his autobiography that he and his teammates at first believed Coach Dick Harp's explanation that he wanted to keep the team "together in a quiet spot, away from the big city." They were, however, disabused of that notion when "someone burned a cross in the vacant lot across from our motel."[81] Teammate John Parker described the team's accommodations as "a dingy motel miles away in Grand Prairie" and lamented that "no restaurant would serve" the team, so the players "took all [their] meals together in a private room."[82] Although the integrated Kansas squad would be permitted to play in the upcoming tournament games, these and other signs indicated how unwelcome the team was, how symbolically threatening some found them to be. They also reflected the intransigence of the South—although national opinion was gradually turning against segregation, white southerners clearly had not relented in their views on Jim Crow.

The team's reception was even worse on the court. In the team's first game in Dallas, they struggled to a hard-earned overtime win over SMU, as a hostile crowd verbally abused the Kansas players and threw trash and other objects at them.[83] According to Chamberlain, the "hostile" fans "booed and jeered" and used a variety of derogatory terms, including "'nigger' and 'jigaboo' and 'spook' and a lot of other things that weren't nearly that nice."[84] Pleased to escape with the win, which they earned in part because King had blocked a last-second shot in regulation, the players assumed the worst was over, since the hometown SMU team had been eliminated.

They were wrong. In fact, the team's second game against Oklahoma City University (OCU) involved even worse crowd behavior. Dallas fans, outraged that an integrated team had defeated their school, switched allegiance to

OCU and continued to taunt and harass the KU squad. To make matters worse, Oklahoma City coach Abe Lemmons and several of his players participated in the unruly behavior. Before the game, Lemmons warned referee Al Lightner that there would be problems "if that big nigger [Chamberlain] piles onto any of my kids."[85] As the game proceeded, the scene verged on bedlam, as Oklahoma City players deliberately attempted to injure Chamberlain and King by tripping them and continued to employ derogatory terms.[86] At one point, according to the *Call*'s description of events, Lemmons "charged one of the officials and said, 'If you don't call some fouls on that big n——r [their dashes] we will get him.'" The normally mild-mannered Harp charged at Lemmons and nearly engaged in a fistfight on the court.[87] As Kansas pulled away to a convincing victory in the second half, the chaos became even more intense. Not even pleading from the SMU athletic director and other public officials could calm the outraged fans, who threw a variety of objects, including coins, paper airplanes, seat cushions, and food, onto the court. After the game, an armed cadre of police officers led the team off the court and traveled with them to the airport.[88]

Considering the magnitude of the unruly fans', players', and coaches' behavior, the belated and minimal coverage of the incidents in the local newspapers was striking. In the immediate aftermath of the story, the major newspapers in the area (the *Capital* and the *Star*) made no mention of the racial abuse suffered by the KU team. In the *Star*, Bob Busby referred, offhand, to a "partisan crowd" during the SMU game; in covering the OCU game, he said the "raucous crowd of 7,600 was slightly out of hand."[89] In neither case did he acknowledge any racial overtones. In the *Capital*, writer Stu Dunbar also commented on "the partisan" nature of the crowd in the OCU game, writing that it was "nearly 100 percent against Kansas," although he did not indicate that Chamberlain's and King's race was almost certainly the main reason why the Dallas fans adopted OCU. Instead, as Snider had done, he attributed the crowd's behavior to complaints about the officiating.[90] Only the *Journal-World*, the town newspaper, even hinted at any racial implications in its coverage of the weekend's games. In describing the SMU game, for example, writer Earl Morey seemed disturbed that the crowd "vented a lot of its displeasure at the two K.U. Negro stars."[91]

There were likely a number of reasons why the mainstream newspapers were hesitant to condemn, or even describe, the Dallas crowd's antipathy for Chamberlain and King. On the one hand, it was clear that some readers of these newspapers were sympathetic to those in support of segregation, and so taking a firm stand against it would have seemed a potentially risky business move.[92] On the other hand, even sympathetic newsmen might have feared that calling extra attention to the racial abuse suffered by the black players would only lead to more taunting in future games and would potentially cause wider conflicts between blacks and whites in the region.[93] Finally, given the supposedly egalitarian values embodied in sports—the idea that the "level playing field" enabled the best to succeed, regardless of race, creed, or color—sportswriters were uncomfortable acknowledging the harsh realities that belied those ideals. Even the *Call* had seemed hesitant to acknowledge the racism Chamberlain and King faced throughout the regular season, never dwelling on the ongoing slurs from unruly fans. For black leaders such as Davis, integrated sports offered so much potential for broader change because they showed that integrated society could work. Emphasizing bigotry's tenacious hold among fans could have lent credence to those who believed that segregated society was the best option because it avoided the racial conflict created by putting blacks and whites into close contact with one another.[94]

In the end, even the mainstream newspapers had no choice but to cover the racial angle of the story; the day after the game, Lightner expressed his disgust with the crowd and the OCU players and coaches in an Associated Press story that received nationwide coverage. In addition to describing Lemmons's pregame threat regarding Chamberlain, Lightner also said that OCU players consistently referred to Chamberlain and King as "those niggers."[95] Although Lemmons vigorously denied the accusations, Lightner, a sports editor from Oregon, refused to back down: "The real trouble seemed to be that Chamberlain and King were dark-skinned. . . . I didn't ask to go down there. They asked me to come. I didn't intend going 2,000 miles to fight the Civil war [*sic*] all over again."[96]

As the story developed, the local newspapers faced the decision of how best to cover the explosive situation. Although clearly aware of the racist behavior of the fans, players, and coaches, writers balked at directly criticizing the melee's participants. Although Bob Busby, writing in the *Star*, acknowledged that "the behavior of the crowd at the Dallas basketball regional hit an all-time low," he refrained from discussing the scene's evident racial bigotry.[97] In fact, he even printed lengthy excerpts from a story by Bill Rives, the sports editor for the *Dallas News*, who argued that "any player as tall and skilled as Chamberlain would have been the target of tough treatment" and that "the racial aspect, which Lightner so unwittingly and so unfortunately brought up, had nothing whatsoever to do with the conduct of the Kansas–O.C.U. game."[98] Although Busby clearly thought the fans were out of line, he perhaps felt obligated to allow the "maligned South" to defend itself. In doing so, he minimized the very real racial threats and intimidations faced by these black players, and, by extension, the racial abuse suffered by black people across the country. An editorial in the *Journal-World* also seemed to miss the point; instead of criticizing the racism of the fans in Dallas, the editorial board instead used the admittedly "disgusting spectacle" of the fan behavior to chastise Lawrence fans for games earlier in the season when they had thrown coins and debris onto the floor at the Allen Fieldhouse. The editorial obliquely mentioned that the OCU players "caused their share of unpleasantness with untimely remarks," and referred to "unethical" practices by the OCU team, but in not naming those remarks and practices, the story did not call attention to the bigotry on display. In effect, they let the South dictate the terms by which racial prejudice would or would not be discussed.[99]

Similarly, in the *Capital*, Dick Snider wrestled with expressing his disgust toward the game's racial ugliness even as he attempted to moderate his critiques. He harshly criticized Lemmons for his on-court agitation, and he lambasted the fans as being "juvenile" because they "booed and threw things and conducted themselves in a manner which would make Elvis Presley fans look and sound intelligent"—strong words, indeed. However, when it came to race, Snider toed a narrow line. Instead of acknowledging the circumstances, he wrote, "Oklahoma City players, they say, had plenty to say to Wilt and Maurice King, KU's Negro players." He did not make clear who "they" were or indicate the credibility of the claims. Similarly, he refused to condemn Lemmons, even when he could have easily verified Lightner's claims by talking, off the record, to any number of sources. He thought that only a fraction of the crowd fit into "the pitifully ignorant group" of bigots who took "added delight in" berating officials and players "if color is involved." Snider wrapped up his column by comparing Chamberlain to baseball great Jackie Robinson, arguing that Wilt was "getting a trial by fire" as the first black superstar in college basketball.[100] If that was the case, why not overtly condemn Lemmons, the OCU players, and the fans? Why hesitate to denounce them publicly as racists? Snider belied his own critique of the situation only a few days later, when he discussed a conversation he had with Lemmons, who "shrugged off the racial charges that came out of the game as 'ridiculous.'" Snider appeared to take him at his word instead of pressing the issue—another example of his discomfort with public discussion of racial inequality and bigotry.[101] In this case, sports served as a rather clumsy language, unable to channel meaningful discussions of race. The mythology of sports—of fair play and meritocracy—doesn't allow for people to behave badly. When fans, players, and coaches violated these ideals, white writers struggled to respond in meaningful ways.

One final sign of the *Star*'s ambivalence toward this event appeared in a curious newspaper advertisement six days after the OCU game, on the day of KU's semifinal game against the University of San Francisco. A simple black-and-white cartoon featured Chamberlain in his Kansas uniform dunking the basketball. Two columns wide and the entire height of the page, the image was explained by a "poem" beneath it: "There was a young man named The Stilt / Who for basketball playing was bilt [*sic*]. / When he dunked one to score / There went up a roar / Of 'Bravo!' or 'He ought to be kilt' [*sic*]."

Beneath the poem was another line of text: "It takes a *man* to do a *man's* job [their italics]. In basketball, Wilt (The Stilt) Chamberlain—In selling goods, the *Kansas City Star*."[102] This cartoon has a number of extraordinary features: the advertisement expresses admiration for Chamberlain on some level and explicitly identifies Chamberlain as a manly man who gets the job done, a remarkable development given Chamberlain's race and the weight of long-held stereotypes about black men. But it also suggests the intense negative reaction to his achievements, in the "joking" line that some believed Chamberlain "ought to be kilt." Given the strong reactions to Chamberlain, it is no wonder that these writers engaged in an elaborate verbal dance around issues of race and inequality. Taking a firm stand regarding the crowd's behavior in Dallas would have required staking out a position on the place of black men in society and on racial integration in general. Demanding fair treatment for Chamberlain from fans and officials would not only have acknowledged the inequalities still present in sports; it would also have given ammunition to the enemies of the United States in the Cold War, who could have used the incidents to criticize the nation's claims of equality. Finally, enumerating the extent of racial prejudice and bigotry faced by Chamberlain and King would have undermined the white faith in black uplift to solve the "race problem." Simply providing opportunities would not be enough—systemic changes would have to occur in order to root out the racial prejudice that prevented black Americans from getting fair treatment from many whites.

Anxiety over elaborating those beliefs may explain why a number of journalists, players, and fans alike appeared to believe that not talking about the game's unpleasantness was the best strategy for dealing with the situation's tension. Snider contended that it was "of relatively little importance what Lemmons is alleged to have called Wilt" during the OCU game. What was important was "that the coach felt it necessary to talk before and after the game, and that the official felt it necessary to reply publicly."[103] Bigotry was not the central issue: instead, it was the *publicity* of it that concerned Snider. KU student Del Haley went a step further. In a *Kansan* column, he complained that "the area newspapers have done more harm than good in relation to" the issue of desegregation by "[pinning] the racial prejudice label" on the behaviors of the fans and the players. Brushing aside the suggestion that players on Oklahoma City had "been making derogatory remarks about our two Negro team members," Haley praised the players and coaches of KU for staying "silent on the whole affair." From his perspective, the media's decision to devote so much attention to the story "only hurt the team's reputation."[104] Even Mayer, who would level some of the harshest criticism of the Dallas fans and the OCU players and coaches, also praised the Kansas players and coaches for "remaining sensibly mum" about the controversy, believing that strategy was good "public relations."[105]

Although these men did not explicitly indicate how the team's "reputation" would be improved by ignoring the racial barbs, they seemed to believe that discussing conflict would create an image of the team (and perhaps the university and region) as agitators, as radicals looking to stir up trouble. Remaining silent would prevent that reputation and a possible backlash against the team and school. That attitude fit in well with the stance toward civil rights of Kansas native and U.S. president Dwight D. Eisenhower. Although Eisenhower believed that all deserved equal protection under law, he was uncomfortable with direct government intervention in issues of segregation, stating, after the decision in *Brown v. Board of Education*, that it was not possible to "change the hearts of men with laws or decisions."[106] Even his decision to use U.S. National Guard troops to integrate Central High School in Little Rock, Arkansas, in September 1957 was undertaken with great reluctance, as Eisenhower hoped to avoid confrontation over the issue. Eisenhower and other like-minded white civic leaders believed that African Americans needed only to be patient, to wait for changes in white Americans' racial attitudes. Activism, or public protestations regarding inequalities in American life, even in the wake of extreme events such as the Texans' boorish behavior, served only to hurt African Americans' cause according to this line of thinking. That attitude surfaced again in discussions of racial injustice in sports and would be criticized more frequently by African Americans as the twentieth century progressed.

There were those, however, who rejected this cautious approach to the situation and who unabashedly criticized the boorish behavior of fans, players, and coaches. The *Call*, for example, emphasized the crowd's racial bias, as the unnamed writer noted that fans "abused Chamberlain because of his race and tried in many ways to hamper his play." Their story also described, and did not allege, Lemmons's use of the term *nigger* in connection to Chamberlain. The story refused to elide the obvious racism and unequal treatment that Chamberlain and King faced.[107] *Star* reader Ray Cain, in a letter to the editor headlined "Texas Insult Offends Him," praised Chamberlain for being "a credit to his race and to basketball" in contrast to the fans and Lemmons, who he said were anything but "good sports."[108] Their poor behavior, in other words, violated the tenets of sportsmanship: the players were not treated equally and with respect on that night, a potential sign of the limitations of sports as a model for a civil society and racial egalitarianism.

Bill Mayer, in the *Journal-World*, reemphasized those points. First, he contradicted Lemmons's claim that he and his players had not used racial slurs. According to Mayer, "courtside observers Saturday said they heard at least one unfavorable racial reference each to Chamberlain and King by the O.C.U. boys, on the court and on the bench."[109] Mayer also criticized the crowd and the region in general, arguing that the "coins and other debris on the court along with insults, many of them with racial overtones," proved that the fans did not deserve another NCAA tournament game, as did the necessity of the KU team having to stay in Grand Prairie because of segregated hotels. These factors taken together spoke poorly of sports in general and, according to Mayer, revealed the fallacy of sports as an arena of fair and open competition: "Supposedly, there's equality, based on ability, in sports, or at least the salesmen try to peddle that bill of goods."[110] The other local papers were hesitant to acknowledge the limitations in this vision of sports. There was too much at stake: admitting rampant inequality in sports meant acknowledging the persistent barriers to equal opportunity in various other aspects of life, including those directly connected to sports, such as public accommodations and educational opportunities. If sports could not serve as an ideal realization of that goal, what hope was there?

After the turmoil of the regional games in Dallas, KU players, coaches, and fans all eagerly looked forward to the national semifinal game and national championship game to be played in Kansas City's Municipal Auditorium. But their hopes were dashed. Although KU easily defeated the defending champions, the University of San Francisco, in its semifinal game on Friday, March 22, the team lost 54–53 in three overtimes to the undefeated team from the University of North Carolina. After the turmoil of the previous weekend, the final two games of the season were largely uneventful.

Given the criticism Chamberlain would face later in his career that he was a "loser," incapable of "winning the big one," the sympathy and praise for Chamberlain by area writers following the three-overtime loss to UNC was somewhat surprising. As with their coverage of KU's earlier defeats, sportswriters largely exonerated Chamberlain from blame, despite the fact that he missed a key free throw in the second overtime that could have won the game. Writing in the *Journal-World*, Earl Morey, for example, believed Chamberlain "probably should be awarded some sort of a sportsmanship honor this season for his splendid actions on the court," and emphasized his twenty-three points and fourteen rebounds, the highest totals of the night for either team.[111] The *Star*, meanwhile, published a sympathetic photograph of Chamberlain walking out of the auditorium following the loss. In the image, taken from behind, Chamberlain looks down, carrying his warm-up pants and jacket. His reflection is visible next to him on a partially mirrored wall. The image suggests a forlorn, exhausted player lamenting his team's loss. The caption, headlined "Alone with His Reflections," indicated that the "downcrest" Chamberlain "was so engrossed" in his reflections on the game "that he almost left the building before putting on his warmup pants and topcoat."[112] Acknowledging the heavy burden Chamberlain felt for the loss, the photograph fit well with a general narrative that Chamberlain had done all he could to will his team to win.[113]

Two subtleties, however, complicated this trend. The first involved a racial incident after the game that only the *Journal-World* and the *Capital* reported. At the game's conclusion, King approached the UNC bench to offer his congratulations to the players and coaches. As he did so, an unknown spectator yelled out a racial slur. King had to be restrained from going after the fan, who quickly darted out of sight into the crowd.[114] For that one fan, at least, the victory of the all-white UNC team had racially significant implications. Although the writers were quick to assert that the fan was not associated with the UNC team and that the UNC players had been complimentary of KU and Chamberlain in particular, it seems likely that the white fan was a southerner, perhaps from North Carolina, who saw validation of Jim Crow segregation in UNC's triumph. The lack of coverage and commentary on the incident suggests that people were not interested in exploring that symbolic aspect of the game.

The *Call*, in fact, viewed the championship weekend through an entirely different lens. UNC's victory over KU and Chamberlain did not dampen the *Call*'s enthusiasm. Sports editor John I. Johnson instead celebrated the widespread attention the tournament had received as fans filled the stands and radio, television, and newspaper coverage reached unprecedented levels for the final game. He took pride in the fact that black athletes could not "be kept off the squads when they get an even break." To Johnson, the presence of Chamberlain and King, along with fellow black players John Green of Michigan State and Art Day and Gene Brown of the University of San Francisco, showed that basketball was a "fine democratic process" that would have wider implications "throughout the nation."[115] The presence of black athletes on three out of four of the final teams showed that once restrictions to access were removed from sports, African Americans would excel, a lesson many black leaders hoped would be extended to other realms of "democratic" life.

One reason the newspaper's editors might not have been too disappointed by the outcome of the KU-UNC game was the success Tennessee State had enjoyed the previous week in winning the NAIA title. Indeed, the newspaper printed photographs of Tennessee State's celebration on the next page after coverage of the KU game, including one image of a white NAIA official handing the championship trophy to McLendon while the runner-up Oklahoma State squad looked on. The caption called the trophy "the biggest prize ever won by an all-Negro college basketball team."[116] The faith that sports achievement would have wide-ranging positive effects was a long-held one in the black community, as we have seen. By this time, though, one may wonder if the black writers were being overly naïve in their assessments. The slow pace of integration in Major League Baseball, the harsh treatment Chamberlain and King had received in Texas, and the persistence of southern resistance to the civil rights movement all suggested that the model of sports had serious limitations. Having staked their claim to this line of thinking, though, the members of the black press appeared loath to withdraw their support, at least at this moment.

While the black press celebrated the significant presence and high-level performance of black players during the NCAA championship weekend, the area's white newspapers consistently praised the "poise" of UNC's all-white team, apparently picking up on the stereotypes that celebrated white men as calmer and more rational than their black counterparts. Mayer noted the trend and responded with exasperation, "You hear so cotton-pickin' much about the 'tremendous poise' demonstrated by" UNC in the national championship game. Mayer pointed out that Kansas had lost by only one point in three overtimes, a sure sign that their team had to play with "poise" as well. Although acknowledging that "Kansas made errors, blew free throws and was guilty of bad passes in the clutch," he pointed out that the UNC players made the same mistakes: "There certainly was no fantastic 'poise differential' as far as we could see," Mayer wrote.[117] Although Mayer did not make the case that these alternate interpretations were based on race, it is almost certain that racial stereotypes of coolly rational Caucasians and overly emotional Negroes influenced the discourse surrounding the game—one more example of the limitations of sports in effecting change.

To Stay or Go? Chamberlain's Difficult Decision, "Amateur" Athletics, and Race Relations

After the disappointing conclusion to a remarkable season, Chamberlain pondered his future in Lawrence. Although he still had two more years of school remaining, rumors began to swirl that he would end his education early and join the Harlem Globetrotters, a popular traveling troupe of black basketball players who dazzled crowds with comedic routines. Chamberlain did, in fact, consider the possibility. Privately, he complained to some of the KU alumni about the pressures he faced as the star athlete at the school: "It's a job . . . and as long as it's a job, I might as well be paid. . . . Here at Kansas the pressure is on me—we have to win."[118] Surely those pressures were heightened by his race. As he weighed his options, the press followed the story closely.

Publications such as the *Call* clearly had a vested interest in having Chamberlain stay in school and finish his degree. Chamberlain could serve as a "race man," as a leader in bringing about integration, only if he played by the rules. Leaving school early would not only remove him from the area spotlight but also mark him as a dropout, a quitter. Jerry Dawson, writing in the *Kansan* about Chamberlain's impending decision, indicated that some worried "that if Wilt leaves, integration in Lawrence will suffer a 25-year setback."[119] The editors of the *Call*, almost certainly led by Davis, were so anxious to see Chamberlain stay that they devoted an editorial to the matter, despite the fact that the newspaper almost never discussed sports on its editorial page. Headlined "Don't Do It, Wilt!" the editorial expressed "hope that Wilt the Stilt will not let the lure of big money take him away from college basketball." The editorial board wanted Chamberlain to "turn down all offers to enter the professional ranks until after he graduates." The *Call* argued that Wilt would be "a bigger man" if he finished his education.[120]

Others ignored the racial implications of Chamberlain's pending decision and emphasized its business implications. Bill Brower, writing for the Associated Negro Press, defended Chamberlain's right to play professionally if he chose to do so, unworried over any damage to the race at large. Comparing Chamberlain's situation with "the bonus babies in major league baseball" who often left college when offered contracts by major-league teams, Brower argued that there was "no great hue and cry over their cashing in on their athletic potential" and wondered why it should be different in Chamberlain's case. Brower believed it would make sense for Chamberlain to "make hay while the sun shines" and to take the $15,000-a-year offer from the Globetrotters.[121] Mayer, meanwhile, painted Chamberlain's ruminations in a positive light: "Many persons admire the youngster for even considering the situation, for they contend that the average person would leap at the chance to make" the considerable amount of money Chamberlain could earn with the Globetrotters.[122]

What bothered many about Chamberlain's potential decision to leave school, however, was its reflection on the state of (supposedly) amateur college athletics. In the *Capital*, Snider thought it was "a sad commentary" on college sports that Chamberlain was thinking of leaving, and cynically pondered whether Chamberlain had actually asked KU alumni for "advice, or a raise."[123] Now that Chamberlain was on the verge of leaving KU, sportswriters felt no obligation to maintain his image as a well-meaning celebrity. Instead, the black star was depicted as a hired gun who had come to KU not to excel in school or make a difference in race relations, but rather to cash in on alumni gifts. In the *Kansan*, George Anthan also thought that Chamberlain's consideration of a professional offer was distasteful. He worried that college basketball was "becoming tainted, ever so slightly, by this aura of professionalism."[124]

Meanwhile, even as Chamberlain took his time in making up his mind, he was barraged by newsmen wanting to get the scoop on the story. Frustrated by the constant telephone calls from reporters, he hung up on the *Star*'s Lawrence correspondent and then on sports editor Busby himself. Busby did not take kindly to the slight:

Chamberlain has become quite sensitive in talking about the matter, but as long as he leaves his answers on a hazy leaving-the-door-open basis, he will continue to be queried by sportswriters and broadcasters and getting huffy about it and hanging up the telephone won't do him any good with public relations. . . . He is a public figure and what he does is of public interest and his advisers should certainly remind him of that fact.[125]

Although the newspapers had generally praised Chamberlain's character throughout the season, this one act of defiance was enough to generate a chiding comment from Busby. The warning to Chamberlain to behave appropriately as a "public figure" constituted another pressure, another voice telling Chamberlain what he should or should not do. It was also rather patronizing—the white editor telling the black athlete to know his place. Seemingly everyone had advice for Chamberlain, including basketball legend George Mikan, who was in town for a speaking engagement and urged the KU star to remain in school.[126] Those were considerable pressures to level on a college sophomore, and they reveal the extremely narrow path black stars had to tread. As some of the few black men to gain access to positive public press coverage, stars like Chamberlain could ill afford slipups that would put their race in a bad light—an extra burden that white athletes did not have to consider.

With all of these competing forces attempting to push him in one direction or the other, Chamberlain finally made up his mind to return to school and announced it in a press release. Nearly everyone breathed a sigh of relief. The local white newspapers heaped praises on Chamberlain for making the right decision.[127] Although they emphasized the benefits of education and Chamberlain's potential as a role model, they were surely equally excited to have Chamberlain's celebrity presence for at least one more year. For KU coach Dick Harp, of course, Chamberlain's return would only aid his team's fortunes on the court. He could now plan for the coming season, secure that Chamberlain would be at the center of the team's campaign. Chamberlain would also, of course, remain at the center of a host of conflicting interests and watchful eyes. The pressures that had caused him to ponder leaving school early would remain unabated.

The Disappointment of 1958 and the Decision to Leave

The fervor over Chamberlain, even in the *Call*, had subsided by fall 1957. There were fewer stories and photographs of him in the area's newspapers, and only seven thousand fans showed up for the varsity-freshman scrimmage that year. Although the editors of the *Call* expected great things, predicting that Chamberlain and his teammates could "wear the crowns as kings of the NCAA" that year, the sudden death of Dowdal Davis at age forty-three over the summer perhaps explained a shift in the newspaper's sports coverage.[128] New sports editor James C. Brown approached sports simply as entertainment to be reported on; the statements about democracy and the higher value of sports were largely absent. The other area newspapers all continued to follow Chamberlain, but, as with the *Call*, the number of photographs and front-page stories declined considerably. However, when Kansas defeated highly regarded Kansas State to win the preseason tournament, the newspapers lauded Chamberlain and ratcheted up expectations for the team once again. Snider, in the *Capital*, praised Chamberlain for improving his game and included unsigned comments from other coaches such as "He's working harder, getting better shots. . . . He's shooting better. . . . He's hustling, defending and rebounding harder than ever before." Snider thought that Chamberlain's improved performance on the court and his high character ("Success hasn't ruined him") made Kansas "the team to beat" once again.[129] That positive assessment of Chamberlain's character would be revised in later months, but as the season progressed, the praise of Chamberlain remained generally consistent, with writers and coaches still marveling at the big man's on-court exploits.

KU's promising season started to unravel, however, in part because of an injury Chamberlain suffered when he was accidentally kneed in the groin during the preseason tournament. Chamberlain's testicles became infected, and he was bedridden in the hospital for nearly a week. Given standards of propriety at the time, the school referred to Chamberlain's illness as a "glandular infection," a phrase most of the newspapers used. By and large, the public coverage of Chamberlain's illness was positive, and the newspapers expressed hope that he would recover quickly.[130] However, another unpublished story lingered under the surface of this pleasant dialogue. Although the university never specifically identified Chamberlain's condition, after a short time, according to Chamberlain's recollection, rumors began to spread: "It seemed like everyone on campus knew the precise anatomical location of my problem . . . and the rumor that I had the clap swept the campus. Kids started snickering and referring to me as 'The Big Dripper.'"[131] Although the gossip was most likely harmless in intent, it nonetheless fit into the stereotype of the sex-crazed black male.

Stereotypes infected other representations of Chamberlain as well, part of the, in Goudsouzian's words, "unthinking racism" that "still governed campus race relations." Even before the season started, a number of events showed the persistence of demeaning stereotypes in white Kansas culture. The Phi Gamma Delta fraternity's "Fiji Island Party," in which white fraternity brothers essentially dressed in blackface, was one such occasion. Another appeared in a photograph in the *Kansan*. Two art class students held up puppets they had made—one, on the left, pale-skinned, smiling, and well defined, and the other, on the right, "black with beady eyes." The caption read, "No offense intended, Mr. Chamberlain, but that's you on the right." An understandably disgusted Chamberlain wrote Chancellor Murphy to complain, and the chancellor expressed his sympathy and urged him to focus on his fellow students' overwhelmingly positive feelings for him.[132] In anticipation of KU's first regular-season game against the Kansas State Wildcats, meanwhile, the *Kansan* published a front-page cartoon of Chamberlain shaking two wildcats, one in each hand, with a caption that read, "Wilton the Wildcat Killer."[133] Chamberlain's long legs were emphasized in the cartoon—but his lips and white teeth were also exaggeratedly large. The minstrel qualities to the front-page drawing show how pervasive stereotypes could creep into representations of Chamberlain and other black men, even in cases when the intent was to express admiration.

Chamberlain infiltrated the broader culture in a number of other ways, as various local residents used him as a form of cultural currency to which they attached a number of meanings. One such instance occurred in the spring of 1957. As the disappointed KU players and fans recovered from the national championship loss and eased their way back into the spring semester, a campaign to end segregation in the town of Lawrence generated a considerable amount of public dialogue and inevitably drew in the town's biggest star, Chamberlain. When Chester Curtice, the owner of the Green Lantern Café, asked readers of the *Journal-World* to support him in his effort to keep his restaurant segregated, he must have been dismayed at the response he received, as those who wrote in overwhelmingly disapproved of segregation.[134] The first reader to respond, Kathryn Harris, used the cases of Wilt Chamberlain and Maurice King to support her argument for integration. Harris argued that people in the South "must be laughing at a town that will make colored boys athletic heroes, and then, not be able to order a meal in a downtown restaurant." To that end, she thought that those in favor of segregation ought to try living as a black person for a day, to see what it would be like. By experiencing the unequal treatment black people routinely received, such as the "rude and insulting remarks and deeds" that King and Chamberlain encountered in the NCAA tournament, white segregationists might better understand the effects of institutionalized racism. Since KU's two black players kept their calm in the face of such bigotry, Harris believed "they both showed themselves to be better sportsmen and gentlemen than their opponents." If these athletes could be not only equal to whites on the basketball court but also morally superior to some bigoted white fans, players, and coaches, then it made no sense to exclude African Americans from other aspects of everyday life.[135]

There were numerous other examples of Chamberlain's value as a form of cultural capital. Chamberlain's on-campus radio show, "Flip 'er with Dipper," debuted in February 1958 and featured his own selections of music and his commentary on a variety of subjects. In representations of Chamberlain as a DJ, newspapers inevitably linked him to the "hip" culture of rhythm and blues music.[136]

Because of his status as a celebrity, people were naturally interested in what the big man liked on and off the court, and his music and fashion choices made their way into the local culture. A letter to the editor in the *Capital* gives some idea just how much Chamberlain had influenced the lingua franca of Kansans. W. W. Graber, administrator of the Kansas Wheat Commission, wrote to complain about a recent editorial in which the board called for a new state slogan (to replace "the Wheat State") because the state was not the number-one producer of wheat in 1957. He argued that basing a change on one year would be foolish: "Do you think that Wilt Chamberlain will be left off of anyone's All-American basketball team if he fails to be high point man in one game this season?"[137] Chamberlain's image also pervaded selected advertisements as well. Independent Laundry and Dry Cleaners employed a photograph of Chamberlain jumping high in the air, with ad copy that read, "Far Above All the Rest! . . . And so is your wardrobe When You Give It Independent Care."[138] Even as Chamberlain could be used to uphold damaging stereotypes, he could also represent excellence and achievement. That cultural malleability, though, could be dangerous; just because Kansans used Chamberlain to discuss a wide range of issues did not necessarily mean that they would engage in a sophisticated assessment of race or any other issue.

As the 1958 season wound down, the team struggled to stay in contention for the conference crown. But when starting guard Bob Billings missed three late-season games with a back injury, the team's hopes for a return to the NCAA tournament were quashed as the team fell out of contention with two straight losses. Although the finally healthy Jayhawks ended the season on a positive note by decisively defeating first-place Kansas State 61–44, disappointment pervaded the team and its fans. As it turned out, the contest turned out to be the last game of Chamberlain's college career. He had decided to turn pro months before, contacting *Look* magazine to set up an exclusive deal to announce his decision. Chamberlain received $10,000 for the rights to his story, but when the news leaked just before he left town for good, he faced an awkward situation. Bound by the terms of his contract, which prevented him from speaking to other media outlets about any of the story's details, Chamberlain bashfully dodged questions from members of the local media, a group he had become well acquainted with over the course of his three years in Lawrence. Finally getting into his red convertible, Chamberlain stopped by to chat with Chancellor Murphy and Coach Harp before heading back to his hometown of Philadelphia.

Reactions to Chamberlain's decision were mixed, with some supporting him and others expressing bitterness at his early departure. In either case, the story of Chamberlain's role as a race man, as a leader sent to improve race relations in the area, was largely forgotten. In the *Call*, James C. Brown supported Chamberlain's decision, thinking it made good financial sense to "learn some more about" basketball as a professional "while he can cash in on it."[139] Bill Brower of the ANP also defended Chamberlain, saying he "made a smart move" by turning pro and wondering how anyone could "criticize Chamberlain's desire to help his family."[140] Ernest Mehl, in the *Star*, generally supported Wilt's decision as well, since Chamberlain "was not being taught . . . the points which would enhance his value as a professional basketball player."[141] Although Mehl had misgivings about college basketball serving as a stepping-stone to professional sports, he did not fault Chamberlain's logic. Similarly, a lengthy editorial devoted to the news in the *Journal-World* was also sympathetic to Chamberlain, wondering "how many persons in their early 20s would bypass that kind of money for one year of college and a degree—especially if they feel they can pick up the degree later?"[142]

Still, others expressed bitterness with Chamberlain's decision and the way he left the university. Busby broke the news by observing that Chamberlain "has washed his hands of collegiate basketball and herded his $5,500 fire-red convertible back home to Philadelphia." Busby was particularly irked, and felt betrayed, that Chamberlain had "issued [a] strong denial" when the story about his decision had been leaked in April.[143] By not being properly deferential to the local news media, apparently, Chamberlain earned their scorn. In the *Capital*, Snider suggested that Chamberlain "let down some people . . . who think he should have stayed and completed his education. Some will think he owed it to KU to remain for his final year of eligibility, and some will say he represents an investment on which the school deserves three years of service." He also took shots at Chamberlain's character, writing that he "may be most disappointing now to those who had the most faith in him." Although Chamberlain had always "been praised by those close to him as a model boy," Snider indicated that he had not always lived up to that reputation, mentioning "stories being circulated" that showed "Wilt was beginning to consider himself bigger than the institution he represented." According to these stories, Chamberlain sometimes made "his own travel arrangements, arriving for a game a full day behind the rest of the team."[144] Even KU students, who had delighted in the big man's presence, grumbled when he made his decision. Chamberlain's teammate and friend Billings recalled students making comments such as the following: "He left school just for the money!" "He was too dumb to ever graduate anyway." "The team will be better off without him."[145] No longer a surefire attraction to draw reader interest, Chamberlain became instead the target of accumulated resentment from Snider and others. This quick reassessment of Chamberlain spoke to an issue that would gain increasing attention among black leaders, scholars, and critics—the exploitation of black athletes for white institutions' gain.

In most of the discussions of his departure, Chamberlain's importance as a basketball player took precedence over his impact as a racial leader. In his own account in *Look* magazine, Chamberlain made clear that he had come to Kansas to "promote interracial good will," and thought that by keeping control of his emotions on court he had done so to some degree but offered little other assessment. He also downplayed the racism he encountered, lamenting select incidents, but generally describing a positive experience (and making no mention, for example, of Lawrence's ongoing segregation).[146] Such omissions were characteristic of his own politics. As Goudsouzian argues, although Chamberlain made it a point to eat wherever he liked, he did so out of a sense of individual "entitlement" rather than as a political "symbol." Former assistant coach Jerry Waugh agreed with that assessment: "I never for one moment felt that Wilt, when he came to Kansas, was coming to be a leader in race relations," no matter what had been said during his recruitment.[147]

Editorials and columns in the *Star*, the *Journal-World*, and the *Capital* similarly tended to reflect on Chamberlain's achievements, speculate on the almost-certain drop in attendance for the following season, and lament the impacts of his departure on the school's basketball team. His impact on race relations was never assessed.[148] As Chamberlain headed for Philadelphia in his convertible, he left behind fans and foes, some who lamented his loss and others who criticized his decision. Most school administrators and fans nervously awaited the NCAA's inevitable punishment for the inducements Chamberlain received during his time at the school.[149] Had he "promoted interracial good will" as he had hoped to? It appeared that no one was willing even to ask that question at this moment, perhaps a reflection of the ongoing racial tensions that divided the nation and the region. To engage that debate would have required a frank assessment of racial prejudice in the supposedly "free state" of Kansas. It would have meant alienating readers like Curtice, who hoped to maintain segregation. And for black leaders, it would have meant acknowledging that the hopes they'd pinned on Chamberlain had largely failed to come to fruition.

Conclusion: A Weight Too Heavy

Wilt Chamberlain cast a lengthy shadow in Kansas when he left Lawrence in 1958. Although he had failed to lead his team to an NCAA championship title, he had mesmerized countless observers with his unique combination of height, strength, skill, and agility. During his three years in the town, black and white people clamored to see him, in person or on television. They besieged him with autograph requests. They attempted to copy his fashions (his usual hat, an Ivy League cap, became remarkably popular on KU's campus and in Lawrence) and wanted to know as much as they could about his habits and dress. Readers frequently wrote in to ask sportswriters about the pads he wore on his shins and the rubber bands around his wrists. In short, he was an icon, a celebrity to starstruck basketball fans.

He was also a black man dominating a game that, until recently, had seen few black faces on its courts. In this way, he augured the future of the game, as more and more African American stars would move to the forefront at the collegiate and professional levels.[150] As Chamberlain overpowered his (mostly white) opponents, and as he worked with his integrated team to achieve individual, team, and school honors, he engendered numerous reactions from those who watched him. He shouldered the expectations of diverse groups as best he could: the hardcore KU basketball fans who expected him to lead the team to the conference title and the NCAA championship each year; the black leaders such as Dowdal Davis who hoped he would erase the color line in the still-segregated region; the white leaders who thought he would set a good example for other African Americans and who wanted his success to paint a positive picture of the school and region; ordinary black residents who fervently wished his success would enable them to eat in any restaurant they chose; all these and many more. It is little surprise that he could not meet all these expectations, their aims too broad, their goals too far-reaching for just one young man. His long, spindly legs could not hold up under so many heavy weights.

Still, in people's discussion of his actions on the court and his life off of it, we can hear how diverse groups attempted to use this giant man to express their hopes, their anxieties, their visions of equality, and their notions of manliness. When people celebrated his leadership, snickered about his sexual behavior, or praised his example as "race leader," they offered concrete and compelling definitions of phrases such as "separate but equal," "deliberate speed," and "equal opportunity." As more and more—although by no means all—white Americans refuted racial segregation in the wake of World War II and in the climate of the Cold War, these conflicting responses to Chamberlain revealed central tensions among those in favor of a more egalitarian society. Many white observers hoped for a society in which black Americans had access to public accommodations but hesitated to support legislation or civil rights activism that forced recalcitrant whites to follow through on this vision of American society, trusting that a gradual change in attitudes inspired by black achievement would be enough. These figures were less likely to consider black men such as Chamberlain as leaders of white men, hoping instead to integrate African Americans into a white-dominated society. On the other hand, although black leaders and some socially conscious whites certainly hoped that Chamberlain's performance could have symbolic value, they nonetheless pushed for more extensive changes. Extraordinary individuals such as Chamberlain could play a leading role in society, steering white and black Americans alike to a promised land of racial equality that took black accomplishments seriously. Still hopeful that integrated team sports could model this equal opportunity society, these leaders minimized racial conflict to show that whites and blacks could get along, even when the starring role was played by an African American man. In these ways, Wilt Chamberlain, at the center of attention in the nation's heartland, forced countless people to consider the nature of the civic, democratic, and multiracial culture of which they were all a part.

4

"Our Colored Boy" and "Fine Black Athletes"

Charlie Scott at the University of North Carolina,
1965–1970

Charlie Scott was a harbinger of things to come in more ways than one. On the basketball court, Scott augured a different style of play and a new model of player. Previously, guards had been little guys, quick and skilled with the ball, but floor-bound and focused on outside shooting. Big men, like Chamberlain, stayed closest to the basket, shooting hook shots over their shoulder or making layups and dunks. They were often lumbering and bruising. Scott was a hybrid of these players. He did not stay rooted to the floor, but his skills were not limited to dunks and tip-ins close to the basket. As fast as the quickest guards but big enough to fight for rebounds, Scott was also a leaper, someone who could rise above the crowd to dunk the ball, grab caroms, or shoot over the outstretched arms of defenders. Agile and graceful, his six-foot, six-inch, thin frame was akin to that of players to come—a link in a chain that extended backward to Oscar Robertson and forwards to David Thompson, Clyde Drexler, Michael Jordan, and Kobe Bryant. Watching Scott dribble past a defender and elevate for a jump shot was like watching the future rise out of the present, leaving the past grounded and obsolete.[1]

Scott marked the future in another way. When, in May 1966, he decided to become the first black scholarship athlete at the University of North Carolina (UNC) at Chapel Hill, the *Carolina Times*, an African American newspaper in nearby Durham, North Carolina, took notice. Although pleased that the state's flagship public university was now welcoming black athletes, the newspaper's editors worried that area black colleges and black businesses would face stiffer competition to retain talented African Americans. An editorial mused, "The Charlie Scott case is but the forerunner of the raids that are certain to be made on Negro society."[2] This cautious tone reflected the changing times. In the same year that Stokely Carmichael popularized the phrase *Black Power,* and as many black activists became increasingly disenchanted with the benefits of integration into white society, Charlie Scott's decision to play for UNC no longer engendered the seemingly untroubled optimism that many in the black press had expressed when Jackie Robinson integrated Major League Baseball. Indeed, when Robinson signed with the Brooklyn Dodgers in 1945, columnist W. L. Greene for Raleigh's *Carolinian,* another local black newspaper, had argued the opposite of the *Carolina Times* editorial. According to Greene, black readers should not "grudge the Jackies the chance" to earn higher pay by playing in the white league, and Greene chastised readers who disagreed.[3] By the spring of 1966, that integrationist optimism had been replaced by concern over the fate of black-run institutions. The editorial's headline, "The Diminishing Returns of Integration," indicated the growing reticence of black leaders to believe that equal opportunity on the athletic field led to broader social and cultural gains and reflected the increasing radicalism of African Americans across the country. Given the long-standing faith that many in the black press had expressed in sports—from Robeson to Chamberlain—this turn marked a significant moment in black Americans' sense of American equality and the ideal of equal opportunity.

As one of the few black athletic stars at any of the major predominantly white southern universities, Scott engendered a number of different responses from observers when he entered UNC.[4] On one level, his arrival augured a bright future on the basketball court for the Tar Heels and spelled trouble for the team's rivals, such as Atlantic Coast Conference (ACC) counterparts Duke University, North Carolina State University, and the University of South Carolina.[5] But his decision clearly had wider impacts: as a black man playing basketball for a nearly all-white school in the South, against almost exclusively white southern opponents, Scott incited a range of responses that revealed tensions over racial integration, issues of fairness and equality, and the place of sports in the broader culture.

Three key moments in Scott's career—his decision to attend UNC, his involvement with the nascent campus Black Student Movement (BSM), and his anger at being denied the ACC Player of the Year award in the spring of 1969—illustrate the contentious meanings of race that crept into his story. In the varying degrees of praise and condemnation, outright jubilation and cautious silence, we can see some of the conflicted lessons that people at the time drew from Scott's achievements on the court and his social activism off it. Although the mainstream media, in line with North Carolina's progressive reputation, attempted to minimize Scott's race in an effort to ease unrest (and in tacit support of the status quo), numerous alternate publications, including the local black press, used Scott's career to probe the limits of the transformative capabilities of sports amid the day-to-day realities of integration.[6] These reactions to Scott's athletic career provide a window into the challenges ordinary people faced as they came to grips with new public representations of race and masculinity in the turbulent late 1960s. They also reflected the reticent South's reluctant acknowledgment of social change—and the bitter lengths to which many would go to preserve the status quo. The ascension of black *men* into positions of prominence would continue to be an especially thorny issue, one further tangled by the South's legacy of bigotry and discrimination.

Race, Popular Culture, and Athletics in "Progressive" North Carolina

North Carolina's reputation as a racially progressive state significantly affected how white observers assessed Scott. One of the most notable features of the dialogue surrounding Scott's career at UNC was a certain pattern of silence and avoidance by both mainstream newspapers and the university administration. Both hesitated to emphasize Scott's race and his significance in breaking down integration because of what William Chafe refers to as the "mystique" of North Carolina "progressivism."[7] North Carolina had long enjoyed a reputation as a moderate state in the South, and V. O. Key's influential study of southern politics, *Southern Politics in State and Nation*, first published in 1949, helped perpetuate the idea that North Carolina was a haven of tolerance in the region, with a "progressive outlook and action in many phases of life" including "race relations."[8] As Chafe has argued, however, that ideal did not always match up with reality, with the state's policies toward blacks keeping African Americans in inferior social and economic positions. Beholden to an image of North Carolina as a progressive state, various white civic leaders in North Carolina tried to minimize any signs of dissent, believing "that conflict over any issue . . . [would] permanently rend the fragile fabric of internal harmony." Instead of fostering public debate about issues, white North Carolina leaders instead emphasized the importance of "civility," which was "a way of dealing with people and problems that made good manners more important than substantial action."[9]

Two episodes reveal the limits of North Carolina's "progressive" outlook toward race and the emphasis on civility over meaningful change, in particularly evocative ways: the failed reelection campaign of Senator Frank Porter Graham in 1950 and Chapel Hill's tumultuous sit-ins in 1963 and 1964. Graham, long known as a progressive force in North Carolina in his position as the president of the University of North Carolina and a popular figure statewide, was appointed to the U.S. Senate by Governor Kerr Scott after the death of Senator J. Melville Broughton in March 1949. When Graham had to run for reelection in 1950, he lost the primary election to corporate lawyer Willis Smith, who successfully characterized Graham as a pro-Communist, pro-black public figure. In the campaign, Smith's supporters harped on the fact that Graham had selected an African American youth as an alternate candidate for the U.S. Military Academy in West Point, New York; handouts indicated that Graham favored integration of public facilities and schools; and Graham's membership in the ACLU supposedly revealed his Communist leanings. Reactionary politics, largely centered on the racial issue, doomed his chances to win, indicating the power of racial politics in North Carolina.[10]

The town of Chapel Hill's own struggles with integrated public accommodations also reveal the seething racial tensions that lingered well into the 1960s. Although long considered a haven of liberal thought and progressive outlook in the South, Chapel Hill had numerous businesses that retained segregated facilities in 1963 and 1964, including eateries on Franklin Street, the town's main thoroughfare. Starting in January 1963, a number of like-minded groups, including the Congress on Racial Equality (CORE) and the Student Peace Union, helped form the Chapel Hill Freedom Committee and began to picket segregated businesses and eventually stage sit-ins.[11] The response in the supposedly liberal town surprised many: in one case, the owner of a grocery store locked his doors to trap protesters sitting in and then dumped bleach and ammonia on them, leading to hospitalization and serious injury; in another case, a female employee of a segregated restaurant urinated on a sit-in protester.[12] Although the activists received behind-the-scenes support from some "white Chapel Hill establishmentarians,"[13] by and large, local publications largely ignored the protests or condemned them, with the exception of the student newspaper the *Daily Tar Heel*.[14] Protester Charles Thompson commented on this community silence in later years: "Almost no one from the town or the University signaled any support. Some local liberals said that we had done both the town and the University a disservice by moving too fast. People were not yet ready for desegregation."[15] Echoing President Eisenhower's cautious approach to civil rights in the wake of the *Brown* decisions, these white Chapel Hill residents trusted that gradual, nonconfrontational change was possible, an attitude viewed with increasing distrust by African Americans across the country.

Chapel Hill residents' violent response to integration demands, the refusal of the town government to pass a public accommodations bill, and the widespread community apathy toward achieving integration revealed the limits of progressivism. As the novelist John Ehle described Chapel Hill in his account of the sit-ins, *The Free Men*, Chapel Hill proved itself as "a Southern town proud of its reputation as a liberal community," which, when worried about "tarnishing that reputation," drew "back from being a genuinely liberal community." Instead of viewing the sit-in movement as a wake-up call "for corrective action," Chapel Hill townspeople "just wanted all the trouble to go away."[16] Hemmed in by the standards of progressivism, Chapel Hill community members avoided acknowledging racial conflict and inequality, preferring to emphasize the moderate and civil nature of their town.

This emphasis on civility helps explain why both the mainstream newspapers and the university hoped to limit dialogue regarding issues of race in college athletics. Unlike sportswriters and administrators in other regions, North Carolinians and other southerners usually refrained from praising the world of sports as a color-free meritocracy. To do so, after all, would have actually contradicted the dominant southern conceptions of equality, which always assumed black inferiority—especially regarding black men. As a result, these white community leaders largely ignored the social barriers being broken by people such as Scott, unwilling to broach the subject of racial equality or note the differences between the newly color-blind realm of sports and the realities of day-to-day southern life. By avoiding these topics, these white civic leaders limited Scott's impacts to the basketball court. Counterexamples such as the area's black newspapers (the *Carolinian* and the *Carolina Times*); the student newspaper, the *Daily Tar Heel*; the local town paper, the *Chapel Hill Weekly*; and even some national publications all covered Scott's experiences as a black athlete with a greater degree of frankness, finding hope in the broadening of opportunity for African Americans, but also probing some of the limits that African Americans still faced even as Jim Crow laws died out.

Other events nationwide affected Scott's reception by blacks and whites. As the once-impermeable walls of Jim Crow segregation began to crack, following events such as Robinson's signing with the Dodgers in 1945, President Truman's decision to integrate the military in 1948, the 1954 *Brown v. Board of Education* decision, and widespread public support for the Montgomery bus boycott of 1955–1956, anxious southerners, black and white, tried to give shape to an integrated culture that fulfilled their needs and desires. With the Civil Rights Acts of 1964 and 1965 providing a federal mandate to end segregation, the often illusionary walls dividing the worlds of black and whites crumbled. But new tensions and conflicts arose out of the rubble. By the time Scott came to Chapel Hill, the broader civil rights movement had reached a moment of transition as new and old leaders clashed over the direction the movement would take. Integration and laws regarding equal opportunity did not easily address the most pressing issues facing the black community, such as extreme poverty, inadequate housing, and barriers to job promotion and advancement. By 1966, younger leaders such as Stokely Carmichael, of the Student Nonviolent Coordinating Committee (SNCC), and Floyd McKissock, of CORE, aggressively pushed for black solidarity and federal economic aid and expressed a willingness to abandon strategies of nonviolence.[17]

In this climate, the integration of popular sports could provide an outlet for nervous observers, a test case for the possibilities of a desegregated South. Certainly, North Carolinians had looked to sports in the past as one way to tease out ideas regarding racial equality. The animated response from local journalists to Robinson's signing in 1945, even though there were no Major League Baseball teams in the South at the time, offers a baseline to compare to Scott's reception twenty years later, in addition to reaffirming the importance of sports to notions of race, masculinity, and equality. The area's black newspapers (and black newspapers across the country) saw Robinson's signing as a pivotal event that indicated that black Americans would gain broader access to a number of areas of life previously restricted to them. Although the story broke too late to make it into the weekly black newspaper the *Carolinian* until November 3, nearly two weeks after the signing, the paper's editors still featured it as the top news item on the front page, highlighting the signing with a banner headline.[18] The paper also featured two columns on its editorial page about the event, both expressing hope that Robinson's signing would lead to greater advances for African Americans in general.[19]

Such hopes were not expressed in the mainstream papers. Sports editorials from the *Charlotte Observer* and the *Durham Morning Herald* provide an interesting glimpse at the tactics mainstream white journalists in the area would use in dealing with the significance of racial pioneers in sports.[20] Jack Wade, writing in the *Observer*, gave voice to a position that his paper and others would often use in later years by attempting to minimize the event's significance and potential for conflict. He argued that although the signing of Robinson was "revolutionary," "it was inevitable" as well. According to Wade, "it was merely a question of when and where." In downplaying the event's significance, Wade attempted to paint a picture of a racially harmonious South, one unblemished by the ugly stains of racial conflict. Indeed, Wade took issue with Dodgers minor league director Branch Rickey, Jr., for saying at the press conference announcing the signing "that he expected widespread 'repercussions'" from the signing, particularly in the South. Wade disagreed, arguing that prejudice was nearly eliminated in the region and that he expected Robinson's entrance into the big leagues to be smooth. He argued that southern white athletes' exposure to black athletes in other sports would ease the transition:

> Times have changed. In recent years southerners have played alongside of and against great Negro football players. They have competed in many a track meet in which great Negro trackmen have competed. They have boxed against great Negro fighters. In most cases, these things have been done as a matter of course.

Indeed, from Wade's perspective, the attempt to single out the South for a bitter reaction would not pan out as Rickey believed it would:

> Let us reiterate our opinion that if the Dodgers organization looks for any great smell to be raised, with "repercussions" to establish it as a martyr, it is apt to be disappointed. . . . [T]he reaction, we believe, especially in the press, will be dignified and restrained, even if there may exist some misgivings and a slight confusion in our hearts.

We can read Wade's analysis as either an extraordinarily naïve case of wishful thinking on his part, or, more likely, as a deliberate attempt to paint a positive picture of what he called the "maligned South."[21] Chafe's description of North Carolina's "progressive" image certainly helps explain Wade's dismissive tone. By crafting an image of the South as moderate and willing to go with the times, Wade fell back on the trope of North Carolina as a state unfettered by racial tensions. This strategy, characteristic of North Carolina, was also often employed by other southerners who dismissed any suggestion that their region had a problem with race relations.

Jack Horner, in the *Herald*, on the other hand, more overtly lamented the signing of Robinson, musing over its implications for segregation at large. Willingly admitting that "there would be complications in the South" if there were an integrated team, Horner chided Rickey for his antisouthern remarks and criticized the Dodgers for raiding the Negro Leagues without compensating them for their players. Using the "separate but equal" logic of *Plessy v. Ferguson*, Horner wondered whether "Negro baseball players want to enter the white leagues." Indeed, he highlighted the "interesting comments" of former All-Star white baseball player Rogers Hornsby as being particularly appropriate:

> The Negro leagues are doing all right and Negro players should be developed and then remain as stars in their own leagues. A mixed baseball team differs from other sports because ball players on the road live much closer together. The way things are it will be tough for a Negro player to become a part of a close-knit group such as an organized ball club. I think Branch Rickey was wrong in signing Jackie Robinson and that it won't work out.

Building on Hornsby's comments, Horner argued that the Robinson signing would cause "friction" and that it would "not help the Negro's cause."[22] Emphasizing the presence of the Negro leagues as a perfectly legitimate place for African Americans to play, Horner lamented that Robinson's signing would create strife where there was none and would upset what had been a perfectly appropriate situation. In other words, Horner feared the consequences of Robinson's signing for the status quo and attempted to suggest that both blacks and whites in general supported the conventions of Jim Crow society.

Men such as Horner and Hornsby saw a society in balance, with black and white carefully circumscribed. Sports modeled not a color-blind meritocracy to these men, but, rather, a functioning segregated society. Horner and Hornsby were either unable or unwilling to acknowledge the pervasive inequalities that relegated blacks to inferior positions legally, politically, and economically. Even looking more closely at the Negro leagues would have revealed that black players played more, earned less, and experienced tougher treatment on the road than their white peers, all inevitable results of segregated society more broadly.[23] In later years, as actions of the federal executive, legislative, and judicial branches of government increasingly struck down Jim Crow laws, columns such as Horner's would disappear, to be replaced by a silence more characteristic of Wade's approach. And yet it seems clear that beneath the veneer of acquiescence, opinions such as Horner's would remain very much in the consciousness of many white southerners.

Although the Robinson signing thrust the issue of integrated athletics into prominence in North Carolina, at the local level minor cracks had already started to develop even before 1945 and would continue to do so before Scott's arrival. Of course, North Carolinians and other southerners had known about black athletic achievements for decades before Scott enrolled at UNC. The exploits of boxers Johnson and Louis, track star Owens, baseball legend Robinson, and other black athletes such as basketball star Chamberlain—against whom UNC played in the 1957 NCAA championship game, of course—had all gained national attention.[24] But there were more direct signs that the weight of the South was losing its power as racial attitudes changed nationally and as African American athletes because more important to the success of white schools in the North and West. By the time of Scott's arrival, ACC schools had already faced black athletes in a variety of contests. Following UNC's lead in 1936, when the Tar Heels went to New York and played against New York University and their star black halfback Ed Williams, a policy gradually evolved among many schools in the upper South whereby it was acceptable for schools to play against blacks as long as the games were not in their home stadiums. Over time, even this policy became more liberal; by the early 1950s, the University of Virginia and Duke had both played racially integrated schools at home. Although many schools in the Deep South states of South Carolina, Georgia, Louisiana, and Mississippi resisted competing against black athletes well into the 1960s, the upper South schools of the ACC proved more amenable to integrated competition.[25] When black athletes did come to the South in the 1950s, however, they often faced humiliating conditions in which they were forced to stay in segregated hotels and eat meals at segregated restaurants, unable to dine and stay with their teammates.[26] Although these conditions gradually improved, Scott's experiences indicate that many in the South still resisted change.

Mixed Reactions to Scott's Big Decision and Groundbreaking Debut

Scott was a blacktop phenomenon in New York City before deciding to move south to attend Laurinburg Institute, a black prep school in south-central North Carolina. A bright student, Scott earned an academic scholarship to Laurinburg and then quickly demonstrated his considerable skills on the basketball court. After initially accepting an academic scholarship to play for Lefty Driesell, then coach at small Davidson University, Scott changed his mind and decided to sign an athletic grant-in-aid with head coach Dean Smith at UNC.[27] Scott chose UNC in part because he liked the team's coaching staff and the other players but also because he felt more comfortable in Chapel Hill as a black man than he did in tiny Davidson. After Scott encountered discrimination in one of Davidson's area stores, he visited UNC, making sure to "walk the town and the campus by himself" in order to "see how a single black man would be treated in Chapel Hill."[28] Not encountering any problems, Scott soon signed a binding letter of intent to attend UNC and play basketball.

Scott's decision to attend UNC would not have been possible without the trailblazing of other black students in the previous decade. Although UNC liked to present itself as a progressive institution ahead of its time in terms of race relations, the university dragged its feet when it came to integrating the school, sluggishly admitting some graduate and professional students before 1954 and only slowly opening its doors to African American undergraduates in the post-*Brown* era. Indeed, UNC got into some trouble when it tried to force its first black students—law students in 1951—to sit in the segregated Jim Crow section at football games instead of in the regular student section. The school eventually relented when various groups protested this action.[29] But as late as 1959, the school continued to segregate black students at football games and other on-campus events.[30] Going against long-held traditions of Jim Crow segregation meant that even watching sports proved a challenge for the integration process. Playing sports would be another matter altogether. As black undergraduates first trickled into UNC in 1955, coaches, for the first time in the South, had to deal with the possibility that black athletes could potentially compete on their teams.[31]

The integration of black students, and undergraduates in particular, was a problematic process for many university administrators who nervously tried to integrate the campus while minimizing racial conflict. Chancellor William B. Aycock attempted to monitor the integration of the student body closely—he kept detailed records on the number of African American students and tracked their progress throughout their time at UNC.[32] Aycock also considered the possibility of sports integration early on, asking athletic department officials in 1957 to keep him posted with the latest developments.[33] By 1964, students were pressuring the administration to integrate sports teams, but it was not until spring 1966 that Scott signed with the school, and not until 1968 that UNC finally integrated its football team.[34]

The university's sluggish pace in enrolling black athletes reveals school leaders' concerns over the implications of integrating the "big-time" sports of men's basketball and football. UNC followed the University of Maryland's lead in recruiting black athletes, although, to the university's credit, it pushed ahead of most other ACC schools. Still, why was there a delay between admitting black undergraduates and recruiting black athletes for major sports programs? As historian Charles H. Martin notes, "It was one thing to admit a small number of African Americans into the classroom but something far more sensitive to accept them into what was arguably the single most important campus activity: big-time sports."[35] Indeed, the integration of football and/or basketball, both popular among students and the community at large, was sure to be controversial—after all, even scheduling games against integrated teams from outside the region had caused consternation well into the 1960s for many schools in the South.[36] Thus, the delay in admitting black athletes can be understood as evidence of the university's desire to avoid public conflict and any controversy that would potentially alienate students, fans, and/or alumni. In this context, it makes sense that the university would allow black students to attend football games but would then try to make them sit in the blacks-only section instead of with their fellow students. The university could suggest that black students enjoyed equal access to university events even as they were cordoned off from their white peers according to the customs of Jim Crow society.[37]

One behind-the-scenes letter, although unrelated to sports, perhaps most clearly highlights the university's integrationist policies. In 1957, J. A. Williams, the personnel officer for the university, outlined the policy of the Carolina Inn (a whites-only on-campus hotel and restaurant) for serving African Americans attempting to eat there. Williams recommended that the staff's first goal should be to try to guide blacks to alternative locations. However, failing that, the staff should not deny blacks service because "a law suit would probably focus the attention of the negroes on the situation in Chapel Hill."[38] Williams wanted to preserve the appearance of civil cooperation, or, in Chafe's terms, "civility," in order to both avoid negative press coverage of the town and foster an image of progressive policies toward blacks on campus.[39]

This attitude carried over to matters related to sports. A potential opportunity for the university to take the lead in integrating the town of Chapel

Hill occurred in the midst of the Chapel Hill sit-ins in December 1963, when Daniel H. Pollitt, a professor in UNC's law school, sent a letter to secretary of the faculty A. C. Howell, requesting a resolution at the next faculty council meeting that "the Administration cease utilizing" segregated businesses "for official university functions," including the use of the Pines restaurant for sports-related press conferences.[40] The resolution apparently came to Aycock himself, because he drafted a letter back to Howell—and his response is instructive in considering the university's stance on integration as a whole. Aycock refused to bend, even slightly. Although Aycock noted that segregated facilities were already avoided for student functions since they would not allow all students to attend, he demurred against extending that policy more broadly. Since the Pines required neither student nor black staff presence for the press conferences held there, the university would not prevent its use for those functions.[41] Given the opportunity to make a relatively minor stand against segregation in Chapel Hill, the chancellor balked, apparently unwilling to create any kind of stir by rebuking this popular restaurant. Using a loophole to get out of the situation, the chancellor simply sidestepped the issue, keeping issues of race and segregation out of the spotlight.[42]

Elements of this mind-set can be seen in Charlie Scott's case as well. After Scott committed to UNC in the spring of 1966, Chancellor Carlyle Sitterson wrote Scott a letter, commending him on his choice—the first and only time the chancellor welcomed any individual incoming student in this manner. Although clearly acknowledging the importance of Scott's decision by personally writing to him, Sitterson did not make any mention at all of the significance of Scott's race in his letter, instead simply observing that he was sure that Scott "carefully considered all of the important factors in making [his] college decision."[43] By ignoring Scott's race, Sitterson perhaps attempted to make Scott feel like just any other student, but he also seemed uncomfortable using Scott's example as a way to promote discussions of integration and racial equality on campus, perhaps fearful that these dialogues would suggest conflict or strife. Scott's race disappears in discourse such as this, even though it obviously had profound influences on his life throughout his time at UNC.

The official athletic department pamphlets previewing each upcoming men's basketball season similarly minimized the significance of the team's gradual integration. The 1964–1965 preview, for example, made no mention of African American walk-on Willie Cooper's race when he played for the freshman team.[44] Although listed on the roster for the freshman team that year, he was one of five team members not pictured in the team photo.[45] Similarly, the athletic department materials covering Scott's four years at UNC made no mention of his race or his pioneering role. The preview issue for his freshman season simply indicated that he was "a highly-rated player from New York City" (although a photograph was included, providing visual evidence of his race).[46] Subsequent editions praised Scott's skills and spot-lighted him as the team's star, but none discussed his integrationist legacy.[47] There may be many reasons why the university hesitated to take this step, perhaps fearing that people would believe the school was pulling a public-ity stunt or trying to generate extra "business" for its supposedly amateur sports teams—or perhaps the university feared the vitriolic response of pro-segregationist alumni. Nevertheless, this silence over Scott's race fits a broader pattern among school leaders.

These examples of the university's relative silence regarding Scott's social significance—and, indeed, to the integration of the student body and the uni-versity town in general—point to one strategy employed in response to inte-gration by white administrators in positions of power. What mattered to these leaders was not necessarily the broader cultural effects of integration—that is, what these small steps meant for the changing character of the institution—but rather how public reaction to these changes might lead to conflict and thus a negative image for the school. The school's, and the state's, progressive image was at stake. Scott arrived on campus after the nationally witnessed turmoil of Birmingham, Alabama, in 1963; Selma, Alabama, in 1964; and the 1965 Watts Riot in Los Angeles. The outpouring of negative response from northern whites as a result of these events made it imperative that the university avoid any ugly scenes as it tried to bring black students peaceably into the academic fold.

The local mainstream newspapers' coverage of Scott's decision to attend UNC similarly showcase how race-minimizing discourse predominated in white public forums, spotlighting the ways in which white southerners attempted to frame integrated sports in ways that did not challenge long-held ideas regarding segregation and black male inferiority. The *Herald*, for exam-ple, mentioned that Scott was "the first of his race to receive an athletic grant-in-aid," but offered no opportunity for Scott to discuss his feelings about his role as a trailblazer.[48] The *News and Observer* was even less open to this type of dialogue; printing a story by the Associated Press, not one of its own writers, the *News and Observer*'s coverage mentioned that Scott was a "bespectacled New York City Negro" but did not point out that Scott was UNC's first black scholarship athlete and the first one in the area.[49] Neither paper offered any editorial or letters to the editor in subsequent days speculating on what Scott's actions portended for racial change in the South. The reluctance of the local papers to discuss Scott's story seemed to indicate the misgivings of many whites; in an article in the *Charlotte Observer*, Mel Derrick wrote that Scott "wanted to go to college down South, not as a crusading Jackie Robinson burning to crack a color line, but as a young man honestly seeking an edu-cation. He wants to be a doctor."[50] Attempting to assuage his readers' fears, Derrick openly discussed Scott's decision, but attempted to circumscribe its far-reaching effects, emphasizing Scott's limited goals as a student-athlete and his unwillingness to agitate for broader changes in racial equality. Sports competition would not model equal opportunity more broadly for these writers, as many black and white writers had argued throughout the twentieth century; instead, sports were merely a minor realm of entertainment that had little impact outside the court and field.

Although mainstream newspapers such as the *News and Observer* and the *Herald* tried to minimize any issues about Scott's race, alternate media voices engaged Scott's story more frankly, allowing for at least the potential of real dialogue to emerge out of Scott's experiences, and giving us some insight into how students and African Americans felt about Scott as a pioneer. The *Chapel Hill Weekly*, the *Daily Tar Heel*, and the black newspapers the *Carolinian* and the *Carolina Times* all dealt with Scott's race more openly, discussing controversy and speculating on Scott's story in relation to changing racial politics in the region. These various alternate media voices help illustrate the critical possibilities largely smothered by the veil of silence so characteristic of North Carolinian "progressivism."

The two in-town newspapers, the *Daily Tar Heel* and the *Chapel Hill Weekly*, both provided a sharper focus on race in their coverage of Scott's decision to attend UNC. The *Weekly*'s headline announced Scott's pioneering role more boldly than any mainstream publication: "Carolina Makes Big Catch: 1st Negro Signs UNC Grant."[51] More significantly, a story one week later about Sitterson's appointment as permanent chancellor for UNC noted that Sitterson "had received a letter from an out-of-state alumnus who refused any more financial aid to the University" because of Scott's recruitment.[52] The letter was a stark reminder that racial conflict still existed and that Scott's transition to UNC would not necessarily be smooth. It was not mentioned in any of the other local newspapers—after all, it would have revealed implicitly that there *was* a connection between sports and politics, something the southern media attempted to avoid as sports became less and less beholden to Jim Crow.

Although the *Tar Heel* did not report that specific incident, the campus newspaper did address Scott's race more thoroughly than the mainstream papers, suggesting that the student body was more willing to welcome black students and black student-athletes into their midst.[53] In their story about Scott's decision to attend the school, Smith was quoted as saying that "the atmosphere for a Negro student" at UNC was the key factor in Scott's decision to attend the school. In particular, Scott and Smith wanted to emphasize Scott's academic goals as well as his athletic ones, and one telling comment from the article engaged the possibility of Scott's exploitation as an entertainer: "[Coach Dean] Smith said that Scott saw that he could be a part of the student body here and 'not just a gladiator.'"[54] Speculating on the significance of UNC's racial climate and mentioning Scott's concern with the status of black athletes at large, the story thoughtfully considered issues ignored by the mainstream press.[55] The article also addressed the basketball team's policy toward recruiting black athletes in general—again, something none of the mainstream papers bothered to report—with Smith saying that he would "recruit Negroes if they can fulfill the academic requirements at UNC and also do the job athletically."[56] Although this engagement with racial issues may have been motivated by students' hopes regarding the positive effects that black athletes would have on their teams' success, as had been the case with Chamberlain at Kansas, even in pursuing that rather prosaic goal the paper still opened up space for dialogue about race relations.

The area's black newspapers approached the story of race and its intersection with Scott's career in two ways that differed from both the white mainstream and the white alternative presses. First, these black publications tended to emphasize black athletic milestones in greater detail; and second, they explicitly challenged the ideal of sports as a model for broader social equality. Although the *Carolinian* did not make special mention of Scott as the first black scholarship athlete in the area, it paired the story with a large photograph of Scott and J. C. Melton, the dean of students at Laurinburg, thus emphasizing the role a black institution played in preparing Scott academically for college.[57] The *Carolina Times* was more thorough in its coverage, devoting a front-page story to Scott's announcement, even though sports matters rarely achieved such prominent placement. Although the story itself merely mentioned that Scott was "the first of his race to receive an athletic grant-in-aid at UNC," it also mentioned Cooper's brief stint with the freshman team in 1964–1965.[58] The prominence given to this story in both papers indicates that many took pride in—and a measure of hope from—Scott's ability to attend and play for the state's flagship public institution. Of course, the *Carolina Times* editorial, "The Diminishing Returns of Integration," also made clear the limits of Scott's symbolic role. Recognizing that integration would not in and of itself provide equality for African Americans, the paper's editors also implicitly questioned the virtue of sports as a model of fairness and egalitarianism, anticipating the widespread athlete revolt of 1968.

With all of these conflicting hopes and fears in the background, Scott started his basketball career at UNC. After a disappointing freshman season in which he was limited by a foot injury, Scott flourished in his first year with the varsity squad as a sophomore. In his first game that season, Scott led a second-half rally that pulled his team to a victory over Virginia Tech University, making a key steal and driving the length of the court for a layup. Scott's pioneering role generated little discourse, with only the *Herald* mentioning (erroneously) that he was "the first Negro athlete ever to play a varsity sport at UNC."[59] Otherwise, his debut created nary a ripple, part and parcel of the progressive strategy. In not discussing the changing racial makeup of the team at any length, the newspapers cordoned off the basketball team from larger political dynamics. But no one could deny Scott's impacts on the basketball court. In the games that followed, Scott and senior standout Larry Miller paced the team to a 28–4 record, with Scott averaging 17.6 points a game, good for second place on the team behind Miller. Agile, graceful, and a good leaper, Scott was a versatile talent who made the Tar Heels a dangerous team for opponents.[60]

But even within the dynamics of the UNC team, racial politics and the progressive mystique affected Scott's experiences significantly. Head coach Dean Smith's way of handling Scott's status as the lone black player on the team could be seen in a similar light to the university's strategy of avoiding any racial controversy. According to Scott, "Coach Smith always tried to keep the race thing out of it." Although Scott understood that Smith wanted to avoid making race an issue within the team by creating an atmosphere in which Scott's race did not matter—in which he was the same as everyone else on the team—the approach left Scott feeling slightly disgruntled in later years. "He was right in saying, if I don't make it an issue, then it won't become an issue within my team," Scott admitted, but "the thing is I had to live outside that team."[61] Although Smith attempted to make Scott feel the same as any other player, the reality was that he was *different* from all the other players, playing with extra scrutiny from the fans and media and unable to enjoy a social life with his teammates outside the basketball court. As a black man dominating whites on the court, Scott inevitably drew extra and often unpleasant attention. White southerners were not used to black men attaining positions of prestige and earning accolades from mixed-race audiences, and the responses of some observers could be vitriolic and brutal.

Teammate Dick Grubar lamented the abuse Scott suffered on the courts, particularly when the team played at the University of South Carolina: "The man put up with more than I think anybody could ever put up with. Just in terms of the racial taunts, the spit, the water, the N-word. It was horrible. It was *horrible*." Scott said in later years that although he appreciated his teammates' concern, he realized that they were probably upset because their teammate and friend was being verbally assaulted—not because of the broader circumstances of racial prejudice. Even in moments of joy—such as the celebration following Scott's brilliant performance in the 1969 ACC Tournament championship game—Scott's race isolated him from his teammates: "We had great fun in the locker room. After that we walked out of the locker room; everybody went one way, and I went another way. I had to celebrate it by myself."[62]

Smith's attempt to minimize racial issues within the confines of his team—his model of a "collective silence" about it—let Scott just be another basketball player on the court, but it ignored the social isolation Scott faced outside the confines of the basketball program and may have limited the outlets for Scott to express his anxieties and frustrations.[63] Smith was certainly sincere in his beliefs in racial egalitarianism and appalled at the treatment Scott received. During one game in South Carolina, for example, the normally mild-mannered coach charged at a white fan who called Scott a "black baboon."[64] However, Smith faced a difficult situation, fearful of alienating players unaccustomed to being teammates with a black man, let alone one who garnered a significant portion of the team's accolades.[65] The experiences of UNC player and North Carolina native Ricky Webb, a teammate of Scott, illustrate the discomfort many had with the idea of a racially integrated society. According to Webb, "the first thing" residents of his hometown would ask him about his experiences as a UNC basketball player was, "How can you shower with a nigger?"[66] As a result of these tensions, Smith may have been concerned that discussing Scott's race too often with his team would suggest that the player was receiving special privileges.[67] Downplaying Scott's race was tactically savvy for Smith and the success of his team, but the heavily burdened Scott could not avoid the additional pressure he felt as a racial pioneer in the spotlight.

The local mainstream press coverage not only largely ignored these additional pressures that Scott faced; they also often channeled white frustrations in subtle ways. One anecdote provides a valuable glimpse into the seething tensions and bitter prejudices that lingered just below the surface of the local white papers' muted coverage. A few days after Scott's varsity debut in the fall of 1967, *Herald* sports editor Hugo Germino passed along a quote from former South Carolina basketball coach Chuck Noe: "Referring to Charlie's speed and quickness, Noe says: 'He'd make a fortune as a pickpocket in New York.'"[68] Stereotypes of lawless black men retained cultural currency, even as sportswriters seemingly accepted Scott as a student-athlete. The paper did not print any letters to the editor or qualifications in the following days.

Activism, Awards Controversy, and the Impacts of the Black Athlete Revolt

Despite the occasional jabs in the media, Scott continued to excel for the Tar Heels. In his first season, UNC made it all the way to the NCAA national championship game before being blown out by UCLA's powerhouse squad, led by coach John Wooden and All-American center Lew Alcindor. The following year, with Miller graduated, Scott assumed the role as the team's unquestioned star, scoring 22.3 points as a junior to lead the team to a 27–5 record. If fans and observers had been able to stomach Scott's success because he played second fiddle to Miller the preceding year, they would have no such luxury in the 1968–1969 season.[69] Although Scott's teammates were talented and experienced, there was no doubt that he was the one who drove the team to victory, as late-season events would make especially clear.

Scott's starring role took on heightened significance because of the changing position of black athletes in predominantly white sports organizations. Although many early pioneers in professional and amateur sports had shied away from pushing for political, social, and economic change, black athletes in the 1960s increasingly became more politically engaged. Black athlete activism would peak in the so-called black athlete revolt of 1967 and 1968, a series of protests and boycotts led by San Jose State sociology professor (and former Division I track athlete) Harry Edwards. The "revolt," best remembered for the "black power salute" of sprinters Tommie Smith and John Carlos on the medal stand during the 1968 Summer Olympic Games, heightened racial tensions and divided athletes, black and white, over the place of politics in sports.[70]

Although few black athletes heeded Edwards's call to boycott the 1968 Summer Olympic Games, numerous public events connected to Edwards's efforts galvanized the American public, including well-publicized protests at track meets at the New York Athletic Club, which permitted black athletes to perform at meets but denied blacks the right to belong to the club. These efforts made Edwards, and his organization the Olympic Project for Human Rights, controversial and unsettling to many who hoped to distance sports from politics.[71] As controversy swirled around black athletes' participation in the Olympics, Jack Olson's series on the "Black Athlete" in *Sports Illustrated*, published over five issues in July 1968, further shattered the illusion that sports were free from racial prejudice and were a model of equality. One of the most widely read series in the history of *Sports Illustrated*, Olson's articles spotlighted the inadequate academic assistance given to black athletes, social taboos against interracial dating, the practice of "stacking" black athletes at certain positions to keep their numbers limited on the playing field, and other examples of bigotry and discord in the sports world. Olson's series was jarring in part because most black and white sportswriters had, as Edwards argued, tended to avoid racial issues in their coverage. The local mainstream North Carolina media took that trend to an extreme in this time of heightened black athletic activism and political awareness.[72]

Scott was certainly not immune to the changing expectations regarding black athlete activism. Pressured to boycott the Olympics, Scott demurred, explaining that he wanted to show his faith in integration. He won a gold medal with the team and was the fifth-leading scorer on the squad.[73] However, he later acknowledged that 1968 "was the time of the militant black" and said he supported athletes who publicized African Americans' continuing efforts toward equality.[74] These same national political pressures made their way to UNC's campus. When Scott was approached by members of the BSM to become involved in various political activities, he found himself in an awkward position as he struggled to balance his desire to help fellow black students and still be a moderate enough figure, in his words, "that other blacks could come [to UNC] after" him.[75]

Only four months after the Olympics concluded in October 1968, Scott had a chance to act on his beliefs regarding activism. In February 1969, Scott became involved with UNC's newly formed BSM. When Chancellor Sitterson appeared to dismiss many of the group's demands for changes on campus—which included the establishment of a Department of African and Afro-American Studies, the abandonment of SAT scores for admission decisions, intensified recruitment of black students, and better financial aid packages for minorities—Scott and black freshman basketball player Bill Chamberlain joined a group of four BSM members to discuss their cause with the university's head administrator on February 18, 1969.[76] Coming in the wake of violent confrontation at nearby Duke, where black students occupied a campus building and fought with local police, Scott's involvement in BSM activities generated considerable media coverage. The *Herald*'s front-page story about the meeting published thumbnail photographs of Scott and Chamberlain with its story and noted Chamberlain's statement at a rally afterward: "If I'm going to represent this university on the basketball court, I think the university should go to bat for me and take some positive action soon." Scott said nothing at the actual event but released a more diplomatic statement later in the day from Maryland, where he had traveled for a game. Saying that he and Chamberlain participated "to serve . . . in helping to close the communication gap" between the BSM and university administrators, Scott emphasized that he was happy at the school, and that his "concern grew out of the situation in which black students have found themselves at universities throughout the country."[77] Even in staking out that rather moderate position, Scott received no support from the editors of the *Herald* or the *News and Observer*, in either the news or sports section. Instead, both newspapers printed editorials that ridiculed the demands of the BSM and praised Sitterson and UNC system president William Friday for taking a firm line against on-campus activism.[78] Neither supporting nor condemning Scott's actions, the mainstream newspapers refused to take a stand regarding the place of political activism in athletics, although the tenor of their coverage—their critiques of the BSM, their support of Sitterson and Friday—criticized the athletes by default.

The pressure continued to build for Scott from both sides, as members of the BSM even asked him to boycott a game in support of their efforts. An anguished Scott approached Smith about the matter. Although the head coach had publicly supported Scott's role in the meeting with Sitterson, he hesitated to give his blessing to a one-game boycott, fearful that he would be fired if he condoned such an action. Scott, too, worried how his team-mates and others would respond to such a dramatic step.[79] In many ways, the youthful Scott was in an extremely delicate position. In essentially the same role Robinson had played in MLB in the late 1940s—acting as a racial trail-blazer in a previously all-white institution—Scott faced pressures the baseball pioneer had not. Most black leaders and activists had been content for Robinson to let his on-field actions suffice as a political statement, especially in his first three years in MLB, on the assumption that outspoken activism would close opportunities to other black athletes. However, the political climate had shifted by the time of Scott's career. By 1968, black activists wanted athletes to use their prestige to advocate on behalf of issues relevant to the African American community. But Scott had many of the same worries that Robinson had in the late 1940s—namely, that politically charged incidents involving the first black athletes in the ACC would prevent other black athletes from following in his footsteps.

Despite these distractions, Scott continued to perform admirably on the court, leading the team to a third consecutive ACC championship and a berth in the NCAA's Final Four. Two remarkable performances astounded local and national basketball observers. In the ACC Tournament champion-ship game against Duke, Scott scored forty points, including twenty-eight in the second half alone, to lead UNC to a come-from-behind 85–74 victory. One week later, he scored thirty-two points, including a last-second, game-winning shot, to lead the Tar Heels to an 87–85 victory over Davidson, a victory that vaulted his team into the national semifinals. Teammates, fans, and area newsmen reveled in his athletic accomplishments, with headlines labeling him "Great Scott."[80]

But Scott's jubilation at these moments was tempered. Only two days before his stunning performance in the ACC championship game, Scott found out that he was denied the ACC Player of the Year award, losing out to John Roche, a white sophomore guard for South Carolina. Roche had cer-tainly played well that season and had scored thirty points in leading South Carolina to an early-season victory over UNC. Traditionally, however, the Player of the Year Award had been given to the best player on the best team—in this case Scott. The Tar Heels had also rebounded to win the rematch with South Carolina later in the season, a game in which Roche committed a cru-cial late-game gaffe that helped UNC clinch a 68–62 victory.[81] Given Scott's more advanced status in school—another factor voters usually considered—Scott appeared to be a shoo-in for the award. When the votes were tallied, however, Roche earned fifty-six votes to Scott's thirty-nine.

The unexpected second-place finish almost certainly stemmed in part from Scott's activism. Scott publicly fumed at the decision and indeed almost boycotted his team's NCAA tournament games, feeling that the vote was racially motivated. Given the fact that five of the sportswriters selecting the All-ACC teams for that year left Scott off of their ballots entirely—an absurdity, given Scott's stellar season-long performance—his accusations seemed well founded. As Scott later recalled, he received little public support for his stance: "I don't remember anyone vocally supporting me on that one." Although Smith told Scott in private that he felt that Scott should have won the award, few public voices joined to condemn the apparently racist vote.[82]

Indeed, despite Scott's protests about the injustice of the Player of the Year voting, the local mainstream newspapers did little to report the snub or, if they did, covered it in measured ways that enabled them to avoid taking a stand. The aura of the progressive mystique continued to limit full discussion of racial politics. The *Herald*, for example, actually covered Scott's complaints—devoting a fairly large story to the topic a few days after the snub. In the story, Scott expressed his disappointment that the sportswriters voted for Roche "because he's white."[83] This engagement with racial issues seems impressive at first glance; the *Herald* printed a story featuring a black player's perspective of race and racism. However, the story still reveals an unwillingness to directly engage issues of race and the challenges to insuring equal opportunity. For example, no editorials or letters to the editor appeared in issues in the following days. Even more damning, the story itself was not written by a local writer: its byline was the *Washington Post–Los Angeles Times* News Service. Ironically, this *local* story was covered by a *national* news service—apparently because it hit too close to home. The *Herald* may have printed its story to at least partially appease its black readership (Durham had, and has, a higher percentage of black residents than Raleigh) but was clearly unwilling to support Scott or to criticize those who had snubbed him. Although one *Herald* writer asked Scott whether he thought his BSM activism had anything to do with the voting, no editorial columnists—on the sports page or elsewhere—argued the position in the newspaper.[84] At least the *Herald* allowed Scott to vent his frustrations; the *News and Observer* failed to mention Scott's complaints at all. Its uncredited article announcing the ACC Player of the Year mentioned that Roche had beat out Scott but indicated nothing about any controversy. The newspaper failed to mention Scott's disgust in subsequent days as well.[85]

There were likely a number of reasons why these newspapers did not grapple with Scott's situation in any depth. Writers who did not buy into the idea of sports as a model of equal opportunity (or who had very race-specific ideas as to what equal opportunity meant) often looked to sports as entertainment removed from politics. Scott's griping about the voting would have seemed inappropriate because political issues such as racial equality were meant to be separate from sports—if they were separate, after all, then the changes that occurred in sports did not have to happen in other aspects of life. Perhaps some of these writers also hoped to minimize racial conflict as a way of protecting black athletes from extra scrutiny, but the strategy of avoiding any discussion of racial issues nonetheless encouraged a dualistic response from white fans who could celebrate black athletic achievement without considering the still-unequal nature of post–Jim Crow society.[86] After all, sports hardly provided a model for equal opportunity in American life when rewards were based on race instead of performance.

The technique of using national media sources to cover local issues of race in athletics was not unique to that one story about Scott's frustration in the *Herald*. Indeed, the *News and Observer* and the *Herald* both printed an Associated Press story around this time that discussed Scott's experiences in context with two other area basketball stars who had come from the North: Davidson's Mike Malloy and Wake Forest's Charles Davis.[87] This story explicitly addressed the issues involved with "Negro athletes at predominantly white Southern colleges," discussing the difficulties in having a fulfilling social life with few other African Americans at their schools, talking about the dilemma of trying to stay "loyal" to both their team and their race, and discussing the importance of "a deep sense of racial pride" for all three athletes.[88] As with the story about Scott's complaints in the *Herald*, however, the national byline of this story distanced the local newspaper from any controversy. Doing so minimized conflict but also stifled dialogue. As Chafe notes, civility and its associated silence had power in this way "to crush efforts to raise issues of racial injustice."[89] Although the presence of these AP stories in the *Herald* and the *News and Observer* reveals a victory of sorts for dissenting voices and anticonsensus perspectives, that victory was far from complete.

Alternate responses to the controversy surrounding Scott's snub as Player of the Year reveal that some whites, students, and African Americans were more willing to use athletic contests as opportunities to bring up broader racial issues regarding sports, equality, and masculinity. Both the *Weekly* and the *Tar Heel* discussed the injustice of the voting and allowed for some discourse regarding racial inequality. Although, curiously, none of the sports-page articles in the *Weekly* offered any commentary on the unfair voting, both an editorial and a letter to the editor offered caustic critiques of the situation. An editorial titled "Great Scott's Late Returns" called the decision of five journalists to leave Scott off the ballots an "incredible miscarriage of justice."[90] The editorial not only disparaged the unfairness of the vote but also accused the writers of being disingenuous by lying to avoid any racial controversy—although the paper did not, it should be noted, ever mention race explicitly. F. Wilton Avery's letter to the editor on the same page, however, did tackle racism directly. After rhapsodizing about Scott's skills and unselfishness on the basketball court, Avery—a white medical school student[91]—rhetorically asked whether Scott's "ability and value to his team and conference could not have been overlooked simply because of his color, could it?"[92] Avery's letter suggested that the failure of the Player of the Year voting was offensive because it did not hold up to the standard of equal opportunity. The rhetoric of athletic integration had been that sports would provide a model where equal access would determine success regardless of race. However, as Avery noted in his critique, that ideal did not hold true in Scott's case. The lingering legacy of prejudice prevented Scott from achieving the respect and admiration he deserved. Taken together, the editorial and the letter to the editor both show a willingness on the part of this marginal, local paper to tackle issues of racism and injustice head on. In effect, they affirmed the link between sports and politics, welcoming the opportunity to use sports to address contested racial issues.

The *Tar Heel* similarly questioned the long-held ideal of athletic equal opportunity in an opinion piece titled "An Extreme Injustice" by sports columnist Art Chansky. In the column, Coach Smith expressed his displeasure with the writers who left Scott off their ballots, accusing them of being either "anti–North Carolina or anti-black." Chansky himself sternly criticized "anyone that can let personal feelings like these effect [sic] judgment of a player's performance on the court."[93] The writers who left Scott off their ballot, in other words, did not follow through on the idealistic vision of sports being free from prejudice and solely based on merit.

As Scott's career progressed, the area's black newspapers continued to hesitantly applaud black athletic achievement in predominantly white schools such as UNC, even as they grew increasingly skeptical about the far-reaching implications of athletics. Although the *Carolina Times* offered no coverage of the ACC voting—not surprising, given that the paper was biweekly, had a fairly brief sports section in general, and seemed more interested in covering the historically black schools in the area—the paper did at least engage Scott's race more openly in its stories about him and the UNC team during this later period of his career. For example, in previewing UNC's appearance in the NCAA tournament regional finals, the paper highlighted "three very fine black athletes" who would be at the center of competition: Scott, Davidson's Malloy, and St. John's University's Johnny Warren.[94] Even that recognition of the presence of black star athletes was missing in coverage from papers such as the *Herald* and the *News and Observer*. The *Carolinian* similarly highlighted race more directly, pointing out that Scott's claiming of the ACC Tournament Most Outstanding Player award was "the first time this honor has been bestowed upon a Negro."[95] None of the other papers mentioned this fact. In this way, these black newspapers saw Scott's milestones and achievements as one more stepping stone on the pathway of progress, following the familiar strategy employed by so many black writers over the course of the twentieth century.

In contrast to this tradition and to the white mainstream presses, however, these African American newspapers also acknowledged the very real limits of sports to effect broader changes. A few weeks after Scott's snub, the *Carolinian* published a Negro Press International article by Joseph L. Turner about the impact of the black athlete on integration. The issue would have had particular relevance to those who had watched Scott's story unfold. Offering insightful commentary about the limits of change possible through the success of black athletes, Turner argued that the apparent widespread "distinction" given to black athletes was only "token acceptance" of an elite few. Granting the popular embrace of black sports stars such as NBA great Bill Russell and tennis player Arthur Ashe, Turner pointed out that "acceptance" as an athlete did "not imply that the same respect [would] be given" to African Americans in more mundane professions. Turner also highlighted racism's continuing manifestations in the sporting world, where there were no black baseball managers, only one black quarterback in professional football, and other rampant "signs of racial discrimination." Thoughtful and probing, Turner's article was another sign that by the late 1960s many African Americans had become disenchanted with the potential of sports integration to initiate broader changes, another reflection of the changing climate of the civil rights movement. Observers saw Scott's snub as one more example of the failure of the egalitarian model of sports, particularly as it related to black men. After all, the hopes had been for athletics to open doors for male breadwinners, to earn respect, to earn Shklar's sense of citizenship as standing. That those opportunities had not been made available to black men, in sports and elsewhere, frustrated black activists and made some question the efficacy of sports in effecting social change.[96]

The national news media, in covering Scott's story, also showed a growing disenchantment with the possibilities of sports integration. Although Jim Crow's shadow had prevented the national media from taking on issues of racial discrimination in earlier years, by the mid- to late 1960s publications such as the *New York Times* and *Sports Illustrated* showed a greater willingness to spotlight ongoing racial bigotry. And because of UNC's prominence as a college basketball powerhouse—and the team's success in the nationally covered NCAA tournament—Scott had the opportunity to provoke dialogue about race and integration in a wider realm than just North Carolina or even the southern states of the ACC. *Sports Illustrated*'s Curry Kirkpatrick, writing a year after Scott's snub, described the heightened level of vitriol levied by opposing North Carolina State fans on Scott and fellow African American teammate Bill Chamberlain, as State fans "spat" on the players. He also observed that "in several key games [in the ACC that season] the ugly old racial epithet [apparently, "nigger"] has been heard from the stands."[97] Unwilling to varnish the racist ugliness that still marred the gradually integrated ACC,

Kirkpatrick refused to succumb to the "progressive" policy of smoothing over any signs of racial conflict.

That sense of disenchantment also pervaded *New York Times* writer James T. Wooten's March 1969 article about Scott's reception by white North Carolina fans. A cautionary assessment of the transformative capabilities of sports, Wooten's article balanced the coverage of white fan esteem for Scott with a darker side of white fans' responses.[98] Thus, Wooten pointed out that a white student who shouted "Charlie for God!" after Scott's dramatic last-second shot to beat Davidson in the NCAA tournament, also observed that "'niggers' choke in the clutch" after Scott's subpar performance against Purdue in the national semifinal game a week later.[99] This story reveals the duality of some white sports spectators—both their idolization and appreciation of Scott as a basketball star and their loathing of him as a member of a supposedly suspicious and inferior race. That one incident was not an isolated event. Lawyer Dan Pollitt recalled that a few years into Scott's career at UNC, after Wake Forest had brought in black players Charlie Davis and Norwood Todmann, a Tar Heel fan yelled, "'Hey, ref! Hey, ref! Them Wake Forest niggers are after our colored boys!'" Pollitt ruefully observed, "Charlie Scott was now our colored boy."[100] Despite Scott's achievements on the court, some white fans persisted in falling back on damaging stereotypes and using derogatory names regarding African Americans.

In his article, Wooten speculated optimistically that Scott would, in general, help encourage the integration of universities in the South and a lessening of racial stereotypes, but his inclusion of the still-present racism among fans cautioned that such gains were never made without serious conflict. That Wooten would adopt this paternalistic attitude—seeing the South as a wayward child that needed more integrated sports competition in order to see the light of racial harmony—was laden with irony. The belief that sports had worked elsewhere and would now work in the South ignored all the ongoing racial problems in sports and life in general in *all* regions of the country—from the Northeast to the Midwest to the West Coast. After all, big-time college sports competition had been integrated in the Northeast since the 1910s, on the West Coast since the 1930s, and in most sections of the Midwest by the early 1950s, but some of the worst race riots in American history took place in 1965 in the Watts section of Los Angeles, and in 1967 in Detroit and Newark, New Jersey.[101] Economic misery, racial prejudice, inadequate housing, and other social woes associated with the long history of racial inequality in America could not be easily solved by sports accomplishments, no matter the optimism of northern white sports reporters.

Scott's willingness to get involved in the BSM reflected an awareness that these larger issues facing the black community needed to be publicly addressed. But he was also certainly cognizant, as were other observers, that his activism could have serious negative impacts on his career, given many whites' concerns with the link between sports and racial politics. After the flare-up over the Player of the Year voting, Avery, in his letter to the editor, pondered whether his activism had cost him votes.[102] *Charlotte News* writer Bill Ballenger also wondered if Scott's work with the BSM had influenced voting, noting that Scott was "under pressure from black militant groups to quit basketball as a gesture against inequality in the system."[103] Similarly, a *Herald* reporter asked Scott if the skewed voting had anything to do with his involvement in the BSM. He angrily replied, "That has nothing to do with that. . . . That's for all black students. This only concerns basketball."[104] Some white fans (who disdained black political activism as a sign of the failure of "progressivism") and black students (who often felt Scott was not doing as much as he could for social issues) would have disagreed.[105] Indeed, Wooten noted that bar patrons in Hickory, North Carolina, watching the national semifinal game against Purdue, cheered for Scott early in the game, but then later entertained the theory that Scott purposefully played poorly because he was "mad at the school" because of the ongoing protests led by the BSM.[106]

The one local press outlet to support Scott's activism was the *Daily Tar Heel*. After Scott and Chamberlain met with Sitterson in February 1969, the newspaper published an editorial that praised the players for their decision to "use their positions as basketball stars as a club to force the Administration to act," even though their actions would likely "gall a lot of people."[107] Sports editor Owen Davis similarly praised the two, writing that he supported black athletes who decided to "take their stand," and he did so in language that criticized the tenets of North Carolina progressivism. Although he guessed that the two would "be branded as troublemakers," Davis encouraged them to persevere, writing that "few achieve greatness by avoiding controversy." He also noted that the school was not the "spiritual nirvana" that many believed it to be. Davis encouraged the athletes to speak frankly, to engage issues directly, and to follow their "conscience," arguing, "the day of the dumb jock is fast fading."[108]

That the fans in Wooten's article and this *Daily Tar Heel* columnist could respond so differently to Scott's activism spoke to the particular pressures Scott faced at a school, and in a region, torn by racial divides and yet known for its racially progressive atmosphere. As a star athlete, a celebrity, Scott was assigned often-competing roles by observers. Some hoped that he could help bridge the gap between the myth and reality of race relations by pushing for ever-greater political and economic gains for minorities. Others, beholden to the status quo, with its veneer of racial progressiveness amid white domination, hoped to limit his achievements to the basketball court and took offense to any activism he did off of it. It is no small wonder he bore up under the constant expectations as well as he did.

Conclusion: The 1970 Season, Sports, and the Changing Meanings of Race

The year following the Tar Heels' Final Four loss and the controversies surrounding the BSM protests and the ACC voting turned out to be a season of ups and downs for Scott. Before the season, the team's players voted Scott and fellow seniors Eddie Fogler and Jim Delaney tri-captains—a significant symbolic victory for the team's first-ever black player. The willingness of Scott's teammates and coaches to recognize him as a leader spoke well for the possibilities for sports to model social changes, to reveal to casual observers that black men were not the caricatures passed down in stereotypes and conventions.

The *Daily Tar Heel* also published a lengthy feature story about the star in its season preview that painted a fuller picture of the man. Art Chansky wrote that Scott had "come a long way" as a person during his time in Chapel Hill. Noting that Scott had been scrutinized "athletically, socially, politically and racially" during his time on campus, he praised the player for handling all of the pressure as well as he did. Scott credited his "more serious" demeanor to "the Olympics . . . and, oh yes, the ACC writers," a jibe at the disappointment he had encountered the previous spring. He also acknowledged his growing political consciousness: "I cast away the privileged characteristics that I inherited when I came here. . . . I have taken my place as an average American black man in society. In doing so, I've become much more aware, but I've gained far more responsibility."[109] A reflective Scott certainly did not shy away from the activism that may have cost him votes the year before, no matter the anxieties of the coaches or the press.

On the court, the team surged to an impressive record early in the season, only to stumble later. Failing to make the NCAA tournament, the team lost in the first round of the National Invitational Tournament. For Scott personally, however, it was another year of on-court excellence. Leading the league in scoring, Scott dazzled fans across the country with skillful all-around play and was named to either the first team or the second team of nearly every major All-America squad. Once again, however, he lost out to Roche for player of the year honors. This time, voters decided to reward the best player on the best team, even though Roche's individual scoring, passing, and rebound numbers were not nearly as impressive as Scott's. Campus voices, again, cried foul. Chansky argued that no "other criteria" besides race could explain why Roche won the award that year. At least one other *Daily Tar Heel* staff member agreed. Beneath Chansky's column, the newspaper printed an untitled cartoon that showed Ku Klux Klan members, in full regalia, putting pieces of paper marked "Roche" into a box that said "ACC Player of the Year."[110]

Mainstream media reporters again kept their silence. Scott was eventually selected as the ACC Athlete of the Year in 1970, leading him to speculate in later years that "something must have touched a nerve."[111] His peers rewarded him as best they could; the campus yearbook editors selected him as one of four seniors to earn the Frank Porter Graham Award for academic excellence, a commitment to the university, and public service.[112] As Scott left the school for a lengthy (and successful) career in professional basketball, he offered his final thoughts on his trailblazing role at the school in an interview with Chansky: "I've never regretted going to North Carolina. . . . I'd do it again. It was fun and that's part of what going to college is supposed to be. If I have a son, I hope he goes to North Carolina."[113]

When Scott decided to attend UNC to play basketball, he surely knew that he was embarking on a challenging four years. As a racial pioneer at a school where basketball was tremendously popular, he would be subject to intense scrutiny. The eyes of an entire state—even an entire region—would be focused on him as he visibly altered one of the last public bastions of segregation in the South. As Scott acknowledged in looking back on his experiences, he felt burdened by the pressure that went along with his career: "I couldn't just be an ordinary basketball player. . . . I had to be better. I also had to be better academically—I couldn't just be an ordinary student."[114] He also had to navigate the turbulent racial politics of the era, testing the limits of acceptable activism. Even as he did so, people around him were contesting what integrated sports competition meant for their local communities and the southern region as a whole. Black men's roles in society earned special attention. Would black men continue to be held out of jobs and positions of authority? Would black stars be welcome in the realm of entertainment, including sports? Could those starring roles lead to changes for black men in everyday life? Even as Scott's teammates voted him a captain, white southerner newsmen and others attempted to mark out the world of sports as an exception, instead of viewing it as a model to follow. These issues followed Scott wherever he went and whatever he did on and off the court.

Still, for all the courage his decision required as a political and social action, it's worth remembering the human dimension to his experiences. His struggle was often a lonely one. "I gave away my whole social life for college," Scott lamented in later years. "At that time [white] people did not associate with blacks. . . . And blacks did not socialize with whites. So, therefore, my social life was very limited to what North Carolina had to offer."[115] Isolated; barraged with racial taunts, particularly on the road; and always subjected to a higher standard of scrutiny than white players—as the ACC Player of the Year awards from 1969 and 1970 reveal—Scott deserves immense credit for his courage in choosing to be such an important trailblazer in the Jim Crow South.

His importance as a role model cannot be underestimated. One of the first black football players at UNC, Charles Waddell, a first-team All-American, said he decided to go to UNC in part because of Scott. According to Waddell, Scott's status as the first black scholarship athlete at UNC made him "the guy that . . . we [black athletes at UNC] looked up to."[116] Collis Temple, a black basketball player who lived in the Louisiana bayous, "watched the Tar Heels on television" and aspired to mimic Scott's success, eventually becoming the first black player at Louisiana State University.[117] Scott himself believed that his success at the school had changed young people's perceptions of race, as white fans aspired to measure up to black athletic heroes: "I think that having little white kids wanting to be like blacks had a more direct effect on race relations than anything else. Then you're changing people's ideologies."[118] Nearly forty years after he had played his last game for UNC, "people . . . especially black people, but also whites" approached him to "talk about the significance" that his UNC career "had on their lives."[119]

And yet measuring Scott's influence may prove less profitable than considering the terms by which white and black observers used his career to different ends in a tumultuous time period. Cautious white leaders—including newspaper editors and university administrators—may have welcomed Scott's contributions on the court but were deeply anxious about his broader significance off of it. In minimizing opportunities for open dialogue about race and the inequalities of the Jim Crow South, these leaders clearly feared a negative reaction from white patrons, whether these were newspaper readers, university students, parents, or wealthy alumni. Hiding behind the veil of progressivism and distancing themselves from open discussion of Scott's racial significance enabled them to avoid conflict, even as it tended to limit Scott's contributions to the basketball court. In a sense, these white leaders probably fulfilled the desires of many whites who wished to circumscribe integration. By not exploring the racist implications of Scott's voting, for example, newspaper editors managed to avoid controversy even as they prevented an opportunity to question just how far-reaching athletic integration could be for social change. The myth that simply providing blacks with equal access to previously cordoned-off areas of life would erase centuries of racism would have been easily disproved by acknowledging the distressing continuities in white fans' reactions to Scott.

At the same time, numerous alternate voices, from the black press, from the university press, and even from the local town newspaper, all pushed for a more frank engagement with changing racial politics. By the time Scott arrived at UNC, many blacks and whites had begun to lose faith in the transformative power of athletics to alter society. In their calls for recognition of the validity of Scott's political work with the BSM, in their support of his cries of racism when he was left off of the all-ACC ballot, and even in their continued willingness to discuss his racial significance, these alternate sources suggest that others took Scott's model as a cautious test case of the promise of integration and equality suggested by the Civil Rights Act of 1964 and the Voting Rights Act of 1965. More often than not, black writers noted the continuity of racism instead of the change, and they worried about the negative effects of integration on thriving all-black institutions. Scott's success alongside white teammates was inspiring to some degree for these black and white audiences, but it was not an endpoint for the struggle for equality. Rather, they hoped to use his stardom to push for more awareness of continuing racism and the ongoing political and economic inequalities that still limited African Americans' possibilities.

There was no one way to read Scott's story, nor were there necessarily two ways equally divided between black and white fans. Instead, Scott's story brings to mind some of the various forces merging, colliding, and glancing off of one another in the late 1960s. Students, alumni, and other fans wanted a team that would win and embraced integration as a way to level the playing field against teams that had already done so. Some black activists hoped to use the celebrity of athletes to push for larger social, economic, and political gains for African Americans. Nervous whites beholden to Jim Crow feared what the recognition of black athletes meant for long-held standards about the "appropriate" behaviors of black men. White community leaders worried athletic integration would lead to ugly racial conflict, giving their region a negative public image. Some black community leaders, alternatively, feared that Scott's example would lead to a drain of talented African Americans from black colleges and other institutions. Far from an exhaustive list, this summary nonetheless suggests the many symbolic weights Scott's career could bear and perhaps indicates why so many paid such close attention to his brilliant achievements. As one player out of five Tar Heels on the court, Scott stood out because of his race. As fans followed the trajectory of his career, they framed his exploits against a changing time when what it meant to be black in the South no longer seemed to apply. As the path to the goal of racial equality seemed, to some distressingly and to others gloriously, at least partly open, various sets of eyes followed Scott, hoping and fearing just what his successes would mean.

5

"Those Nigras" and "Men Again"

Bear Bryant, John Mitchell, and Wilbur Jackson
at the University of Alabama, 1969–1973

In August 1970, A. M. "Tonto" Coleman, the commissioner of the Southeastern Conference (SEC), the athletic association of the most prominent (and predominantly white) universities of the Deep South, wrote an impassioned column in which he described the moral worth and intrinsic values of college football. Published in the annual college football preview in the *Birmingham News*, Coleman's column would have had special resonance with the newspaper's local readers, who ranked among the most passionate fans in the nation. Many rooted enthusiastically for the University of Alabama (UA), located only sixty miles from Birmingham in Tuscaloosa. The school's football team had won three national championships in the 1960s under celebrated head coach Paul "Bear" Bryant and had brought considerable pride to state residents. In his column, Coleman earnestly described college football as "a universal language wherein the doctor, the lawyer, the minister, the baker, the candlestick-maker, and even the town drunk can get together and talk"; "an opportunity for an education" for football players and the other athletic programs funded by football's revenues; "the common denominator of the faculty, the student body, the alumni, and 'Joe Fan'"; and a vital force in "the building of a competitive spirit and character." He believed that athletic competition would, in a tumultuous time period, "result in building the leadership . . . which will keep America strong." He saw it counteracting the "selfishness . . . complacency . . . [and] apathy" he believed was infecting the nation.[1]

Although people had often ascribed a range of virtues to athletic competition, Coleman's lengthy missive took on an especially urgent tone because of the increasingly radical activism that characterized the civil rights and anti–Vietnam War movements. In the realm of sports, moreover, desegregation had finally reached the schools of the Deep South, another destabilizing shift for both whites and blacks. Bowing to public and competitive pressures, most schools in the SEC had begun to integrate their athletic teams by 1970, placing black athletes in positions previously reserved for white athletic heroes.[2] Although UA had not yet fielded a black player on its varsity squad, change was coming in that regard, and readers of the *Birmingham News* likely knew it. Meanwhile, across the nation, antiwar protests, civil rights demonstrations, affirmative action policies, and black athletic boycotts combined, in the eyes of many whites, to undermine the values of American society. With distress, the local mainstream media reported on the activities of groups such as the Black Panthers, regularly devoting front-page stories to gatherings of black radical groups even when their meetings took place far from Alabama. Upset by the perceived upheaval in society, and the revolutionary boasts of these and other groups, many whites looked to athletics as a salve, a restoration of order in a chaotic time.

For local African Americans, college football offered another possibility—a recognition of black achievement in the South and a welcome opportunity for upward mobility. College football's popularity in the state inspired black leaders and civil rights activists to campaign for African American athletes' inclusion in UA's prominent football program. But black leaders had their own concerns. Anxieties regarding the preservation of black-run institutions, such as universities, heightened as the 1960s ended and the 1970s began. As a result, many in the black press promoted college athletic teams from historically black schools with an increasing sense of urgency.

As the UA football team sluggishly integrated its football team, these hopes and anxieties would color public discussion of the team's changing character. A number of key moments surrounding the team illuminated these debates in particularly evocative ways: a 1969 lawsuit filed by the school's student-run Afro-American Association that called for the school to recruit black athletes with the same diligence as whites; a humiliating season-opening defeat to the integrated University of Southern California (USC) team in the fall of 1970; and public discussion of the recruitment, and debuts, of the team's first black players, Wilbur Jackson and John Mitchell. The presence of Bear Bryant—a respected and beloved coach for many white Alabamians—loomed over all of these events, as his actions had the potential to set an example for integration across the state.[3] As the civil rights movement fractured and lost steam with the dawning of the 1970s, the University of Alabama's highly esteemed and publicly visible football team offered a compelling opportunity to test how racial integration might work in the Deep South. Would white southerners accept black players on a team that had been a source of regional (white) pride? Would southern blacks welcome the chance to play, or even cheer, for the prestigious program, or would they maintain their loyalty to the black institutions that had been central to their community in previous years? Could black and white southerners work together to achieve success, and, if so, under what terms?

The discourse surrounding the UA football team provided some answers to these questions, revealing the depth of white resistance to affirmative action and the continuing challenges in building broad support for civil rights activism. Although blacks and whites had always interacted in the Deep South, this was the region of the nation in which racial lines were drawn most clearly. The cautious test case of this sports team took on heightened significance, and it called special attention to the place of leaders in the community—both the failings of whites with power, such as Bryant, and the anxieties over losing black leaders as a result of integration. Paradoxically, in its successes and failures, the team shed new light on the heartening possibilities—and discouraging limitations—of college sports to model an equal-opportunity society. In the end, even the relatively peaceful integration of the UA team offered little solace to everyday black Alabamians still struggling to overcome a legacy of discrimination and poverty—a lesson that many observers in the press, on both sides of the color line, seemed to miss.

Bear Bryant, Black Athletes, and the Changing Climate of Civil Rights

The Alabama football team, because of a confluence of factors, offered a particularly rich site to test racial integration in the Deep South. As a state, Alabama had been the site of some of the most famous, and infamous, moments in the civil rights movement. Together with its neighbor Mississippi, Alabama had one of the worst reputations with regard to the treatment of its African American residents. The Montgomery bus boycott of 1955 and 1956, which called attention to Jim Crow policies in public transportation, had marked an important early victory for civil rights activists (and led to the ascension of a young newcomer to the city, the Reverend Martin Luther King, Jr.). The Birmingham campaign of the Southern Christian Leadership Conference (SCLC) in April and May 1963 had been another important event, galvanizing northern white support for the black struggle for equality. Millions across the nation watched in horror as police officers, led by notorious white commissioner Eugene "Bull" Connor, sprayed nonviolent protesters and marchers with fire hoses and unleashed police dogs on demonstrating high school students. These events, along with a host of others, placed the state at the center of the national civil rights struggle.

The University of Alabama itself entered national discussions of race relations on June 11, 1963. When black students Vivian Malone and James Hood attempted to enroll at the school, Alabama governor George Wallace stood in the doorway to the university's main building to prevent their entrance into the school, defying a court order. Wallace was an avowed supporter of segregation, announcing in his inaugural address only five months previously that he would keep segregation alive in Alabama "forever." With a large crowd of journalists and pro-segregation Alabamians on hand, and Americans across the nation watching, scores of National Guard soldiers ensured the two students' safety when Wallace finally stood aside.[4] The events at the school inspired President John F. Kennedy to address the nation that night, calling for a new civil rights bill that would outlaw discrimination in public accommodations and public education.[5] On campus, Hood and Malone received a relatively peaceful welcome once Wallace stood aside (Malone, in fact, graduated from the school in 1965—the first African American to do so) and national publications praised the school's leadership. However, black students certainly faced their fair share of racial epithets and poor treatment, and many white residents wrote UA president Frank Rose to complain that he had not been firm enough in his support of segregation. Many white Alabamians were clearly quite distressed to see the university integrated, fearful of what this change meant for long-standing social customs regarding the "proper" places of blacks and whites.[6]

As the school admitted a trickle of black students in the years following the stand in the schoolhouse door, football coach Bear Bryant continued to succeed with all-white teams. Bryant was known for his fiery temper and tough demeanor (he had earned the nickname "Bear" for reportedly wrestling a captive bear as a thirteen-year-old), and his players in later years nearly unanimously agreed that they were frightened of the gruff coach.[7] According to historian Andrew Doyle, white Alabamians took special pride in Bryant's squads, as they provided "undeniable proof of achievement and legitimacy for a state that historically led the nation only in adult illiteracy and infant mortality." Given the racial makeup of his teams, Bryant also served as a symbol for a defiant South in the face of increasing pressure to integrate.[8] Yet Bryant himself was actually something of a racial moderate, having had black friends while growing up poor in Arkansas. In his 1974 autobiography, Bryant even insisted that he had tried to integrate the University of Kentucky football team in the late 1940s, when he served as the team's head coach, but had been denied by the university president. Be that as it may, by the mid-1960s, the coach hesitated to recruit black players for his Alabama squad, knowing that the state's governor was a staunch segregationist and fearing that white fans might not be willing to accept black players.[9] According to former recruiting coordinator Clem Gryska, Bryant hoped to find players who would blend in seamlessly without causing "another schoolhouse door episode" but was frustrated that Wallace's race-baiting made it difficult for him to act on his desire to have black players on the team.[10]

Regardless of the coach's personal feelings, Bryant hardly took a leadership role in those tumultuous years following the schoolhouse door incident.[11] In fact, it was a desire to keep his team competitive more than any change in the racial atmosphere that inspired Bryant to integrate, just as it had been the case with Allen at KU. As national opinion turned against segregation, Bryant's all-white team paid the price in bowl games and in polls determining the national champion. The 1966 season was especially important. Jim Murray of the *Los Angeles Times*, a heavy-handed and opinionated syndicated columnist, protested bitterly when Alabama won the national championship again in 1964, suggesting that the team merely won the "Front-of-the-Bus championship" because of its refusal to schedule integrated teams for regular-season contests.[12] Although Alabama residents wrote letters to Bryant declaring their support for him and ridiculing Murray, the writer's protestations appeared to work. In 1966, Alabama did not win the national championship, despite being undefeated, while Notre Dame, with one tie on its record, claimed the title.[13] Although white Alabamians expressed their outrage in a variety of forms, they appeared uninterested in calling for more games against integrated teams—or for the integration of the team itself.

Only three months after the disappointment of 1966, Bryant first addressed the subject of black football players with university administrators, explaining that he and his staff had no plans "to recruit colored athletes from out-of-the-state at this time, but certainly would be interested in any who qualify within the State."[14] The "lost championship" of 1966 seemed to light a fire under the longtime head coach.[15] The coaching staff had the opportunity to act on their supposedly egalitarian ideals only one month later. When spring practice opened on April 2, 1967, five black players showed up to try out for the team, an event the local media covered with some interest.[16] However, because none of the players ever made the varsity squad, the incident did not generate much lasting discussion. The experiences of Andrew Pernell, a black student from Bessemer, Alabama, however, revealed how the team's lackluster efforts at recruiting black athletes impeded blacks' opportunities to make the team, even as walk-ons. Although Pernell was gifted enough to make the squad and participated in spring practice in 1967 and 1968, he had to leave the team because NCAA regulations prohibited walk-on football players from receiving outside scholarships. In order to stay on the team, Pernell would have had to give up his private scholarship, an option he could not afford. The other possibility would have been for the football team to give Pernell a football scholarship, but Bryant and the coaching staff insisted that the team was at the limit allowed by the NCAA—even though the school was permitted to provide up to 125 players with scholarships at that time.[17] The unwillingness to make room for Pernell, to free up a spot for the following season by offering one less white freshman a scholarship, raises questions about Bryant's sincerity in recruiting black players.

By 1968, Pernell and the other black players had found allies in their quest to integrate the UA squad: the Afro-American Association (AAA), a student group formed that year.[18] Although the number of black students remained low—even by the spring of 1971, there were approximately 340 black students out of a total population of about 13,000 students—those who had managed to gain admittance to the university found support and solidarity through the AAA.[19] Pernell's experiences and the football team's policies toward black athletes provided some of the first opportunities for the group to organize. When Pernell was prohibited from playing in the team's annual "A-Day" game in 1968, an intersquad scrimmage at the conclusion of spring practice, because of his scholarship situation, the group distributed leaflets accusing the school of racism.[20] As the start of the fall semester approached, the group also published an open letter to the university community that called for a number of initiatives, including one that emphasized that the university should "actively" recruit black athletes and offer them scholarships.[21] Two weeks later, on August 15, 1968, AAA leaders Edward Nall and Moses Jones met with Bryant to discuss black athlete recruitment. According to Willard F. Gray, the chairman of the Faculty Committee on Intercollegiate Athletics, who was in attendance at the meeting, the conversation "was a most cordial one and the students left with a pledge to assist with recruitment of outstanding, well-qualified, black athletes."[22] Still, the AAA's participation indicated that black students were getting impatient with the football team's half-hearted efforts to integrate.

Pressure for Bryant to integrate also came from a familiar source—the local black press, who kept up their decades-long push for integrated athletic competition by calling on UA and other schools in the SEC to seek out talented African American athletes. When UA's chief rival, Auburn University, signed its first black players for the 1968–1969 school year, *Birmingham World* sports editor Marcel Hopson praised the school, while criticizing UA's athletic department for continuing "to drag its feet on fielding outstanding Negro athletes on its freshman and varsity football and basketball teams."[23] Hopson kept up his efforts throughout the spring of 1969. In March, he criticized UA and other SEC schools for "ignoring the 'very good prospects' from the all-Negro or formerly all-Negro oriented high schools" in the state. He believed that SEC schools used test results "as an excuse" for not recruiting black athletes, because it was clear to him that white athletes were also "not necessarily geniuses," but were still given scholarships.[24] Although the late 1960s showed a tendency toward black solidarity, these comments, and the efforts of black players to join the UA football team, show that African Americans clearly wanted to participate with whites in a variety of public activities. Black Power did not kill integrationist hopes altogether, not even among young African Americans.

That goal went unrecognized by many whites as the 1960s ended and the 1970s began. As various people considered the potential integration of UA's football team, the changing climate of the civil rights movement significantly affected their response to these events. Stokely Carmichael's impromptu call for "Black Power" in the summer of 1966 had inspired, or at least coincided with, a massive shift in white public perception of the civil rights movement. By 1967, according to historian Peniel Joseph, "Black Power" and not "civil rights" came to "[frame] public perception" of black activism.[25] The mainstream media emphasized radical black activities, including armed takeovers of campus buildings by black students at Columbia University, Duke University, and other schools, and the actions of groups such as the Black Panthers, who proudly carried weapons and spoke of revolutionary overthrow.[26] These developments caused great anxiety in the mainstream white media, prompted calls for an end to black separatism and so-called reverse racism, and led to a white retreat from the civil rights movement.[27] President Nixon's 1968 election campaign for "law and order" built on these fears, coding resistance to black activism with a call for a crackdown on lawless radicals.[28] Bryant would have to navigate this terrain as he welcomed black athletes in a time of upheaval and strife.

Affirmative action plans also affected people's perceptions of race and the goals of the civil rights movement—and colored discourse surrounding the football team's integration. President Lyndon Johnson had actually employed a sports metaphor to justify affirmative action in 1965: "You do not take a person who, for years, has been hobbled by chains and liberate him, bring him up to the starting line of a race and then say, 'You are free to compete with all the others,' and still justly believe that you have been completely fair." Despite the president's warning, most white Americans appeared to believe that this effort was indeed sufficient.[29] As the economy began a downturn in 1970, resistance to affirmative action grew, as whites believed that black economic advancement came at the expense of whites. In this climate, prominent labor organizations and many Jewish Americans—two core groups of supporters for the civil rights movement in the 1950s and early 1960s—turned their backs on their coalition partners, uncomfortable with plans that seemed to rely on racial "quotas" or "hiring guidelines" for minorities.[30] As black activists pushed for representation on Alabama's football team in proportion to their presence in the state, white football leaders and press members carefully delineated a policy that eschewed any "taint" of affirmative action.

Thus, as black activists attempted to retain black cultural institutions while simultaneously breaking down the remaining barriers of Jim Crow segregation, and as white leaders attempted to integrate blacks into white society without giving up the privileged position they inhabited, UA's football team proved to be a particularly important symbolic battle ground.

The AAA Lawsuit and Recruiting UA's First Black Players

The battle over the integration of UA's football team came to a head in July 1969. At the start of the month, the AAA, in conjunction with local civil rights activists, filed suit against the school for failing to recruit black football players in earnest. The lawsuit, and responses to it, raised compelling questions regarding the limits of racial integration. Would token acceptance of black athletes be enough? Or would the university and the white community have to make significant changes in the ways they sought out and evaluated black achievement?

The lawsuit itself stemmed from the efforts of the AAA and two lawyers: Harvey Burg, a white graduate of Columbia Law School who moved to Alabama in 1967 to get involved in the civil rights movement, and Jim Baker, an African American lawyer from the area. Although Burg and his associates could not find "a conscious effort to bar blacks" from the team, they also discovered that the school tended to recruit white players "through a whole old-boy network of whites who had played at Alabama" or had coached at the school. This network generally did not include traditionally black high schools and the numerous talented players on those teams, thus denying those players the opportunity to play for the school. Burg faced a dilemma in pursuing any action against the school, however, as he struggled to find any black athlete willing to risk being labeled "a troublemaker."[31]

The AAA proved to be the perfect solution. Although members of the group had been buoyed by their August 1968 meeting with Bryant, believing that he would conscientiously seek out talented black athletes, the coaching staff had signed no black players to scholarships in the ensuing months. As a result, the group issued a press release in January 1969 headlined "Is This Institutionalized Racism?" Calling the athletic department a bastion of "white supremacy," the group wondered whether "a black man" had to "be a 'Superman' or an O.J. Simpson" to get a scholarship at Alabama. They then called on Bryant to offer the remaining four scholarships to black players.[32] When their efforts proved fruitless, the group turned to Burg and his associates to pursue the matter legally. U. W. Clemon, an African American classmate of Burg's from Columbia, took up the case and filed the lawsuit in federal court on July 2, 1969.[33] The suit named Bryant, in his capacity as athletic director and football coach; the University of Alabama; its board of trustees; UA president F. David Mathews; and Robert Finch, U.S. Secretary of the Department of Health, Education, and Welfare (HEW) as defendants. These men, according to the suit, had failed to uphold the Civil Rights Act of 1964 and the Fourteenth Amendment to the U.S. Constitution by denying African Americans "equal opportunities and rights . . . to education and participation in interscholastic athletics."[34]

At a time of heightened white concerns regarding black separatism and affirmative action, the plaintiffs emphasized the need to ensure equal opportunities for blacks. Thus, the lawsuit accused Bryant and the school of violating African Americans' constitutional rights by "failing to seek out with equal diligence" talented African Americans from integrated and all-black high schools and by failing to reward black athletes with scholarships in proportion to their population in the state. Taken together, these failings denied "black high school students the right to equal opportunity, and benefits to higher public education."[35]

In explaining why they were seeking redress, the plaintiffs linked sports accomplishments to broader issues of respect and economic opportunity. According to the language of the suit, the school's discrimination against black athletes prevented them from getting "a college education" along with the "recognition and status" that came with participation "on prominent athletic teams"—another example of how Shklar's idea of citizenship as standing influenced activists. The plaintiffs then tied their case to dreams of upward economic mobility: black athletes were not able to access the monetary rewards that came with education and with professional sports success. Token efforts toward black athletic recruitment would not suffice. Although acknowledging that one black student, James Owens, had been offered a football grant-in-aid, the lawsuit dismissed that one incident, indicating that the talented player was recruited only "belatedly, after he had been recruited by rival Auburn University" and in response to pressure from the AAA. That one effort was not enough: the football program would have to intensify its recruitment, to match the fervor with which it sought out the state's and nation's premier white football players. The time had come, in other words, for the most prestigious football team in the state to fully recognize black athletic achievement and provide for African Americans the same chance to earn prestige and financial success open to white athletes.[36]

News of the lawsuit earned significant attention in the local mainstream media and also helped clarify the AAA's position. Locally, the *Tuscaloosa News* and the *Crimson White* printed articles about the legal matter as the lead story on their respective front pages, while the *Birmingham News* put the story on page two, what it referred to as the "Second Front Page." Clearly, the area press believed the story to be significant.[37] But as had been the case in North Carolina during Charlie Scott's career, the local mainstream newspapers in Tuscaloosa and Birmingham offered no commentary on the lawsuit's merits, in either the sports pages or editorial sections, nor did they print any letters to the editor on the subject. Even the black newspaper the *Birmingham World* refrained from commenting on the subject, a surprising omission for a paper that had only months before, on multiple occasions, called for black athletes at the school.[38] Only the *Crimson White*, the very liberal on-campus newspaper, expressed its support for the lawsuit. In an impassioned editorial, the newspaper's editors said that they joined "the Afro-Americans on this campus in demanding that something be done to correct a situation long overdue for change." Defending the AAA's decision to file a suit, the newspaper's editors argued that the AAA had "quietly sought to alleviate the situation through conversations with University officials" but had "received nothing but platitudes." As a result, the *Crimson White* staff indicated that it "fully" supported the black students in their efforts for "full equality in all phases of University life." However, the editors were also careful to articulate the limits of their support, avoiding the language of racial quotas: "Like many black students on this campus, the *Crimson White* does not feel a Negro should be signed for sports here merely because he happens to be black." The shadow of affirmative action hung over even these supportive white students.[39]

That support assuredly did not represent the only opinion on the matter. Jack Gurley, a graduate of the university in 1950, wrote an agitated letter to the editor in response to the *Crimson White* editorial, expressing his displeasure with the newspaper's "rotten views." Gurley believed that the editors did not represent "the majority" of students and he thought that it was "a disgrace" that the editors were "[representatives] of the University of Alabama in any matter whatsoever."[40] Clearly, the integration of the football team, or at least the tactics employed by the AAA, did not sit well with Gurley. He was not alone. Activist Frye Gaillard's 1970 report on the desegregation of SEC athletics included some of the frustrations white Alabama fans had with the suit. According to the author, one "irate alumnus" said, "It just burns me up for those nigras to try to tell the Bear who to recruit."[41] What appeared to gall many whites was that African Americans would attempt to usurp power from the team's beloved (white) head coach. If white southerners were gradually getting more accustomed to desegregated life, many were clearly not amenable to having African Americans assume leadership roles or shape the direction of integration in any way.

Although Bryant had been out of town when the lawsuit was filed, and thus unavailable for comment, he addressed the situation at his annual midsummer press conference three weeks later. Bryant refuted the central claims of the lawsuit, that he and his staff had been negligent in recruiting black players, insisting that they were interested only in recruiting "winning play-ers," regardless of whether they were "white or black or any other color." Perhaps because, presumably for pro-segregationist whites, the emphasis on building "winning football teams" provided a plausible reason for Bryant's recruitment of black athletes, the editors of the *Birmingham News* reprinted his statement at the top of the sports page: "We're going to attempt to recruit players who are winning players, not because they're white or not because they're black."[42] But Bryant also clearly felt that the lawsuit was out of line, saying, "We ask our alumni and friends to help us recruit, but not to help us select" players. In doing so, he reaffirmed his power as head coach (and his leadership role as a white man), implicitly chiding the AAA for attempting to encroach on his territory.[43]

In making these announcements, Bryant was most likely being genuine; behind the scenes, the head coach relayed the same message to his assistants. The day the lawsuit had been filed, Bryant had sent a memo to his coaching staff telling them that the team's "recruiting policy shall continue just as it has been in the past—with the lone purpose of recruiting WINNING STUDENT-ATHLETES, regardless of color." He also told his assistants that although they would "welcome individuals and groups to call . . . attention to prospective student-athletes," he and his staff would "reserve the right" to decide whom they would recruit.[44] Far from Wallace's cry of "segregation forever," Bryant's own declarations acknowledged that integration was approaching but refused to give black activist groups any credit in spurring his decisions. Integration would occur on Bryant's terms, a reflection of larger white recalcitrance in accepting black influence on policy decisions in the South.

Bryant further outlined his opinions on integrating his team the follow-ing summer when he gave a deposition in the lawsuit to Clemon on July 8, 1970. Bryant admitted that his staff had targeted black athletes for only "three or four years," and he was also candid that competitive factors motivated the change in policy. He explained that he and his staff did not want the best in-state black players "to get away" to other schools, hence the decision to start with local black athletes.[45] Defending his record while also acknowledging that he and his staff could have been more thorough in earlier years, Bryant made no secret of his desire to improve his team by recruiting talented Afri-can American athletes.

If competition explained the recent changes in the team's recruiting, an anecdote he shared with Clemon suggested one reason for the delay in sign-ing black scholarship players. Bryant recalled:

Four or five years ago . . . I was in Mobile and a . . . very fine [African American] coach came to me and said he had a real terrific [black] athlete that wanted to come to the University and he would like to play. . . . I told him if he comes up there we are going to treat him just like anybody else, but from one coach to another, if he was my kid, right now I believe it is a little too soon, I would direct him some place else. I said, we want to win, color doesn't mean anything to us, but . . . we are going to have to play in Starkville, Mississippi, and Oxford, Mississippi, and Tuscaloosa, Alabama, and it might be just a year or two from now, but I said, right now if he was my kid, I would try to direct him some place else, but if he comes, he would be treated like anybody else, and the coach, we visited quite awhile, and he understood and agreed with me.[46]

Was Bryant being honest here, or had he deflected the unnamed athlete away for other reasons? It is impossible to say with certainty, but there were certainly elements of truth to Bryant's answer—black players would have faced brutal treatment from fans in Alabama and Mississippi.

But the phrase "too soon" was all-too familiar for black Americans, who had been told on countless occasions by white leaders that racial progress could not be rushed, that African Americans need only be patient. This idea motivated Martin Luther King's famous April 1963 "Letter from Birmingham Jail," in which the civil rights leader rebuffed white southern ministers who called his tactics "unwise and untimely."[47] King and other civil rights leaders had recognized this language of moderation as code for a continuing deferral of black rights and aspirations and had demanded immediate change. Likely aware of these frustrations in the black community, Bryant nonetheless pursued a cautious strategy similar to that used by President Eisenhower, who had hesitated to enforce the *Brown v. Board of Education* verdict. Instead of taking the lead in recruiting black players, the coach waffled, delaying long enough that his school's football team integrated after more than half of the other teams in the conference had done so. Given the coach's stature in the state, in the SEC, and in the nation, many wonder whether Bryant could have accelerated the process by leading the way instead of following others. Bryant's hesitance to act in this regard is especially ironic because of Bryant's tough-as-nails demeanor with his team. Bryant played the role of a tyrant on the football field but was not willing to take his leadership outside that realm.[48] Sports thus remained separate from civic issues in significant ways.

Bryant consistently affirmed in the deposition that he would treat players the same regardless of race. When a black student named Doc Roane asked Bryant about trying out for the team in the spring of 1967, Bryant "told him to get his physical and shave that mustache off and come on out there." Bryant then talked with his team about having black players try out for the squad, explaining that he "was trying to do it in a way that nobody could get hurt . . . and the squad handled it and I think our kids, we respected Doc."[49]

When another black athlete, a junior college transfer named Ralph McGill, visited, Bryant had one of the homecoming queens show him around town, hoping to interest the talented athlete in Tuscaloosa and the team. He also cautioned McGill that "we never had a black football player on our squad and there might be problems," but he urged the player to come to him with any issues he encountered. Although McGill chose instead to attend the University of Tulsa, Bryant's efforts suggest that he was feeling out how to best bring black and white players together on his squad.[50] Well aware of the depth of racial animosity in Alabama and the likelihood of uncomfortable interactions between his players and unruly fans, Bryant sought to ease his program gradually into the integrated era.

In contrast to Bryant's gradual, cautious approach, however, the lawsuit called for direct action by the school, clearly frustrated that the coach had not taken a leadership role in desegregating big-time athletics. The AAA and their supporters insisted that the time had already come for the football team to seek out talented black athletes and provide them with equal opportunities to their white counterparts. The AAA followed their lawsuit in November 1969 with a list of seven demands that called for significant changes to the school's institutional culture, including the establishment of an Afro-American Cultural Center, a separate orientation for black students, and the hiring of more black faculty. The school's new president, David Mathews, expressed his concerns that the group was seeking to separate itself from the university's white population, writing in a letter to the group that in addressing the "many real and serious problems" for black students at a school "where most students are white," the university should not "return to separatism." The school, and black and white students, had to face "the hard task of having to live together."[51] However, the AAA's seventh and final demand contradicted that assessment: "Action should be taken by the administration to end the racist and discriminatory practices of its athletic department."[52] Presumably, that meant bringing black and white athletes together on the university's teams, hardly a separatist endeavor. But the university resisted even that integrationist goal, as administrators attempted to have the lawsuit dismissed on multiple occasions. The contradictions spoke to "the hard task" blacks and whites faced in learning how to live with one another in new ways and how to share beloved cultural institutions.

As the lawsuit progressed—with the university officially denying the charges in the fall of 1969, Bryant's deposition in July 1970, and a postponement of the trial until July 1971—Bryant and his staff made the first major strides in securing black players for UA's squad. The recruitment of the two black pioneers—Wilbur Jackson and John Mitchell, who both debuted with the varsity squad in the fall of 1971—reveals how important athletic competition could be symbolically, and practically, to many in the local community.

Jackson and Mitchell took widely divergent paths to UA, although their backgrounds were, in many ways, quite similar. Jackson was from Ozark, a small town in Alabama's hinterland. Brought up in a working-class family (his father worked on railroad lines), Jackson played only two years of high school football—his junior year at an all-black school and his senior year in a newly integrated high school. His recruitment by UA's coaches resulted from a rather accidental set of circumstances. On hand to keep tabs on two players from Jackson's high school team who had already made commitments to the program, assistant coach Pat Dye spotted footage of Jackson playing in the high school's spring football game and began to recruit the wide receiver as well.[53]

Mitchell's route to the school was more circuitous. He grew up in Mobile, a city on Alabama's Gulf Coast, where his father served in the U.S. Coast Guard and his mother was a homemaker. As a child, he eagerly tuned in to Alabama and Auburn football games on the radio and on television, dreaming of attending either of the in-state powerhouses. However, with a rather thin frame, Mitchell did not attract interest from many big-time football programs. Instead, his academic exploits—he and three other black students had won a state science fair competition—had earned him academic scholarship offers from UA and other SEC schools. Hoping to play football, Mitchell instead accepted an athletic scholarship to Eastern Arizona Junior College, where his inspired play during the 1969 and 1970 seasons drew the attention of a number of big-time programs, including USC. When USC coach and longtime Bryant friend John McKay mentioned offhandedly that he was about to sign a talented end from Alabama, Bryant tracked him down and began recruiting Mitchell as well.[54] Although Mitchell's and Jackson's recruitments did not meet the AAA's call for the team to actively seek out black players from traditionally black high schools (and, indeed, effectively validated the AAA's charge that the team continued to recruit through the "old boys" network), the staff's efforts to land the two talented black players showed that the team was actually willing to take on African American players.

Both players remembered Bryant's recruiting pitch in similar ways, and the tactics the coach used show how he attempted to welcome the black players while limiting the potential for disruption of his program. According to Jackson, the UA coaches never mentioned his pioneering role, but they made a point of telling him, "Look, you're going to be treated like everybody else."[55] Similarly, when Bryant visited with Mitchell and his family, he told the skilled defensive end, "You are gonna be treated like anybody else. I don't have black players, white players, I have just players."[56] He also assured Mitchell's mother that her son would be "treated fairly . . . like all the other players."[57] Undoubtedly, Bryant was being sincere, letting the players know that they would not be discriminated against because of their race—a real concern for black athletes at the time across the country. But Bryant's emphasis that he would not give the black players any special treatment also fit in well with the white backlash against affirmative action and other policies that gave minority groups "special treatment."

That defensiveness came through clearly in the second point Bryant emphasized with the two black pioneers. He told both players that if they encountered any problems because of their race, they should bring the issues to him, that he would "get it solved." He urged them not to "go to the press first."[58] The coach probably had a number of reasons for that philosophy, but he almost certainly wanted to avoid dissension within the team and the distractions that a public discussion of racial attitudes would have incurred—a very real possibility, given the widespread black athletic activism across the country. As Bryant explained in his autobiography, he "damn sure wouldn't stand for [his first black athlete] showing up with a bunch of photographers and some big-talking civil rights leader trying to get publicity."[59] Like many whites, Bryant clearly disapproved of the changes in civil rights activism in the late 1960s, as advocates moved away from sit-ins and marches to more localized dramatization and publicity of individual incidents of discrimination. While Bryant disdained what he saw as the media hoopla surrounding civil rights activism, he did not dissuade his players from becoming involved in issues on campus. Jackson was a member of the AAA and said he "usually attended their meetings on campus."[60] But Bryant was clearly intent on keeping politics out of his football team. In this way, Bryant effectively reduced Mitchell and Jackson's ability to use their positions as star football players to push for broader issues of black justice and equality, and to draw attention to debates regarding black masculinity.

In any case, both players said that Bryant's warnings regarding racism on the team were unnecessary, that they never had any problems with their teammates. Mitchell believed that this was the result of Bryant's stature: "I think it was so much because of Coach Bryant. . . . I think they were afraid of what he might do to them."[61] He was probably correct. According to offensive lineman Jimmy Rosser, Bryant stood up after the conclusion of the team's spring practice in 1970 and gave his assessment of the team and what it needed to work on before the start of the next season. He added one unexpected message: "He told us that he was going to get the best athletes available to play for us and that included black players. He then proceeded to tell us that if any of you didn't like that then you could get the hell out of here."[62] Given Bryant's stature and imposing presence, it is little wonder that his players avoided antagonizing their new teammates.[63] Would the broader community have responded with the same fear and reverent awe had Bryant insisted on integrating his team at an earlier date? Because Bryant failed to use his clout outside the boundaries of the practice field, that question remains unanswerable.

When the team finally did integrate, the responses of people outside the team did not occasion any public outcry. In the white mainstream press, the news of Jackson's decision to sign a scholarship offer with the school in December 1969 generated considerable attention. The *Tuscaloosa News* covered Jackson's signing in the most detail, with a front-page story announcing Jackson's decision.[64] Sports editor Charles Land opened his story by announcing that UA would "shatter its all-white tradition this fall."[65] Referring to Jackson as "a fleet wingback from Ozark's Carroll High," Land seemed excited that Jackson would play for the team. When asked about being the school's first black football player, Jackson said, "It doesn't bother me. . . . I've been up there to visit twice, and everything seemed okay to me. I feel pretty good about it."[66] The *News* certainly did not shy away from Jackson's trailblazing role, and Land even speculated that the school would likely attract more black players before the official signing day.

Others in the mainstream media were more hesitant to celebrate the event. The *Birmingham News* did not report Jackson's announcement that he would sign with the school, instead waiting until the official signing date. That decision was an odd one, especially considering that one day after the Tuscaloosa story, the newspaper had an ideal opportunity to comment on Jackson's decision. Sports editor Alf Van Hoose devoted his column to Alabama's prospects for the future and its need for better players on the varsity squad. The column would have been a logical forum to discuss the arrival of black players on the UA team, but Van Hoose said nothing about Jackson, perhaps hesitant to point to black players as saviors of the program.[67] White fans' sense of connection to the UA team might have been shaken if black players came in to save the team from its downward spiral. When the newspaper reported the signing of letters of intent one week later, the news that Alabama had signed its first black player was certainly not the lead of the story. That information was relegated to the second page, where writer Jimmy Bryan noted in passing the signing of Jackson and another black player, Bo Mathews, a six-foot, three-inch, 235-pound fullback from Butler High in Huntsville.[68] As with North Carolina's "progressive" media, the *Birmingham News* downplayed integrationist developments in athletics in order to minimize their impacts on racial politics more broadly.[69]

The local black press, on the other hand, cautiously celebrated the event as a hopeful sign of progress. The *Birmingham World* reprinted an editorial from the *Chicago Daily Defender* under the headline "Crumbling Barriers?":

> If signing up a black athlete is an index to racial and social progress in the Deep South, then a new day is dawning in the old confederate state of Alabama in whose capital George Wallace, when he was

Governor, personally tried to keep a black girl from registering at the University of Alabama, just about five years ago.

Today, matters seem to be taking a different racial twist. Wilbur Jackson, a black football player has been a tendered a football scholarship by officials at the University of Alabama. He will become the first Negro football player to sign with Alabama. . . .

. . . This may well be a sign that race barriers are beginning to crumble. Or is this unjustified optimism?[70]

The cautious tone in the wake of Jackson's signing was understandable. White Alabama's recalcitrance toward black civil rights and its dismal record of violence against blacks made many African Americans skeptical of signs of progress. Still, Jackson's signing offered a glimpse of a future in which "race barriers" no longer impeded black progress.

Many white Alabamians were not as pleased by Jackson's signing, and a letter from UA alumnus A. B. Porter to President David Mathews reveals the distaste some felt as a result of the decision to recruit black players. Opening his letter, "Strongly protest our school giving athletic scholarship to colored football player," Porter believed that the decision to provide a scholarship to a black football player stemmed from the "desire to win at any cost," and he called that motivation "a terrible thing." Although Bryant had often couched his decision to integrate in terms of its competitive advantages, Porter dismissed that argument, upset that the team had sacrificed its white racial purity. He hoped that the squad would "lose all games in which this darkie and any others . . . participate." An Alabama native and a property owner in Gadsden, Porter wrote it was "doubtful" that the school would "ever get another buck" from him in donations as a result of Bryant's decision.[71] Although Bryant did not retain any letters he received in response to his decision to recruit black players, it seems clear that Porter was not alone, that the act of aiding African Americans with full scholarships and a place on the prestigious football team was too much for some to bear. What would it mean for white fans to root for a "darky"? How could white segregationists get behind the team, how could they find refuge in the team's success like they used to? When black players actually took the field, the stakes would get even higher.

Of Myth and Memory: The USC Game, or Sam Cunningham's Magic Bullet

The season-opening game between USC and Alabama on September 12, 1970, has taken on almost mythic proportions among some college football fans, as it is often remembered as being the game that brought integration to Alabama's football program. Before a packed stadium at Birmingham's

Legion Field, the integrated USC team throttled Alabama 42–21, with black players scoring every one of the Trojans' five touchdowns on the day. USC sophomore fullback Sam Cunningham made a lasting impression on the fans and press who watched the game; he scored three touchdowns and seemed to overpower any Alabama defender who attempted to stop him. In the conventional telling of the story, the drubbing persuaded a recalcitrant Bryant to integrate his football team. There are many problems with this story, which scholars and journalists have identified, but the tale's most important flaw is that it is factually untrue.[72] Wilbur Jackson was already on the freshman team in the fall of 1970, and the team's coaching staff was eagerly seeking out black players. Further, as discussed earlier, Bryant had welcomed the opportunity to add black players to his team, hoping to restore competitive balance. However, despite these inaccuracies, the 1970 contest between the schools offers rich material for considering issues of race and equality as they affected Alabama football. In the buildup to the game and in its aftermath, blacks and whites, Alabamians and non-Alabamians, could not help seeing the game's racial implications.

Ironically, the game against USC was a last-minute addition to UA's schedule, as the NCAA had only recently ruled that schools could play eleven regular-season games in a season. Bryant traveled to California to set up a home-and-away series with his good friend McKay. If he had any intentions of using the game to introduce Alabama fans to integrated competition, he certainly kept those opinions to himself. In the weeks leading up to the game, reporters frequently asked the coach why he had scheduled such a difficult opponent for the first game of the year, and Bryant consistently listed the same reasons: that he wanted to give his players the opportunity to travel to other parts of the country, and that he wanted to play against the best programs. He never brought up race, although it was surely behind some of the frequent questioning directed at him.[73] Regardless of Bryant's intentions, it was obvious to all who followed the sport that the USC team would feature black players—even their quarterback, the position considered the most prestigious on the field, was an African American player named Jimmy Jones.

These black players, their white teammates, and even the school's cheerleaders all shared apprehensions about traveling to Birmingham for the game, knowing the state's (well-deserved) tarnished image regarding racial bigotry. Bill Holland, a white fullback, recalled in later years, "All most of us knew about Alabama was lynchings and burning crosses. . . . And we didn't want to know much more than that."[74] A USC cheerleader told a local reporter after the game that squad members "were told to expect anything down here in the South."[75] The black players on USC's team had conflicted feelings about the game. Some were especially anxious and even smuggled weapons—including guns and knives—on the trip. Others saw the game as an opportunity to prove what they could do, seeing it as an opportunity to give "a real demonstration of . . . Black Power" to Alabama whites. Black players' apprehensions about white fans' responses to them were well-founded; when the USC players arrived, some white Alabamans gawked as the "USC nigguz" (the term one white woman used to refer to the players as she nervously gathered up her children) checked into their hotel. When the USC players took the field to warm up before the game, fans shouted "catcalls and racial slurs."[76]

That reception was not the one intended and carefully orchestrated by Birmingham's civic leaders. Eager to distance themselves from images of civil rights brutality, the city's elites attempted to make the visiting team welcome. As planes bringing players, families, and fans from Los Angeles arrived, they were met by Birmingham's mayor, George Seibels; the Banks High School band, playing "a medley of California and Alabama tunes"; and "the Birmingham Arlington Belles, a group of 20 of the city's lovlies [sic] dressed in long and frilly antebellum dresses and near-umbrella-sized bonnets."[77] Considering the racial dynamics of the game, the choice of an "Old South" theme represented a curious decision. No doubt many thought it was quaint and charming, but it almost certainly added to the anxieties of USC's black players. Meanwhile, the editors of the *Birmingham News* also attempted to make their California visitors feel welcomed, expressing in an editorial the "hope that Southern Cal's trip to Birmingham is just the first of many such visits by the Trojans and other leading teams from other sections of the country." One can imagine these "progressive" leaders crossing their fingers that all would go smoothly and that the city would bolster its reputation. The editorial concluded by expressing the hope that "everything about [USC's] stay is enjoyable except the final score."[78]

The final score actually turned out to be quite pleasant for USC, as they drubbed UA in a game that most felt was not even as close as the twenty-one-point margin indicated. The dominating performances by USC's black players must have made the game's outcome especially jarring—one of USC's scores had been a touchdown reception by halfback Clarence Davis, a Birmingham resident who had been unable to attend his home state's premier football program. One final event, after the last whistle had sounded and the teams were heading to their dressing room, would have likely pushed some white Alabama fans over the edge. As the USC players left the field, they celebrated by throwing Confederate money in the air.[79] Even in the moment, these players saw larger ramifications to their victory than just a regular-season game. USC's victory was an affirmation of a racially integrated society, a rejection of the Jim Crow mentality that had its long roots in slavery.

Although Warren Coon of the *Tuscaloosa News* lamented the Confederate money incident as "the final insult" of the contest, on the whole the local white press said nothing about the game's racial significance in its immediate aftermath.[80] However, they certainly did not shy away from crediting USC's black players. Writers from both the *Tuscaloosa* and *Birmingham News* praised Cunningham effusively, and both newspapers featured photographs of the big back in action.[81] Only when Murray and other writers outside the region used the game to critique Alabama's segregated squad did Charles Land of the *Tuscaloosa News* respond. Land criticized "a West Coast writer who was feeling rather smugly about it all." According to Land, this writer (likely Murray) suggested that "Alabama . . . get some black players, too. . . . Look out the winder and there's no telling how many football players you'll find." Land was not impressed: "It seemed the only racial stone the man could find to throw, for Alabama's football team certainly did not insult any Southern Cal players of any color."[82] Indeed, Land and others in the local press emphasized the local citizens' civility. Land's coworker Delbert Reed was delighted to report that USC's nervous cheerleaders found that "none" of the "bad things" they had heard about Alabamians "were true." One USC cheerleader praised the locals as being "really nice."[83] These writers played along with the image of a progressive South, refusing to permit the game to be an indication of the superiority of an integrated team and a denigration of southern society.

The local black newspaper the *Birmingham World*, however, considered the game in precisely those terms. Marcel Hopson noted that although "thousands of words" had been said regarding the lack of black football players at UA, the USC game had "intensified" those discussions. Hopson then printed lengthy excerpts from Murray's column about the contest, clearly supporting its sentiments: "Alabama has finally joined the Union. They ratified the Constitution, signed the Bill of Rights. . . . They now hold these truths to be self-evident, that all men are created equal in the eyes of the creator."[84] Although the staff of the *World* had been skeptical of the capacity of sports to model a fair society in recent times, they saw this game nonetheless as a pivotal turning point—an affirmation of black male abilities.

Others in the black community similarly celebrated the game's outcome. One young African American waiter remembered being "too distracted to focus clearly on his tables" while the game played. Black teens from Birmingham explained to a white UA fan that they supported USC because there were "brothers on the [USC] team." According to one account, a barbershop in Birmingham had an aging clipping of the game story hanging on its wall in the late 1990s—nearly thirty years after the contest.[85] The performance of black players in an integrated setting, playing against one of the premier all-white teams in the nation, had symbolic importance to these observers. Their performance constituted, as the USC players had hoped, "a real demonstration of . . . Black Power" to Alabama whites.

For many local white fans, the game served to inspire a desire to add black players to the UA squad. U. W. Clemon, the lawyer in the AAA lawsuit, remembered his African American friends telling him after the game that white Alabama fans responded to the drubbing with the "universal" idea that the school needed to "get . . . some of those black football players." *Los Angeles Times* writer Jeff Prugh reported a comment that came from a group of four white Alabama fans the morning after the game: "I sure bet the Bear wishes he had two or three of them Nigra boys on his team *now*. They were huge!"[86] That the comment spoke to a rather prosaic, and demeaning, reason to integrate a football team is certain. And it clearly suggested the possibility that black athletes would be exploited for their athletic ability with little thought given to their development as students (or race leaders). But it also reveals the resonance the game had with a wide circle of observers. On the whole, the USC-Alabama game marked a prelude to the team's integration. Observers on both sides of the color line grappled with what an integrated team might look like and considered the terms under which that team would perform. The following season, black and white fans alike would finally have an integrated UA team to cheer for.

Rising Tide: Integrating the UA Football Team

The struggle to integrate UA's football team was a long one. John Mitchell took the field as the first black varsity football player in the school's history more than four years after the abortive attempts of blacks to walk onto the team in the spring of 1967, more than two years after the filing of the AAA lawsuit in July 1969, and a long year after the loaded dialogue surrounding the USC game. Responses to that long-awaited debut—and that of his teammate Wilbur Jackson the following week—reveal football's potential to model how blacks and whites could work together successfully.

Two events preceding the black players' varsity debuts set the stage for the football team's integration: Jackson's starting role with the freshman football team in the fall of 1970 and both players' participation in spring practice in April and May 1971. Although limited by a lingering ankle injury, Jackson played in all five of the freshmen team's contests that season and served as one of three game captains for the team's matchup with Tennessee.[87] Jackson's debut created only a ripple; the speedy player appeared in photographs and articles in both of the local dailies, so even casual fans could see that change was coming to the varsity team's makeup.[88] If some thought that the black players' impact on the team would be minimal the following season because of Jackson's injury and reduced role, Mitchell's presence in spring practice in 1971 and Jackson's improved health made it quite clear that black players would play significant roles.

Mitchell's presence was even more significant because, unlike the recovering and youthful Jackson, Mitchell was an experienced player likely to contribute immediately. Earning a position with the first-team defense during practice, Mitchell quickly became integral to the team's fortunes. Fans would have to support him if they wanted their team to succeed. According to one anecdote, fan acceptance of the talented end came quickly. During that first spring practice with the team, Mitchell accompanied some teammates to a bar in town called the Tide, a traditional watering hole for the football players. At first, the patrons stopped and stared, stunned that a black person had entered the establishment. However, according to historian Raymond Hughes, once "Mitchell was introduced as a football player, everybody went back to what they were doing." Some patrons even offered to buy him drinks. Only one year later, Mitchell's picture hung on one of the bar's walls.[89] These early experiences—Jackson's participation with the freshman team and both players' important roles in spring practice and the A-Day Game—likely acclimated many white Alabamians to black players' presence on their beloved team.

Preseason press coverage during fall practice in August and early September 1971 served a similar function. Jackson and Mitchell both appeared in the team's official media guide that fall. As with all the other players, the two had paragraph-length write-ups and a thumbnail photograph—so there was no doubt as to their race even though the guides made no mention of their trailblazing roles. Mitchell's write-up even indicated that the talented defensive end "quickly established himself as one of the top contenders for a starting job this fall."[90] Photographs of the two from fall practice regularly appeared in both the Tuscaloosa and *Birmingham* newspapers as well, so readers were not caught unaware of their presence on the squad. But it remained unclear how accepting Alabama's fans would be—and the two players must surely have been nervous as the season approached.

The *Tuscaloosa News* printed individual feature stories on both black players in the weeks leading up to the start of the 1971 season. Although Delbert Reed's article regarding Mitchell focused on his contribution to the team's depth at defensive end and made no mention of his race,[91] Tom Couchman's article about Jackson, headlined "The Times, They Are a 'Changin,'" more explicitly addressed Jackson's experiences as the first black player in the school's history, a surprising engagement with racial politics given the media's usual silence on such issues. Couchman wrote that Jackson did not represent the traditional stereotypes of football players as "a bunch of numbers with faceless faces (white around these parts)." Couchman explained, "For one thing, [Jackson] happens to be black, the first black football player to sign a scholarship with the University of Alabama." The other thing that made Jackson different, according to the youthful Couchman, was his reason to attend UA. According to Couchman, Jackson did not come to UA solely to "eat, drink, and sleep football." Jackson agreed: "Now you have guys concerned with getting an education first, and then with social problems and things like that. Football just isn't the most important thing now." Reflecting the spirit of black athlete activism that had engulfed the nation in the late 1960s, Jackson's comments might have proved unsettling to some—would the team face unrest with black athletes? Jackson's assessment of his experiences to that point would have mitigated those concerns: "No problems. . . . I don't notice anything different, that I get any different treatment. Everything seems to be okay." Although Couchman wondered whether "a black man in Wilbur Jackson's position" could offer any other answer, he seemed assured by the ease with which Jackson interacted with his white roommate, Danny Taylor.[92]

A rather frank analysis of Jackson's trailblazing role, Couchman's article showed both the interest in black players and the awareness of the potential for disruption and disharmony. It also expressed the familiar hope that sports could provide a venue for blacks and whites to come together peaceably.[93] Left unsaid was the idea that the team's integration offered any sort of model for broader society. This nervous test case showed that these particular players got along as teammates, but there was no outright call for these lessons to be extended into other realms of life. Just as North Carolina's mainstream media had attempted to circumscribe athletic integration, to mark it as distinct from everyday life, the discourse surrounding Jackson and Mitchell had the potential to imply the same limiting message.

On the whole, mainstream press coverage leading up to the season veered haphazardly between assessing the changes to the team's racial makeup and ignoring the significance of the squad's new players. On the one hand, Van Hoose of the *Birmingham News* spoke with pride before the team's season-opening rematch with USC that "two fine black athletes, end John Mitchell and flanker Wilbur Jackson," would be "making historic debuts." He seemed especially delighted to point this out, since "professional cynic" Jim Murray had suggested that the Tide was "out of its class" in taking on USC.[94] On the other hand, as practice started that fall, Van Hoose had identified "two obvious look-changes" in that year's team—and neither had to do with the presence of black players on the varsity for the first time. Instead, he commented on the larger size of the players and their longer hair, which Bryant assured reporters would not change the team's core values: "sacrifice, dedication, work, unselfishness, [and] desire."[95] Presumably, having black players on the squad would also not affect those ideals, but neither Bryant nor Van Hoose discussed that change in any depth, apparently feeling that longer hair was more worthy of comment. And yet emphasizing longer hair over the team's racial integration minimized (perhaps unintentionally) the real discrimination that Alabama's blacks had faced for hundreds of years.

One final preseason anecdote suggests how the team's integration fit into broader dialogues regarding racial equality and even affirmative action policies. In the midst of a *Tuscaloosa News* story about the silliness of media day, in which players posed for countless (and often rather strange) photographs, writer Charles Land described this scene:

> The *News'* Calvin Hannah and Dan Meissner stacked up nine players, three deep, to distract the railbirds for a moment.
> "That's an HEW shot," one writer quipped, noting the only black player was on the top row.
> One looked over the group and observed that only six of the nine players appeared to be enjoying the pose. "The guys on the bottom don't seem to be smiling," he said.[96]

HEW stood for the U.S. Department of Health, Education, and Welfare, at the time the branch of the federal government known for enforcing laws against segregation and discrimination. One could read the comment in a number of ways. In putting the black player at the top of the formation, the photographers were giving blacks an unfair advantage, just as HEW and government programs, such as affirmative action, supposedly did. Or, in including a black player at all, the photographer emphasized the squad's newly integrated character, with the jibe about the HEW suggesting that many saw federal pressure and interference affecting the team's makeup. At the very least, the anecdote revealed how Alabama's football team could channel some people's frustrations with the process of integration, even as it could offer hope to others.

Finally, after weeks of practice, the season started, with Alabama taking on USC in Los Angeles on September 10, 1971. The game marked Mitchell's debut with the team, and it was an auspicious beginning for the newly integrated squad.[97] Despite being underdogs, Alabama earned a 17–10 win that marked the start of a successful 11–1 season. Area newspapers gleefully celebrated the victory. In the *Birmingham News*, UA's triumph over USC shared top billing on the front page with the death of Soviet premier Nikita Khrushchev.[98] One day later, Van Hoose indicated that the victory had been tremendously important to community members—estimating that between five thousand and ten thousand people showed up to greet the team when they arrived at the Birmingham airport late that Saturday night, including "old men . . . with their ladies," "middleagers [*sic*]," "kids," and even "babes in arms." Van Hoose ascribed a good deal of meaning to the game, believing the victory "proved" to the Alabama players that "they are men again." He also argued that the "conquest of Southern Cal" had regional implications: "Dixie football, beginning to be suspect in other regions lately, needed it. Alabama's record under Bryant, sagging in tough games the last three years, needed it."[99] For all of the gender, regional, and personal implications ascribed to the contest, nowhere, not in this article nor in any in the following days in either the *Birmingham* or *Tuscaloosa News*, did these writers make the point that a black male athlete had played a key role in the momentous win and had helped restore the reputation of "Dixie football."[100] It would have been difficult for white writers to broach that subject. If the win proved that the players were "men again," and the win was earned in part because of the contribution of black players, what did that say about conventional beliefs in white male supremacy?

As the season progressed, the mainstream media generally treated the black players the same as their teammates. Mitchell and Jackson certainly earned praise. As a starting defensive end, Mitchell used his speed and relentless drive to hound quarterbacks and running backs, slipping past blockers to bring down the opponents. Jackson, although relegated to a backup role, nonetheless showcased the skills that had made him a top recruit. Combining excellent speed with strength and guile, Jackson broke off a number of long runs in the season, twisting past defenders and powering through tackles. As a result of their performances, Mitchell and Jackson both appeared in action photographs from the team's games, and the local white writers certainly noted the important roles the two played. The *Birmingham News*, for example, praised Mitchell for his performance against Louisiana State University, when he sacked the quarterback and caused a fumble late in the 14–7 victory.[101] Similarly, Jackson earned accolades for his sixty-seven-yard touchdown run in Alabama's 31–3 win over the University of Miami.[102] Jimmy Bryan, of the *Birmingham News*, even devoted a feature story to Mitchell in late September 1970, discussing his improving play at defensive end. Mentioning Mitchell's pioneering role only in passing, near the conclusion of the story, Bryan had high praise for the junior college transfer, writing that he had "as much potential as any man who ever lined up at a Tide flank." Bryan certainly took Mitchell seriously, quoting the black player's opinions regarding the team's upcoming opponent and his own role in the defense.[103] In many ways, the local mainstream press followed a course similar to that of North Carolina's progressive newspapers, seamlessly incorporating the achievements of Mitchell and Jackson into their regular coverage and minimizing discourse regarding race. But the Alabama papers acknowledged the two athletes' pioneering roles more openly than did their counterparts to the north.

Perhaps these local newspapers were following Bryant's lead. After all, the coach had promised to treat the players the same as any other, and he appeared to follow through on his pledge. The coach regularly credited the black players for their performance in games and often did so in ways that acknowledged their effort and not just their ability, not falling trap to the white media convention wherein white players worked hard and black players succeeded because of "natural" talent. For example, after Jackson's long run against Miami, Bryant praised the running back not for his speed but for his determination when he "broke those tackles on the sideline."[104] As the end of the season approached, Bryant told a group of athletic boosters that Mitchell had "been a great defensive end" and had been vital to the team's success.[105] Bryant certainly did not shy away from crediting the team's black players, and he also attempted to reach out to his black players in other ways. On one occasion, he scheduled the popular film *Shaft*—an action film starring black actor Richard Roundtree—for one of the team's outings that fall, and black and white players alike loved the movie.[106]

Behind the scenes, the team's first black players felt they were treated fairly as well. According to Mike Washington, who played with the freshman team in 1971, Bryant told the team the first time they gathered that "he didn't care who we were, he didn't care who our mama and daddy were, and he didn't care what color we were. He said we were going to get an education and we were going to play football—in that order. And he stuck to his promise."[107] Mitchell and Jackson, both at the time and in later years, recalled having "no problems" as the squad's first black players and praised Bryant for his equitable treatment of them. Jackson said in later years, "It was a tough experience on the field, but it was tough on everyone. . . . I felt as though I was treated like everyone else, and I also felt that is how it should have been."[108] His teammate Sylvester Croom—like Washington, a freshman in 1971—echoed that perspective: "Coach Bryant didn't have black players or white players. . . . He just had football players. The only thing he cared about was your effort; he didn't care about the color of your skin."[109] Certainly, the black players faced additional pressure from outside the coaching staff because of their race. According to Washington, some black residents told him he "wouldn't have a chance at Alabama and white people . . . said" he and the other black players "should go to a black school."[110] But he also insisted that within the confines of the team, Bryant created an environment in which race did not determine recognition or status, and he meted out praise and punishment accordingly.

But for all of Bryant's fairness in his treatment of the team's black players, he also refrained from using these players to argue for more integration and more recognition of black achievement more broadly. As a beloved coach, he clearly could have done so, using the examples of Mitchell and Jackson and others to call attention to black efforts geared to improving black life in education and the economy. That he did not do so explicitly enabled athletics to remain a separate universe that did not impact day-to-day life.

Although the mainstream white press picked up on the color-blind attitude Bryant took toward his team, and thus kept athletics isolated from local politics, the local black press made a determined effort to keep black players, and black schools, in the spotlight. However, that decision did not entail focusing on the exploits of Jackson and Mitchell. Indeed, the *World* rarely mentioned the UA team during the 1971 season, instead concentrating their sports reporting on the local historically black colleges and universities. The history of black athletic achievement in Alabama helps explain that emphasis. The *World* devoted considerable attention to an organization called the Grid Forecasters, who held an annual banquet to honor local black athletes in order to inspire college coaches "throughout the nation" to recruit these players and offer them scholarships.[111] That the group still existed in the early 1970s spoke to the ongoing inequalities in the black sporting world. In August 1972, the newspaper's editors justified the Forecasters' continuing work, expressing distress that integration of schools and sporting conferences had not led to "a corresponding utilization of black coaches, black administrators, and black school athletes into the established broader structures of athletics."[112] Bryant and most white UA fans did not concern themselves with these issues. Instead, they welcomed black athletes as saviors of their program but made them fit into previously existing white-run institutions.

The emphasis on protecting black athletes and black athletic institutions dominated the *World's* sports coverage. If North Carolina's black press coverage of Charlie Scott's debut had been tinged with anxiety regarding the fate of African American institutions, the *World's* analysis overtly lamented the effects of integration on historically black schools. In January 1971, *World* columnist Marion Jackson noted the troubles that black college football teams were facing as they were "no longer able to recruit the top athletes of their race."[113] Jackson also bemoaned the fact that the integration of high schools usually led to the retention of white football coaches, who steered their top athletes to their own schools and not black colleges.[114] By June 1971, Jackson was calling on small black colleges to hold games in downtown stadiums so that "Negro football competition" could be "rescued."[115] The *World* was not alone in this bleak assessment. A December 1970 article by Lacy Banks in *Ebony* magazine expressed similar concerns. Although pleased that African American athletes were finally being given the opportunity to play at schools such as "Mississippi State and the University of Alabama, sworn bastions of white supremacy," Banks noted that many in the black community expressed misgivings. Some worried that black athletes would be exploited for their athletic ability. Others noted that stereotypes relegated black athletes to certain positions, excluding them from roles such as the quarterback. Prairie View College coach Alexander Durley and Grambling University coach Eddie Robinson also lamented the loss of quality athletes from black schools, noting the impact this trend had on attendance and revenues. Robinson also pleaded that he could mold an African American youth into "a man, a fighter, a producer . . . better than the white man."[116] Implicitly, these commentaries recognized the potential of black athletes to be exploited at majority white schools. Instead of being developed into productive men, black athletes might only bolster white institutions' athletic fortunes without attaining the other lasting benefits traditionally associated with college athletics.

The loss of attendance at black football games proved particularly troubling to many black leaders. Hopson was outraged when the Health Bowl Benefit Football Classic, a game whose proceeds provided financial aid to poor, sick children, had been canceled in November 1971 because of declining interest. The annual affair, which pitted two local black high school football teams against one another, had been played on Thanksgiving Day for twenty-nine years. The decision to cancel inspired Hopson to call Birmingham "the 'Grave Yard' of Negro 'Firsts.'" Officials blamed "the advent of school (racial) integration" for canceling the game, citing a decline in income from a net of $21,248.02 in 1965 to only $13,474.76 in 1970.[117] Hopson still seethed one week later, writing this scathing indictment: "No one (especially . . . ethnic minority groups) can 'merge' with the so called 'Power Structure' in any walk of life. The minority group merely gets 'swallowed up.' Results: Not even the bones or skin are left to show any trace of . . . existence." Hopson also expressed anger that some of the premier, previously all-black high school football teams were not ranked by the Alabama High School Athletic Association (AHSAA), despite fine records, arguing that after the Negro Alabama Interscholastic Athletic Association "merged" with the AHSAA, it was actually "'buried' into oblivion."[118] These, then, were the stakes of racial integration. In the same year that black players made their debuts with the UA squad, at the same time that Jackson and Mitchell were helping lead the Crimson Tide to an undefeated regular season, sports were not providing a blueprint for a racially equitable society in which black male achievement was recognized, as many in the black community had hoped for so long. Instead, desegregated sports provided another case of white majority culture subsuming black culture, obliterating cherished African American institutions, and removing black men from leadership positions in the community.

The first year of an integrated team at UA, then, conveyed a wide range of meanings, providing hope to some and anxiety to others as Alabamians tried to bring blacks and whites together in the post–Jim Crow Deep South. A late October 1971 photograph in the *Tuscaloosa News* captured both the possibilities and the challenges sports provided as a model of that ideal of interracial equality.

In the picture, Johnny Musso, UA's star running back, and John Mitchell talked with three African American boys, who smiled and looked in wonder at the football players. According to the caption, the two players told the youths to "keep working and stay in school," a positive lesson, certainly, and symbolic of how UA's prestigious football team could reach out to an even wider audience with black players now on the team. The arrangement of the principles in the photograph may have conveyed another message, however. Mitchell sat in a chair and talked with a black boy holding a football. Musso stood behind Mitchell and had one hand on his shoulder and one hand on the shoulder of another black student who looked intently at Mitchell. Although clearly meant to be an image of racial harmony, the image nonetheless conveyed a paternalistic message. Musso stood in a position of authority, benevolently guiding the proceedings.[119] Blacks and whites had come together, yes, but there were still issues to be ironed out—who was in charge of this newly ordered society, and who would shape the terms of integration, remained very much undecided.

Expanding Opportunity: 1972 and After

John Mitchell and Wilbur Jackson broke through the color barrier in Alabama football in 1971, and there would be no going back. Although the squad lost the de facto national championship game to the University of Nebraska on January 1, 1972, the following year proved to be another successful season for the university's football team and its black athletes. During the 1972 season, Mitchell served as game captain on multiple occasions, was selected by his peers as one of three permanent captains at the season's conclusion, and earned first-team All-American honors on the Eastman Kodak squad (a team selected by the American Football Coaches Association). That same year, Jackson led the team in rushing yards and earned significant media coverage. And the two were not alone, with four black sophomores and two black freshmen (just made eligible by the NCAA) joining the varsity squad and playing significant roles. Although the squad would come up short in its quest for another national championship, it added an SEC title to the school's already impressive collection and reaffirmed Alabama's place as one of the top football programs in the nation.

As in the previous season, issues related to race and college football offered signs of both hope and despair regarding race relations. Positive signs involving racial integration abounded. Bryant continued to live up to his color-blind pledge, praising his black players consistently in the press, including young underclassmen such as Ralph Stokes, Mike Washington, and Tyrone King. The head coach even named freshman linebacker Woodrow Lowe one of three game captains for the 1972 team's second game of the year to reward the young player for his effort on special teams.[120] The mainstream press praised the team's black players as well: Mitchell was often asked for his insights regarding the team's performance; the Associated Press named Mitchell to the first-team All-SEC squad; and the local media praised Mitchell for his All-American selection.[121] Support seemed strong in the community as well. At the regular season's conclusion, Mitchell, along with the other seniors on the squad, received a watch from the Jefferson County Chapter of the University of Alabama Alumni Association. A small gesture, to be sure, but a visible sign that traditions were changing. The group had given watches to the senior players every year since 1923, and Mitchell was the first black player to share in the event.[122]

The conclusion of Mitchell's career provided an impetus for his hometown community and for the local media to assess racial progress. In February 1973, one month after his final game with the Tide, the city of Mobile celebrated "John Mitchell and Bobby McKinney Day," honoring the black star and one of his white senior teammates. Both players received "crimson and white" cars at the dinner held in their honor, and Bryant, the event's guest speaker, effusively praised both players, saying that they had "represented" their home town "very, very well" on and off the football field. When discussing Mitchell's career, Bryant rued that the UA football team had not fielded black athletes "long before" it eventually did. The coach also continued to employ a discourse that minimized racial distinctions among his players. When asked how many black players were on his team, Bryant replied, "None. . . . [W]e don't have any white ones either. We just have players. I just wish it had been that way all along." Mitchell himself expressed his positive feelings regarding his time at the school, saying that he was "readily accepted by the players, coaches, students and fans" and praising Bryant for having a positive influence on his life. Mitchell said his career at the school was full of "great memories."[123]

The press picked up on these positive feelings. In a story in the *Birmingham News* regarding the end of Mitchell's trailblazing career, Van Hoose was delighted to report that "quietly, with dignity, and very effectively" Mitchell had been "a sociological pioneer" on the team. He was also pleased to write that there would be "no book" written by Mitchell to chronicle his experiences because "the trail he blazed . . . completely lacked dramatics." Thus, "no publisher has banged Mitchell's door to commercialize on the popular theme of violence."[124] Clearly, Van Hoose was relieved that the unrest that had occurred at other schools across the country did not take hold at UA. A story in the *Crimson White* about Jackson's and Mitchell's experiences in 1971 and 1972 supported these positive assessments. Jackson said that "for the most part everybody was friendly" during his time at the school. He believed that coaches' emphasis on winning would make discrimination and tokenism on football teams a thing of the past. Mitchell went one step further, saying that the black and white players on the UA team "have a beautiful relationship."[125] These comments must have been heartening to those who looked to football to model blacks and whites working together in an integrated society. Whites who resented radical black activism could get behind black athletes who merged into white-run institutions with little complaint—these players did not need to be corralled by Nixon's call for law and order.

Some were still skeptical. As the regular season came to a close for the 1972 UA squad, *Crimson White* features editor Nathan Turner wrote a column about black students' sense of the campus and its racial climate. He situated their responses in light of the ninth anniversary of Wallace's stand at the schoolhouse door, wondering why it took the university so long to admit black students and how much, or little, racial attitudes had changed in the previous nine years. Although many of the black students he interviewed expressed doubts about the school's racial climate, Turner cited the lawsuit regarding black athletes as proof that progress had been made. At that point, according to an athletics department official, there were eighteen black athletes, including ten on the football team. All ten had "either played or dressed out" that season, including the four black freshmen. But Turner cautioned that some still doubted the university's commitment, believing that black athletes were "being used" or that athletics department officials recruited black athletes only because they realized "that they [could not] win without blacks." Turner saw that skepticism as a sign that black students were still "trying to come to grips with a school which many say has not lived down its past."[126] The worries about black athlete exploitation were very real, and students had apt reasons to be skeptical about the nature of change at UA.

The media's response to a racially charged situation in late September 1972 at nearby Troy State University also suggested some of the limitations of sports for addressing the more complex issues at the heart of the changing civil rights struggle. Six black football players at the school, located approximately 180 miles from Tuscaloosa and 140 miles from Birmingham, had left the team at halftime of a game against Ouachita College, protesting what they believed to be unfair conditions and biased treatment from coaches and athletics officials. Head coach Tom Jones immediately dismissed the players from the team and gave them no opportunity to return—a stance that delighted *Birmingham News* writers Jimmy Bryan and Alf Van Hoose. Describing the behavior of the players as a "mutiny," Bryan insisted that Jones was not being racist in kicking the black players off the team: "Coach Jones," he wrote, "does not judge a man by the color of his skin. He judges him by the color of his blood and backbone." What defined these players was their decision to "quit." Neither Jones nor Bryan took seriously the players' list of grievances—which included unfair distribution of work-study jobs, false statements in recruiting, and inferior medical treatment for the team's black players.[127]

Other (white) observers across the country also enthusiastically supported Jones's decision. In an era when youth activism, and especially black athlete activism, was at an all-time high, Jones proved heroic to many, who likely saw his actions as another example of the "law and order" that President Nixon had promised in his 1968 election campaign. The enthusiastic reactions to

Jones's firm response also fit in well with Nixon's "southern strategy" in the 1972 election, in which the president aggressively courted southern white voters who felt betrayed by desegregation and affirmative action policies.[128] Van Hoose believed that the coach's decision entailed a "landmark stand"— a curious choice of words given Wallace's infamous gesture in the schoolhouse door. To Van Hoose, sports had "shown the way" in a "turbulent era" in American history, and he saw Jones's actions as one more sign of that leadership. Van Hoose cautioned his readers not to interpret his article as "applause for a coach jumping on black athletes." He insisted that he praised Jones for punishing athletes of any color for "trying to test solid rules of conduct" that had been established over the long history of organized sports. Although Van Hoose argued that his enthusiasm for Jones stemmed from the treatment of youth revolt (and on some level, that was surely true), other signs belied that interpretation; in the article, Van Hoose chose coaches Jim Owens at Washington; Ben Schwartzwalder at Syracuse; and Lloyd Eaton, former coach at Wyoming—who all dealt with black athlete uprisings—as people who would have been gratified by Jones's stand.[129] Clearly, racial issues were important to Van Hoose. Despite his plea to read his article differently, one could easily interpret it as a call for white leaders in positions of authority to put blacks back in their "proper" place. Sports had "shown the way" to put any uppity blacks, in any walk of life, in their place.

Still, there were many ways that sports—and Alabama's football team in particular—did offer hope for people concerned about racial integration. When Mitchell narrowly missed earning a spot with the San Francisco 49ers of the National Football League, Bryant offered him a position as an assistant coach—the first black assistant coach at any major university in the South. Mitchell held that position for a number of years and is currently an assistant coach with the NFL's Pittsburgh Steelers. Meanwhile, as increasing numbers of black players joined the Crimson Tide, the team's fortunes rebounded. Although the squad had finished 6–5 in 1969, and 6–4–1 in 1970, disappointing by Bryant's high standards, the first integrated teams of 1971 and 1972 bounced back to 11–1 and 10–2, respectively. One year later, the team would claim a share of the national championship. There was no doubt that black players contributed to that success, but so, too, did Bryant's emphasis on equal treatment. His players consistently recalled the fairness with which he treated black players. Walter Lewis, who was UA's second black quarterback in the early 1980s, said the coach told the players that they "bled the same blood and sweated the same sweat," which helped create "a bond among the players."[130] Ozzie Newsome, who played at UA, had a Hall of Fame career in the NFL, and is currently the general manager of the NFL's Baltimore Ravens, said of Bryant, "[Martin Luther] King preached opportunity . . . but without people like Coach Bryant who gave us the opportunity and really treated us as equals, where would we be?"[131] Bryant's thoroughness in integrating his team—naming black captains, putting black players in key positions, and hiring black assistants (Croom was hired as an assistant not long after Mitchell)—spoke to his sense of fairness and his commitment to winning.[132] It also opened up a number of new opportunities for his black players. As Wilbur Jackson commented in later years, "Being a football player at Alabama puts you into a select network that will help you throughout your adult life."[133]

Of course, those opportunities did not necessarily translate to other black Alabamians or to other African Americans in the South in general. When Mitchell looked back on his first season with the varsity, he was pleased to report that he had "no troubles" at the school but admitted that "being an athlete really helps."[134] And that would be the real challenge for the 1970s and beyond—how to reshape everyday life so that ordinary black citizens could participate equally with their white peers. The black students who sued the school, the black athletes at Troy State University, even radical groups such as the Black Panthers, all pushed for African Americans to enjoy the same standard of living, the same treatment, the same recognition of their past and their culture that most white Americans enjoyed without ever acknowledging their privileged position. Where white newspapers anxiously saw "radical" behavior and "separatist" politics, many African Americans saw the obliteration of their cultural institutions and the loss of positions of prestige to black professionals—from high school football coaches to university presidents and everything in between. How could people extend the positive treatment and experiences of Mitchell, Jackson, Newsome, and the other black Alabama football players to more people in the black community, to a wider circle? These athletes entered into one old-boy network and benefited. But that was only one of many such networks that gave white men a leg up on their competition. Would white men in the worlds of business and politics be so agreeable? The effusive praise for Tom Jones and the white backlash in the 1972 presidential election—which rolled back many affirmative action policies and other programs designed to help minorities—suggested that those transformations remained unlikely.

In fact, the experiences of the UA football team and the changing climate of racial politics both suggested that sports failed to model an equal opportunity society, something that many blacks and whites appeared not to recognize. If increasing numbers of black writers and commentators were critical of the broader implications of sports, others continued to see integrated sports as a sign of progress in broader life. These supporters included many of the privileged athletes themselves, who did not seem to get that they were exceptions to the rule. Many white sportswriters missed this point as well. When *Crimson White* sports editor Rick Young argued in March 1972 that the integrated Alabama football team showed sports to be "one of the perilously few segments of society that shows us integration works, and how it works," he was merely echoing the words of countless commentators before him.[135] That old familiar dream of sports as a color-blind meritocracy proved too appealing to let go.

Conclusion

What We Talk about When We Talk about Sports

The centrality of sports to debates over race and equality would continue in the years after 1973, but the early 1970s marked an important era of transition—with the integration of the last SEC schools, racial segregation in big-time college athletics (at least among players) had ended. This era also saw the gradual demise of the modern civil rights movement, as the fractures exposed in debates over affirmative action and black nationalism proved too wide to heal entirely. Nonetheless, the movement wrought remarkable changes in American civic life. African Americans could no longer be denied access to public spaces because of their race, including business establishments and modes of transportation. Voting rights, too, became a reality for all Americans, regardless of race and ethnicity, as the federal government stepped in to ensure that voter registration practices were fair and terror free. Culturally, Black Power ushered in a new awareness of black beauty and racial pride that affected mainstream media coverage, advertising, television and film depictions, and countless other cultural outlets, although troublesome stereotypes remained. On the whole, though, these sweeping changes essentially sounded the death knell of the Jim Crow South, that arbitrary and surprisingly powerful set of rules and customs that had affected so many Americans across the country for more than one hundred years.

Although racial integration had come to athletics and to many other aspects of American life, much work remained to be done. Black players continued to face racial barriers at the collegiate level, including coaches who restricted them from certain positions, fans who continued to cling to negative stereotypes of black men, and university officials who welcomed black athletes' financial contributions to the school via sports but who made no effort to ensure their education. While many still turned to sports as proof of the American dream of equal opportunity, the same frustrations reappeared time and again.

Leadership positions in college sports proved to be a particularly thorny issue. Although John Mitchell became an assistant coach with Alabama in 1973 and parlayed that experience into coaching jobs at other schools and in the NFL, most black athletes were not so fortunate. The traditional network of white college administrators and coaches made available few opportunities for black players when their careers ended. As of March 2010, only 13 out of 119 Division IA college football teams had black head coaches. When organizations such as the Black Coaches and Administrators (BCA) called attention to this dismal record and asked that universities with openings for head coaches interview at least one minority coach, public response again showed how sports issues could channel debates regarding equality in American life.[1] On one sports-themed Internet message board, the call for interviews of black candidates led to an impassioned discussion. One reader lamented that the BCA was asking for a "double standard," arguing that if schools were required to interview African Americans for coaching positions, "then there should be requirements on offering scholarships to white players." Others defended the organization, insisting that granting interviews did not infringe on whites' rights and that the process was one small step that schools could take to overcome the "institutionalized belief that White-Americans are somehow better suited to be head coaches than are African-Americans."[2] These debates highlighted the ongoing vitality of college athletics to channel anxieties and aspirations regarding American democratic society and suggested the barriers black men face in securing leadership positions in the realm of athletics and beyond.

New bodies and institutions contributed to the dialogue as well. With the passage of Title IX of the Educational Amendments Act in 1972, Congress mandated that schools fund men's and women's on-campus activities—including athletics—equally. Although the implementation of Title IX has been controversial, and spending on men's athletic programs continues to outpace funding of women's sports, the legislation nonetheless spurred the creation of women's college teams across the country, providing numerous opportunities previously out of reach.[3] One sign of this change appeared in a brief November 1972 story in the *Crimson White*. That month, UA approved a budget for women's sports for the first time in the school's history, allocating the laughably small sum of $13,000 for that purpose.[4] As schools across the nation slowly began to implement women's sports programs, these teams and athletes channeled new debates regarding gender and sexual equality. The spring 2007 controversy surrounding radio talk show host Don Imus, who called the Rutgers women's basketball players "nappy-headed hos," spoke to the ways women's athletics could be the site for discourse regarding the intersections of race, sex, gender, and even class. Imus's comments lampooned the women players for being unfeminine, called attention to their race, and simultaneously poked fun at what he saw as their lower-class appearance.[5] The outrage in the mainstream media showed that such observations would not go uncontested.

As these and numerous other contemporary examples suggest, the debates over American equality—and the centrality of sports to those discussions— continue on into the present day. Because the model of the level playing field has had such long-lasting resonance in American culture, and because economic, racial, and gender inequalities persist (and, in some cases, have become even more extreme), many people continue to turn to sports as a model for American society, as a realization of the ideal of equal opportunity. The varied case studies of this project suggest that college sports in particular can work well to channel discussions regarding equality and opportunity. Deeply resonant in local communities, and free from the relatively abstract language characteristic of the realms of law and public policy, integrated team college sports inspired dialogue regarding race relations in a variety of ways.

First, these pioneering athletes provided specific examples for people to articulate their beliefs regarding the contours of American democratic society. When Kathryn Harris pondered how her fellow Lawrence residents could applaud Wilt Chamberlain and Maurice King on the court and then refuse other African Americans service in local restaurants, she turned to sport to make her point because of its popularity, no doubt, but also because of its long-standing ideals of fair play. Harris had specific material with which to grapple with the racial paradoxes in American life—the embrace of African Americans in one arena in society and their utter rejection in another. Warren Morton's response to the USC homecoming display in 1939, that it reflected the trials faced by minorities in American society, similarly showcased the potential for sports to channel intelligent discussion regarding the nation's racial politics. Sports provided the common ground for Morton to critique a nation he saw falling short of its egalitarian ideals.

College athletes also opened up spaces for people's beliefs to be momentarily suspended—and perhaps lastingly altered—as observers cheered athletes from groups they might have otherwise disparaged. Although some have rightfully expressed skepticism over the capacity of sports to make bigots into racial liberals, there were moments that suggested sports could effect change in people's attitudes. John Mitchell's welcome in a Tuscaloosa watering hole was perhaps one small step to a greater recognition of black male achievement.

Charlie Scott's hopes for integrated basketball—that white children pretending to be black players would have lasting change—may well have been valid, as the younger generation certainly accepted changing racial politics much more quickly than their parents.[6] Indeed, as *Crimson White* sports editor Rick Young noted in March 1972, sports could model even prosaic advances in daily life. Young contrasted the ongoing tensions over the busing of students to integrate public elementary and high schools with the accepted busing taking place in sports—of integrated squads, such as UA's, traveling together to games. As whites in the North and South fought school busing and affirmative action vigorously, and as black activists struggled to retain cultural institutions and gain access to new economic opportunities, sports held out some hope. They taught Americans, as Young noted, "that different races can ride the bus together."[7]

The discussion of these pioneering college athletes also inspired conversations regarding racial equality because they illuminated the players' struggles, and in the process called attention to the barriers African Americans faced in other areas of life. Clearly, the racial vitriol endured by these players spoke to the extreme verbal, emotional, and physical abuse encountered by African Americans across the nation, even if the mainstream media failed to report these instances as vigorously as the black press. But even more subtly, these athletes showed the varied pressures and issues facing the black community, for those attuned to such things. Strode's economic plight, which drove him to leave school early, clearly revealed the economic distress facing many in the black community. That his brother and father could not find work, in particular, spoke to the particular burdens faced by black men who for so long had been denied employment and access to the role of male breadwinner. Similarly, when the national newswires reported that southern basketball players Charlie Scott, Mike Malloy, and Charles Davis all faced pressure to represent their school and team while still being "loyal" to their race, they inevitably called attention to the changing racial politics of the 1960s. Readers had to engage, on some level, with the tension between integrationist politics and that of black pride and black nationalism.

And, finally, the achievements of these college sports teams proved that blacks and whites could work together to attain success. In all of these cases, black and white athletes came together to achieve a common goal—team success in the highest levels of college athletic competition. Paul Robeson and his white teammates took Rutgers football to new heights, earning national acclaim. The multiracial, multiethnic 1939 UCLA football team achieved great success, landing near the top in national polls and generating excitement across the country. Wilt Chamberlain and Charlie Scott led their mostly white teams to berths in the final rounds of the NCAA men's basketball tournaments. And Alabama's integrated football team returned the squad to national prominence, playing for the national championship in the second year that John Mitchell and Wilbur Jackson were eligible for varsity competition. For those who hoped that sports offered a model for broader society, there was hope to be found in these accomplishments. On some level, the team success enjoyed in all five of these case studies validated arguments that blacks and whites could work together. Success in these sports demanded more than just occasional games together—teammates had to practice countless hours with one another, travel for games together, and share rooms on the road. On the field, these team sports required players to work in concert with one another. Just as Robeson had to block for his Rutgers teammates running the football, Wilt Chamberlain depended on his fellow Jayhawks to pass him the ball in prime scoring position. None of these athletes could do it alone. When these players put aside racial differences, they provided visual evidence contradicting the cries of bigots who said racial integration could not work.

But the limitations faced by these pioneers over the course of the twentieth century also revealed the inadequacies of college sports to deal with some of the complicated issues related to the ideal of equality—issues that continue to divide Americans. Coaches who recruited black players simply to remain competitive could, and did, exploit black athletes, failing to support these players' academic endeavors and ignoring them when their playing careers ended. Although NCAA statistics indicate that student-athletes graduate at a higher rate than students on the whole, there have been a number of examples of prominent basketball and football programs that have succeeded athletically while graduating meager numbers of their players.[8] One 2007 study conducted by the University of Central Florida's Institute for Diversity and Ethics in Sports revealed that prominent NCAA basketball programs—including the national runner-up that year, the Ohio State University—had four-year graduation rates of 10 percent or lower.[9] Stories such as that of Creighton University basketball player Kevin Ross, who, in 1982, after four years at the school, was unable to read, revealed that exploitation of athletes continued beyond the 1960s.[10] As cultural analyst Nelson George noted in *Elevating the Game*, "For the scores of moneyed NBA superstars there are literally hundreds of . . . African-American men who are undereducated by teachers yet advanced so their school can reap financial or promotional benefit."[11] Even small-college athletic programs outside the glitz and big-money of Division IA sports have seen their athletes underperform academically.[12] Countless athletes also ended up in poverty after their college careers, unable to use their sports background to find gainful employment.

At the same time that college athletics failed—and continues to fail—black players with regard to their academic progress and postcareer life, some white fans continue to praise black athletic achievement but circumscribe its meanings, falling back on stereotypes of intellectual inferiority and primitive passions. Charlie Scott's story offers a cautionary lesson in this regard. The fact that the same fan could view Scott as "God" after one victory and claim that "niggers choke in the clutch" after one loss reflected the persistence of long-held stereotypes. These dual readings of athletic achievements did not end with the integration of professional and college sports. Contemporary sports coverage, especially reader feedback on Internet message boards and comment sections, is replete with comments linking black athletes to a wide range of supposedly inherent failings. When ESPN.com columnist L. Z. Granderson penned a column criticizing sportswriters and fans for stereotyping both black and white athletes in regard to their athletic skills, a number of fans responded positively, but many others missed the central message. One respondent, FYE34, argued that "whites are more likely to hustle" than black players, evoking the old familiar stereotype of hardworking whites versus naturally gifted but lazy blacks.[13] That these and other stereotypes persist in public discourse reveals the limits for integrated sports competition to undo long-held beliefs and prejudices.

Furthermore, the esteem and opportunities given to athletes did not necessarily translate to other African Americans. Athletic success did little to rectify centuries of poverty in the black community. The income gap between whites and blacks, on the whole, remains wide, a reminder that centuries of discrimination cannot be undone simply by removing legal and political barriers to black opportunity. Although prominent black athletes have cashed in on their stardom with huge paychecks and glamorous lives, African Americans as a group have continued to languish behind white Americans in economic standing.[14] When *Forbes* magazine unveiled its list of the top ten highest-paid athletes in the world in 2011, African Americans occupied the top three spots, with golfer Tiger Woods and basketball players Kobe Bryant and LeBron James heading the list.[15] And yet the accompanying *Forbes* story failed to note the extreme gap between these super-earners and ordinary African Americans. While athletes such as Woods, Bryant, and James have earned considerable mainstream media coverage, the discussion of these athletes' fabulous wealth rarely spurs dialogue regarding the ongoing problems of the income gap between blacks and whites. Even stories assessing black athletes' rise from poverty to wealth often celebrate the individual's successful story but offer little sense of the complexities that account for the high rate of poverty in the African American community. Gawking at black athletes' lavish homes and expensive cars does not, and cannot, engage the struggles that ordinary African Americans face in their attempts to rise in American society.

Further, the hopes that the success of integrated team sports would enable all black men to access all the privileges of U.S. male citizenship have been dashed. Many African Americans, especially in the black press, had hoped that athletics would enable new models of black masculinity, with increased access to the rights and responsibilities of manhood. All five of the case studies in this book feature athletes who believed that would happen—from Robeson at Rutgers to John Mitchell and his peers at Alabama. However, a number of facts, and the nature of public discourse regarding sports, appear to undermine that faith. As historian Michele Wallace has argued, although black men achieved more cultural prominence and could more readily date and marry white women as a result of the civil rights movement, one of the most important markers of manhood—economic independence—remained elusive.[16] Furthermore, according to 2006 U.S. Department of Justice statistics, one in every fifteen adult black men, and one in every nine black men between ages twenty and thirty-four, was in prison, compared to the national average of one in every ninety-nine adults.[17] Although John Hoberman's *Darwin's Athletes* inspired much controversy, he makes a valid point that the focus on black male athletes "has done much to perpetuate the invisibility of the black middle class."[18] Instead of sports opening doors to other professions— to black doctors, lawyers, and professors—black male athletes largely remain the exception. The success of John Mitchell at Alabama, in other words, did not lead to a flood of black doctors in that state or in the nation at large.

Depictions of black athletes have also continued to lean heavily on stereotyped representations of black men. In his essay about 1960s baseball star Dick Allen, historian Matthew Frye Jacobson calls attention to "an imagined political spectrum of 'good' and 'bad' Negroes" in the white media. This limited vision of black manhood depicted a black athlete as a "bad boy" if he dared to claim that race *mattered* in how people treated him or responded to him.[19] That attitude continues to inflect coverage of contemporary sports stars, as can be seen in the disdainful coverage of athletes such as LeBron James, who suggested that the negative response to his decision to switch teams stemmed in part from racial power dynamics.[20]

Even earnest attempts to engage issues of black manliness through sports have missed the mark. In the spring of 2011, ESPN Films released a documentary called *The Fab Five*, which detailed the college careers of the five extraordinarily talented black basketball players who attended the University of Michigan in the early 1990s. The film occasioned controversy because in it, one of the players, former NBA professional Jalen Rose, indicated that he resented Duke University because the school recruited only black players who were "Uncle Toms." Grant Hill, a former Duke player and NBA star, responded with an editorial in the *New York Times* in which he criticized Rose for denigrating African Americans "from two-parent, middle-class families." Sports again served as a vehicle for discussing issues related to manliness and citizenship, but the back-and-forth between Hill and Rose failed to illuminate the intense pressures faced by black men as a result of systematic discrimination and oppression. And while Hill cautioned Rose to "avoid stereotyping me and others . . . in much the same way so many people stereotyped" Rose and his teammates "for their appearance and swagger," he did not make clear that the image created by Rose and his teammates constituted a kind of activism.[21] Rose and the other members of the Fab Five deliberately challenged conventions of propriety as a way to affirm their pride and self-direction. In a way, they followed football star Jim Brown's sense of his responsibility "in a culture where black manhood has been kicked around and threatened for generations" to "tell the truth like I see it" and to "walk tall."[22] A more thorough analysis of this story would have involved an engagement with the models of manhood available, or unavailable, to black male public figures. After all, some scholars, such as Todd Boyd, have found empowerment in the "nigga" persona embodied by the Fab Five and some professional black athletes—a tough, working-class black man who refuses to cow to white norms. However, others have fretted that depictions of black male athletes as hypersexualized and brazen individuals harms perceptions of black men more generally.[23] Those kinds of debates remain largely unaddressed in the popular media coverage of sports.

Questions of leadership remain especially thorny issues that have been extremely difficult to resolve through sports. In nearly all major organized sports leagues—at the college and professional levels—significant gaps remain between blacks and whites in leadership positions, including head coaches, athletics directors, and front-office positions. The dearth of black head coaches in college football is perhaps the most extreme example of this trend, but it is by no means the only one. As of the 2009–2010 academic year, minorities accounted for only 7.4 percent of athletics directors at NCAA Division 1 schools. Although the number of black head coaches in basketball is significantly better, with 21 percent, much work remains to be done.[24] When white Los Angeles Dodgers executive Al Campanis, a former teammate of Jackie Robinson, infamously observed in 1987 that blacks "may not have some of the necessities to be, let's say, a field manager, or, perhaps, a general manager," he undercut the lofty hopes black leaders had for athletic achievement. Campanis acknowledged black excellence on the field, but he believed it unlikely that African Americans could effectively assume leadership positions.[25] Although Campanis's remarks incited a firestorm that led to his dismissal, and in the process generated discussion of the position of black coaches, his attitude spoke to the ways in which white fans and executives could accept black athletic achievement without embracing black leadership. In all these ways, the level playing field of sports remained a utopia whose example could not easily be duplicated in other aspects of American life.

When Americans talked, and continue to talk, about sports, then, they almost inevitably engage issues of racial equality, fairness, and justice. And yet these discussions, illuminating as they can be, are not a shortcut for earnest discussions of policy and practice. Sports may help Americans think about fairness and equality, but the model of sports cannot be made to stand in for the complexities of modern American life. As these numerous examples show, just because people praised sports as a model—or criticized it as a model—did not mean they were necessarily saying the same thing. The danger in channeling discussions of racial politics through sports is a loss of subtlety, a missed opportunity for earnest discussions of the difficult issues that continue to cloud the quest for equality in American life.

It was not enough to say that Paul Robeson's recognition as an All-American athlete showed the capacity of sports to model a merit-based society in the 1910s. As we have seen, he had to undergo far more challenges than his white peers and received far less recognition than he deserved. And it is still not enough to say that sports show the nation how the American democratic system "works." The discourse surrounding college football and basketball has not engaged, and cannot possibly engage, the complex issues at the heart of American inequality. But it can help. As we appreciate brilliance on the field and court, as we celebrate mixed-race bodies moving in concert with one another, with black hands high-fiving white hands, let us not forget the stories that place each individual in context. When we talk about the big games afterward, let us remember the millions living in poverty, the ones still shut out of leadership opportunities, and the persistence of stereotypes. We don't have to stop loving sports or celebrating its beauties, as long as we keep our eye on a more compelling goal than a game-winning score. And, most important, as long as we don't stop talking about those larger issues once the games end.

Fundamentally, we need to recognize that President Johnson's warnings to white America about the need for affirmative action, about the many steps necessary before African Americans would be capable to compete on equal terms with whites, retain their currency in contemporary times. Although black athletes and entertainers represent some of the most popular and beloved celebrities in American culture, their exceptional success does not mean that all is equal in American life. In truth, the ideal of equal opportunity will never be realized. There will never be a starting line where everyone in society, regardless of race, family wealth, ethnicity, and religion, is on equal footing. But sports offer a sign of how change can occur, how progress can be made. As black college athletes took to fields and courts previously restricted to them, their bodies spoke to the possibilities of transcending barriers to equal opportunity. By chipping away at other examples of discrimination—such as stacking, exclusion from certain positions, and leadership roles on and off the field—these athletes modeled the exhausting, never-ending effort required to make the playing field of sports less uneven. They represented, and continue to represent, the long struggle to make American society live up to its egalitarian ideals. If we take that single-minded pursuit, through discrimination, setbacks, media bias, and other obstacles, and move it *outside* the realm of sports, we may yet come closer to that elusive ideal of equality.

Notes

INTRODUCTION

1. "Editorials: Football Honor Roll," *The Crisis* 46, no. 11 (November 1939): 337.

2. Throughout this book, I use the term *integration* to refer to the process by which black athletes fought for the right to play for athletics teams at predominantly white universities and colleges. Although some civil rights scholars argue that *desegregation* is a more appropriate term, because true and equitable integration remain an unrealized ideal in American life, most of the commentators I discuss in this project believed in, and articulated, a vision of racial integration. Indeed, that faith, as expressed through college sports, lies at the heart of this study.

3. A number of works consider the cultural implications of popular entertainment. Especially noteworthy are Elliott J. Gorn, *The Manly Art: Bare-Knuckle Prize Fighting in America* (Ithaca, NY: Cornell University Press, 1986); John F. Kasson, *Amusing the Million: Coney Island at the Turn of the Century* (New York: Hill and Wang, 1978); W. T. Lhamon, *Deliberate Speed: The Origins of a Cultural Style in the American 1950s* (Washington, DC: Smithsonian Institution Press, 1990); Lary May, *Screening Out the Past: The Birth of Mass Culture and the Motion Picture Industry* (New York: Oxford University Press, 1980); Kathy Peiss, *Cheap Amusements: Working Women and Leisure in Turn-of-the-Century New York* (Philadelphia: Temple University Press, 1986); Lynn Spigel, *Make Room for TV: Television and the Family Ideal in Postwar America* (Chicago: University of Chicago Press, 1992); and Warren I. Susman, *Culture as History: The Transformation of American Society in the Twentieth Century* (Washington, DC: Smithsonian Institution Press, 2003).

4. Many excellent scholarly works address the confluence of sports and race. See, for example, Joseph Dorinson, "Black Heroes in Sport: From Jack Johnson to Muhammad Ali," *Journal of Popular Culture* 31, no. 3 (1997): 115–135; D. Stanley Eitzen, *Fair and Foul: Beyond the Myths and Paradoxes of Sport*, 3rd ed. (New York: Rowman and Littlefield, 2006); Elliott Gorn and Warren Goldstein, *A Brief History of American Sports* (New York: Hill and Wang, 1993); C. Richard King and Charles Fruehling Springwood, *Beyond the Cheers: Race as Spectacle in College Sport* (Albany: State University of New York Press, 2001); Patrick B. Miller, *Sporting World of the Modern South* (Chicago: University of Illinois Press, 2002); Patrick B. Miller and David K. Wiggins, eds., *Sport and the Color Line: Black Athletes and Race*

Relations in Twentieth-Century America (New York: Routledge, 2004); Jules Tygiel, *Baseball's Great Experiment: Jackie Robinson and His Legacy* (New York: Oxford University Press, 1983); Jules Tygiel, *Extra Bases: Reflections on Jackie Robinson, Race, and Baseball History* (Lincoln: University of Nebraska Press, 2002); and David K. Wiggins, *Glory Bound: Black Athletes in a White America* (Syracuse, NY: Syracuse University Press, 1997).

5. John Bloom and Michael Nevin Willard, eds., *Sports Matters: Race, Recreation, and Culture* (New York: New York University Press, 2002), 2. For a good summary of some of the principal works on sports and race, see Jeffrey Sammons, "'Race' and Sport: A Critical, Historical Examination," *Journal of Sport History* 21, no. 3 (Fall 1994): 203–278. See also Steven A. Reiss, "The New Sport History," *Reviews in American History* 18, no. 3 (September 1990): 311–325.

6. Bloom and Willard, *Sports Matters*, 2; John Hoberman, *Darwin's Athletes: How Sports Has Damaged Black America and Preserved the Myth of Race* (New York: Houghton Mifflin, 1997), xiv. Hoberman's book—particularly his critique of the black middle and upper class—generated a firestorm of controversy and protest. For an effective critique, see Jeffrey T. Sammons, "A Proportionate and Measured Response to the Provocation That Is *Darwin's Athletes*," *Journal of Sport History* 24, no. 3 (1997): 378–388. For examples of other scholars and commentators skeptical of the ability of sports to change racial beliefs, see Robert Lipsyte, *SportsWorld: An American Dreamland* (New York: Quadrangle, 1975); William C. Rhoden, *Forty Million Dollar Slaves: The Rise, Fall, and Redemption of the Black Athlete* (New York: Crown, 2006); Earl Smith, *Race, Sport and the American Dream* (Durham, NC: Carolina Academic Press, 2007); Donald Spivey, "The Black Athlete in Big-Time Intercollegiate Sports, 1941–1968," *Phylon* 44, no. 2 (June 1983): 116–125; and Neil J. Sullivan, "Baseball and Race: The Limits of Competition," *Journal of Negro History* 83, no. 3 (1998): 168–177.

7. Book-length treatments include Nelson George, *Elevating the Game: Black Men and Basketball* (Lincoln: University of Nebraska Press, 1992); Kurt Edward Kemper, *College Football and American Culture in the Cold War Era* (Urbana: University of Illinois Press, 2009); Charles H. Martin, *Benching Jim Crow: The Rise and Fall of the Color Line in Southern College Sports, 1890–1980* (Urbana: University of Illinois Press, 2010); Michael Oriard, *Bowled Over: Big-Time College Football from the Sixties to the BCS Era* (Chapel Hill: University of North Carolina Press, 2009); and Rhoden, *Forty Million Dollar Slaves*. Hollywood films include Boaz Yakin, dir., *Remember the Titans* (Buena Vista Pictures, 2001); James Gartner, dir., *Glory Road* (Buena Vista Pictures, 2006); and Gary Fleder, dir., *The Express* (Universal Pictures, 2008).

8. See Sheila Tully Boyle and Andrew Bunie, *Paul Robeson: The Years of Promise and Achievement* (Amherst: University of Massachusetts Press, 2001); Lloyd Brown, *The Young Paul Robeson: "On My Journey Now"* (Boulder, CO: Westview Press, 1997); and Martin Duberman, *Paul Robeson* (New York: Knopf, 1989).

9. Demas focuses on the team in his article, "'On the Threshold of Broad and Rich Football Pastures': Integrated College Football at UCLA, 1938–1941," in *Horsehide, Pigskin, Oval Tracks and Apple Pie: Essays on Sports and American Culture*, ed. James A. Vlasich (Jefferson, NC: McFarland, 2006), 86–103. He also discusses the team in his recent book, *Integrating the Gridiron: Black Civil Rights and American College Football* (New Brunswick, NJ: Rutgers University Press, 2010). Oriard mentions the team briefly in *King Football: Sport and Spectacle in the Golden Age of Radio and Newsreels, Movies and Magazines, the Weekly and the Daily Press* (Chapel Hill: University of North Carolina Press, 2001).

10. Aram Goudsouzian, "'Can Basketball Survive Wilt Chamberlain?': The Kansas Years of Wilt the Stilt," *Kansas History: A Journal of the Central Plains* 28 (Autumn 2005): 150–173.

11. Barry Jacobs, *Across the Line: Profiles in Courage: Tales of the First Black Players in the ACC and SEC* (Guilford, CT: Lyons Press, 2008).

12. See John David Briley, *Career in Crisis: Paul "Bear" Bryant and the 1971 Season of Change* (Macon, GA: Mercer University Press, 2006); Andrew Doyle, "An Atheist in

Alabama Is Someone Who Doesn't Believe in Bear Bryant: A Symbol for an Embattled South," in *Sporting World of the Modern South*, ed. Patrick B. Miller (Chicago: University of Illinois Press, 2002), 247–275; and Don Yaeger, with Sam Cunningham and John Papadakis, *Turning of the Tide: How One Game Changed the South* (New York: Center Street, 2006).

13. For a concise summary of the particular issues facing black men, see Steve Estes, *I Am a Man! Race, Manhood, and the Civil Rights Movement* (Chapel Hill: University of North Carolina Press, 2005), 5–7. See also Gail Bederman, *Manliness and Civilization: A Cultural History of Gender and Race in the United States, 1880–1917* (Chicago: University of Chicago Press, 1995); Robert Staples, *Black Masculinity: The Black Male's Role in American Society* (San Francisco: Black Scholar Press, 1982); and Michele Wallace, *Black Macho and the Myth of the Superwoman* (New York: Dial Press, 1978).

14. Pamela Grundy, *Learning to Win: Sports, Education, and Social Change in Twentieth-Century North Carolina* (Chapel Hill: University of North Carolina Press, 2001), 282.

15. Judith N. Shklar, *American Citizenship: The Quest for Inclusion* (Cambridge, MA: Harvard University Press, 1991), 2. By *standing*, Shklar means "one's place in a hierarchical society"; for Americans, "their relative social place, defined by income, occupation, and education." Citizenship as standing requires at least "a minimum of social dignity," or what I have referred to as "respect."

16. Estes, *I Am a Man!* 7.

17. For more on the history of the black press, see Stanley Nelson, dir., *The Black Press: Soldiers without Swords* (San Francisco: California Newsreel [distributor], 1998); Armistead S. Pride and Clint C. Wilson II, *A History of the Black Press* (Washington, DC: Howard University Press, 1997); and Todd Vogel, ed., *The Black Press: New Literary and Historical Essays* (New Brunswick, NJ: Rutgers University Press, 2001).

18. Patrick B. Miller, "To 'Bring the Race Along Rapidly': Sport, Student Culture, and Educational Mission at Historically Black Colleges during the Interwar Years," in *Sporting World of the Modern South*, ed. Patrick B. Miller (Chicago: University of Illinois Press, 2002), 129–152 (quotation from p. 131).

19. Bernard Williams, "The Idea of Equality," in *In the Beginning Was the Deed: Realism and Moralism in Political Argument*, ed. Geoffrey Hawthorn (Princeton, NJ: Princeton University Press, 2005), 97–114 (quotation from p. 100).

20. B. Williams, "The Idea of Equality," 109. Noted political theorist Ronald Dworkin makes a similar point about equality. In *Sovereign Virtue*, he writes, "equality is a contested concept: people who praise or disparate it disagree about what it is they are praising or disparaging." Ronald Dworkin, *Sovereign Virtue: The Theory and Practice of Equality* (Cambridge, MA: Harvard University Press, 2000), 2.

21. This example is akin to the definition outlined by economist and political theorist John Roemer. He writes, "Thus, there is, in the notion of equality of opportunity, a 'before' and an 'after': before the competition starts, opportunities must be equalized, by social intervention if need be, but after it begins, individuals are on their own. The different views of equal opportunity can be characterized according to where they place the starting gate which separates 'before' from 'after.'" John E. Roemer, *Equality of Opportunity* (Cambridge, MA: Harvard University Press, 1998), 2.

CHAPTER 1

1. Lester A. Walton, "Robeson Latest Football Star," *New York Age*, November 29, 1917, p. 6.

2. Clifford Putney, *Muscular Christianity: Manhood and Sports in Protestant America, 1880–1920* (Cambridge, MA: Harvard University Press, 2001), 2.

3. Ibid., 1.

4. See Gail Bederman, *Manliness and Civilization: A Cultural History of Gender and Race in the United States, 1880–1917* (Chicago: University of Chicago Press, 1995), 4; Peter

Filene, *Him/Her/Self: Gender Identities in Modern America*, 3rd ed. (Baltimore: Johns Hopkins University Press, 1998), 74–122; and John F. Kasson, *Houdini, Tarzan, and the Perfect Man: The White Male Body and the Challenge of Modernity in America* (New York: Hill and Wang, 2001).

5. See Martin Summers, *Manliness and Its Discontents: The Black Middle Class and the Transformation of Masculinity, 1900–1930* (Chapel Hill: University of North Carolina Press, 2004); and Warren Susman, "'Personality' and the Making of Twentieth-Century Culture," in *Culture as History: The Transformation of American Society in the Twentieth Century* (Washington, DC: Smithsonian Institution Press, 2003), 271–286.

6. Patrick B. Miller, "To 'Bring the Race Along Rapidly': Sport, Student Culture, and Educational Mission at Historically Black Colleges during the Interwar Years," in *Sporting World of the Modern South*, ed. Patrick B. Miller (Chicago: University of Illinois Press, 2002), 131.

7. See Al-Tony Gilmore, *Bad Nigger! The National Impact of Jack Johnson* (Port Washington, NY: Kennikat Press, 1975); Thomas R. Hietala, *The Fight of the Century: Jack Johnson, Joe Louis, and the Struggle for Racial Equality* (Armonk, NY: Sharpe, 2002); Randy Roberts, *Papa Jack: Jack Johnson and the Era of White Hopes* (New York: Free Press, 1983); and Geoffrey C. Ward, *Unforgivable Blackness: The Rise and Fall of Jack Johnson* (New York: Knopf, 2004).

8. Bederman, *Manliness and Civilization*, 5.

9. Ibid., 42.

10. Putney, *Muscular Christianity*, 163.

11. See Wanda Ellen Wakefield, *Playing to Win: Sports and the American Military, 1898–1945* (Albany: State University of New York Press, 1997), 6–7. Some took this belief in the wartime practicality of sports even further; one commentator, for example, believed that throwing a baseball was good practice for tossing a hand grenade. In some baseball games in army camps, players for both teams wore gas masks, to diminish their fear of gas and get them used to performing while wearing them. See Wakefield, *Playing to Win*, 26.

12. See Wakefield, *Playing to Win*, 12–14.

13. See Mark Ellis, *Race, War, and Surveillance: African Americans and the United States Government during World War I* (Bloomington: Indiana University Press, 2001), 4–14 (quotation from p. 13). See also Piero Gleijeses, "African Americans and the War against Spain," in *A Question of Manhood: A Reader in U.S. Black Men's History and Masculinity*, vol. 2, *The 19th Century: From Emancipation to Jim Crow*, ed. Earnestine Jenkins and Darlene Clark Hine (Bloomington: Indiana University Press, 2001), 320–346.

14. Wakefield, *Playing to Win*, 20–21.

15. I have focused on four different African American publications: the *New York Age*, which covered Robeson's and Pollard's exploits largely because they played in the New York area and were thus a local attraction; the *Crisis*, the official voice of the NAACP, which was white-owned but was edited by noted black leader W.E.B. Du Bois and purported, at least, to speak for and to African Americans; and two national black newspapers, the *Baltimore Afro-American* and the *Chicago Defender*.

16. In the local community, I have used the Rutgers College student newspaper, the *Targum*, the New Brunswick (N.J.) *Daily Home News*, letters of university administrators, scrapbooks, and yearbooks. I have also analyzed three mainstream papers from New York: the *Tribune*, which covered sports in the most depth of the New York papers; the *Times*; and the *Sun*. I have also noted articles from other white publications, including newspapers from other cities and alumni magazines.

17. Martin Duberman, *Paul Robeson* (New York: Alfred A. Knopf, 1989), 15.

18. Enrollment totals fluctuated during Robeson's four years at the school, with the number of students never reaching six hundred. Two other black students attended the school alongside Robeson in later years, but the school's all-male environment and lack of racial diversity made the campus a space dominated by white masculinity. For enrollment

totals, see *Rutgers College Catalogue for 1915–1916* (New Brunswick, NJ: Self-published, 1916), 266, and subsequent volumes.

19. Robeson originally related this account of his attempts to join the Rutgers team in a 1944 article in the *New York Times*. See Robert van Gelder, "Robeson Remembers," *New York Times*, January 16, 1944, p. X1. When this account was published, Robeson's teammates denied the charges, believing that Robeson had been treated the same as any other "scrub" attempting to make the squad. Duberman contends that the evidence supports Robeson's version of events. See Duberman, *Paul Robeson*, 20–21.

20. Eslanda Goode Robeson, *Paul Robeson, Negro* (New York: Harper, 1930), 30.

21. Kimmel argues that while many feminist scholars have seen in American manhood a "drive for power, for domination, for control," anxiety was actually more characteristic of white manliness. Indeed, Kimmel sees "the fear of others dominating . . . [or] having power or control over" white men as being a more apt description of American manliness. See Michael Kimmel, *Manhood in America: A Cultural History* (New York: Free Press, 1996), 6.

22. M. A. Blake to William H. S. Demarest, October 23, 1917, Records of the Rutgers College Office of the President (William H. S. Demarest) 1890–1928, Special Collections and University Archives, Rutgers University Libraries, Box 3, folder 36. See also M. A. Blake to William H. S. Demarest, December 10, 1917, Demarest Papers, Box 3, folder 36.

23. M. A. Blake to William H. S. Demarest, October 29, 1917, Demarest Papers, Box 3, folder 36.

24. See "President's Statement," Celebration: 150th Anniversary, 1916–1918, Demarest Papers, Box 6, folder 18. See also "Rutgers College, 1915–1918," in Duberman, *Paul Robeson*, 19–30.

25. See, for example, "Rutgers 13, Washington and Lee 13," *Targum*, October 18, 1916, pp. 40–41.

26. Duberman, *Paul Robeson*, 23. According to Fritz Pollard, Robeson "was still mad as anything" about the Washington and Lee game when Rutgers and Brown squared off against one another the following week, even though he often faced other racial slights such as segregated eating establishments while traveling with the football team. See Sheila Tully Boyle and Andrew Bunie, *Paul Robeson: The Years of Promise and Achievement* (Amherst: University of Massachusetts Press, 2001), 54–55, 60.

27. James D. Carr to William H. S. Demarest, June 6, 1919, Demarest Papers, Box 43, folder 6.

28. For a good account of the decision to sit Robeson for the game, see Boyle and Bunie, *Paul Robeson*, 59.

29. Carr to Demarest, June 6, 1919. Demarest responded to Carr's letter, writing that he was "sorry that there was any incident such as you relate." He emphasized "the highest regard" that people at the school had for Robeson, noting that "if there was a single untoward incident in his four year's record, I am sorry." William H. S. Demarest to James D. Carr, June 16, 1919, Demarest Papers, Box 43, folder 6.

30. Contrary to some published accounts, Robeson lived on campus with his fellow white students. Although some, including Robeson's son Paul Robeson, Jr., and his eulogist, Bishop J. Clinton Hoggard, indicated that Robeson was forced to live with an African American family because of his race, university records list him living in three different dormitory rooms on campus throughout his time at the school, all in Winants Hall. For a copy of Robeson's eulogy, see Records of the Rutgers College Office of the President (Richard P. McCormick), "Paul Robeson" folder. Paul Robeson, Jr., wrote that his father had to live off campus for his freshman year but then lived in the dorms the remainder of his time at college, citing Hoggard as a source. See Paul Robeson, Jr., *The Undiscovered Paul Robeson: An Artist's Journey 1898–1939* (New York: Wiley, 2001), 20, 26. For Robeson's official on-campus addresses, see *Rutgers College Catalogue* for each year. According to Boyle and Bunie, in Robeson's first two years, he lived in a dorm room by himself. His junior year, he lived with the other two black students at the school: Robert Ritter Davenport of Orange, New Jersey

(class of 1920), and Leon Harold Smith of Saugerties, New York (class of 1921). In his senior year, he lived with a white Jewish student named Herbert Miskend (class of 1922). See Boyle and Bunie, *Paul Robeson*, 55–56.

31. "Syracuse Triumphs," *Targum*, October 17, 1917, pp. 64–65 (quotation from p. 64).

32. "The 1917 Season," *Targum*, December 19, 1917, pp. 273–285 (quotation from p. 282).

33. "1917 Season," p. 285.

34. Boyle and Bunie argue that Robeson was never in the glee club at Rutgers "because of the socializing (with female choruses from other schools with whom Rutgers would sing in joint concerts) that followed performances." See Boyle and Bunie, *Paul Robeson*, 54.

35. Two scrapbooks in the Rutgers archives suggest that Robeson did, indeed, insinuate himself into everyday campus life, at least in his role as athletic star. Both Paul Rexford Molineux and Royal F. Nichols, white students who were contemporaries of Robeson, had photographs and newspaper stories dealing with Robeson's athletic success in their scrapbooks, alongside photographs of white Rutgers athletes. Indeed, one of the few sports clippings in Nichols's scrapbook was a story about Rutgers's 5–1 victory over Princeton in June 1919 that emphasized that the game was Robeson's last sporting event for the school (and Rutgers's first victory over Princeton in any sport in nearly fifty years). The scrapbooks are located in the Special Collections and University Archives, Rutgers University Libraries.

36. See Titus B. Maxwell, ed., *The Scarlet Letter* (East Orange, NJ: Abby Printshop, 1918), 83; and Clifford N. Baker, "Review of the 1918 Football Season," in *The Scarlet Letter* (East Orange, NJ: Abby Printshop, 1919), 143–146 (quotation from p. 145).

37. "Paul Leroy Robeson, '19," *Targum*, June 1919, p. 566.

38. Francis E. Lyons, "Prophesy of the Class of '19," *Targum*, June 1919, p. 574.

39. "Rutgers Triumphs," *Targum*, November 28, 1917, pp. 223–225, 228 (quotation from p. 224).

40. "The Season," *Targum*, December 4, 1918, p. 173.

41. Paul Robeson, Jr., *Undiscovered Paul Robeson*, 30. Boyle and Bunie list a number of other reasons why Robeson was not selected as team captain: "Robeson as team captain would have presented one problem after another: a black man doing the coin toss before games, speaking at pep rallies, meeting alumni, shaking hands with opponents—all almost impossible to imagine." See Boyle and Bunie, *Paul Robeson*, 68.

42. Even before these two men achieved national renown, other black athletes had been successful in integrated sports. William Henry Lewis, who would become the assistant attorney general under President William Howard Taft, earned All-American status for the Harvard football team in the 1890s, and George Jewett starred for the University of Michigan in the 1900s. However, black athletes were still a rarity by the time Robeson and Pollard played, and both men were distinct minorities at their respective schools. Lewis actually played a pivotal role in helping Pollard get admitted to Brown University. See John M. Carroll, *Fritz Pollard: Pioneer in Racial Advancement* (Chicago: University of Illinois Press, 1992), 41–56. For more on Lewis, see Gregory Bond, "The Strange Career of Will Henry Lewis," in *Out of the Shadows: A Biographical History of African American Athletes*, ed. David K. Wiggins (Fayetteville: University of Arkansas Press, 2006), 38–57.

43. For more information about Pollard's early years, see Carroll, *Fritz Pollard*, 1–40.

44. Although there had been other black football players at Brown, none had been as successful as Pollard would become. Pollard actually met Robeson in the summer of 1915 while working at Narragansett Pier (where Robeson was also working) and became good friends with the burly athlete. See ibid., 41–60.

45. See ibid., 103–106, 111–119.

46. Miller, "To 'Bring the Race along Rapidly,'" 131.

47. "Fred Pollard," *New York Age*, November 23, 1916, p. 4.

48. "Football Stars with Eastern School," *Chicago Defender*, December 18, 1915, p. 7.

49. "Pollard Sensation of Football Season," *New York Age*, November 23, 1916, p. 6.

50. "Fredrick Douglas Pollard," photograph, *Chicago Defender*, December 30, 1916, p. 1.

51. "Pollard Given Place on 'The All-American,'" *Chicago Defender*, December 30, 1916, p. 5.

52. "Rutgers Too Strong for Holy Cross Men," *New York Tribune*, November 5, 1916, p. II-3.

53. "Robeson on All-American," *New York Age*, December 8, 1917, p. 6. For Robeson's size relative to his teammates, see Duberman, *Paul Robeson*, 20. For photographs of Robeson's body from the 1920s and 1930s, see Hazel Carby, *Race Men* (Cambridge, MA: Harvard University Press, 1998), 48–66.

54. "Sporting Gossip: Robeson Stars Again," *Baltimore Afro-American*, December 1, 1917, p. 6.

55. Robeson starred in baseball and basketball in addition to football at Rutgers. See "Men of the Month: Paul Le Roy Robeson," *The Crisis* 15, no. 5 (March 1918): 230–231.

56. "The Horizon: Education," *The Crisis* 18, no. 3 (July 1919): 150–151.

57. Boyle and Bunie, *Paul Robeson*, 66–67.

58. See Ellis, *Race, War, and Surveillance*, 4–5, 10, 14. Those who were suspicious had good reason to be so inclined; during the Spanish-American War in the 1890s, black leaders had pursued a similar plan, encouraging blacks to enlist and promoting African American participation and service in order to inspire whites to grant more rights and reward black achievement. Those hopes were dashed, with returning black servicemen (and supporters of black troops) encountering fierce rioting and abuse. See Gleijeses, "African Americans and the War against Spain."

59. Edwin B. Henderson, "The Season's Basket Ball," *The Crisis* 12, no. 2 (June 1916): 66.

60. See M. A. Blake to William H. S. Demarest, November 15, 1917, Demarest Papers, Box 3, folder 36; and M. A. Blake to William H. S. Demarest, October 23, 1917, Demarest Papers, Box 3, folder 36.

61. "Football," *Targum*, June 20, 1917, p. 692. Indeed, Robeson won the Senior Competitive Extemporaneous Speaking Contest by orating on the subject of "The War's Effect on American Manhood." See "Robeson Wins Extemporaneous Speaking Contest," *Targum*, April 30, 1919, p. 515.

62. "Pollard: That's All!" *The Crisis* 13, no. 5 (March 1917): 230. For more on Young and his struggles against discrimination, see Gleijeses, "African Americans and the War against Spain," 324–325.

63. Carroll, *Fritz Pollard*, 118–119.

64. Boyle and Bunie, *Paul Robeson*, 71.

65. "Football Season Ends," *Targum*, December 4, 1918, p. 170.

66. "Partiality in the Navy," *New York Age*, November 29, 1917, p. 4.

67. James W. Johnson, "Views and Reviews: There Is Also a Navy," *New York Age*, November 29, 1917, p. 4.

68. Lester A. Walton, "Robeson Latest Football Star," p. 6.

69. Phil Waters, "A Foot Ball Wizard," *New York Age*, December 23, 1915, p. 6.

70. Carroll, *Fritz Pollard*, 106.

71. See, for example, "Gridiron Notes," *Baltimore Afro-American*, November 18, 1916, p. 4; "Pollard Sensation of Football Season," p. 6; and "Pollard a Sure All-American Man," *Baltimore Afro-American*, November 25, 1916, p. 4.

72. "Pollard Given Place on 'The All-American,'" p. 5.

73. "Fredrick Douglas Pollard," photograph, p. 1.

74. "To Banquet Football Star," *New York Age*, November 30, 1916, p. 6.

75. "Pollard Guest of Forty Boys Club," *Chicago Defender*, December 30, 1916, p. 5.

76. See, for example, "An All-Eastern Football Eleven," *New York Tribune*, December 10, 1916, p. II-3; Dan Daniel, "High Lights and Shadows in All Spheres of Sport:

Sanford in Ecstasies over Rutgers Eleven," *New York Sun*, October 12, 1918, p. 17; Frank O'Neill, "Only One Team Left in Brown's Pathway," *New York Tribune*, November 26, 1916, p. II-4; and "Vermont Weak, So Brown Wins Easily," *New York Tribune*, October 31, 1915, p. II-2.

77. Louis Lee Arms, "George Foster Sanford Again Attains the Heights as Football Coach: Rutgers a One-Man Team and His Name Is Robeson," *New York Tribune*, November 26, 1917, p. 13.

78. Louis Lee Arms, "Rutgers Blanks Newport Navy: Dashing Robeson Humbles Black's Noted Warriors," *New York Tribune*, November 25, 1917, p. II-1.

79. "A Whirl through Sportdom," *Daily Home News*, June 16, 1919, p. 10.

80. Clipping from *Yale Alumni Review*, undated, reprinted in "The Looking Glass: Pollard," *The Crisis* 13, no. 3 (January 1917): 139. The term *dark eel* certainly has phallic implications as well, particularly since so much white anxiety focused on black men's supposedly insatiable sexual drive and phallic power.

81. "Gridiron Notes," p. 4.

82. Charles A. Taylor, "Maroon Grid Warriors Smothered by Rutgers: Robeson, Giant Negro, Plays Leading Role for Jersey Eleven in Defeating McCaffrey's Charges by 28 to 0—Sanford Team Plays Brilliantly," *New York Tribune*, October 28, 1917, p. II-1.

83. Arms, "Rutgers Blanks Newport Navy," p. II-1.

84. "Rutgers Too Strong for Holy Cross Men," p. II-3.

85. Harold O'Neill, "Rutgers Team's Great Victory Sends Thrills throughout City," *Daily Home News*, November 26, 1917, p. 9.

86. Bederman, *Manliness and Civilization*, 23. See also Putney, *Muscular Christianity*, 6.

87. "Rule Pitches Rutgers to Win over Princeton," *Daily Home News*, undated, in Royal F. Nichols scrapbook.

88. Harold O'Neill, "Rutgers Depending on Closer Unity of Play to Defeat Black's Newport Eleven," *Daily Home News*, November 23, 1917, p. 18.

89. *Brooklyn Eagle* excerpt, reprinted in Harold E. O'Neill, "Sporting Topics," *Daily Home News*, December 18, 1917. Although the use of the term *boy* often had racial connotations—being used to denigrate black manhood—newspapers consistently employed the term *boy* with white college athletes as well.

90. "Rutgers and West Virginia in Tie Game: Sanford Team Escapes Defeat by Only Two Yards," *New York Tribune*, November 4, 1917, p. II-1.

91. For example, the *Crisis* made note of "protests" against "the use of the word 'darky' by the white press when referring to Negroes" and celebrated that some white papers had agreed to no longer use the term. See "The Horizon: Social Progress," *The Crisis* 16, no. 5 (September 1918): 242.

92. Louis Lee Arms, "Eleven Stars of Gridiron Picked from Year's Crop," *New York Tribune*, December 2, 1917, p. II-3.

93. "Five College Stars among the Top-Notchers," photograph, *New York Tribune*, December 2, 1917, p. II-3.

94. Harold E. O'Neill, "Rutgers Loses to W. and J. . . . ," *Daily Home News*, December 1, 1916.

95. "Line-Up of Rutgers Football Team and Five of Their Star Players," *New York Tribune*, October 6, 1918, p. II-2.

96. See Carroll, *Fritz Pollard*, 29–30.

97. See, for example, "Brown Crushes Harvard, Pollard Leading Attack," *New York Tribune*, November 19, 1916, pp. II-1, II-3; and "Three Remarkable New Backfield Men of Present Gridiron Season," photograph, *New York Tribune*, November 19, 1916, p. II-4.

98. See, for example, Mr. Fan, "Brown's Wizard Defeats Harvard," *Chicago Defender*, November 25, 1916, pp. 1, 5.

99. "The Tufts-Harvard Football Game," photograph, *Chicago Defender*, October 21, 1916, p. 7.

100. On the flip side, whites gleefully printed photographs that showed white athletes in triumph over blacks. For example, a photograph of white boxer Jess Willard standing over a defeated Jack Johnson at the conclusion of their 1915 heavyweight championship bout was a regular feature of white bars across the country. See Bederman, *Manliness and Civilization*, 4.

101. Black commentators also championed efforts to reestablish integrated boxing in order to give African Americans an equal opportunity to pursue the fame (and prize money) associated with the popular sport. See Lester A. Walton, "Mixed Bouts Now Permitted in New Jersey," *New York Age*, October 5, 1918, p. 6; and "The Horizon: Social Progress," *The Crisis* 17, no. 2 (December 1918): 87.

102. "Fred Pollard," p. 4.

103. "Robeson, Star at Rutgers," *New York Age*, December 28, 1916, p. 6.

104. See Carroll, *Fritz Pollard*, 105.

105. "Princeton May Bar Tufts from Games," *Chicago Defender*, October 28, 1916, p. 5.

106. "Robeson Stars, Although Rutgers Is Defeated," *Chicago Defender*, November 30, 1918, p. 5.

107. Carroll, *Fritz Pollard*, 72.

108. After all, the term *nigger* had been used as a term of derision for African Americans since the early decades of the nineteenth century. For a legal history of hate speech, see Samuel Walker, *Hate Speech: The History of an American Controversy* (Lincoln: University of Nebraska Press, 1994). For the origins of the term *nigger* and its negative connotations, see Randall Kennedy, *Nigger: The Strange Career of a Troublesome Word* (New York: Pantheon Books, 2002), 4–5.

109. See Judith N. Shklar, "The Liberalism of Fear," in *Liberalism and the Moral Life*, ed. Nancy L. Rosenblum (Cambridge, MA: Harvard University Press, 1989), 21–38 (quotation from p. 27).

110. Of course, some white newspaper writers may have been as bigoted as the worst fans in the stands and thus saw no issue with the poor behavior.

111. Harold E. O'Neill, "West Virginia Tried Eighteen . . . ," *Daily Home News*, November 13, 1916, p. 10.

112. Robeson indicated that one of the West Virginia players warned against touching him and called Robeson a "black dog." Documentary filmmaker and critic Pare Lorentz, at the time a young fan of West Virginia, attended the game, and his recollections support Robeson's: soon after the start of the game, "a number of West Virginia fans began hollering 'Kill that nigger! Kill that nigger!'" See Boyle and Bunie, *Paul Robeson*, 64.

113. O'Neill, "West Virginia Tried Eighteen . . . ," p. 10.

114. As mentioned previously, Robeson's topic for his senior year address, for example, dealt with "the war's effect on American manhood."

115. *Targum*, June 1918, p. 727.

116. *Targum*, June 1918, p. 727. The *Daily Home News* coverage agreed that he "held the audience spellbound." See "Robeson Gets First Honors at Junior Ex.," *Daily Home News*, May 21, 1918.

117. Robeson's honors thesis pursued a slightly different tactic toward expanding the terms of American citizenship and making equal opportunity a more attainable goal. Robeson argued that "the hope of the American people lies in the strength of the Fourteenth Amendment," that the equal rights clause of the Fourteenth Amendment was vital to protecting American citizens. Paul S. Robeson, "The Fourteenth Amendment, 'The Sleeping Giant of the American Constitution'" (bachelor's thesis, Rutgers College, 1919), 23.

118. Robeson gave the speech at the request of Rutgers president William Demarest, who invited him after the first student in line became ill. The text of Robeson's speech was reprinted in the June graduation issue of the *Targum*. See Paul Robeson, "The New Idealism," *Targum*, June 1918, pp. 570–571.

119. Official estimates placed the death toll at thirty-nine African Americans, although the total was probably closer to one hundred. Many more were injured and, as Malcolm McLaughlin notes, "thousands effectively became refugees" when their homes were destroyed. See Malcolm McLaughlin, *Power, Community, and Racial Killing in East St. Louis* (New York: Palgrave Macmillan, 2005), 2. See also Elliott M. Rudwick, *Race Riot at East St. Louis, July 2, 1917* (Carbondale: Southern Illinois University Press, 1964).

120. Robeson's use of the phrase "clasp friendly hands" also riffed on Washington's famous "Atlanta Exposition Address" of 1901. Washington appeased nervous whites by noting that "in all things that are purely social we can be as separate as the fingers, yet one as the hand in all things essential to mutual progress." Here Robeson saw a more meaningful connection of white and black hands. For alternate interpretations and analysis of Robeson's address, see Boyle and Bunie, *Paul Robeson*, 76–77, and Paul Robeson, Jr., *Undiscovered Paul Robeson*, 35–39. For Washington's address, see Booker T. Washington, *Up from Slavery*, with related documents, ed. W. Fitzhugh Brundage (New York: Bedford/St. Martin's, 2003), 142–145.

121. Robeson became a controversial figure in the post–World War II era, as he openly supported Soviet Communism, believing that it offered a more egalitarian society. The House Un-American Activities Committee held special hearings about Robeson in 1949, and he had his visa revoked by the state department in 1950. See Duberman, *Paul Robeson*, 359–362, 388–390.

122. For more on the summer race riots of 1919, see William M. Tuttle, Jr., *Race Riot: Chicago in the Red Summer of 1919*, repr. ed. (1970; repr., Chicago: University of Illinois Press, 1996).

CHAPTER 2

1. Sam Lacy, "UCLA Makes Bowl Bid," *Washington Afro-American*, November 18, 1939, p. 26.

2. Historian Lane Demas discusses the integration of the UCLA football program, and the 1939 team in particular, in his essay "'On the Threshold of Broad and Rich Football Pastures': Integrated College Football at UCLA, 1938–1941," in *Horsehide, Pigskin, Oval Tracks and Apple Pie: Essays on Sports and American Culture*, ed. James A. Vlasich (Jefferson, NC: McFarland, 2006), 86–103.

3. See Douglas Flamming, *Bound for Freedom: Black Los Angeles in Jim Crow America* (Berkeley: University of California Press, 2005), 4–5; and Josh Sides, *L.A. City Limits: African American Los Angeles from the Great Depression to the Present* (Berkeley: University of California Press, 2003), 11–26.

4. Rachel Robinson, with Lee Daniels, *Jackie Robinson: An Intimate Portrait* (New York: Abrams, 1996), 24.

5. See Woody Strode and Sam Young, *Goal Dust* (New York: Madison Books, 1990), 10; and Jackie Robinson, with Ed Reid, "Jackie Robinson Tells His Own Story," *Washington Post*, August 21, 1949, pp. C-1, C-3.

6. Strode, *Goal Dust*, 11, 50, 61–62.

7. See "Brother of Jackie Robinson Mauled," p. 1-A; Arnold Rampersad, *Jackie Robinson: A Biography* (New York: Knopf, 1997), 60–61, 64–65; J. Robinson, "Jackie Robinson Tells . . . ," p. C-3; Jackie Robinson and Alfred Duckett, *I Never Had It Made* (New York: Putnam, 1972), 17; and Strode, *Goal Dust*, 11.

8. University enrollment totals are from Verne A. Stadtman, ed., *The Centennial Record of the University of California* (Berkeley: Regents of the University of California, 1967), 221–222. For more on joining the PCC, see Andrew Hamilton and John B. Jackson, *UCLA on the Move: During Fifty Golden Years 1919–1969* (Los Angeles: Ward Ritchie Press, 1969), 172–173. USC had two black players on its team under longtime head coach Howard Jones, including an All-American tackle named Bryce Taylor (1925) and another player named

Bert Richie. According to Strode, however, after Richie had "got involved in some sort of scandal involving a white woman . . . Howard Jones vowed he would never let another black kid play on his team." See Strode, *Goal Dust*, 29. Other incidents reveal that USC athletic teams on the whole were not welcoming of African Americans and other minorities. In the fall of 1936, USC track coach Dean Cromwell, in a speech to the German-American Alliance, said he wished he "could only be that handsome boy Hitler in New York for one hour" so that he could deal with the overwhelming "foreign population" in the city. See "Hot Demand for Removal of Dean Cromwell as Troy Track Head," *Pasadena Post*, September 15, 1936, p. 14.

9. For general assessments of the reception given to Owens and Louis, see William J. Baker, *Jesse Owens: An American Life* (New York: Free Press, 1986); Mark Dyreson, "Jesse Owens: Leading Man in Modern American Tales of Racial Progress and Limits," in *Out of the Shadows*, ed. David K. Wiggins (Fayetteville: University of Arkansas Press, 2006), 110–131; Anthony O. Edmonds, "Joe Louis, Boxing, and American Culture," in Wiggins, *Out of the Shadows*, 132–145; Donald Spivey, "The Black Athlete in Big-Time Intercollegiate Sports, 1941–1968," *Phylon* 44, no. 2 (June 1983): 116; David K. Wiggins, "The 1936 Olympic Games in Berlin," in *Glory Bound: Black Athletes in a White America* (Syracuse, NY: Syracuse University Press, 1997), 61–79.

10. The *News and Observer* story was reprinted in a story from the *California Eagle*, a black paper led by Charlotta Bass. See "Owens, Louis Praised by Dixie Daily," *California Eagle*, August 28, 1936, p. 11. Bass took over the *Eagle* in 1912, just before the newspaper's founder died. Bass later ran for vice president as a Progressive Party candidate in 1956. See Charlotta A. Bass, *Forty Years: Memoirs from the Pages of a Newspaper* (Los Angeles: Self-published, 1960); and Regina Freer, "L.A. Race Woman: Charlotta Bass and the Complexities of Black Political Development in Los Angeles," *American Quarterly* 56, no. 3 (2004): 607–632.

11. See Baker, *Jesse Owens*, 129–145; and Jeremy Schapp, *Triumph: The Untold Story of Jesse Owens and Hitler's Olympics* (New York: Houghton Mifflin, 2007), 231–234.

12. As Demas argues, the experiences of black athletes in team competition such as football complicate the traditional "race hero" approach to sports history, in which historians spotlight an individual such as Louis for his pioneering role: "There was never a single 'color line' or integrating figure in college football, but rather a tediously slow, arduous, and non-linear process—one that spanned nearly 80 years and countless players." He argues that this integration process "more closely resembled the broader African American struggle for civil rights during the 20th century." See Demas, "On the Threshold," 88; Lewis A. Erenberg, *The Greatest Fight of Our Generation: Louis vs. Schmeling* (New York: Oxford University Press, 2006), 4; Gary Gerstle, *American Crucible: Race and Nation in the Twentieth Century* (Princeton, NJ: Princeton University Press, 2001), 139; and David W. Stowe, *Swing Changes: Big-Band Jazz in New Deal America* (Cambridge, MA: Harvard University Press, 1994).

13. The school's racial attitudes were the not the only incentives for these athletes to choose UCLA. Strode acknowledged that he and Washington (and presumably Robinson, who was one of the most sought-after players in the country) received extra inducements to play for UCLA. In addition to his tuition and stipend, school officials also gave him "twenty bucks under the table so I could pay the bills at home." He and Washington were also given a car to share in addition to free books and clothes. See Rampersad, *Jackie Robinson*, 68; Vincent Rice, "Once Over Lightly," *Daily Bruin*, September 28, 1937, p. 3; and Strode, *Goal Dust*, 32, 62, 64–65.

14. According to Strode, when UCLA played the University of Oklahoma later that same season, Wyrick approached the Oklahoma players before the game and told them that Washington and Strode were his "friends" and that the Oklahoma players "better respect them for the good players they are." See J. Cullen Fentress, "Down in Front: On the Grid Front," *California Eagle*, October 12, 1939, p. 3-B; "Report of Student-Alumni Football Committee, January 17, 1938," p. 7, Series 359, Chancellor's Office, Box 56, folder 209;

Rube Samuelsen, "Sport Volleys," *Pasadena Post*, November 22, 1938, p. 8; and Strode, *Goal Dust*, 64–65.

15. See Charles W. Paddock, "Bruins Down Missouri by 13–0 Score," *Pasadena Post*, November 28, 1937, pp. 1, 23, 25 (quotation from p. 23); Strode, *Goal Dust*, 65; United Press, "Bruins' Negro Foes 'Passed' by Mustangs," *Pasadena Post*, November 16, 1937, p. 6; and B. J. Violett, "Teammates Recall Jackie Robinson's Legacy," *UCLA Today*, April 25, 1997, available at http://www.today.ucla.edu/portal/ut/970425TeammatesRecall.aspx.

16. Strode, *Goal Dust*, 63.

17. Tom Bradley, "Minorities Considered," *California Eagle*, November 9, 1939, p. 8-B.

18. Many African Americans enjoyed the radio series and thus might not have found anything offensive in Washington's nickname. Not all whites would have seen anything inappropriate in its use, either; white Louisiana politician Huey Long actually embraced the title "Kingfish," although his whiteness mitigated some of the moniker's negative qualities. However, the *Eagle*'s avoidance of "Kingfish" in connection with Washington showed that many in the black community were troubled by its use, and a number of African American groups protested the radio show (and its later television incarnation) for its demeaning representations of black people. For more on the controversy surrounding the show, see Melvin Ely, *The Adventures of Amos 'n' Andy: A Social History of an American Phenomenon* (New York: Free Press, 1991).

19. As with Pollard and Robeson, white writers also linked black athletic performance to the primitive and natural in their writing. In the *Examiner*, for example, Bob Hunter referred to Robinson as a "grease-dipped lightning bolt" on one occasion, part of a broader pattern of language usage. Hunter also called Washington "the one-man typhoon" following another game. See Bob Hunter, "Stanford Shocks U.C.L.A., 14 to 14," *Los Angeles Examiner*, October 15, 1939, pp. II-2, II-4; and "Bruins Belt Grizzlies!" *Los Angeles Examiner*, October 22, 1939, pp. II-2, II-5.

20. United Press, "U.C.L.A.'s Eleven in 26–13 Win," *Pasadena Post*, September 25, 1937, pp. 6–7 (quotation from p. 6).

21. United Press, "Stanford Has 'Washington,'" *Pasadena Post*, October 7, 1937, p. 10.

22. Braven Dyer, "The Sports Parade," *Los Angeles Times*, November 5, 1937, p. A-19.

23. "First in Pay-Dirt," photograph, *Daily Bruin*, September 27, 1937, p. 1.

24. Michael Oriard, *King Football: Sport and Spectacle in the Golden Age of Radio and Newsreels, Movies and Magazines, the Weekly and the Daily Press* (Chapel Hill: University of North Carolina Press, 2001), 319.

25. "Kenny Turns In an All-American Performance," *California Eagle*, November 4, 1937, p. 6-A.

26. See, for example, Associated Press, "Pass Traveled 62 Yards," *New York Times*, December 6, 1937, p. 20; J. Cullen Fentress, "Kenny Washington Astounds 'Experts' with Longest Heave," *California Eagle*, December 9, 1937, p. 3-B; David Orro, "U.C.L.A. Back Makes Year's Record Pass," *Chicago Defender*, December 11, 1937, p. 9; and Rube Samuelsen, "Washington Shatters Muller's Pass Mark," *Pasadena Post*, December 5, 1937, pp. 22–23.

27. "Kenny's Herculean Toss," *California Eagle*, December 9, 1937, p. 2-B. As their careers continued, Washington and Strode became celebrities to both blacks and whites, participating in parades, getting into clubs for free, and meeting celebrities such as musician Fats Waller and actress Jane Wyman. See Strode, *Goal Dust*, 73, 83. The two were also invited to a variety of events in the black community, including special appearances alongside the likes of Louis Armstrong at winter Negro League baseball games. See "Giants Whip Kings 10–4; Kenny Guest," *California Eagle*, December 9, 1937, p. 3-B; and "Royal Giants to Battle Detroit Today," *Los Angeles Times*, December 19, 1937, p. A-11.

28. Braven Dyer, "The Sports Parade," *Los Angeles Times*, October 13, 1938, p. A-11.

29. Almena Davis, "Down in Front," *California Eagle*, November 17, 1938, p. 3-B.

30. Shavenau Glick, "Robinson's 104-Yard Run Tops P.J.C. Win," *Pasadena Post*, November 24, 1938, pp. 8–9 (quotation from p. 8).

31. "50,000 Cheer Jack Robinson in Pasadena Rose Bowl Win," *California Eagle*, November 3, 1938, p. 3-B.

32. Rube Samuelsen, "Sport Volleys," *Pasadena Post*, October 30, 1938, pp. 20–21 (quotation from p. 20).

33. Shavenau Glick, "Robinson Named 'Most Valuable Player,'" *Pasadena Post*, December 7, 1938, p. 6. Black teammate Ray Bartlett, who would join Robinson at UCLA, also received an award, leading Strode to recall that Robinson's and Bartlett's postseason accolades with PJC were "pretty unusual: the two guys who got all the honors were black." Strode, *Goal Dust*, 85.

34. C. Mallery, "His Award Just a Matter of Form," cartoon, *Pasadena Post*, December 7, 1938, p. 6.

35. "They Gave Him a Dose of His Own Grid Medicine," photograph, *Pasadena Post*, December 14, 1938, p. 6.

36. "Jackie Robinson to Lead All-Stars," *California Eagle*, December 8, 1938, p. 3-B.

37. "Pasadena Civic Groups Honor Jackie Robinson with Loving Cup," *California Eagle*, December 22, 1938, p. 3-B.

38. A white player named Frank Spratt was captain instead. See Shavenau Glick, "Do You Really Know Your Bulldogs?" *Pasadena Post*, November 7, 1938, p. 8. Neither Washington nor Strode was elected team captain for UCLA either.

39. See, for example, Rube Samuelsen, "Sport Volleys," *Pasadena Post*, December 13, 1938, p. 6.

40. "Brother of Jackie Robinson Mauled," p. 1-A. The local branch of the NAACP filed a formal protest with the city in the matter, although apparently nothing ever came of it. The *Pasadena Post*, the mainstream newspaper most likely to report on the arrest, made no mention of either Edgar Robinson's situation or the NAACP protest. See "55 Arrested during Fete," *Pasadena Post*, January 3, 1939, p. 13.

41. Rampersad, *Jackie Robinson*, 61.

42. Although Robinson remembered his time at UCLA as being "happy days," Strode and UCLA graduate manager Bill Ackerman both recalled Robinson as being a loner. See Jackie Robinson, with Wendell Smith, *Jackie Robinson: My Own Story* (New York: Greenberg, 1948), 9; and Strode, *Goal Dust*, 86–89. Rampersad argues that Robinson was more well liked than Strode acknowledged, but the alternate perspectives may have been a matter of timing; given the troubling events Robinson experienced just before the start of the fall semester in 1939, it is not surprising that he would seem withdrawn and troubled to Strode during the one year they played together. See Rampersad, *Jackie Robinson*, 71–72.

43. Rampersad, *Jackie Robinson*, 66. Rampersad borrows from film historian Donald Bogle, who defined "the brutal black buck" as the "big, baadddd niggers, over-sexed and savage, violent and frenzied," one of five major stereotypes in Hollywood film representations of blacks. See Donald Bogle, *Toms, Coons, Mulattoes, Mammies, and Bucks: An Interpretive History of Blacks in American Films* (New York: Continuum International, 2002), 9–14.

44. Strode, *Goal Dust*, 89. White teammate Don McPherson also said in later years that Robinson had "a little bit of a chip on his shoulder." See Demas, "On the Threshold," 91; and Violett, "Teammates Recall."

45. See "A Bronze Hercules," photograph, *Chicago Defender*, September 9, 1939, p. 10; and "A Star Reports—Robinson Enters U.C.L.A. and Students Are Happy," *Chicago Defender*, September 16, 1939, p. 8.

46. "61 Huskies to Answer Grid Call at UCLA," *California Eagle*, September 7, 1939, p. 3-B.

47. Atlas Photo Service, "Four Bruins and 'Papa' Bruin," photograph, *California Eagle*, September 21, 1939, p. 3-B.

48. For more of the *Eagle*'s enthusiasm, see "UCLA Football Squad Made Up of 'Home Town' Talent," *California Eagle*, September 14, 1939, p. 3-B; and J. Cullen Fentress, "Down in Front: A Colorful Outfit," *California Eagle*, September 21, 1939, p. 3-B.

49. J. Cullen Fentress, "Down in Front: Those Enthused Bruins," *California Eagle*, September 28, 1939, p. 3-B.

50. "Gold Dust Trio," photograph, *Daily Bruin*, September 29, 1939, p. 5.

51. "Bruins Impress Horrell," *Los Angeles Examiner*, September 18, 1939, p. II-7.

52. Although most contemporary observers consider the quarterback position the most prestigious role, in earlier years the halfbacks earned more fame, as forward passing was less common. Indeed, in the "single-wing" offense run by UCLA in 1939, the left halfback (Washington's position) usually received the ball from the center on offense, either running with it, handing it off to another back, or throwing it downfield. For a description of UCLA's offense, see Strode, *Goal Dust*, 58.

53. See Bob Hunter, "Bruins Boast of Night Grid Mark," *Los Angeles Examiner*, September 25, 1939, p. II-7; and Rube Samuelsen, "Sport Volleys," *Pasadena Post*, September 29, 1939, p. 6.

54. "Pasadena Grid Player Arrested," *Los Angeles Times*, September 7, 1939, p. I-14.

55. Jackie Robinson, with Ed Reid, "Being an Athlete Gets Robinson out of a Jam," *Washington Post*, August 22, 1949, pp. 8–9 (quotation from p. 8). See also Rampersad, *Jackie Robinson*, 66; and Strode, *Goal Dust*, 89.

56. Letter from Billie C. Schindhelm to Dear Sirs, Series 359, Chancellor's Office, Box 71, folder 101, undated.

57. Letter from James R. Bowen to Robert G. Sproul, Series 359, Chancellor's Office, Box 71, folder 101, November 6, 1939. To his credit, UCLA vice president and provost E. R. Hedrick did not give Bowen much satisfaction in his reply, writing that he "had known of the situation" mentioned in the letter and that he hoped that Robinson would "learn through his contacts here to conduct himself in such a way that he may re-establish himself in the community." Although acknowledging that Robinson acted inappropriately (which is debatable), Hedrick did not suggest that he would punish Robinson in any way or that he deserved punishment. Letter from E. R. Hedrick to James R. Bowen, Series 359, Chancellor's Office, Box 71, folder 101, November 13, 1939. The letter was returned as undeliverable.

58. Davis J. Walsh, "I Speak My Mind," *Los Angeles Examiner*, September 27, 1940, p. II-4.

59. An incident in Robinson's sophomore year revealed this aspect of Robinson's personality clearly. While playing basketball for UCLA against Cal in Berkeley in February 1940, Robinson was subjected to racial abuse from fans in the stand. Black UCLA graduate Tom Berkeley, then at Hastings Law School in San Francisco, attended the game and reported to a university administrator that Robinson provoked the crowd by talking back to them instead of laughing off the insults. Although he wished that Robinson could have restrained himself, he sympathized with his plight, writing, "It is not always easy to smile at 'Take the nigger out of there,' 'Down with the colored race,' 'Look out eightball' and so on." See Jim Lash to Robert Sproul, March 6, 1941, Series 369, Chancellor's Office, Box 124, folder 101.

60. "Case against Jackie Dismissed," *California Eagle*, October 19, 1939, p. 1-A.

61. TCU had finished the previous season ranked number one in the Associated Press (AP) poll, making the team, to most observers, the national champion for that year. The final AP poll is available for viewing at College Football Poll.com, a site dedicated to college football rankings and predictions of future games. See http://www.collegefootballpoll.com/polls_1936_present.html (accessed January 3, 2012).

62. See "General Kenny Washington Goes to Town," photograph, *Chicago Defender*, October 7, 1939, p. 8, and "Kenny Washington-Jackie Robinson Help Beat T.C.U.," *Chicago Defender*, October 7, 1939, p. 9.

63. Associated Negro Press, "Work of Washington and Robinson Brings Victory to UCLA," *Washington Afro-American*, October 14, 1939, p. 26.

64. See Bob Hunter, "Overlin Scores Touchdown in Third after Long Drive," *Los Angeles Examiner*, September 30, 1939, p. II-3; and "Cantor Saves Bruins," *Los Angeles Examiner*, November 26, 1939, pp. II-3, II-6 (quotation from p. II-3).

65. J. Cullen Fentress, "Down in Front: Those Surprising Bruins," *California Eagle*, October 5, 1939, p. 1-B.

66. "Seattle Jam Session Fetes UCLA Grid Heroes," *California Eagle*, October 12, 1939, p. 5-A. The band itself was likely named in honor of Joe Louis, whose nickname was the Brown Bomber.

67. Al Santoro, "To the Point," *Los Angeles Examiner*, November 27, 1939, p. II-3.

68. Demas, "On the Threshold," 93. See Paul Zimmerman, "Sports Post-Scripts," *Los Angeles Times*, October 9, 1939, p. A-11.

69. J. Cullen Fentress, "Down in Front: On the Grid Front," *California Eagle*, October 19, 1939, p. 3-B.

70. "Do You Know?" *California Eagle*, November 2, 1939, p. 8-B.

71. J. Cullen Fentress, "Down in Front: Bruins and the Bowl," *California Eagle*, November 9, 1939, p. 3-B.

72. "Claims Undesirable Policy Comes to Light on Campus," *California Eagle*, November 30, 1939, p. 3-A.

73. J. Cullen Fentress, "Down in Front: Commendable Spirit," *California Eagle*, November 16, 1939, p. 3-B.

74. United Press, "New Grid Machines Get Test," *Pasadena Post*, October 14, 1939, p. 6.

75. "Washington Tops Scorers," *Los Angeles Examiner*, October 23, 1939, p. II-3.

76. One prime example of this tendency came before the Santa Clara game, when the *Post* featured a large photograph of reserve lineman Mladin Zarubica in action, an unlikely choice, to say the least. See "How Burly Bruin Would Ride Santa Clara Bronco," *Pasadena Post*, November 18, 1939, p. 6.

77. Rampersad, *Jackie Robinson*, 70–71.

78. Bob Hunter, "Robinson Hurt in Practice," *Los Angeles Examiner*, November 2, 1939, pp. II-7, II-8 (quotation from p. II-7). The next day, when Hunter reported on Robinson's injury status, he similarly wrote that Robinson was injured "when tackled viciously by two goof squad members." Bob Hunter, "Robinson Limps," *Los Angeles Examiner*, November 3, 1939, p. II-5.

79. Letter from Billie C. Schindhelm to Robert G. Sproul, Series 359, Chancellor's Office, Box 71, folder 101, December 13, 1939. There are actually two nearly identical versions of this letter, one addressed to "Dear Sirs" (cited previously) and one addressed to Sproul.

80. Hart's use of "comrades" fits in well with the growing prominence of the Communist Party in the United States in the 1930s. The popular front embraced various cultural forms—including sport—as a means of promoting the Communist Party's ideology. For a thorough analysis of the effects of the popular front (although one that gives sports little attention), see Michael Denning, *The Cultural Front: The Laboring of American Culture in the Twentieth Century* (New York: Verso, 1998).

81. Letter from Michael Joseph Hart to Robert G. Sproul, Series 359, Chancellor's Office, Box 71, folder 101, December 4, 1939.

82. Demas, "On the Threshold," 90.

83. See, for example, "Bruin Pre-game Rally Friday," *Los Angeles Examiner*, December 5, 1939, p. I-16; and "Trojan Faculty Warns Raiders," *Los Angeles Examiner*, December 5, 1939, p. I-15.

84. USC's poor reputation regarding black athletes added to the drama, particularly for black writers. In the *Eagle*, Fentress had been perturbed when USC coach Howard Jones demurred from giving a definite answer regarding Robinson's skill because he had seen only the night game against TCU that season and "couldn't see Jackie so well" as a result. Fentress interpreted that comment to be a derogatory reference to Robinson's dark skin. See J. Cullen Fentress, "Down in Front: Bruins Continue to Improve," *California Eagle*, November 23, 1939, p. 3-B.

85. Fay M. Jackson, "U.S.C. Officials Quash Nazism Attempt," *California Eagle*, November 30, 1939, p. 1-B.

86. Jackson, "U.S.C. Officials Quash Nazism Attempt," p. 1-B.

87. See Erenberg, *Greatest Fight*, 3, 160–161.

88. Warren Morton, "Preserve Constitution, Bill of Rights," *Pasadena Post*, December 24, 1939, p. 8.

89. Charles Amin, "Discusses Chicago University Football Action," *Pasadena Post*, January 7, 1940, p. 8.

90. In later years, Strode dismissed the incident as a sign of "fear" on the part of the USC fans but saw no racial overtones. However, he seemed not to remember the presence of Cantor and Cohen in the display and clearly did not recall the furor in the *Eagle*, so his memory may have been clouded by the passing of more than forty years. See Strode, *Goal Dust*, 97.

91. Jackson, "U.S.C. Officials Quash Nazism Attempt," p. 1-B.

92. See J. Cullen Fentress, "Down in Front: Shorts in Sports," *California Eagle*, November 16, 1939, p. 3-B; Al Santoro, "To the Point," *Los Angeles Examiner*, November 11, 1939, p. II-3; and Al Wolf, "Washington Nominated for All-American Recognition," *Los Angeles Times*, November 13, 1939, p. A-10.

93. Milt Cohen, "Here's Our Angle," *Daily Bruin*, December 4, 1939, p. 3.

94. J. Cullen Fentress, "Down in Front: Shorts in Sports," *California Eagle*, December 7, 1939, p. 2-B.

95. Dick Hyland, "Hyland Picks All-Coast Team," *Los Angeles Times*, December 17, 1939, pp. A-11, A-13 (quotation from p. A-13).

96. Davis J. Walsh, "I Speak My Mind," *Los Angeles Examiner*, December 3, 1939, p. II-3.

97. See "All-American Football—Bunk!" *Daily Bruin*, December 12, 1939, p. 2; and Milt Cohen, "Here's Our Angle," *Daily Bruin*, December 4, 1939, p. 3.

98. Davis J. Walsh, "I Speak My Mind," *Los Angeles Examiner*, December 3, 1939, p. II-3.

99. Dick Hyland, "Behind the Line," *Los Angeles Times*, November 23, 1939, p. 29.

100. Chester G. Hanson, "Determination Grid's Gift to Washington," *Los Angeles Times*, December 8, 1939, p. 22. See also Bob Hunter, "Washington Dubs Fame Fickle Dame," *Los Angeles Examiner*, December 6, 1939, pp. II-3, II-5.

101. Strode, *Goal Dust*, 96.

102. "Washington on All-Star Team," *Los Angeles Times*, December 27, 1939, p. 22.

103. "Bill Stern Names Kenny Washington All American," *Chicago Defender*, December 2, 1939, p. 24.

104. "Editorials: Wrong Color," *The Crisis* 47, no. 1 (January 1940): 17.

105. Allan Dale, "Washington vs. Lansdell Brings Season's Classic," *Los Angeles Examiner*, December 4, 1939, p. II-6.

106. Sam Lacy, "UCLA Makes Bowl Bid," p. 26.

107. Letter from Hart to Sproul.

108. J. Cullen Fentress, "Down in Front: Shorts in Sports," *California Eagle*, December 7, 1939, p. 2-B.

109. For a sampling of these stories, see George Kirksey, "Sugar Bowl to 'Challenge' Local Classic?" *Pasadena Post*, November 21, 1939, pp. 6–7; Rube Samuelsen, "Troy Still Suffers from Shock but Eyes Rose Bowl Problem," *Pasadena Post*, December 3, 1939, p. 20; "Tennessee to Meet Coliseum Game Winner," *Pasadena Post*, December 7, 1939, p. 10; and Davis J. Walsh, "I Speak My Mind," *Los Angeles Examiner*, November 14, 1939, p. I-18. Demas notes that *New York Times* reporter Allison Danzig reported that Tennessee would "definitely" not play in the Rose Bowl if UCLA earned the West Coast bid. See Demas, "On the Threshold," 94.

110. Mark D. Briggs, "A Tale of Two Pioneers: The Integration of College Athletics in the South during the 1960s in the Age of the Civil Rights Movement" (master's thesis, University of North Carolina, Chapel Hill, 2000), 15–17.

111. Art Carter, "From the Bench," *Washington Afro-American*, November 4, 1939, p. 29.

112. Dawsey Johnson, "When, and If War Comes," *Washington Afro-American*, November 25, 1939, p. 20.

113. J. Don Davis, "Montgomery Won't Play in Cotton Bowl Game; Won't Be Allowed on Bench in Uniform," *Chicago Defender*, December 23, 1939, p. 22.

114. Charles Paddock, "Spikes," *Pasadena Star-News*, November 6, 1939, p. 14.

115. Dick Hyland, "Behind the Line," *Los Angeles Times*, November 28, 1939, p. A-11.

116. Letter from Schindhelm to Sproul.

117. Al Santoro, "Trojans Favored 2–5 over U.C.L.A. in Today's Game," *Los Angeles Examiner*, December 9, 1939, pp. I-1, II-5.

118. "When Robinson Stopped Lansdell's Touchdown Mark," *Chicago Defender*, December 16, 1939, p. 24.

119. Strode, *Goal Dust*, 100.

120. Since all players played both offense and defense, there was no specialized kicker. Someone from the regular team simply stepped in to kick field goals and extra points, making these scoring opportunities much less of a sure thing.

121. Associated Negro Press, "Washington Hailed by Coast Fans," *Washington Afro-American*, December 16, 1939, p. 26. The *Examiner* also considered the tie a "moral victory" for UCLA. See Davis J. Walsh, "Deathless Deadlock, Moral Victory for Bruins," *Los Angeles Examiner*, December 10, 1939, pp. II-2, II-4.

122. See J. Cullen Fentress, "Down in Front: Shorts in Sports," *California Eagle*, December 14, 1939, p. 2-B; and J. Cullen Fentress, "UCLA's Exciting Bruins and USC's Trojans Battle to 0–0 Deadlock," *California Eagle*, December 14, 1939, p. 2-B. Demas notes that writers in the *New York Amsterdam News* lamented that UCLA's tie meant that the "Rose Bowl Remains as White as a New Lily." See Demas, "On the Threshold," 101; and Daniel, "And Rose Bowl Remains as White as a New Lily," *New York Amsterdam News*, December 16, 1939, p. 101.

123. Fay Young, "The Stuff Is Here . . . ," *Chicago Defender*, December 16, 1939, p. 22.

124. See http://www.collegefootballpoll.com/polls_1936_present.html (accessed January 3, 2012).

125. Strode, *Goal Dust*, 104.

126. Robert C. Hume, "Still Hope Here," *Los Angeles Examiner*, December 15, 1939, p. I-16.

127. "103,000 Cheered Him," *California Eagle*, December 28, 1939, p. 4-B.

128. United Press, "Western Football All-Stars Underdogs against East in Annual Shrine Contest," *Pasadena Post*, December 25, 1939, p. 12.

129. "All-Star Selectors Still under Fire," *California Eagle*, 28 December 1939, p. 1-A. The story was picked up by the national black press as well. Fay Young, writing in the *Defender*, lamented "the apparent color line in big time college football." See "The Stuff Is Here . . . ," *Chicago Defender*, December 30, 1939, pp. 18, 20 (quotation from p. 20).

130. J. Cullen Fentress, "Down in Front: Your Answer, Gentlemen," *California Eagle*, December 21, 1939, p. 8-A.

131. Bob Hunter, "Bruin Star Due for Two Games," *Los Angeles Examiner*, December 21, 1939, pp. II-5, II-6 (quotation from p. II-5).

132. See J. Cullen Fentress, "Down in Front: Shorts in Sports," *California Eagle*, December 14, 1939, p. 2-B; Dick Hyland, "Behind the Line," *Los Angeles Times*, January 23, 1940, p. A-11; "Kenny Named Greatest Back of Year; Strode Most Improved," *California Eagle*, January 25, 1940, p. 1-A; and "UCLA Stars Honor Guests at Jefferson Football Rally," *California Eagle*, December 21, 1939, p. 8-A.

133. See Joe Hernandez, "Pros Besiege Trojan Grid Aces," *Los Angeles Examiner*, December 11, 1939, p. II-4.

134. For the Shrine game controversy, see United Press, "Western All-Stars Virtually Selected," *Pasadena Post*, December 14, 1939, p. 10; United Press, "West Shrine Team

Named," *Los Angeles Examiner*, December 14, 1939, p. II-3; and United Press, "Western Football All-Stars Underdogs against East in Annual Shrine Contest," *Pasadena Post*, December 25, 1939, p. 12. For a discussion of the black players' lack of opportunities in contrast to the USC stars, see Joe Hernandez, "Pros Besiege Trojan Grid Aces," *Los Angeles Examiner*, December 11, 1939, p. II-4; and J. Cullen Fentress, "Down in Front: Your Answer, Gentlemen," *California Eagle*, December 21, 1939, p. 8-A.

135. Davis J. Walsh, "I Speak My Mind," *Los Angeles Examiner*, December 29, 1939, p. I-20.

136. J. Cullen Fentress, "Down in Front: Your Answer, Gentlemen," *California Eagle*, December 21, 1939, p. 8-A.

137. "Kenny Washington," editorial, *Chicago Defender*, September 14, 1940, p. 14.

138. Hank Shatford, "Shatford's Sports Slag," *Daily Bruin*, March 5, 1941, p. 3. See also J. Cullen Fentress, "In Behalf of Jackie Robinson," *California Eagle*, March 13, 1941, p. 3-B; and Sam Sale, "Robinson Fails to Make All-League Cage Team: Prejudice 'Rumored' to Have Played Major Role in Selections," *Daily Bruin*, March 5, 1941, p. 3.

139. See letter from L. D. Reddick to Robert Sproul, Series 369, Chancellor's Office, Box 124, folder 101, February 18, 1941.

140. "Kenny Signs 3-Year Pact," *California Eagle*, November 21, 1940, p. 6-A.

141. See Joffre Roberts and Garland Embrey, "Civil Rights in America," *Daily Bruin*, May 17, 1940, p. 8, for the *Bruin's* response to the Klan parade.

142. Milt Cohen, "Here's Our Angle," *Daily Bruin*, May 15, 1940, p. 3.

CHAPTER 3

1. Robert Allen Cherry, *Wilt: Larger than Life* (Chicago: Triumph Books, 2004), 41.

2. Kathryn Harris, "Racial Opinions," *Lawrence Daily Journal-World*, May 7, 1957, p. 4.

3. One example of the special treatment Chamberlain received: the big man's father was a janitor for the *Saturday Evening Post*, and a KU alumnus in a high-up position used his clout to get Chamberlain's father promoted. See Aram Goudsouzian, "'Can Basketball Survive Wilt Chamberlain?' The Kansas Years of Wilt the Stilt," *Kansas History: A Journal of the Central Plains* 28 (Autumn 2005): 150–173.

4. For more on the hoopla surrounding Chamberlain as a high school player, and for an excellent narrative of Chamberlain's career at KU, see ibid., 152. For more on Chamberlain's early years, see Cherry, *Wilt: Larger than Life*, 3–39; and Wilt Chamberlain and David Shaw, *Wilt: Just Like Any Other 7-Foot Black Millionaire Who Lives Next Door* (New York: Macmillan, 1973), 6–47.

5. Amber Reagan-Kendrick, "Ninety Years of Struggle and Success: African American History at the University of Kansas, 1870–1960," (Ph.D. diss., University of Kansas, 2004), 8.

6. Reagan-Kendrick, "Ninety Years," 19, 32, 167.

7. Reagan-Kendrick, "Ninety Years," 34–35. See Loren Miller, "College," *The Crisis* 34 (January 1927): 138. Miller then published another article in the *Crisis* that was deeply critical of Chancellor Ernest Lindley in August 1927. See Loren Miller, "The Unrest among Negro Students at a White College: The University of Kansas," *The Crisis* 34 (August 1927): 187.

8. Reagan-Kendrick, "Ninety Years," 6.

9. Kristine M. McCusker, "The Forgotten Years of America's Civil Rights Movement: The University of Kansas, 1939–1961," (master's thesis, University of Kansas, 1994), 6.

10. Reagan-Kendrick, "Ninety Years," 11. The conference's official (although rarely used) name was the Missouri Valley Intercollegiate Athletic Association (MVIAA). The other member schools in 1912 were Drake University, Iowa State College, the University of Missouri, the University of Nebraska, and Washington University in St. Louis. During Chamberlain's years at KU, the Big Seven consisted of Iowa State, KU, Kansas State University, Missouri, Nebraska, the University of Colorado, and the University of Oklahoma.

11. The YMCA and the YWCA complained, but Chancellor Lindley ignored them and supported Allen. See McCusker, "The Forgotten Years," 29.

12. See Reagan-Kendrick, "Ninety Years," 38.

13. McCusker, "The Forgotten Years," 8–9.

14. Goudsouzian, "'Can Basketball Survive Chamberlain?'" 154. Allen was likely motivated more by competition than by any sense of racial justice. Max Falkenstein, who started as a radio broadcaster for the KU men's basketball team in the early 1950s and knew Allen personally, explained that after Kansas State recruited an excellent black player named Gene "The Jet" Wilson in 1950, Allen responded with the mind-set of "We gotta get us a black player," because he did not want his opponents to have an edge. Author interview with Max Falkenstein, August 10, 2006, Lawrence, Kansas.

15. I use the term *varsity debut* because in that era freshman were ineligible to play varsity basketball. Thus, players could play only three years at the varsity level, starting with their sophomore season.

16. Reagan-Kendrick, "Ninety Years," 167.

17. Dowdal Davis to Roy Wilkins, December 23, 1955, Dorothy Hodge Johnson Papers, Correspondence—General, 1953–1956, Spencer Research Library, University of Kansas.

18. Mary L. Dudziak, *Cold War Civil Rights: Race and the Image of American Democracy* (Princeton, NJ: Princeton University Press, 2000), 12.

19. Chamberlain and Shaw, *Wilt: Just Like Any Other*, 46.

20. Ernest Mehl, "Sporting Comment," *Kansas City Star*, December 6, 1956, p. 22; and Fay Young, "Fay Says," *Chicago Defender*, May 28, 1955, p. 11.

21. Mehl, "Sporting Comment," 22.

22. Kerfords also visited Chamberlain in Philadelphia between Chamberlain's February and April trips to Lawrence.

23. Wilt Chamberlain, with Tim Cohane and I. R. McVay, "Why I Am Quitting College," *Look* 22 (June 10, 1958): 91–101 (quotation from p. 100). Chamberlain echoed this statement years later in his autobiography. See Chamberlain and Shaw, *Wilt: Just Like Any Other*, 47.

24. Roy A. Edwards to Franklin D. Murphy, March 16, 1959, "Dept., Athletic Office—NCAA Chamberlain, 1958/59" folder, Chancellor Franklin Murphy Papers, Spencer Research Library, University of Kansas.

25. Ernest Mehl, "Sporting Comment," *Kansas City Star*, December 11, 1956, p. 12-C.

26. "Jackie Robinson Says Baseball Set Integration Pace," *Kansas City Call*, September 30, 1955, p. 10.

27. See "Phenom Cager, Wilt Chamberlain, to Attend K.U.," *Kansas City Call*, May 20, 1955, p. 10; Dick Snider, "Capitalizing on Sports," *Topeka Daily Capital*, May 14, 1955, p. 14; Dick Walt, "Along the Jayhawker Trail," *University Daily Kansan*, May 16, 1957, p. 4; "Wilt the Stilt Picks Kansas to End Frantic Talent Chase," *Lawrence Daily Journal-World*, May 14, 1955, evening ed., pp. 1–2.

28. "Phenom Cager," p. 10.

29. See, for example, Associated Press, "Star Cager Chooses K.U.," *Kansas City Star*, May 15, 1955, p. 3-S.

30. Bill Mayer, "Bill Mayer's Sport Talk," *Lawrence Daily Journal-World*, May 16, 1955, p. 9.

31. The pervasiveness of white writers' pride in KU's supposedly progressive nature could also be seen the following fall when *Capital* writer Dick Snider related the following anecdote: During Chamberlain's recruitment, "an Oklahoma representative" attempted "to talk Wilt into being the first to crack the color barrier at OU." According to Snider, Chamberlain responded: "Tell 'em I'll let the next guy do that for 'em." Snider seemed to delight in the fact that KU was ahead of Oklahoma when it came to racial integration—despite the fact that the team had integrated only recently and had few black athletes on any of its teams. See Dick Snider, "Capitalizing on Sports," *Topeka Daily Capital*, September 6, 1955, p. 14.

32. See Bill Mayer, "Wilt May Sell 10,000 Ducats for Frosh Fray This Winter," *Lawrence Daily Journal-World*, September 5, 1955, pp. 1–2; and Snider, "Capitalizing on Sports," 14.

33. See Rich Clarkson, "Long and Short of K.U. Sport," photograph, *Lawrence Daily Journal-World*, September 5, 1955, p. 1; Gene Smoyer, "That's the Long and the Short of It," photograph, *University Daily Kansan*, September 12, 1955, p. B-3; "Milt [*sic*] (The Stilt) Chamberlain," photograph, *Kansas City Star*, September 5, 1955, morning ed., p. 9; "Wilt Chamberlain, seven-foot . . . ," photograph, *Topeka Daily Capital*, September 6, 1955, p. 15.

34. Snider, "Capitalizing on Sports," 14.

35. "The 'Stilt' Becomes a Jayhawk," *Kansas City Call*, September 23, 1955, p. 11. In his autobiography, Chamberlain bitterly complained that Kansas recruited Leamon to come with him to school despite the fact that he considered two of his black teammates, Vince Miller and Marty Hughes, to be superior. It proved to him that "a black man has to be twice as good as a white man just to get an even break." See Chamberlain and Shaw, *Wilt: Just Like Any Other*, 49.

36. Chamberlain and Shaw, *Wilt: Just Like Any Other*, 50, 51, 58.

37. Ibid., 51.

38. Goudsouzian, "'Can Basketball Survive Chamberlain?'" 158.

39. NEA Telephoto, "Rest for a Weary 'Stilt,'" *Lawrence Daily Journal-World*, September 7, 1955, p. 13.

40. "Highly Promising K.U. Athletes," *Kansas City Call*, October 7, 1955, p. 12.

41. "K.U. Cage Foes Beware: Big Dipper at Large!" *Lawrence Daily Journal-World*, November 20, 1955, p. 8; "Wilt Makes Non-Spectators Wish They'd Seen the Show," *Lawrence Daily Journal-World*, November 20, 1955, p. 9.

42. See Rich Clarkson, "It's a Long Fall from Way up There to the Floor," *Lawrence Daily Journal-World*, November 22, 1955, p. 11; and Bill Mayer, "Future Bleak for Jay Cage Foes," *Lawrence Daily Journal-World*, November 20, 1955, p. 12.

43. Gordon Hudelson and Jack Fisher, "Wilt the Stilt," photo montage, *University Daily Kansan*, May 21, 1955, pp. 2–3 (special "Picture Supplement").

44. See Bill Moore, "It's a Tall Story for K.U. as the Stilt Makes His Debut," *Kansas City Star*, November 19, 1955, pp. 1, 7; Ed Garich, "Stilt Hits 42 as Frosh Win," *Kansas City Star*, November 19, 1955, p. 22; and "It's Easier from up Here," photograph, *Kansas City Star*, November 19, 1955, p. 22.

45. Goudsouzian, "'Can Basketball Survive Chamberlain?'" 160.

46. For the *Call*'s game story, see "Wilt, the Stilt, Charms K.U. Basketball Fans," *Kansas City Call*, November 25, 1955, p. 11. For photographs of Chamberlain in action from the game, see "Wilt (the Stilt) in Action," *Kansas City Call*, December 2, 1955, p. 12.

47. John I. Johnson, "Sport Light: K.U. Fans Meet Wilt, 'The Stilt,'" *Kansas City Call*, November 25, 1955, p. 10.

48. Goudsouzian, "'Can Basketball Survive Chamberlain?'" 156.

49. See Daryl Hall, "Wilt and Co. Seek First Victory Tonight," *University Daily Kansan*, December 3, 1956, p. 1; Bill Snead, "Big Man on Campus, and Court," *Lawrence Daily Journal-World*, December 3, 1956, p. 1; Dick Snider, "Wilt, KU Make Debut Tonight," *Topeka Daily Capital*, December 3, 1956, p. 13; and "This Is It," photograph, *Kansas City Star*, December 3, 1956, p. 4-C.

50. Before the game, the Northwestern players, including center Joe Rucklick, a talented player who would go on to a productive NBA career, expressed doubts that Chamberlain was as good as advertised. Afterward, they were convinced. A stunned Rucklick called Chamberlain "the greatest" player he had ever seen. See "Wilt Convinces Cats He Isn't Overrated," *Lawrence Daily Journal-World*, December 4, 1956, p. 13.

51. Herschel Nssienson, "Bill Russell Is Gone, but the Stilt Has Arrived," *Kansas City Call*, December 14, 1956, p. 10.

52. "Wilt 52, It's All True," *Kansas City Star*, December 4, 1956, morning ed., p. 22.

53. "The High and Mighty," photograph, *Kansas City Star*, December 4, 1956, morning ed., p. 22.

54. Bill Mayer, "Bill Mayer's Sports Talk," *Lawrence Daily Journal-World*, December 5, 1956, p. 17.

55. Max Falkenstein, with Doug Vance, *Max and the Jayhawks: 50 Years On and Off the Air with KU Sports* (Wichita, KS: Wichita Eagle and Beacon Publishing, 1996), 61.

56. Goudsouzian, "'Can Basketball Survive Chamberlain?'" 161.

57. Bill Snead, "Look Out Below!" photograph, *Lawrence Daily Journal-World*, December 10, 1956, p. 11.

58. See Donald Bogle, *Toms, Coons, Mulattoes, Mammies, and Bucks: An Interpretive History of Blacks in American Films* (New York: Continuum International, 2002), 9–14.

59. Bill Mayer, "Bill Mayer's Sport Talk," *Lawrence Daily Journal-World*, December 28, 1956, p. 8.

60. Falkenstein, *Max and the Jayhawks*, 59–60.

61. "Everyone Is Babbling about the Dipper," *Lawrence Daily Journal-World*, December 4, 1956, pp. 1, 6. According to the story, "telephone calls poured into Lawrence from all over the nation to find out how Chamberlain did" (quotation from p. 1).

62. Bob Lyle, "Wilt Hits 52 for New Record," *University Daily Kansan*, December 4, 1956, pp. 1, 8 (quotation from p. 1).

63. John I. Johnson, "Sport Light: 1956 Has Been Memorable for Many," *Kansas City Call*, December 28, 1956, p. 7.

64. "The Stilt Paces KU Jayhawks Win over Colorado," *Kansas City Call*, March 8, 1957, p. 11.

65. "Tennessee State Tigers Win NAIA Championship," *Kansas City Call*, March 22, 1957, 10.

66. See Board of Health, "Long Reach, but a Good Example," photograph, *Lawrence Daily Journal-World*, December 12, 1956, p. 13; and "Wilt Chamberlain, Who Gave . . . ," photograph, *Topeka Daily Capital*, December 13, 1956, p. 28. In the photograph, a small white woman injects Chamberlain's arm while he looks at the camera. A white basketball player named John Cleland waits in line.

67. See, for example, "KU Ready for League Play after Tourney Sweep," *University Daily Kansan*, January 3, 1957, p. 4; and Bill Mayer, "Bang on Door Fuels K.U. in Vital Game," *Lawrence Daily Journal-World*, March 7, 1957, p. 15.

68. Cliff Long, Jr., "Iowa State's Gary Thompson," cartoon, *Topeka Daily Capital*, December 26, 1956, p. 12.

69. Bill Mayer, "Bill Mayer's Sport Talk," *Lawrence Daily Journal-World*, December 21, 1956, p. 10.

70. See "Jayhawks Fill Field Houses," *University Daily Kansan*, March 4, 1957, p. 1; and "K.U.-Colorado Sellout to Be Televised," *Kansas City Star*, January 25, 1957, p. 23.

71. "K.U. Cagers on Coast," *Kansas City Star*, December 14, 1956, p. 4-D.

72. See Bill Snead, "The Luckiest Kid in the World?" *Lawrence Daily Journal-World*, December 31, 1956, p. 1; and "Young Fan and Friend," photograph, *Kansas City Star*, January 6, 1957, p. 2-B.

73. Falkenstein, *Max and the Jayhawks*, 64–65.

74. Bill Mayer, "Bill Mayer's Sport Talk," *Lawrence Daily Journal-World*, December 24, 1956, p. 8.

75. See, for example, "Chamberlain, Wilt: Freshman Game," videotape, 1 tape; "Kansas University Highlight Footage 1957," videotape, 1 tape; and "Kansas Basketball 'A Century of Tradition,'" videotape, 1 tape, Spencer Research Library, University of Kansas.

76. Chamberlain enjoyed success with the track team that same spring as well; he won the Big Seven championship in the high jump and competed in the shot put, the triple jump, sprint races, and the half-mile. Goudsouzian, "'Can Basketball Survive Chamberlain?'" 171.

77. See, for example, Associated Press, "K.U. Is Choice to Win N.C.A.A.," *Kansas City Star*, March 11, 1957, morning ed., p. 19.

78. See "Congratulations to the Big 7 Champs," advertisement, *University Daily Kansan*, March 12, 1957, pp. 8–9; and "KU Is Proud of It's [*sic*] Basketball Champs!" advertisement, *University Daily Kansan*, March 13, 1957, p. 4.

79. See "Jay Watchers Begin Drive for TV Funds," *Lawrence Daily Journal-World*, March 13, 1957, p. 1; and "TV Beckons All to Watch as Games Snuff Out Studies," *University Daily Kansan*, March 18, 1957, p. 1.

80. See "Kansas Leaves for Dallas, Set for Regional Playoffs," *Topeka Daily Capital*, March 14, 1957, p. 18; and Bill Mayer, "Bill Mayer's Sport Talk," *Lawrence Daily Journal-World*, March 11, 1957, p. 11.

81. Chamberlain and Shaw, *Wilt: Just Like Any Other*, 65. None of the newspapers, nor later accounts of the situation, mention this event. It may be apocryphal, because Chamberlain was known to exaggerate, and some other facts do not add up. Chamberlain claimed that he was not allowed to go to a drive-in movie in his own car while in town, but he had flown down with the rest of the team, and so his car was in Lawrence. Still, it is quite clear that the integrated team was an unwelcome guest in the area at large whether this specific incident is true or not.

82. Falkenstein, *Max and the Jayhawks*, 66.

83. Ibid.

84. Chamberlain and Shaw, *Wilt: Just Like Any Other*, 65.

85. Associated Press, "A Racial Taint in O.C.U. Game," *Kansas City Star*, March 18, 1957, p. 17.

86. Falkenstein, *Max and the Jayhawks*, 66. Chamberlain praised one OCU player, center Hubert Reed, who "came over and apologized to me for him and the fans several times, and that more than offset all the abuse." See Chamberlain and Shaw, *Wilt: Just Like Any Other*, 66.

87. "Roudiness [*sic*] Mars KU-Okla. City Game in Dallas," *Kansas City Call*, March 22, 1957, p. 11.

88. Falkenstein, *Max and the Jayhawks*, 66. The rowdiness of the crowd even inspired unnamed "Mississippi Friends" to send Chamberlain a telegram, urging him to not "mind Texas" and to "keep up [his] wonderful play." See Mississippi Friends to Wilt Chamberlain, telegram, March 22, 1957, "1957" folder, Wilt Chamberlain [Biographical] file, Spencer Research Library, University of Kansas.

89. See Bob Busby, "K.U. Needs Overtime," *Kansas City Star*, March 16, 1957, morning ed., p. 22; and Bob Busby, "K.U. Uses Team Effort," *Kansas City Star*, March 17, 1957, pp. 1-B, 2-B.

90. Stu Dunbar, "Kansas Batters Oklahoma City, 81–61," *Topeka Daily Capital*, March 17, 1957, p. C-1.

91. Earl Morey, "Oread Battlers Avert Third Lightning Bolt," *Lawrence Daily Journal-World*, March 16, 1957, pp. 1–2 (quotation from p. 2). It is likely that the *Journal-World* would have covered the racial subplot of the OCU game in greater detail than the other newspapers, but the paper did not publish an issue on Sunday. Similarly, the weekly *Call* eventually addressed the bigotry in its next issue.

92. For example, one *Capital* reader, Mrs. Margaret Snow, of Manhattan, Kansas, believed that the southern states should be "proud of standing so valiantly for their states' rights and the integrity of both races." She believed that the southern states were supporting "constitutional government as laid down by our founding fathers." See Margaret Snow, "For State's Rights," *Topeka Daily Capital*, January 13, 1957, p. A-16.

93. Falkenstein acknowledged that he had not brought up the behavior of the fans in his role as radio broadcaster because he did not want to "add to the tension of the moment by bringing that stuff up." Author interview with Max Falkenstein, August 10, 2006, Lawrence, Kansas.

94. The mainstream newspapers might have also failed to report the racial taunting encountered by Chamberlain and King in locations such as Missouri and Oklahoma because of the negative image that behavior would have given their region as a whole.

95. Associated Press, "A Racial Taint in O.C.U. Game," p. 17.

96. Associated Press, "O.C.U. Asks an Apology," *Kansas City Star*, March 18, 1957, p. 17. Behind the scenes, Lemmons wrote Chamberlain to explain his team's antics, explaining that he hoped his team could draw charge calls against the big man and thus "slow" him down on the fast break. He also attempted to persuade Chamberlain that he never set out to hurt him or King because of their race, writing that he had "many negro friends in Oklahoma City." Chamberlain replied to the two-page letter with a terse, one-sentence reply: "Thank you very much for your letter of March 18." See Abe Lemmons to Wilt Chamberlain, March 18, 1957, and Wilt Chamberlain to Abe Lemmons, March 29, 1957, both in "1957" folder, Wilt Chamberlain [Biographical] file, Spencer Research Library, University of Kansas.

97. Bob Busby, "On the Level," *Kansas City Star*, March 19, 1957, morning ed., p. 19.

98. Bob Busby, "On the Level," *Kansas City Star*, March 21, 1957, morning ed., p. 30.

99. "Dallas and Lawrence," *Lawrence Daily Journal-World*, March 19, 1957, p. 4.

100. Dick Snider, "Capitalizing on Sports," *Topeka Daily Capital*, March 19, 1957, p. 11.

101. Dick Snider, "Capitalizing on Sports," *Topeka Daily Capital*, March 24, 1957, p. C-1.

102. "There Was a Young Man . . . ," advertisement, *Kansas City Star*, March 22, 1957, p. 35.

103. Snider, "Capitalizing on Sports," March 19, p. 11.

104. Del Haley, "Aiding Segregation in Reverse," *University Daily Kansan*, March 21, 1957, p. 2.

105. Bill Mayer, "Bill Mayer's Sport Talk," *Lawrence Daily Journal-World*, March 20, 1957, p. 18.

106. Michael S. Mayer, "With Much Deliberation and Some Speed: Eisenhower and the Brown Decision," *Journal of Southern History* 52 (February 1986), 43–76 (quotation from p. 61).

107. "Roudiness [sic] Mars KU-Okla. City Game in Dallas," p. 11.

108. Ray Cain, "Texas Insult Offends Him," *Kansas City Star*, March 22, 1957, p. 46.

109. Bill Mayer, "Oread Gang Coolest as Cage Tiff Roars," *Lawrence Daily Journal-World*, March 18, 1957, pp. 1–2.

110. Bill Mayer, "Bill Mayer's Sport Talk," *Lawrence Daily Journal-World*, March 18, 1957, p. 9.

111. Earl Morey, "N.C. Proves Ranking by Edging Jay Quint," *Lawrence Daily Journal-World*, March 25, 1957, p. 10.

112. "Alone with His Reflections," *Kansas City Star*, March 25, 1957, p. 18.

113. Singling out Chamberlain for blame for his one missed free throw would have been outrageously unfair, although still possible given the nature of sports coverage. Chamberlain had scored twenty-three out of KU's fifty-three points. He had also shot a respectable 6–13 from the field; his teammates, by comparison, shot 9–34. Meanwhile, other teammates, including senior co-captain Gene Elstun, also missed pivotal free throws that could have won the game for KU.

114. See Bob Hurt, "Harp Says Rebounds Gave North Carolina Big Victory," *Topeka Daily Capital*, March 24, 1957, p. C-1; and Bill Mayer, "Bill Mayer's Sport Talk," *Lawrence Daily Journal-World*, March 25, 1957, p. 12.

115. John I. Johnson, "Sport Light: NCAA Meet Has Wide Appeal," *Kansas City Call*, March 29, 1957, p. 10.

116. "Receiving the Coveted Trophy," *Kansas City Call*, March 29, 1957, p. 12.

117. Bill Mayer, "Bill Mayer's Sport Talk," *Lawrence Daily Journal-World*, March 27, 1957, p. 19.

118. Bill Mayer, "Wilt, Loneski State They'll Stay at K.U.," *Lawrence Daily Journal-World*, May 4, 1957, pp. 1–2 (quotation from p. 2).

119. Jerry Dawson, "So What?" *University Daily Kansan*, May 7, 1957, p. 2.

120. "Don't Do It, Wilt!" *Kansas City Call*, May 10, 1957, p. 18.

121. Bill Brower, "Beating the Gum," *Kansas City Call*, May 24, 1957, p. 10.

122. Mayer, "Wilt, Loneski, State They'll Stay," p. 2.

123. Dick Snider, "Capitalizing on Sports," *Topeka Daily Capital*, May 5, 1957, p. C-1.

124. George Anthan, "Along the Jayhawker Trail," *University Daily Kansan*, May 7, 1957, p. 6.

125. Bob Busby, "On the Level," *Kansas City Star*, May 23, 1957, morning ed., p. 25.

126. Bill Mayer, "Mikan Asks Wilt to Refuse Pros; Athletes Lauded," *Lawrence Daily Journal-World*, May 21, 1957, p. 13.

127. See, for example, "R-o-c-k C-h-a-l-k—Wilt to Stay!" *Topeka Daily Capital*, May 27, 1957, p. 4; and "Wilt's Big Decision," *Lawrence Daily Journal-World*, May 25, 1957, p. 4.

128. James C. Brown, "Sport Light," *Kansas City Call*, December 13, 1957, p. 10. For the story of Davis's death, see "Dowdal H. Davis Dies Suddenly," *Kansas City Call*, June 28, 1957, pp. 1, 4.

129. Dick Snider, "Capitalizing on Sports," *Topeka Daily Capital*, January 1, 1958, p. 13.

130. "One-Man Team? Jayhawks Say No," *Kansas City Star*, January 7, 1958, p. 14.

131. Chamberlain and Shaw, *Wilt: Just Like Any Other*, 74.

132. Goudsouzian, "'Can Basketball Survive Chamberlain?'" 163–165 (quotations from pp. 163, 164).

133. Bob Sweet, "Wilton the Wildcat Killer," cartoon, *University Daily Kansan*, February 3, 1958, p. 1.

134. Chester Curtice, "Restaurant Problems," *Lawrence Daily Journal-World*, May 4, 1957, p. 4.

135. Kathryn Harris, "Racial Opinions," p. 4.

136. See Bob Busby, "On the Level," *Kansas City Star*, February 18, 1958, morning ed., p. 17; "'Dipper' Turns 'Flipper,'" *University Daily Kansan*, February 14, 1958, p. 8; and "Sorting the Platters," *Kansas City Star*, February 21, 1958, p. 30.

137. W. W. Graber, "Says Kansas Still Leading Producer," *Topeka Daily Capital*, January 5, 1958, p. A-14.

138. "Far above All the Rest!" advertisement, *University Daily Kansan*, January 14, 1958, p. 7.

139. James C. Brown, "Sport-O-Rama," *Kansas City Call*, May 30, 1958, p. 10.

140. Bill Brower, "Beatin' the Gum," *Kansas City Call*, June 13, 1958, p. 10.

141. Ernest Mehl, "Sporting Comment," *Kansas City Star*, May 25, 1958, p. B2.

142. "Best of Luck Wilt," *Lawrence Daily Journal-World*, May 24, 1958, p. 4. Lawrence residents generally appeared to be supportive as well. The following Monday, a front-page story dealt with local reaction to Chamberlain's decision, saying that "Downtown Lawrence conversation . . . centered around the departure of . . . Wilt Chamberlain" on Friday and Saturday. According to the unbylined story, "most showed no resentment over his decision" and many "added they probably would have done the same thing." See "Fans Switch from Wilt after Football Preview," *Lawrence Daily Journal-World*, May 26, 1958, p. 1.

143. Bob Busby, "On the Level," *Kansas City Star*, May 27, 1958, morning ed., p. 23.

144. Dick Snider, "Capitalizing on Sports," *Topeka Daily Capital*, May 24, 1958, p. 16.

145. Bob Billings, "My Friend, Wilt Chamberlain," "1959" folder, Wilt Chamberlain [Biographical] file, Spencer Research Library, University of Kansas.

146. Chamberlain, "Why I Am Quitting College," 94.

147. Goudsouzian, "'Can Basketball Survive Chamberlain?'" 165.

148. See "Best of Luck, Wilt," p. 4; "The Great Wilt Leaves K.U.," *Kansas City Star*, May 26, 1958, p. 28; Dick Snider, "Capitalizing on Sports," *Topeka Daily Capital*, May 24,

1958, p. 16; and Dick Snider, "Capitalizing on Sports," *Topeka Daily Capital*, May 31, 1958, p. 14.

149. Goudsouzian, "'Can Basketball Survive Chamberlain?'" 172.

150. Ibid., 168.

CHAPTER 4

1. Barry Jacobs makes a similar observation in *Across the Line: Profiles in Courage; Tales of the First Black Players in the ACC and SEC* (Guilford, CT: Lyons Press, 2008), 100.

2. See "The Diminishing Returns of Integration," *Carolina Times*, May 7, 1966, p. A2.

3. W. L. Greene, "Lest We Forget," *The Carolinian*, November 3, 1945, p. 4.

4. There had been other black scholarship athletes in the South, although they were still rare in 1966. Some Texas schools, such as the University of North Texas, integrated their athletic squads as early as the late 1950s. See Ronald E. Marcello, "The Integration of Intercollegiate Athletics in Texas: North Texas State College as a Test Case, 1956," *Journal of Sport History* 14, no. 3 (Winter 1987): 286–316. Western Texas College—now the University of Texas at El Paso—featured an all-black starting five that won the NCAA basketball championship in 1966. However, most men's basketball and football teams at major southern universities and colleges remained segregated, and Scott was the first black star player in the ACC.

5. At the time of Scott's arrival on campus, the schools in the ACC were the University of Maryland, the University of Virginia, North Carolina State University, Duke University, UNC, Wake Forest University, Clemson University, and the University of South Carolina.

6. The principal mainstream publications explored in this article are the *Durham Morning Herald* and the *News and Observer*. Alternate publications include the campus newspaper the *Daily Tar Heel*, the *Chapel Hill Weekly*, the *Carolinian*, and the *Carolina Times*.

7. William Chafe, *Civilities and Civil Rights: Greensboro, North Carolina, and the Black Struggle for Freedom* (New York: Oxford University Press, 1981), 7.

8. V. O. Key, with Alexander Heard, *Southern Politics in State and Nation* (New York: Knopf, 1949), 206.

9. Chafe, *Civilities and Civil Rights*, 4–8 (quotations from pp. 7, 8). Paul Luebke has echoed this point in recent years, noting that to black North Carolinians, "the state's racial moderation was always problematic." Indeed, according to Luebke, "the moderate path that the white elite chose nevertheless institutionalized and legitimated a segregated society in which blacks could not expect either political or economic equality." See Paul Luebke, *Tar Heel Politics: Myths and Realities* (Chapel Hill: University of North Carolina Press, 1990), 102.

10. See Warren Ashby, "Campaign Ordeal," in *Frank Porter Graham: A Southern Liberal* (Winston-Salem, NC: John F. Blair, 1980), 257–271.

11. For a thorough account of the sit-in movement in Chapel Hill and its aftermath, see John Ehle, *The Free Men* (New York: Harper and Row, 1965). For recent reflections on the sit-in movement, see "A Challenge to the Old Order," 30; Charles L. Thompson, "Standing Up by Sitting Down," 32–43; Carolyn Edy, "Segregation's Last Stand," 44–47; and Carolyn Edy, "Town and Gown," 46, all in *Carolina Alumni Review* 95, no. 2 (March/April, 2006).

12. For accounts of the former incident, see Ehle, *The Free Men*, 141–143; and Thompson, "Standing Up," 32–34. For accounts of the latter incident, see Ehle, *The Free Men*, 144; and Thompson, "Standing Up," 41–42.

13. Thompson, "Standing Up," 39.

14. See Ehle, *The Free Men*, 152; and Thompson, "Standing Up," 39.

15. Thompson, "Standing Up," 43.

16. Ehle, *The Free Men*, 325–326.

17. See Clayborn Carson, *In Struggle: SNCC and the Black Awakening of the 1960s*, rev. ed. (Cambridge, MA: Harvard University Press, 1995), 215–306; Alan Matusow, *The Unraveling of America: A History of Liberalism in the 1960s* (New York: Harper and Row,

1984), 345–375; and Harvard Sitkoff, *The Struggle for Black Equality 1954–1992*, rev. ed. (New York: Hill and Wang, 1993), 184–209.

18. Associated Negro Press, "Nat'l League Signs 1st Negro; Club Owners Jubilant but Want Robinson Paid For," *The Carolinian*, November 3, 1945, pp. 1, 8. See 1.

19. See C. D. Halliburton, "Second Thoughts," *The Carolinian*, November 3, 1945, p. 4; and Greene, "Lest We Forget," p. 4.

20. See Jack Horner, "Robinson Case Starts Hot Stove Gossip," *Durham Morning Herald*, October 25, 1945, p. II-2; and Jack Wade, "Jack Wade's Sports Parade; Revolutionary, But It Was Inevitable," *Charlotte Observer*, October 25, 1945, p. II-2.

21. Wade, "Revolutionary, But It Was Inevitable," p. II-2.

22. Horner, "Robinson Case Starts Hot Stove Gossip," p. II-2.

23. For a brief but apt summary of the negro leagues, see Jules Tygiel, *Baseball's Great Experiment: Jackie Robinson and His Legacy* (New York: Oxford University Press, 1983), 16–29. For a more expansive history, see Neil Lanctot, *Negro League Baseball: The Rise and Ruin of a Black Institution* (Philadelphia: University of Pennsylvania Press, 2004).

24. For more on North Carolinians' knowledge of integrated athletic competition, see Pamela Grundy, *Learning to Win: Sports, Education, and Social Change in Twentieth-Century North Carolina* (Chapel Hill: University of North Carolina Press, 2001), 262.

25. The first black to compete in a game in the South was football player Chester Pierce, who played for Harvard against the University of Virginia (UVA) in 1947. Duke then hosted the integrated University of Pittsburgh football team in 1950. See Mark D. Briggs, "A Tale of Two Pioneers: The Integration of College Athletics in the South during the 1960s in the Age of the Civil Rights Movement" (master's thesis, University of North Carolina, Chapel Hill, 2000), 15–17.

26. Grundy, *Learning to Win*, 264. The experiences of these black athletes was comparable to black musicians who played fraternity parties at southern schools in the late 1950s and into the 1960s. As music historian Brian Ward has noted, white southern students could revel in black music even as they continued to relegate black musicians to second-class status. See Brian Ward, *Just My Soul Responding: Rhythm and Blues, Black Consciousness, and Race Relations* (Berkeley: University of California Press, 1998), 232.

27. Scott's change of heart did not come without controversy. Driesell was so upset that he actually ambushed Scott, "jumping out of the bushes the next day [after Scott's commitment] to confront [him] as he walked to a movie." See Art Chansky, *Dean's Domain: The Inside Story of Dean Smith and His College Basketball Empire* (Marietta, GA: Longstreet, 1999). In fact, the president of the Davidson College Alumni Association, William White, even sent university president William Friday and Smith a letter complaining about UNC's recruitment of Scott. See William White to William Friday and Dean Smith, May 5, 1966, and J. Carlyle Sitterson to William White, May 9, 1966, both in Box 15, "Athletics—Basketball" folder, Chancellor's Records: J. Carlyle Sitterson Papers, #40022, Southern Historical Collection, Wilson Library, University of North Carolina, Chapel Hill.

28. Briggs, "Tale of Two Pioneers," 69.

29. Charles H. Martin, "The Rise and Fall of Jim Crow in Southern College Sports: The Case of the Atlantic Coast Conference," *North Carolina Historical Review* 76 (July 1999): 263–265.

30. One NYU administrator specifically lamented the "segregation of" black students "at football games and other activities" at UNC as particularly disheartening. See letter from Sydney G. Roth to William B. Aycock, November 9, 1959, Box 2, "Integration—Negroes 1957–1959" folder, Chancellor's Records: William B. Aycock Papers, #40020, Southern Historical Collection, Wilson Library, University of North Carolina, Chapel Hill.

31. Martin, "Rise and Fall of Jim Crow," 265.

32. Although there are many examples of papers such as this, the first example in Chancellor Aycock's papers comes from 1957. See Roy Armstrong to William B. Aycock, July 31, 1957, Box 2, "Integration—Negroes 1957–1959" folder, William B. Aycock Papers.

33. See William B. Aycock to Sam McGill, July 6, 1957, Box 2, "Integration—Negroes 1957–1959" folder, William B. Aycock Papers.

34. See Student Legislature's Special Committee on Discriminatory Practices to William B. Aycock, March 2, 1964, Box 2, "Integration—Negroes 1964" folder, Aycock Papers. Maryland integrated its football team in 1963. Other African Americans had participated on sports teams on UNC's campus before Scott—the first black to compete at UNC was Edwin Okorama, who played for the soccer team in 1963. See Briggs, "Tale of Two Pioneers," 15–16. However, football and men's basketball were the dominant sports on campus, and integrating these teams carried much more symbolic weight.

35. Martin, "Rise and Fall of Jim Crow," 265.

36. For example, in 1963, Mississippi State University basketball coach James H. "Babe" McCarthy sneaked his team across the state line to participate in an NCAA tournament game against the integrated squad from Loyola University of Chicago. See Russell J. Henderson, "The 1963 Mississippi State University Basketball Controversy and the Repeal of the Unwritten Law: 'Something More Than the Game Will Be Lost,'" *Journal of Southern History* 63, no. 4 (November 1997): 827–854.

37. Wake Forest first signed an African American basketball player the same year as UNC, in the spring of 1966. The other schools in the conference followed, starting with Duke and North Carolina State the following year. Recruitment of African American football players occurred more slowly. Again, North Carolina (along with North Carolina State) was second behind Maryland and Wake Forest, when they signed Ricky Lanier in 1968. It took the University of Virginia and Clemson University until 1971 to follow suit. See Martin, "Rise and Fall of Jim Crow," 265.

38. J. A. Williams to William B. Aycock, July 19, 1957, Box 2, "Integration—Negroes 1957–1959" folder, Aycock Papers.

39. Chafe, *Civility and Civil Rights*, 8.

40. See Daniel H. Pollitt to A. C. Howell, December 17, 1963, Box 2, "Integration—Negroes 1961–1963" folder, Aycock Papers.

41. See William B. Aycock to A. C. Howell, January 17, 1964, Box 2, "Integration—Negroes 1964" folder, Aycock Papers.

42. Head basketball coach Dean Smith is often credited with integrating the town of Chapel Hill by going out to lunch at the Pines (where the basketball team usually had its pregame meals) with his minister and a black friend in the late 1950s. Smith downplayed the incident in his autobiography, noting that he was only an assistant coach at the time and thus not tremendously influential, but the memory of the event has had staying power. See Dean Smith, with John Kligo and Sally Jenkins, *A Coach's Life* (New York: Random House, 1999), 95–96.

43. See J. Carlyle Sitterson to Charlie Scott, May 9, 1966, Box 15, "Athletics—Basketball" folder, J. Carlyle Sitterson Papers.

44. According to various sources, Smith and the rest of the coaching staff had hoped that Cooper would be the first black player on the varsity team as a walk-on. However, Cooper failed an accounting exam early in his sophomore year and decided to concentrate on his studies instead. See Briggs, "Tale of Two Pioneers," 71; Chansky, *Dean's Domain*, 63; Smith, *A Coach's Life*, 99.

45. Bob Quincy, ed., *The 1964/1965 UNC Basketball Blue Book* (Chapel Hill, NC: Self-published, 1964), 8–9. Alternate title: *University of North Carolina Basketball, 1964–65 Basketball: Our Men in Outer Space.*

46. Jack Williams, ed., *The 1966/1967 UNC Basketball Blue Book* (Chapel Hill, NC: Colonial Press, 1966), 41.

47. See Jack Williams, ed., *The 1967/1968 UNC Basketball Blue Book* (Chapel Hill, NC: Colonial Press, 1967), 17; Jack Williams, ed., *The 1968/1969 UNC Basketball Blue Book* (Chapel Hill, NC: Colonial Press, 1968); and Jack Williams, Sybil Smith, Rick Brewer, and Chris Cobbs, eds., *The 1969/1970 UNC Basketball Blue Book* (Chapel Hill, NC: Colonial

Press, 1969). Season previews also made no special note of Billy Jones, the ACC's first black basketball player, who played for the University of Maryland from 1964 to 1968.

48. See Don Shea, "Laurinburg's Scott Signs with Carolina; Negro Youth Accepts Scholarship," *Durham Morning Herald*, May 4, 1966, p. B3.

49. See "UNC Gets Laurinburg Star Scott," May 4, 1966, p. 17.

50. Mel Derrick, "Charlie Scott: Basketball Star . . . Student . . . and Tar Heel Prize," *Charlotte Observer*, May 4, 1966, p. D6.

51. See "Carolina Makes Big Catch: 1st Negro Signs UNC Grant," *Chapel Hill Weekly*, May 4, 1966, p. 6.

52. See Lawrence Maddry, "I Have Tremendous Optimism: Sitterson," *Chapel Hill Weekly*, May 11, 1966, p. 2. Such responses were not uncommon. Head football coach Bill Dooley received a letter from a fan calling him "a traitor to his southern heritage" after signing Lanier. See Keith Patrick Howard, "Desegregation of College Football in the Southeastern United States" (master's thesis, University of North Carolina, Chapel Hill, 2001), 29.

53. Alone among area publications, the *Tar Heel* also covered walk-on Cooper's first game with the freshman team in the fall of 1964, identifying him as "the first Negro to score two points for the Blue and White." See "Freshmen Cagers Drop Baby Tigers by 87–56 Count," *Daily Tar Heel*, December 2, 1964, p. 1.

54. See Barry Jacobs, "Campus Atmosphere Helps Bring Charlie Scott Here," *Daily Tar Heel*, May 5, 1966, p. 5.

55. The specific term *gladiator* was often used by Edwards and perhaps showed Smith's awareness of his efforts.

56. See Jacobs, "Campus Atmosphere," p. 5.

57. See "Cage Star Going to Carolina," *The Carolinian*, May 21, 1966, p. 15.

58. See "Scott to Attend UNC with Full Scholarship Agreement," *Carolina Times*, May 7, 1966, pp. 1A, 6A.

59. Jack Horner, "Carolina's Second Half Comeback Trips Virginia Tech: Miller Hits 30 in 89–76 Win," *Durham Morning Herald*, December 3, 1967, final ed., C1.

60. Jacobs, *Across the Line*, 116.

61. Briggs, "Tale of Two Pioneers," 77.

62. Jacobs, *Across the Line*, 101–102.

63. Briggs, "Tale of Two Pioneers," 78.

64. See Chansky, *Dean's Domain*, 64; and Jacobs, *Across the Line*, 102.

65. Smith himself acknowledged that he and his players "felt our way along, and we grew closer over time," as they tried to adjust to an integrated environment that both Scott and the white players were unaccustomed to. See Smith, *A Coach's Life*, 102.

66. Briggs, "Tale of Two Pioneers," 78–79.

67. In fact, Scott said in later years that Smith's decision to limit the discussion of racial issues with the team made sense: "If I would have kept it on my mind all the time, it would have been very hard." See Jacobs, *Across the Line*, 115.

68. Hugo Germino, "Gathering Up the Dope," *Durham Morning Herald*, December 5, 1967, afternoon ed., p. B2.

69. Jacobs, *Across the Line*, 118.

70. See Amy Bass, *Not the Triumph but the Struggle: The 1968 Olympics and the Making of the Black Athlete* (Minneapolis: University of Minnesota Press, 2002); Harry Edwards, *The Revolt of the Black Athlete* (New York: Free Press, 1969); Michael Lomax, "Revisiting *The Revolt of the Black Athlete*: Harry Edwards and the Making of the New African-American Sports Studies," *Journal of Sport History* 29, no. 3 (Fall 2002): 469–479; Jack Scott, *The Athletic Revolution* (New York: Free Press, 1971); and David K. Wiggins, "'The Year of Awakening,'" in *Glory Bound: Black Athletes in a White America* (Syracuse, NY: Syracuse University Press, 1997), 104–122.

71. For more on Edwards's efforts, and the responses to them, see Harry Edwards, *The Struggle That Must Be: An Autobiography* (New York: Macmillan, 1980), 174–188.

72. Edwards, *Revolt of the Black Athlete*, 31–37. Olson's articles formed the basis of his book *The Black Athlete: A Shameful Story; The Myth of Integration in American Sport* (New York: Time-Life Books, 1968).

73. Jacobs, *Across the Line*, 118.

74. Briggs, "Tale of Two Pioneers," 96–98 (quotation from p. 98). Scott was not alone in rejecting the boycott. See "Should Negroes Boycott the Olympics? Ebony Poll of Athletes Indicates Majority Prefer to Participate in This Year's Mexico City Sports Spectacular," *Ebony* 23, no. 5 (March 1968): 110–116.

75. Briggs, "Tale of Two Pioneers," 100–103.

76. The BSM may have been partially motivated to act by a campus visit from Stokely Carmichael on November 21, 1968. Carmichael implicitly attacked the progressive mystique in his speech, saying that the "main goal" of white liberals was "to prevent confrontation and conflict," which led to the continuation of "the status quo." See J. D. Wilkinson, "Carmichael Attacks Liberals, Explains Need for Violence," *Daily Tar Heel*, November 22, 1968, p. 1.

77. Dale Gibson and Ross Scott, "New Demands, Ultimatum Presented by UNC Blacks," *Durham Morning Herald*, February 19, 1969, morning ed., pp. 1A, 2A.

78. See "Threat in Black Student Demands," *Durham Morning Herald*, February 21, 1969, p. 4A; and "Not 'Revolution,'" *News and Observer*, February 20, 1969, p. 4.

79. Jacobs, *Across the Line*, 119. Scott did not begrudge Smith his hesitance, arguing that the idea of a boycott was more of "a power move by the black students" than a genuine good cause.

80. See, for example, Owen Davis, "Great Scott. Scott's End-of-Game Bucket Leads Carolina to Regional Title over Davidson, 87–85," *Daily Tar Heel*, March 16, 1969, p. 1.

81. Art Chansky, *The Dean's List: A Celebration of Tar Heel Basketball and Dean Smith* (New York: Warner Books, 1996), 48.

82. Briggs, "Tale of Two Pioneers," 81–83 (quotation from p. 82).

83. See "Scott Sore at ACC Coach, Player Picks," *Durham Morning Herald*, March 16, 1969, p. 2C.

84. "Scott Sore," p. 2C.

85. See "Roche Player of the Year," *News and Observer*, March 13, 1969, p. 39.

86. The one exception to this trend was the story in the *Charlotte News*, where writer Bill Ballenger noted that the issue involved in Scott's voting was "essentially a racial one." He also printed an exchange with Scott in which the black star pointedly commented, "White writers did this." See Bill Ballenger, "Scott Hints He May Quit; Miffed by All-ACC Voting," *Charlotte News*, March 14, 1969, p. 16A.

87. See "For Scott, Malloy and Davis, Schooling in North Carolina Story of Extremes," *Durham Morning Herald*, March 15, 1969, p. 3B; and "Negro Stars Live in Two Worlds," *News and Observer*, March 15, 1969, p. 14.

88. "For Scott, Malloy and Davis," p. 3B.

89. Chafe, *Civilities and Civil Rights*, 8.

90. "Great Scott's Late Returns," *Chapel Hill Weekly*, March 23, 1969, p. B2.

91. University of North Carolina at Chapel Hill, *Yackety Yack: The Yearbook of the University of North Carolina at Chapel Hill* (Dallas, TX: Taylor, 1967), 461.

92. F. Wilton Avery, "The Greatest Scott of All," *Chapel Hill Weekly*, March 23, 1969, p. B2.

93. Art Chansky, "An Extreme Injustice," *Daily Tar Heel*, May 19, 1969, p. 4.

94. See Sam Davis, "UNC Beats Duke for Title on Scott's 40 Points," *Carolina Times*, March 15, 1969, p. A7.

95. See "'Great' Scott Leads All in ACC Scoring," March 15, 1969, p. 21.

96. See Joseph L. Turner, in "Spotlight on Sports" section, *The Carolinian*, March 29, 1969, p. 23.

97. See Curry Kirkpatrick, "One More War to Go," *Sports Illustrated*, March 2, 1970, 12–15. For his discussion of these racial incidents, see p. 15.

98. See James T. Wooten, "Negro Basketball Star a Hero to Many North Carolina Whites," *New York Times*, March 22, 1969, p. 20.

99. Wooten, "Negro Basketball Star," p. 20. That one fan was not the only one to blame Scott for the team's loss to Purdue. In a column following the game, Chansky chastised UNC fans for "badmouthing" the team after the loss. He reminded students "that Charlie Scott nearly won the Atlantic Coast Conference Tournament single handedly" and had led the way against Davidson. Apparently, many assigned responsibility for the loss to Scott, an additional burden for a player already weighted down with many pressures. See Art Chansky, "Not Typical of Carolina," *Daily Tar Heel*, March 22, 1969, p. 4.

100. Jacobs, *Across the Line*, 113.

101. For an apt summary of these three riots—and their consequences—see Matusow, *Unraveling of America*, 360–367.

102. Avery, "Greatest Scott of All," p. B2.

103. Bill Ballenger, "Scott Hints He May Quit," p. 16A.

104. "Scott Sore," p. 2C.

105. Briggs, "Tale of Two Pioneers," 102–103.

106. Wooten, "Negro Basketball Star," p. 20.

107. "Scott, Chamberlain Right in Supporting Demands," *Daily Tar Heel*, February 19, 1969, p. 2. The *Daily Tar Heel* was also the lone area newspaper to support the demands brought forth by the BSM. Even the *Chapel Hill News* expressed bemusement at on-campus black activism. An editorial commented ironically that the aims of the BSM seemed to be "flatly opposed to those . . . of the civil rights movement" of the recent past. See "A Most Confusing Situation," *Chapel Hill News*, February 19, 1969, p. II-2; and "University Has No Case for Racial Complacency," *Daily Tar Heel*, February 5, 1969, p. 2.

108. Owen Davis, "Heel Prints," *Daily Tar Heel*, February 21, 1969, p. 5.

109. Art Chansky, "All-American Charles Scott Has Travelled a Long Way," *Daily Tar Heel*, November 25, 1969, p. 1, "Basketball Preview."

110. Art Chansky, "Writers 'Ran' True to Form," *Daily Tar Heel*, March 11, 1970, p. 4.

111. Chansky, *Dean's List*, 53.

112. See University of North Carolina at Chapel Hill, *Yackety Yack* (Winston-Salem, NC: Hunter, 1970), 94.

113. Art Chansky, "A Lone Victory," *Daily Tar Heel*, March 18, 1970, p. 4. Scott was certainly well prepared to pursue a career in professional basketball following his four years at UNC. He earned numerous accolades during his ten-year professional career in the American Basketball Association and the National Basketball Association, including the ABA's Rookie of the Year Award in 1971, and an NBA championship with the Boston Celtics in 1976. He became a successful businessman when his playing career ended.

114. Jacobs, *Across the Line*, 114.

115. Briggs, "Tale of Two Pioneers," 91.

116. Howard, "Desegregation of College Football," 28.

117. Jacobs, *Across the Line*, 98.

118. Briggs, "Tale of Two Pioneers," 86.

119. Jacobs, *Across the Line*, 99.

CHAPTER 5

1. Tonto Coleman, "Football? What Is It? . . . ," *Birmingham News*, August 23, 1970, p. F-14.

2. The first SEC school to integrate its football team was the University of Kentucky, in 1966. Six other schools followed suit between 1968 and 1970 before UA integrated in 1971. See Mark D. Briggs, "A Tale of Two Pioneers: The Integration of College Athletics in the South during the 1960s in the Age of the Civil Rights Movement" (master's thesis, University of North Carolina, Chapel Hill, 2000), 173.

3. Bryant was so beloved by Alabama residents that, according to biographer Allen Barra, the day after he died in 1983, "the entire area code for the state of Alabama . . . had been shut down from overload." See Allen Barra, *The Last Coach: A Life of Paul "Bear" Bryant* (New York: W. W. Norton, 2005), xiv.

4. Suzanne Rau Wolfe, *The University of Alabama: A Pictorial History* (Tuscaloosa: University of Alabama Press, 1983), 212–213.

5. For more on the effects of the stand in the schoolhouse door, see Taylor Branch, *Parting the Waters: America in the King Years, 1954–63* (New York: Simon and Schuster, 1988), 822–824.

6. According to the historian Suzanne Rau Wolfe, "the University's subsequent peaceful integration" after Wallace's standoff with federal troops earned Rose acclaim from "publications around the country." See Wolfe, *University of Alabama*, 206. Examples of the anger from locals whites toward Rose can be found in the "Crank Letters" folder, President Frank Rose Papers, William Stanley Hoole Special Collections Library, University of Alabama, Tuscaloosa.

7. For the origins of Bryant's nickname, see Paul W. Bryant and John Underwood, *Bear: The Hard Life and Good Times of Alabama's Coach Bryant* (Boston: Little, Brown, 1974), 23–24.

8. Andrew Doyle, "An Atheist in Alabama Is Someone Who Doesn't Believe in Bear Bryant: A Symbol for an Embattled South," in *Sporting World of the Modern South*, ed. Patrick B. Miller (Chicago: University of Illinois Press, 2002), 247–275 (quotation from p. 250).

9. See Bryant and Underwood, *Bear*, 299–306. Even after Bryant decided to integrate the team, he still worried about public response. Condredge Holloway, an African American quarterback who aspired to attend UA, said that when he met with Bryant in 1970 during his recruitment, the coach told him: "I'd love to have you at Alabama, but Alabama's not ready for a black quarterback." See Keith Dunnavant, *Coach: The Life of Paul "Bear" Bryant* (New York: Simon and Schuster, 1996), 259.

10. John David Briley, *Career in Crisis: Paul "Bear" Bryant and the 1971 Season of Change* (Macon, GA: Mercer University Press, 2006), 36.

11. Bryant believed that integrating his team as a political act, in direct conflict with the governor's desires, was not the appropriate response: "You don't change people's thinking overnight," he wrote. "When folks are ignorant, you don't condemn them, you teach 'em." See Bryant, *Bear*, 300.

12. Doyle, "An Atheist in Alabama," 263. Original citation is *Los Angeles Times*, December 4, 1964, III-1. Bryant advocated for the squad to be permitted to play integrated teams in postseason bowl games, and the team faced an integrated team from Pennsylvania State University in the Liberty Bowl in December 1959. See Bryant and Underwood, *Bear*, 301.

13. This "outrage" inspired Bull Connor to write Bryant a letter commiserating that Bryant and his team had been dealt with unfairly. See Doyle, "An Atheist in Alabama," 265. Keith Dunnavant devoted an entire book to the saga of the 1966 team. See Dunnavant, *The Missing Ring: How Bear Bryant and the 1966 Alabama Crimson Tide Were Denied College Football's Most Elusive Prize* (New York: St. Martin's Press, 2007).

14. Paul Bryant to Frank A. Rose and Jeff Bennett, March 20, 1967, "Athletics, Department of" folder, President Frank Rose Papers. Bryant's decision to start recruiting only in-state African American athletes stemmed from his belief that out-of-state players were unlikely to attend the school because of its negative image in the national media. See Ed Darling, "On Bowls, Recruiting, Coaching, Future," *Tuscaloosa News*, November 18, 1970, p. 7.

15. Bryant admits as much in his autobiography, writing that he was mostly interested in getting "good players" when he attempted to integrate the team. He "wanted to win" and lamented that he could not keep the best black athletes in the state. See Bryant and Underwood, *Bear*, 300.

16. See, for example, "Bryant Checks Negro Hopefuls," *Tuscaloosa News*, April 6, 1967; and Tommy Roberts, "Tide Spring Drills Open with 151 Reporting," *Crimson White*, April 3, 1967, p. 6.

17. For more on Pernell's experiences, see John Croft, "Bear's 'Handicap' of Segregation to Be No More," *Crimson White*, November 26, 1968, p. 2.

18. Organizations dedicated to the interests and concerns of African American students, such as UNC's BSM, flourished in the latter half of the 1960s. For more on these groups, see Fabio Rojas, *From Black Power to Black Studies: How a Radical Social Movement Became an Academic Discipline* (Baltimore: Johns Hopkins University Press, 2007).

19. Don Yaeger, with Sam Cunningham and John Papadakis, *Turning of the Tide: How One Game Changed the South* (New York: Center Street, 2006), 57.

20. Ibid., 63–64.

21. Edward L. Nall, Booker T. Forte, Rosa Moore, and Moses C. Jones, Jr. to University Community, August 1, 1968, Student Organizations, "Afro-American Association 1968–1969" folder, President David Mathews Papers, W. S. Hoole Special Collections Library, University of Alabama, Tuscaloosa.

22. Willard F. Gray to David Mathews, August 19, 1970, "Athletics, 1968" folder, President David Mathews Papers.

23. Marcel Hopson, "Hits and Bits," *Birmingham World*, January 25, 1969, p. 6.

24. Marcel Hopson, "Hits and Bits," *Birmingham World*, March 29, 1969, p. 7.

25. Peniel E. Joseph, *Waiting 'Til the Midnight Hour: A Narrative History of Black Power in America* (New York: Henry Holt, 2006), 174.

26. Harvard Sitkoff, *The Struggle for Black Equality 1954–1992*, rev. ed. (New York: Hill and Wang, 1993), 213.

27. See Joseph, *Waiting 'Til the Midnight Hour*, 205–275.

28. Sitkoff, *Struggle for Black Equality*, 211.

29. Ibid., 217.

30. See Robert J. Weiss, *"We Want Jobs": A History of Affirmative Action* (New York: Garland, 1997), 126, 130–133.

31. Yaeger, *Turning of the Tide*, 60–62 (quotation from p. 62).

32. "Is This Institutionalized Racism?" "Student Organizations, Afro-American Association 1968–1969" folder, President David Mathews Papers. See also James C. Wilder to David Mathews, attached. O. J. Simpson was a prominent black running back from the University of Southern California who had just won the most prestigious college football honor, the Heisman Trophy, in December 1968.

33. Copies of the lawsuit are available in the "Afro-American Association 1968–1969 folder," Mathews Papers.

34. Yaeger, *Turning of the Tide*, 65–67; "Afro-American Association 1968–1969" folder, Mathews Papers.

35. "Afro-American Association 1968–1969" folder, Mathews Papers.

36. Ibid.

37. The prominence of the story in these local newspapers contradicts Briley, who writes that the lawsuit received little press coverage. See Briley, *Career in Crisis*, 27; "Racial Suit Aimed at UA Athletics," *Tuscaloosa News*, July 1, 1969, 2nd ed., pp. 1–2; "Black Students Sue Bama on Athletes," *Birmingham News*, July 2, 1969, metro ed., p. 2; and "Afro Suit Charges Discrimination in Athletic Recruits," *Crimson White*, July 7, 1969, p. 1.

38. The *World's* decision to refrain from commenting on the lawsuit may have had to do with its editors' animosity toward young black radicals. On multiple occasions, the newspaper printed editorials and columns damning the tactics and ideals of groups such as the Black Panthers, clearly falling in line more with old-guard organizations such as the NAACP.

39. "Support for Afros," *Crimson White*, July 7, 1969, p. 2.

40. Jack Gurley, "Editorial Ires Alum: C-W's Views Called Rotten," *Crimson White*, July 21, 1969, p. 2.

41. Frye Gaillard, "Crumbling Segregation in the Southeastern Conference," *The Black Athlete—1970* (Nashville, TN: Race Relations Information Center, 1970), 27.

42. "We're Going to . . . ," *Birmingham News*, July 23, 1969, p. 31.

43. Charles Land, "Recruiting Plan Still the Same, Bryant Declares," *Tuscaloosa News*, July 23, 1969, p. 15.

44. Briley, *Career in Crisis*, 26.

45. Another indication of Bryant's focus on competition occurred later in the deposition. After discussing a number of players his staff was currently trying to sign, Bryant grumbled, "I hope the hell this list doesn't get to our opponents." See Transcript of Bryant deposition, 46.

46. Ibid., 14.

47. The full text of the "Letter from Birmingham Jail" is available at the University of Pennsylvania's African Studies Center. See http://www.africa.upenn.edu/Articles_Gen/Letter_Birmingham.html.

48. See, for example, Barra, *Last Coach*, xxv; and Doyle, "An Atheist in Alabama," 269–270.

49. Transcript of Bryant deposition, 48–49.

50. Ibid., 27. Although it seems implausible that Bryant would ask a white woman to escort the black player on his tour of the university and town, this appears to have been the case. The first black homecoming queen, Terry Points of Birmingham, won the honor in 1973. See Wolfe, *University of Alabama*, 227.

51. See David Mathews to Joseph Mallisham, April 26, 1971, "Afro-American Association 1970–1973" folder, President David Mathews Papers.

52. "Demands on Which Action Is to Be Taken," "Afro-American Association 1970–1973" folder, President David Mathews Papers.

53. Yaeger, *Turning of the Tide*, 157–163.

54. See ibid., 164–168; and Briley, *Career in Crisis*, 111–113.

55. Ibid., 163–164.

56. Briley, *Career in Crisis*, 113.

57. Yaeger, *Turning of the Tide*, 168.

58. Ibid., 167. According to Jackson, Bryant told him, "If you have a problem, come and see me. Don't see anybody else. Just come and see me, and it'll be taken care of." See ibid., 164.

59. Bryant, *Bear*, 302.

60. Briley, *Career in Crisis*, 110.

61. Yaeger, *Turning of the Tide*, 169. Mitchell also noted that his experiences were atypical in some ways: "There were some places I went because I was a football player that a lot of other black students never entered because they were all-white places, where only white students would go."

62. Briley, *Career in Crisis*, 9.

63. Of course, some players treated their black teammates fairly because they harbored no racial prejudice. Mitchell's roommate was Bobby Stanford, a white player from Albany, Georgia. The two became, and remain, best friends. See Yaeger, *Turning of the Tide*, 168.

64. Charles Land, "Negro Picks Bama," *Tuscaloosa News*, November 23, 1969, pp. 1–2.

65. Land, "Negro Picks Bama," p. 1.

66. Ibid., 2.

67. Alf Van Hoose, "Freshmen Promise New Bryant Era," *Birmingham News*, November 24, 1969, p. 13.

68. Jimmy Bryan, "Auburn Out-Signs Tide 37–16 as Recruiting War Begins," *Birmingham News*, December 14, 1969, pp. C-1, C-6. Mathews did not qualify academically and thus never joined the team.

69. This comparison seems particularly apt, as the masthead of the *News* read, "Serving a Progressive South."

70. "Crumbling Barriers," *Birmingham World*, January 3, 1970, p. 4.

71. See A. B. Porter to David Mathews, January 18, 1971, "Athletics, Jan.–March 1971" folder, President David Mathews Papers.

72. A number of authors have debunked the importance of this game. Even Yeager's *Turning of the Tide*, which takes the story of the 1970 game as its central event, acknowledges that the UA team was already on the path to racial integration.

73. Alf Van Hoose, "'Bama Puts on Deeper Red for '70," *Birmingham News*, August 23, 1970, pp. C-1, C-7. Nonetheless, Bud Furillo, a writer for the *Los Angeles Herald-Examiner*, insisted that Bryant intended for the game to ease racial integration at UA. "We all heard that Bryant had come to talk with [USC coach John] McKay about scheduling a game to help him [Bryant] get some black players on his team." See Yaeger, *Turning of the Tide*, 81.

74. Yaeger, *Turning of the Tide*, 111.

75. Delbert Reed, "South's Nice Says Visitor," *Tuscaloosa News*, September 14, 1970, p. 14.

76. Yaeger, *Turning of the Tide*, 114–125 (quotations from pp. 113, 119, 125).

77. Harold Kennedy, "Old South Welcome Greets Southern Cal," *Birmingham News*, September 12, 1970, metro ed., pp. A-1, A-5 (quotation from p. A-1).

78. "Meaty Football Fare," *Birmingham News*, September 12, 1970, metro ed., p. 10.

79. Warren Coon, "That Confederate Money Made Things Even Worse," *Tuscaloosa News*, September 14, 1970, pp. 13–14 (quotations from p. 14).

80. Coon, "That Confederate Money," p. 14.

81. See, for example, Alf Van Hoose, "Trojan Hosses Turn It On," *Birmingham News*, September 13, 1970, pp. C-1, C-5 (quotations from metro ed., p. C-1); Tom Self, "Soph Sam Cunningham . . . ," photograph, *Birmingham News*, September 13, 1970, metro ed., p. C-1; Charles Land, "Tough Trojans Top Tide, 42–21," *Tuscaloosa News*, September 13, 1970, pp. 1, 14; and Dan Meissner, "Trojans' Sam Cunningham . . . ," photograph, *Tuscaloosa News*, September 14, 1970, p. 13.

82. Charles Land, "Looking with Charles Land," *Tuscaloosa News*, September 14, 1970, p. 6.

83. Reed, "South's Nice," p. 14.

84. Marcel Hopson, "Hits and Bits," *Birmingham World*, September 26, 1970, p. 2.

85. Yaeger, *Turning of the Tide*, 130–135.

86. Ibid., 14.

87. "Vols Next for Tide Frosh," *Birmingham News*, November 5, 1970, p. 26.

88. See, for example: Charles Land, "Tide Frosh Open Here Monday," *Tuscaloosa News*, October 4, 1970, p. B-2; "Tide Freshmen Footballers Talking Over That Last Little Detail," photograph, *Tuscaloosa News*, November 20, 1970, p. 7; Alf Van Hoose, "Bama Rookies Bring Speed, Size to Combat," *Birmingham News*, October 6, 1970, p. 10; and "Vols Next for Tide Frosh," p. 26.

89. Raymond Hughes, "Desegregating the Holy Day: Football, Blacks and the Southeastern Conference" (Ph.D. diss., Ohio State University, 1991), 101.

90. Charley Thornton and Kirk McNair, *Alabama Football 1971* (Tuscaloosa, AL: Self-published, 1971), 22, 23, 26, 28 (quotation from p. 28).

91. Delbert Reed, "Mitchell Tightens Tide Loose Ends," *Tuscaloosa News*, September 2, 1971, p. 9. Reed and the coaches he talked with complemented Mitchell. End coach Richard Williamson praised Mitchell for having "a good attitude" and said the end "works hard." Although the article did not address Mitchell's race, the story was accompanied by a file photo of Mitchell running in uniform with no helmet on.

92. Tom Couchman, "The Times, They Are a 'Changin,'" *Tuscaloosa News*, August 23, 1971, p. 6.

93. If fans were upset that UA would have black players on their team, they didn't show it at the box office. Games for the 1971 season sold out quickly. See "Alabama Game Tickets Fast Becoming Scarce," *Tuscaloosa News*, August 15, 1971, p. B-1.

94. Alf Van Hoose, "'One Skeered, Other One Is Glad of It' in Los Angeles," *Birmingham News*, September 10, 1971, p. 9.

95. Alf Van Hoose, "The '71 Tide: Larger, with Longer Hair," *Birmingham News*, August 17, 1971, p. 15.

96. Charles Land, "Picture Day Is . . . Well . . . Like That," *Tuscaloosa News*, August 17, 1971, p. 8.

97. Jackson, like many of the team's reserves, did not play in the first game against USC. He debuted the following week.

98. Alf Van Hoose, "Bryant Beams over Tide in Trenches," *Birmingham News*, September 11, 1971, pp. 1, 11. The *Tuscaloosa News* also printed the game story on the front page. See Delbert Reed, "Terrific Tide Topples Trojans, 17–10," *Tuscaloosa News*, September 11, 1971, pp. 1, 5.

99. Alf Van Hoose, "Cloud 9 Fine, but It's Back to Work Again," *Birmingham News*, September 13, 1971, pp. 23, 27 (quotation from p. 23).

100. As an example, an editorial in the *Tuscaloosa News* three days after the game expressed excitement that "success was attained in starting this new season" of UA football, congratulating the coaches and players, but made no mention of the racial barrier broken when Mitchell took the field. See "Victory Adds Interest to Tide's Home Opener," *Tuscaloosa News*, September 14, 1971, p. 4.

101. Clyde Bolton, "Tiders Out-Tough Bengals 14–7 and Scent Oranges," *Birmingham News*, November 7, 1971, pp. C-1, C-7.

102. Alf Van Hoose, "Relentless Tide Bowls Over Miami 31–3, Sniffs Oranges," *Birmingham News*, November 14, 1971, pp. C-1, C-9.

103. Jimmy Bryan, "'Bama's Mitchell Has Best Day, but Looking for Better," *Birmingham News*, September 29, 1971, p. 23.

104. Jimmy Bryan, "'Bowl Can Wait'; Tide Makes It 10 Down, Big One to Go," *Birmingham News*, November 14, 1971, p. C-8.

105. Clyde Bolton, "Bryant Talks of a Great 'Bama Team," *Birmingham News*, November 16, 1971, p. 22.

106. Briley, *Career in Crisis*, 35.

107. Kirk McNair, *What It Means to Be Crimson Tide* (Chicago: Triumph Books, 2005), 156.

108. Eli Gold, with M. B. Roberts, *Bear's Boys* (Nashville, TN: Thomas Nelson, 2007), 87.

109. Gold, *Bear's Boys*, 47.

110. McNair, *What It Means*, 157.

111. Marcel Hopson, "Hits and Bits," *Birmingham World*, January 13, 1973, p. 4.

112. "Emphasis on Recognition," *Birmingham World*, August 26, 1972, p. 2.

113. Bryant actually anticipated this development in his deposition to Clemon. He told the lawyer that the coaches at traditionally black colleges were "going to be displeased with you all, they used to get all of those athletes." See Transcript of Bryant deposition, p. 86.

114. Marion Jackson, "Views Sports of the World," *Birmingham World*, January 2, 1971, p. 6. Hopson was particularly disgruntled that black football coach William N. Horn, a coach for twenty years at Western Olin High School, was not hired for either one of two vacancies at majority white schools. Instead, white coaches with much less experience were hired. See Marcel Hopson, "Hits and Bits," *Birmingham World*, August 21, 1971, p. 6.

115. Marion Jackson, "World Sports," *Birmingham World*, June 24, 1972, p. 5.

116. Lacy J. Banks, "Black Football Players in the White South," *Ebony* 26, no. 2 (December 1970): 132, 139.

117. Marcel Hopson, "Hits and Bits," *Birmingham World*, November 13, 1971, p. 7.

118. Marcel Hopson, "Hits and Bits," *Birmingham World*, November 20, 1971, p. 5.

119. Dan Meissner, "Keep Working and Stay in School," photograph, *Tuscaloosa News*, October 19, 1971, p. 7.

120. Ronald Weathers, "Kentucky Comes a-Calling . . . It's Turnaround for Bear," *Birmingham News*, September 17, 1972, pp. C-1, C-12.

121. See Clyde Bolton, "One Man's Vote: Hannah," *Birmingham News*, November 30, 1972, p. 25; and "Davis Nips Jones as Tide, Tigers Lead All-SEC," *Birmingham News*, November 29, 1972, pp. 55, 61.

122. Jimmy Bryan, "Crimson Tide Seniors Relive Big Moments," *Birmingham News*, December 9, 1972, p. 13.

123. Ben Nolan, "Glimpses from the Score Book," *Mobile Register*, February 20, 1973, pp. 1C, 2C. The *Crimson White* also reported this celebration, noting that other former UA players attending the event included Lee Roy Jordan, Scott Hunter, Kenny (Snake) Stabler, Bubba Sawyer, and David Chatwood. The presence of those past stars suggests that many former players supported the decision to integrate the team. See Rick Gilliam, "Inside Sports," *Crimson White*, February 19, 1973, p. 12.

124. Alf Van Hoose, "Tide Pioneer Just Member of the Team," *Birmingham News*, January 7, 1973, pp. C-1, C-8 (quotations from p. C-1).

125. Nathan Turner, "Blacks Discuss Football Careers," *Crimson White*, January 18, 1973, p. 5. Mitchell's roommate in 1971, Robin Parkhouse, corroborated his assessment, saying that the two had "become good friends." He added, "We treat each other as men, and believe me, John Mitchell is a fantastic human being and a real man." See Leonard Shapiro, "Mitchell Found 'Good Life' at UA," *Tuscaloosa News*, December 29, 1971, p. 15.

126. Nathan Turner, "Black Attitude Today Reflects Liberalization of Racial Opinions," *Crimson White*, November 30, 1972, p. 5.

127. Jimmy Bryan, "Walkout Terminated Blacks' Football," *Birmingham News*, October 4, 1972, pp. 29, 30.

128. For more on Nixon's "southern strategy," see Sitkoff, *Struggle for Black Equality*, 212–214, 216, 224. Dean J. Kotlowski offers a positive assessment of Nixon's civil rights record in *Nixon's Civil Rights: Politics, Principle, and Policy* (Cambridge, MA: Harvard University Press, 2001), although many scholars dispute his arguments, including Sitkoff, whose review appears in the *Journal of American History* 89 (March 2003): 1611.

129. Alf Van Hoose, "Applause Rings from Afar for Troy's Coach Jones," *Birmingham News*, October 6, 1972, p. 11. In a later story, Jones said that he had received "mail from all over the country" as well as telephone calls supporting his actions. See Jimmy Bryan, "Support from All Over for Jones' Stand," *Birmingham News*, October 11, 1972, p. 36.

130. McNair, *What It Means*, 232.

131. Dunnavant, *Coach*, 265.

132. Barra writes that Bryant's "greatest achievement as a leader was the thoroughness with which he integrated the team and the coaching staff once the commitment was made." See Barra, *Last Coach*, xxv.

133. Briley, *Career in Crisis*, 276.

134. See Shapiro, "Mitchell Found 'Good Life,'" p. 15.

135. Rick Young, "Press Box," *Crimson White*, March 9, 1972, p. 11.

CONCLUSION

1. The Black Coaches and Administrators website catalogs stories featuring the organization and has a number of articles devoted to the issue of interviewing and hiring African American college football coaches. In addition, the NCAA released a story detailing the number of minority head coaches in college football. See the Black Coaches and Administrators website at http://bcasports.org, and "Minority Head Football Coaches" on the NCAA website, available at http://www.ncaa.org/wps/wcm/connect/public/NCAA/Issues/Diversity+and+Inclusion/Minority+Head+Football+Coaches.

2. The discussion took place from November 28 through November 20, 2007, in the Tar Pit forum of the Inside Carolina website, an Internet publication devoted to UNC sports. Discussions are archived for only a limited time, so no permanent record of the discussion exists online, although the author printed a copy for his research.

3. For more on the effects of Title IX and the response to it, see Linda Jean Carpenter, *Title IX* (Champaign, IL: Human Kinetics, 2005); and Susan Ware, *Title IX: A Brief History with Documents* (Boston: Bedford/St. Martin's, 2007).

4. Brad Fisher, "Women's Sports Budget Approved by Athletics," *Crimson White*, November 9, 1972, p. 1.

5. The Imus story was widely reported in the news. The Associated Press story is available through msnbc.com at http://nbcsports.msnbc.com/id/17982146/I/.

6. A plethora of scholarship has explored the generational differences in racial tolerance. See, for example, Caroline Hodges Persell, Adam Green, and Liena Gurevich, "Civil Society, Economic Distress, and Social Tolerance," *Sociological Forum* 16, no. 2 (June 2001): 203–230.

7. Rick Young, "Press Box," *Crimson White*, March 9, 1972, p. 11.

8. For the official graduation rate statistics, see the NCAA website. Graduation rates from 2001 to 2002 are currently available. See "Overall Division 1," http://web1.ncaa.org/app_data/instAggr2008/1_0.pdf.

9. For a brief summary of the report, see Associated Press, "Study Shows Low Graduation Rates," *Washington Post*, March 13, 2007, available at http://www.washingtonpost.com/wp-dyn/content/article/2007/03/12/AR2007031201397.html. For more on poor graduation rates in big-time college athletics, see George H. Sage, "Racial Inequality and Sport," in *Sport in Contemporary Society*, 6th ed., ed. D. Stanley Eitzen (New York: Worth, 2001), 275–284.

10. The ESPN network featured Ross's story as part of its *Outside the Lines* series. For a transcript of the show, see http://sports.espn.go.com/page2/tvlistings/show103transcript.html.

11. Nelson George, *Elevating the Game: Black Men and Basketball* (Lincoln: University of Nebraska Press, 1992), 238.

12. For an excellent study of college athletics at the lower levels of competition, see William G. Bowen and Sarah A. Levin, *Reclaiming the Game: College Sports and Educational Values* (Princeton, NJ: Princeton University Press, 2003).

13. See L. Z. Granderson, "Who Says White Men Can't Jump?" ESPN, April 1, 2008, available at http://myespn.go.com/s/conversations/show/story/3323500.

14. For example, according to U.S. Census data in 2009, the median per capita income for white families totaled $65,545 and only $38,409 for African American families. See "Money Income of Families—Median Income by Race and Hispanic Origin in Current and Constant (2009) Dollars: 1990 to 2009," available at http://www.census.gov/compendia/statab/2012/tables/12s0697.pdf.

15. For the entire list, see Kurt Badenhausen, "The World's Highest-Paid Athletes," *Forbes*, May 31, 2011, available at http://www.forbes.com/sites/kurtbadenhausen/2011/05/31/the-worlds-highest-paid-athletes/.

16. Michele Wallace, *Black Macho and the Myth of the Superwoman* (New York: Dial Press, 1978), 55.

17. See Adam Liptak, "U.S. Imprisons One in 100 Adults, Report Finds," *New York Times*, February 29, 2008, available at http://www.nytimes.com/2008/02/29/us/29prison.html.

18. John Hoberman, *Darwin's Athletes: How Sports Has Damaged Black America and Preserved the Myth of Race* (New York: Houghton Mifflin, 1997), xxiv.

19. Matthew Frye Jacobson, "'Richie' Allen, Whitey's Ways, and Me: A Political Education in the 1960s," in *In the Game: Race, Identity, and Sports in the Twentieth Century*, ed. Amy Bass (New York: Palgrave Macmillan, 2005), 21.

20. J. A. Adande, "LeBron James, Race and the NBA," ESPN, October 1, 2010, available at http://sports.espn.go.com/nba/trainingcamp10/columns/story?columnist=adande_ja&page=LeBronRace-101001.

21. Grant Hill, "Grant Hill's Response to Jalen Rose," *New York Times*, March 16, 2011, available at http://thequad.blogs.nytimes.com/2011/03/16/grant-hills-response-to-jalen-rose/.

22. Scoop Jackson, "Black Athletes: Beyond the Field," ESPN, February 24, 2010, available at http://sports.espn.go.com/espn/commentary/news/story?page=jackson/100224.

23. Todd Boyd, "The Day the Niggaz Took Over: Basketball, Commodity Culture, and Black Masculinity," in *Out of Bounds: Sports, Media, and the Politics of Identity*, ed. Aaron Baker and Todd Boyd (Bloomington: University of Indiana Press, 1997), 123–142.

24. Richard Lapchick, with Brian Hoff and Christopher Kaiser, *The 2010 Racial and Gender Report Card: College Sport* (Orlando: University of Central Florida, 2011), 1, 6. These meager numbers are echoed in the professional ranks, with black head coaches few and far between in the NFL and MLB especially. Although the NBA has seen an increased number of black head coaches in recent years, the percentage of African American players remains much higher than the percentage of black coaches and general managers.

25. For a quick summary of the incident, and to watch the episode of the ABC program *Nightline* in which Campanis made his comments, see http://abcnews.go.com/Nightline/ESPNSports/story?id=3034914.

Bibliography

Unpublished Sources

Aycock, William. Chancellor's Records: William B. Aycock Papers. Southern Historical Collection. University of North Carolina, Chapel Hill.

Bryant, Paul W. Papers. Civil Rights Lawsuit 1969 Collection. Paul W. Bryant Museum. University of Alabama, Tuscaloosa.

Chamberlain, Wilt. Biographical File. University of Kansas Archives, Lawrence, KS.

Clothier, Robert C. Robeson, Paul, 1945–1949. Records of the Rutgers College Office of the President (Robert C. Clothier). Rutgers University, New Brunswick, NJ.

Davis, Dowdal. Correspondence, 1955–1957. Dorothy Hodge Johnson Papers. University of Kansas Archives, Lawrence, KS.

Demarest, William H. S. Robeson, Paul, 1898–1976. Records of the Rutgers College Office of the President (William H. S. Demarest). Rutgers University, New Brunswick, NJ.

Falkenstein, Max. Interview with author, August 10, 2006, Lawrence, KS.

Mathews, F. David. Correspondence, 1969–1975. President Forrest David Mathews Papers. W. S. Hoole Special Collections Library. University of Alabama, Tuscaloosa.

McCormick, Richard C. Records of the Rutgers College Office of the President (Richard C. McCormick). Rutgers University, New Brunswick, NJ.

Molineux, Paul Rexford. Scrapbook. Rutgers University, New Brunswick, NJ.

Murphy, Franklin D. Correspondence, 1952–1959. Chancellor Franklin D. Murphy Papers. University of Kansas Archives, Lawrence, KS.

Nichols, Royal F. Scrapbook. Rutgers University, New Brunswick, NJ.

Rose, Frank. President Frank Rose Papers. W. S. Hoole Special Collections Library. University of Alabama, Tuscaloosa.

Sitterson, J. Carlyle. Chancellor's Records: J. Carlyle Sitterson Papers. Southern Historical Collection. University of North Carolina at Chapel Hill.

Sproul, Robert. Chancellor's Office Papers. UCLA University Archives, Los Angeles, CA.

Newspapers

Baltimore Afro-American, September 1915–December 1918
Birmingham News, July 1969–January 1973

Birmingham World, July 1969–January 1973
California Eagle, August 1936–March 1941
The Carolinian (Raleigh, NC), October 1945, May 1966–May 1970
Chapel Hill News, October 1945, May 1966–May 1970
Charlotte News, March 1969
Charlotte Observer, October 1945, May 1966–May 1970
Chicago Defender, September 1915–January 1973
Crimson White (Tuscaloosa, AL), April 1967–January 1973
The Crisis, December 1910–January 1975
Daily Home News (New Brunswick, NJ), September 1915–June 1919
Daily Tar Heel (Chapel Hill, NC), October 1945, April 1947, May 1965–May 1970
Durham Carolina Times, October 1945, May 1966–May 1970
Durham Morning Herald, October 1945, May 1966–May 1970
Kansas City Call, October 1954–June 1958
Kansas City Star, January 1955–June 1958
Lawrence Daily Journal-World, May 1955–May 1958
Los Angeles Daily Bruin, August 1936–March 1941
Los Angeles Examiner, September 1936–March 1941
Los Angeles Times, September 1936–March 1941
News and Observer (Raleigh, NC), October 1945, May 1966–May 1970
New York Age, February 1915–June 1919
New York Amsterdam News, September 1939–January 1941
New York Sun, September 1915–December 1918
New York Times, September 1915–August 1973
New York Tribune, September 1915–December 1918
Pasadena Post, September 1936–May 1941
Pasadena Star-News, September 1936–May 1941
Pittsburgh Courier, September 1939–January 1941, January 1955–June 1958
Targum (New Brunswick, NJ), September 1915–June 1919
Topeka Daily Capital, January 1955–June 1958
Tuscaloosa News, April 1967–January 1973
University Daily Kansan (Lawrence, KS), January 1955–June 1958
Washington Afro-American, September 1936–March 1941

Books, Theses, and Journal and Magazine Articles

Ashby, Warren. "Campaign Ordeal." In *Frank Porter Graham: A Southern Liberal,* 257–271. Winston-Salem, NC: John F. Blair, 1980.
Badenhausen, Kurt. "The World's Highest-Paid Athletes." *Forbes,* May 31, 2011. Available at http://www.forbes.com/sites/kurtbadenhausen/2011/05/31/the-worlds-highest-paid-athletes.
Baker, Clifford N. "Review of the 1918 Football Season." In *The Scarlet Letter,* edited by George E. Talmage, Jr., 143–146. East Orange, NJ: Abby Printshop, 1919.
Baker, William J. *Jesse Owens: An American Life.* New York: Free Press, 1986.
Banks, Lacy J. "Black Football Players in the White South." *Ebony* 26, no. 2 (December 1970): 131–139.
Barbeau, Arthur E., and Florette Henri. *The Unknown Soldiers: Black American Troops in World War I.* Philadelphia: Temple University Press, 1974.
Barra, Allen. *The Last Coach: A Life of Paul "Bear" Bryant.* New York: W. W. Norton, 2005.
Bass, Amy. *Not the Triumph but the Struggle: The 1968 Olympics and the Making of the Black Athlete.* Minneapolis: University of Minnesota Press, 2002.
Bass, Charlotta A. *Forty Years: Memoirs from the Pages of a Newspaper.* Los Angeles: Self-published, 1960.

Bederman, Gail. *Manliness and Civilization: A Cultural History of Gender and Race in the United States, 1880–1917.* Chicago: University of Chicago Press, 1995.

Bloom, John, and Michael Nevin Willard, eds. *Sports Matters: Race, Recreation, and Culture.* New York: New York University Press, 2002.

Bogle, Donald. *Toms, Coons, Mulattoes, Mammies, and Bucks: An Interpretive History of Blacks in American Films.* New York: Continuum International, 2002.

Bond, Gregory. "The Strange Career of Will Henry Lewis." In *Out of the Shadows: A Biographical History of African American Athletes,* edited by David K. Wiggins, 38–57. Fayetteville: University of Arkansas Press, 2006.

Bowen, William G., and Sarah A. Levin. *Reclaiming the Game: College Sports and Educational Values.* Princeton, NJ: Princeton University Press, 2003.

Boyd, Todd. "The Day the Niggaz Took Over: Basketball, Commodity Culture, and Black Masculinity." In *Out of Bounds: Sports, Media, and the Politics of Identity,* edited by Aaron Baker and Todd Boyd, 123–142. Bloomington: University of Indiana Press, 1997.

Boyle, Sheila Tully, and Andrew Bunie. *Paul Robeson: The Years of Promise and Achievement.* Amherst: University of Massachusetts Press, 2001.

Branch, Taylor. *Parting the Waters: America in the King Years, 1954–63.* New York: Simon and Schuster, 1988.

Briggs, Mark D. "A Tale of Two Pioneers: The Integration of College Athletics in the South during the 1960s in the Age of the Civil Rights Movement." Master's thesis, University of North Carolina, Chapel Hill, 2000.

Briley, John David. *Career in Crisis: Paul "Bear" Bryant and the 1971 Season of Change.* Macon, GA: Mercer University Press, 2006.

Brown, Lloyd. *The Young Paul Robeson: "On My Journey Now."* Boulder, CO: Westview Press, 1997.

Bryant, Paul W., and John Underwood. *Bear: The Hard Life and Good Times of Alabama's Coach Bryant.* Boston: Little, Brown, 1974.

Carby, Hazel. *Race Men.* Cambridge, MA: Harvard University Press, 1998.

Carpenter, Linda Jean. *Title IX.* Champaign, IL: Human Kinetics, 2005.

Carroll, John M. *Fritz Pollard: Pioneer in Racial Advancement.* Chicago: University of Illinois Press, 1992.

Carson, Clayborne. *In Struggle: SNCC and the Black Awakening of the 1960s,* rev. ed. Cambridge, MA: Harvard University Press, 1995.

Chafe, William H. *Civilities and Civil Rights: Greensboro, North Carolina, and the Black Struggle for Freedom.* New York: Oxford University Press, 1981.

"A Challenge to the Old Order." *Carolina Alumni Review* 95, no. 2 (March/April 2006): 30.

Chamberlain, Wilt, with Tim Cohane and I. R. McVay. "Why I Am Quitting College." *Look,* June 10, 1958, 91–101.

Chamberlain, Wilt, and David Shaw. *Wilt: Just Like Any Other 7-Foot Black Millionaire Who Lives Next Door.* New York: Macmillan, 1973.

Chansky, Art. *Dean's Domain: The Inside Story of Dean Smith and His College Basketball Empire.* Marietta, GA: Longstreet, 1999.

———. *The Dean's List: A Celebration of Tar Heel Basketball and Dean Smith.* New York: Warner Books, 1996.

Cherry, Robert Allen. *Wilt: Larger than Life.* Chicago: Triumph Books, 2004.

Demas, Lane. *Integrating the Gridiron: Black Civil Rights and American College Football.* New Brunswick, NJ: Rutgers University Press, 2010.

———. "'On the Threshold of Broad and Rich Football Pastures': Integrated College Football at UCLA, 1938–1941." In *Horsehide, Pigskin, Oval Tracks and Apple Pie: Essays on Sports and American Culture,* edited by James A. Vlasich, 86–103. Jefferson, NC: McFarland, 2006.

Denning, Michael. *The Cultural Front: The Laboring of American Culture in the Twentieth Century.* New York: Verso, 1998.

Dorinson, Joseph. "Black Heroes in Sport: From Jack Johnson to Muhammad Ali." *Journal of Popular Culture* 31, no. 3 (1997): 115–135.

Doyle, Andrew. "An Atheist in Alabama Is Someone Who Doesn't Believe in Bear Bryant: A Symbol for an Embattled South." In *Sporting World of the Modern South*, edited by Patrick B. Miller, 247–275. Chicago: University of Illinois Press, 2002.

Duberman, Martin. *Paul Robeson.* New York: Alfred A. Knopf, 1989.

Dudziak, Mary L. *Cold War Civil Rights: Race and the Image of American Democracy.* Princeton, NJ: Princeton University Press, 2000.

Dunnavant, Keith. *Coach: The Life of Paul "Bear" Bryant.* New York: Simon and Schuster, 1996.

———. *The Missing Ring: How Bear Bryant and the 1966 Alabama Crimson Tide Were Denied College Football's Most Elusive Prize.* New York: St. Martin's Press, 2007.

Dworkin, Ronald. *Sovereign Virtue: The Theory and Practice of Equality.* Cambridge, MA: Harvard University Press, 2000.

Dyreson, Mark. "Jesse Owens: Leading Man in Modern American Tales of Racial Progress and Limits." In *Out of the Shadows*, edited by David K. Wiggins, 110–131. Fayetteville: University of Arkansas Press, 2006.

Edmonds, Anthony O. "Joe Louis, Boxing, and American Culture." In *Out of the Shadows*, edited by David K. Wiggins, 132–145. Fayetteville: University of Arkansas Press, 2006.

Edwards, Harry. *The Revolt of the Black Athlete.* New York: Free Press, 1969.

———. *The Struggle That Must Be: An Autobiography.* New York: Macmillan, 1980.

Edy, Carolyn. "Segregation's Last Stand." *Carolina Alumni Review* 95, no. 2 (March/April 2006): 44–47.

———. "Town and Gown." *Carolina Alumni Review* 95, no. 2 (March/April 2006): 46.

Ehle, John. *The Free Men.* New York: Harper and Row, 1965.

Eitzen, D. Stanley. *Fair and Foul: Beyond the Myths and Paradoxes of Sport*, 3rd ed. New York: Rowman and Littlefield, 2006.

Ellis, Mark. *Race, War, and Surveillance: African Americans and the United States Government during World War I.* Bloomington: Indiana University Press, 2001.

Ely, Melvin. *The Adventures of Amos 'n' Andy: A Social History of an American Phenomenon.* New York: Free Press, 1991.

Erenberg, Lewis A. *The Greatest Fight of Our Generation: Lewis vs. Schmeling.* New York: Oxford University Press, 2006.

Estes, Steve. *I Am a Man! Race, Manhood, and the Civil Rights Movement.* Chapel Hill: University of North Carolina Press, 2005.

Falkenstein, Max, with Doug Vance. *Max and the Jayhawks: 50 Years On and Off the Air with KU Sports.* Wichita, KS: Wichita Eagle and Beacon Publishing, 1996.

Filene, Peter. *Him/Her/Self: Gender Identities in Modern America*, 3rd ed. Baltimore: Johns Hopkins University Press, 1998.

Flamming, Douglas. *Bound for Freedom: Black Los Angeles in Jim Crow America.* Berkeley: University of California Press, 2005.

Freer, Regina. "L.A. Race Woman: Charlotta Bass and the Complexities of Black Political Development in Los Angeles." *American Quarterly* 56, no. 3 (2004): 607–632.

Gaillard, Frye. "Crumbling Segregation in the Southeastern Conference." In *The Black Athlete–1970.* Nashville, TN: Race Relations Information Center, 1970.

George, Nelson. *Elevating the Game: Black Men and Basketball.* Lincoln: University of Nebraska Press, 1992.

Gerstle, Gary. *American Crucible: Race and Nation in the Twentieth Century.* Princeton, NJ: Princeton University Press, 2001.

Gilmore, Al-Tony. *Bad Nigger! The National Impact of Jack Johnson.* Port Washington, NY: Kennikat Press, 1975.

Gleijeses, Piero. "African Americans and the War against Spain." In *A Question of Manhood: A Reader in U.S. Black Men's History and Masculinity.* Vol. 2, *The 19th Century:*

From Emancipation to Jim Crow, edited by Earnestine Jenkins and Darlene Clark Hine, 320–346. Bloomington: Indiana University Press, 2001.

Gold, Eli, with M. B. Roberts. *Bear's Boys*. Nashville, TN: Thomas Nelson, 2007.

Gorn, Elliott J. *The Manly Art: Bare-Knuckle Prize Fighting in America*. Ithaca, NY: Cornell University Press, 1986.

Gorn, Elliott, and Warren Goldstein. *A Brief History of American Sports*. New York: Hill and Wang, 1993.

Goudsouzian, Aram. "'Can Basketball Survive Wilt Chamberlain?': The Kansas Years of Wilt the Stilt," *Kansas History: A Journal of the Central Plains* 28 (Autumn 2005): 150–173.

Granderson, L. Z. "Who Says White Men Can't Jump?" ESPN, April 1, 2008. Available at http://myespn.go.com/s/conversations/show/story/3323500.

Grundy, Pamela. *Learning to Win: Sports, Education, and Social Change in Twentieth-Century North Carolina*. Chapel Hill: University of North Carolina Press, 2001.

Hamilton, Andrew, and John B. Jackson. *UCLA on the Move: During Fifty Golden Years 1919–1969*. Los Angeles: Ward Ritchie Press, 1969.

Henderson, Russell J. "The 1963 Mississippi State University Basketball Controversy and the Repeal of the Unwritten Law: 'Something More Than the Game Will Be Lost.'" *Journal of Southern History* 63 (November 1997): 827–854.

Hietala, Thomas R. *The Fight of the Century: Jack Johnson, Joe Louis, and the Struggle for Racial Equality*. Armonk, NY: Sharpe, 2002.

Hoberman, John. *Darwin's Athletes: How Sports Has Damaged Black America and Preserved the Myth of Race*. New York: Houghton Mifflin, 1997.

Howard, Keith Patrick. "Desegregation of College Football in the Southeastern United States." Master's thesis, University of North Carolina, Chapel Hill, 2001.

Hughes, Raymond. "Desegregating the Holy Day: Football, Blacks and the Southeastern Conference." Ph.D. diss., Ohio State University, 1991.

Jacobs, Barry. *Across the Line: Profiles in Courage; Tales of the First Black Players in the ACC and SEC*. Guilford, CT: Lyons Press, 2008.

Jacobson, Matthew Frye. "'Richie' Allen, Whitey's Ways, and Me: A Political Education in the 1960s." In *In the Game: Race, Identity, and Sports in the Twentieth Century*, edited by Amy Bass, 19–46. New York: Palgrave Macmillan, 2005.

Joseph, Peniel E. *Waiting 'Til the Midnight Hour: A Narrative History of Black Power in America*. New York: Henry Holt, 2006.

Kasson, John F. *Amusing the Million: Coney Island at the Turn of the Century*. New York: Hill and Wang, 1978.

———. *Houdini, Tarzan, and the Perfect Man: The White Male Body and the Challenge of Modernity in America*. New York: Hill and Wang, 2001.

Kemper, Kurt Edward. *College Football and American Culture in the Cold War Era*. Urbana: University of Illinois Press, 2009.

Kennedy, Randall. *Nigger: The Strange Career of a Troublesome Word*. New York: Pantheon Books, 2002.

Key, V. O., with Alexander Heard. *Southern Politics in State and Nation*. New York: Alfred A. Knopf, 1949.

Kimmel, Michael. *Manhood in America: A Cultural History*. New York: Free Press, 1996.

King, C. Richard, and Charles Fruehling Springwood. *Beyond the Cheers: Race as Spectacle in College Sport*. Albany: State University of New York Press, 2001.

Kirkpatrick, Curry. "One More War to Go." *Sports Illustrated*, March 2, 1970, 12–15.

Kotlowski, Dean J. *Nixon's Civil Rights: Politics, Principle, and Policy*. Cambridge, MA: Harvard University Press, 2001.

Lanctot, Neil. *Negro League Baseball: The Rise and Ruin of a Black Institution*. Philadelphia: University of Pennsylvania Press, 2004.

Lapchick, Richard, with Brian Hoff and Christopher Kaiser. *The 2010 Racial and Gender Report Card: College Sport*. Orlando: University of Central Florida, 2011.

Lhamon, William T. *Deliberate Speed: The Origins of a Cultural Style in the American 1950s.* Washington, DC: Smithsonian Institution Press, 1990.

Lipsyte, Robert. *SportsWorld: An American Dreamland.* New York: Quadrangle, 1975.

Liptak, Adam. "U.S. Imprisons One in 100 Adults, Report Finds." *New York Times*, February 29, 2008. Available at http://www.nytimes.com/2008/02/29/us/29prison.html.

Lomax, Michael. "Jackie Robinson: Racial Pioneer and Athlete Extraordinaire in an Era of Change." In *Out of the Shadows: A Biographical History of African American Athletes*, edited by David K. Wiggins, 162–179. Fayetteville: University of Arkansas Press, 2006.

———. "Revisiting *The Revolt of the Black Athlete*: Harry Edwards and the Making of the New African-American Sports Studies." *Journal of Sport History* 29 (Fall 2002): 469–479.

Luebke, Paul. *Tar Heel Politics: Myths and Realities.* Chapel Hill: University of North Carolina Press, 1990.

Marcello, Ronald E. "The Integration of Intercollegiate Athletics in Texas: North Texas State College as a Test Case, 1956." *Journal of Sport History* 14, no. 3 (Winter 1987): 286–316.

Martin, Charles H. *Benching Jim Crow: The Rise and Fall of the Color Line in Southern College Sports, 1890–1980.* Urbana: University of Illinois Press, 2010.

———. "The Rise and Fall of Jim Crow in Southern College Sports: The Case of the Atlantic Coast Conference." *North Carolina Historical Review* 76 (July 1999): 253–284.

Matusow, Alan. *The Unraveling of America: A History of Liberalism in the 1960s.* New York: Harper and Row, 1984.

Maxwell, Titus B., ed. *The Scarlet Letter.* East Orange, NJ: Abby Printshop, 1918.

May, Lary. *Screening Out the Past: The Birth of Mass Culture and the Motion Picture Industry.* New York: Oxford University Press, 1980.

Mayer, Michael S. "With Much Deliberation and Some Speed: Eisenhower and the Brown Decision." *Journal of Southern History* 52 (February 1986): 43–76.

McCusker, Kristine M. "The Forgotten Years of America's Civil Rights Movement: The University of Kansas, 1939–1961." Master's thesis, University of Kansas, 1994.

McLaughlin, Malcolm. *Power, Community, and Racial Killing in East St. Louis.* New York: Palgrave Macmillan, 2005.

McNair, Kirk. *What It Means to Be Crimson Tide.* Chicago: Triumph Books, 2005.

Miller, Patrick B. "To 'Bring the Race Along Rapidly': Sport, Student Culture, and Educational Mission at Historically Black Colleges during the Interwar Years." In *Sporting World of the Modern South*, edited by Patrick B. Miller, 129–152. Chicago: University of Illinois Press, 2002.

Miller, Patrick B., and David K. Wiggins, eds. *Sport and the Color Line: Black Athletes and Race Relations in Twentieth-Century America.* New York: Routledge, 2004.

Olson, Jack. *The Black Athlete: A Shameful Story; The Myth of Integration in American Sport.* New York: Time-Life Books, 1968.

Oriard, Michael. *Bowled Over: Big-Time College Football from the Sixties to the BCS Era.* Chapel Hill: University of North Carolina Press, 2009.

———. *King Football: Sport and Spectacle in the Golden Age of Radio and Newsreels, Movies and Magazines, the Weekly and the Daily Press.* Chapel Hill: University of North Carolina Press, 2001.

Peiss, Kathy. *Cheap Amusements: Working Women and Leisure in Turn-of-the-Century New York.* Philadelphia: Temple University Press, 1986.

Persell, Caroline Hodges, Adam Green, and Liena Gurevich. "Civil Society, Economic Distress, and Social Tolerance." *Sociological Forum* 16, no. 2 (June 2001): 203–230.

Pride, Armistead S., and Clint C. Wilson II. *A History of the Black Press.* Washington, DC: Howard University Press, 1997.

Putney, Clifford. *Muscular Christianity: Manhood and Sports in Protestant America, 1880–1920.* Cambridge, MA: Harvard University Press, 2001.

Quincy, Bob, ed. *The 1964/1965 UNC Basketball Blue Book.* Chapel Hill, NC: Self-published, 1964.

Rampersad, Arnold. *Jackie Robinson: A Biography.* New York: Knopf, 1997.

Reagan-Kendrick, Amber. "Ninety Years of Struggle and Success: African American History at the University of Kansas, 1870–1960." Ph.D. diss., University of Kansas, 2004.

Reiss, Steven A. "The New Sport History." *Reviews in American History* 18, no. 3 (September 1990): 311–325.

Rhoden, William C. *Forty Million Dollar Slaves: The Rise, Fall, and Redemption of the Black Athlete.* New York: Crown, 2006.

Roberts, Randy. *Papa Jack: Jack Johnson and the Era of White Hopes.* New York: Free Press, 1983.

Robeson, Eslanda Goode. *Paul Robeson, Negro.* New York: Harper, 1930.

Robeson, Paul, Jr. *The Undiscovered Paul Robeson: An Artist's Journey 1898–1939.* New York: Wiley, 2001.

Robeson, Paul S. "The Fourteenth Amendment, 'The Sleeping Giant of the American Constitution.'" Bachelor's thesis, Rutgers College, 1919.

Robinson, Jackie, and Alfred Duckett. *I Never Had It Made.* New York: G. P. Putnam, 1972.

Robinson, Jackie, with Wendell Smith. *Jackie Robinson: My Own Story.* New York: Greenberg, 1948.

Robinson, Rachel, with Lee Daniels. *Jackie Robinson: An Intimate Portrait.* New York: Harry Abrams, 1996.

Roemer, John E. *Equality of Opportunity.* Cambridge, MA: Harvard University Press, 1998.

Rojas, Fabio. *From Black Power to Black Studies: How a Radical Social Movement Became an Academic Discipline.* Baltimore: Johns Hopkins University Press, 2007.

Rutgers College Catalogue for 1915–1916. New Brunswick, NJ: Self-published, 1916.

Sage, George H. "Racial Inequality and Sport." In *Sport in Contemporary Society,* 6th ed., edited by D. Stanley Eitzen, 275–284. New York: Worth, 2001.

Sammons, Jeffrey. "A Proportionate and Measured Response to the Provocation That Is *Darwin's Athletes.*" *Journal of Sport History* 24, no. 3 (Fall 1997): 378–388.

———. "'Race' and Sport: A Critical, Historical Examination." *Journal of Sport History* 21, no. 3 (Fall 1994): 203–278.

Schapp, Jeremy. *Triumph: The Untold Story of Jesse Owens and Hitler's Olympics.* New York: Houghton Mifflin, 2007.

Schulman, Bruce J. *The Seventies: The Great Shift in American Culture, Society, and Politics.* New York: Free Press, 2001.

Scott, Jack. *The Athletic Revolution.* New York: Free Press, 1971.

Shklar, Judith N. *American Citizenship: The Quest for Inclusion.* Cambridge, MA: Harvard University Press, 1991.

———. "The Liberalism of Fear." In *Liberalism and the Moral Life,* edited by Nancy L. Rosenblum, 21–38. Cambridge, MA: Harvard University Press, 1989.

"Should Negroes Boycott the Olympics? Ebony Poll of Athletes Indicates Majority Prefer to Participate in This Year's Mexico City Sports Spectacular." *Ebony* 23, no. 5 (March 1968): 110–116.

Sides, Josh. *L.A. City Limits: African American Los Angeles from the Great Depression to the Present.* Berkeley: University of California Press, 2003.

Sitkoff, Harvard. Review of *Nixon's Civil Rights: Politics, Principle, and Policy,* by Dean J. Kotlowski. *Journal of American History* 89 (March 2003): 1611.

———. *The Struggle for Black Equality 1954–1992,* rev. ed. New York: Hill and Wang, 1993.

Smith, Dean, with John Kligo and Sally Jenkins. *A Coach's Life.* New York: Random House, 1999.

Smith, Earl. *Race, Sport and the American Dream.* Durham, NC: Carolina Academic Press, 2007.

Spigel, Lynn. *Make Room for TV: Television and the Family Ideal in Postwar America.* Chicago: University of Chicago Press, 1992.

Spivey, Donald. "The Black Athlete in Big-Time Intercollegiate Sports, 1941–1968." *Phylon* 44, no. 2 (June 1983): 116–125.

———. "'End Jim Crow in Sports': The Protest at New York University, 1940–1941." *Journal of Sport History* 15 (Fall 1988): 282–303.

Stadtman, Verne A., ed. *The Centennial Record of the University of California*. Berkeley: Regents of the University of California, 1967.

Staples, Robert. *Black Masculinity: The Black Male's Role in American Society*. San Francisco: Black Scholar Press, 1982.

Stowe, David W. *Swing Changes: Big-Band Jazz in New Deal America*. Cambridge, MA: Harvard University Press, 1994.

Strode, Woody, and Sam Young. *Goal Dust*. New York: Madison Books, 1990.

Sullivan, Neil J. "Baseball and Race: The Limits of Competition." *Journal of Negro History* 83, no. 3 (1998): 168–177.

Summers, Martin. *Manliness and Its Discontents: The Black Middle Class and the Transformation of Masculinity, 1900–1930*. Chapel Hill: University of North Carolina Press, 2004.

Susman, Warren I. *Culture as History: The Transformation of American Society in the Twentieth Century*. Washington, DC: Smithsonian Institution Press, 2003.

———. "'Personality' and the Making of Twentieth-Century Culture." In *Culture as History: The Transformation of American Society in the Twentieth Century*, 271–286 (Washington, DC: Smithsonian Institution Press, 2003).

Thompson, Charles L. "Standing Up by Sitting Down." *Carolina Alumni Review* 95, no. 2 (March/April 2006): 32–43.

Thornton, Charley, and Kirk McNair. *Alabama Football 1971*. Tuscaloosa, AL: Self-published, 1971.

Tuttle, William M., Jr. *Race Riot: Chicago in the Red Summer of 1919*, repr. ed. 1970. Reprint, Chicago: University of Illinois Press, 1996.

Tygiel, Jules. *Baseball's Great Experiment: Jackie Robinson and His Legacy*. New York: Oxford University Press, 1983.

———. *Extra Bases: Reflections on Jackie Robinson, Race, and Baseball History*. Lincoln: University of Nebraska Press, 2002.

University of North Carolina at Chapel Hill. *Yackety Yack*. Winston-Salem, NC: Hunter, 1970.

———. *Yackety Yack: The Yearbook of the University of North Carolina at Chapel Hill*. Dallas, TX: Taylor, 1967.

Violett, B. J. "Teammates Recall Jackie Robinson's Legacy." *UCLA Today*, April 25, 1997. Available at http://www.today.ucla.edu/portal/ut/970425TeammatesRecall.aspx.

Vogel, Todd, ed. *The Black Press: New Literary and Historical Essays*. New Brunswick, NJ: Rutgers University Press, 2001.

Wakefield, Wanda Ellen. *Playing to Win: Sports and the American Military, 1898–1945*. Albany: State University of New York Press, 1997.

Walker, Samuel. *Hate Speech: The History of an American Controversy*. Lincoln: University of Nebraska Press, 1994.

Wallace, Michele. *Black Macho and the Myth of the Superwoman*. New York: Dial Press, 1978.

Ward, Brian. *Just My Soul Responding: Rhythm and Blues, Black Consciousness, and Race Relations*. Berkeley: University of California Press, 1998.

Ward, Geoffrey C. *Unforgivable Blackness: The Rise and Fall of Jack Johnson*. New York: Knopf, 2004.

Ware, Susan. *Title IX: A Brief History with Documents*. Boston: Bedford/St. Martin's, 2007.

Washington, Booker T. *Up from Slavery*, with related documents, ed. W. Fitzhugh Brundage. New York: Bedford/St. Martin's, 2003.

Weiss, Robert J. *"We Want Jobs": A History of Affirmative Action*. New York: Garland, 1997.

Wiggins, David K. *Glory Bound: Black Athletes in a White America*. Syracuse, NY: Syracuse University Press, 1997.

————. "The 1936 Olympic Games in Berlin." In *Glory Bound: Black Athletes in a White America*, 61–79. Syracuse, NY: Syracuse University Press, 1997.

————. "'The Year of Awakening.'" In *Glory Bound: Black Athletes in a White America*, 104–122. Syracuse, NY: Syracuse University Press, 1997.

Wiggins, William H., Jr. "Jack Johnson as Bad Nigger: The Folklore of His Life." *Black Scholar* 2 (January 1971): 4–19.

Williams, Bernard. "The Idea of Equality." In *In the Beginning Was the Deed: Realism and Moralism in Political Argument*, edited by Geoffrey Hawthorn, 97–114. Princeton, NJ: Princeton University Press, 2005.

Williams, Jack, ed. *The 1966/1967 UNC Basketball Blue Book.* Chapel Hill, NC: Colonial Press, 1966.

————. *The 1967/1968 UNC Basketball Blue Book.* Chapel Hill, NC: Colonial Press, 1967.

————. *The 1968/1969 UNC Basketball Blue Book.* Chapel Hill, NC: Colonial Press, 1968.

Williams, Jack, Sybil Smith, Rick Brewer, and Chris Cobbs, eds. *The 1969/1970 UNC Basketball Blue Book.* Chapel Hill, NC: Colonial Press, 1969.

Wolfe, Suzanne Rau. *The University of Alabama: A Pictorial History.* Tuscaloosa: University of Alabama Press, 1983.

Yaeger, Don, with Sam Cunningham and John Papadakis. *Turning of the Tide: How One Game Changed the South.* New York: Center Street, 2006.

Films

Fleder, Gary, dir. *The Express.* Universal Pictures, 2008.

Gartner, James, dir. *Glory Road.* Buena Vista Pictures, 2006.

Hehir, Jason, dir. *The Fab Five.* ESPN Films, 2011.

Nelson, Stanley, dir. *The Black Press: Soldiers without Swords.* San Francisco: California Newsreel [distributor], 1998.

Yakin, Boaz, dir. *Remember the Titans.* Buena Vista Pictures, 2001.

Websites

Black Coaches and Administrators (BCA), http://bcasports.org

The Carolina Story: A Virtual Museum of University History, http://museum.unc.edu/index.html?tab=UNC%20Virtual%20Museum%20Home

ESPN.com, http://espn.go.com/

InsideCarolina.com, http://northcarolina.scout.com/

Kansas University History Galleries, http://www.kuhistory.com

National Collegiate Athletic Association, http://www.ncaa.org

Paul W. Bryant Museum, http://bryantmuseum.ua.edu/

Paul Robeson Cultural Center, http://prcc.rutgers.edu/

UCLA Athletic Department, http://uclabruins.collegesports.com/genrel/062200aah.html

University of Pennsylvania, African Studies Center, http://www.africa.upenn.edu

Index